Building Generative AI Solutions for Industries with AWS

Improve operational Efficiency and Scalability with AWS

Neel Sendas
Saurabh Saxena
Joseph Sacco

Apress®

Building Generative AI Solutions for Industries with AWS: Improve operational Efficiency and Scalability with AWS

Neel Sendas
Marietta, GA, USA

Saurabh Saxena
Broadlands, VA, USA

Joseph Sacco
North Haven, CT, USA

ISBN-13 (pbk): 979-8-8688-2829-4
ISBN-13 (electronic): 979-8-8688-2830-0
https://doi.org/10.1007/979-8-8688-2830-0

Managing Director, Apress Media LLC: Welmoed Spahr
Acquisitions Editor: Celestin Suresh John
Editorial Assistant: Gryffin Winkler

Cover designed by eStudioCalamar

Distributed to the book trade worldwide by Springer Science+Business Media New York, 1 New York Plaza, New York, NY 10004. Phone 1-800-SPRINGER, fax (201) 348-4505, e-mail orders-ny@springer-sbm.com, or visit www.springeronline.com. Apress Media, LLC is a Delaware LLC and the sole member (owner) is Springer Science + Business Media Finance Inc (SSBM Finance Inc). SSBM Finance Inc is a **Delaware** corporation.

For information on translations, please e-mail booktranslations@springernature.com; for reprint, paperback, or audio rights, please e-mail bookpermissions@springernature.com.

Apress titles may be purchased in bulk for academic, corporate, or promotional use. eBook versions and licenses are also available for most titles. For more information, reference our Print and eBook Bulk Sales web page at http://www.apress.com/bulk-sales.

Any source code or other supplementary material referenced by the author in this book is available to readers on GitHub. For more detailed information, please visit https://www.apress.com/gp/services/source-code.

If disposing of this product, please recycle the paper

To my mother, whose unwavering belief in the power of knowledge and relentless pursuit of excellence shaped not only who I am but how I see the world. Your quiet strength taught me that true innovation begins with curiosity, and your endless encouragement gave me the courage to explore ideas that once seemed impossible. This book, like so much of what I've accomplished, exists because you showed me that the greatest gift we can give is to help others understand what we've learned. Thank you for being my first teacher, my constant inspiration, and the foundation upon which all my work is built.

—Saurabh

To my wife Jill and my children Arianna and Ethan—thank you for your patience, your encouragement, and for always reminding me what matters most.

—Joseph

To my wife Jaya and my kids Preisha and Neevan—you are my heart, my reason, and my home. This book is as much yours as it is mine.

—Neel

Table of Contents

About the Authors

Neel Sendas is Principal Technical Account Manager at Amazon Web Services (AWS). In this role, he serves as the AWS Cloud Operations lead for some of the largest enterprises that utilize AWS services. Drawing from his expertise in cloud operations for multiple industries, Neel presents solutions to common challenges related to ML cloud governance, cloud finance, and cloud operational resilience and management at scale. Neel also plays a crucial role as part of the core team of Machine Learning Technical Field Community leaders at AWS, where he contributes to shaping the road map of AWS machine learning (AI/ML) and generative AI services. Neel is based in the state of Georgia, United States.

Saurabh Saxena is Senior Principal Technical Account Manager at AWS. During the last 12 years, he has provided strategic technical guidance to enterprise customers, helping them navigate complex cloud transformations and maximize their AWS investments. With deep technical expertise across AWS services and a focus on business outcomes, he partners with key stakeholders to architect solutions that drive innovation and operational excellence. Saurabh often leads high-impact customer engagements, developing technical road maps and coordinating cross-functional teams to guarantee successful cloud adoption. He specializes in translating complex technical concepts into business value, helping organizations leverage AWS technologies to achieve their strategic goals.

Joseph Sacco is a Principal Technical Account Manager at Amazon Web Services (AWS), where he serves as a strategic technical advisor to some of the largest healthcare and life sciences (HCLS) organizations in the world. Prior to joining Amazon, Joseph was the Director of IT at a healthcare startup focused on optimizing electronic healthcare data.

Joseph brings over 15 years of experience delivering technology solutions and digital transformations across the HCLS space, from private providers and biopharmaceutical companies to global health systems. Drawing on this experience and his work in generative AI, Joseph provides real-life examples of how AI can help speed up lengthy regulatory and compliance processes, enhance diagnostic accuracy, increase speed in radiology workflows, reduce clinician burnout, improve clinical decision-making, and more.

Joseph is based in Connecticut, United States.

Foreword

The fundamental text of my early career was *The Handbook of Fixed Income Securities* by Frank J. Fabozzi—if you know you know, as they say today. Absolutely essential reading to anyone in the fixed income and structured finance markets I grew up in, but not exactly conversational fodder for dinners with friends and family outside the industry.

Generative Artificial Intelligence is different—it is ubiquitous and its growth and influence outpace the adoption of recent technological advances like the internet, web, mobile phones, and cloud computing.

In the last week alone, I had the unique joy that seems to occur only during summers of hanging out with five of my closest friends from the last 20 years—social connections that have no professional relationship to me or each other. We're all just friends from a previous era of our lives—the one before work. Today, they work in five different industries, and each serves on at least one company board. One ran a marketing agency before founding her own alcohol brand. One runs a large blockchain technology company. One is a chief merchandizing and design executive in the fashion industry. One runs a SaaS company. One is an investment banker in the midst of founding an AI data center company.

Over casual breakfast at our home, the conversation organically turned into one that I might have had in an AWS Executive Briefing Center with customers alongside the authors of this book. Generative AI is fundamentally reshaping how not only AWS customers but each of my friends approaches both their lives and their businesses. And, while each of them pays for multiple AI subscription products that they use daily, they differ widely in how they've deployed AI in their organizations.

Despite the progress they've each made, everyone felt that GenAI could help themselves and their companies move faster, deliver more, and usher their businesses into a new and better age. At the same time, they shared concerns. How does GenAI meet the security and regulatory compliance challenges of systems managing billions of transactions? How does GenAI help a creative process driven by human taste? What does human work look like when AI systems are assessing large volumes of AI-generated business proposals?

Alongside industry-specific issues, the most challenging concerns surrounded leadership and people. How do we enable our people to use GenAI to be more productive while ensuring that we continue to receive the value that comes from high-judgment humans? GenAI is not merely automating what humans do. It is augmenting *how* humans think, decide, and create value. But it can only reshape the cognitive layer of how our organizations operate if we can lead our people and our organizations through that change.

There is a moment in every technological revolution when the question shifts—quietly but irreversibly—from *"Should we pursue this?"* to *"How quickly can we afford not to?"* Consistent personal and professional collisions like my recent breakfast signal these inflection points.

Generative AI is that moment. And it arrived faster than any of us predicted.

I have led global financial industry strategy through multiple technology cycles, and I can say without reservation that what we are experiencing today is categorically different from those of the past. The early GenAI adopters are not simply cutting costs or accelerating workflows. They are rewriting their competitive blueprints. Risk models that once required weeks of analyst time are being iterated in hours. Client-facing interactions that demand armies of relationship managers are being personalized at scale without sacrificing the human touch. Regulatory compliance processes—long the unglamorous but existential backbone of our industry—are being transformed from liability centers into intelligence assets.

But, as my friends and I discussed over breakfast, and what no one seems to talk about in the boardroom: technology is rarely the hard part.

The hard part is leadership. The hard part is deciding where to begin, how to pace the transformation, how to bring your people along, and how to govern a capability that evolves faster than most organizational policies can keep up with. The hard part is translating genuine executive enthusiasm into disciplined, enterprise-wide adoption without falling into the twin traps of paralysis through over-analysis or recklessness through under-governance.

This book addresses that hard part directly—and does so across the industries where these decisions are being made right now.

What distinguishes this work from the flood of GenAI content that has saturated the market is its focus on the executive perspective. This is not a technical manual. It is not a collection of vendor case studies. It is a strategist's guide—written for leaders who must make high-stakes decisions with incomplete information, competing priorities, and boards that are simultaneously demanding bold innovation and rigorous risk management. It is for my friends who run software companies and alcohol brands and fashion companies and investment banks and blockchain companies.

The chapters that follow provide something I have yet to encounter: a coherent, industry-grounded framework for thinking about GenAI adoption at scale. The authors resist the temptation to oversimplify and keep things practical. They acknowledge the genuine risks—hallucination, data governance, talent scarcity, ethical exposure—without allowing those risks to become excuses for inaction. And critically, they ground their guidance in the realities of industries where the stakes of getting this wrong are measured not just in quarterly earnings but in customer trust, regulatory standing, and institutional reputation.

As someone who advises organizations across the global financial ecosystem, I am often asked a version of the same question: *"Where do we actually start?"* My answer, invariably, begins with clarity of purpose—understanding not what GenAI can do in the abstract but what specific problems, at what specific scale, matter most to your organization's strategic trajectory.

This book helps you find that clarity.

Whether you are a CEO charting the long arc of transformation, a Chief Digital Officer building the implementation road map, or a Chief Risk Officer constructing the governance guardrails, you will find this guide to be an honest, well-reasoned, and genuinely useful companion. It will not tell you that GenAI is easy. It will not promise that the journey is without friction. But it will equip you with the frameworks, the vocabulary, and the strategic confidence to lead that journey with intention.

The financial services industry is already being reshaped by those who moved early and moved thoughtfully. The same is true across healthcare, manufacturing, retail, and every other sector explored in these pages. The window for deliberate, first-mover advantage narrows with each passing quarter.

The question is no longer whether to act.

It is how to do so wisely—and soon.

And most hopefully, for you, reader, the fundamental text provided in these pages proves as excellent conversation fodder for your next breakfast with friends as it did for mine.

Stephen Clarke, Director, Global Financial Industries
New York, 2026

Introduction

Intelligence at Scale: Why Generative AI Is the Defining Business Lever of Our Time

A Different Kind of Shift

In the spring of 2023, a hospital in the American Midwest deployed an experimental AI system in three of its primary care clinics. The system did something deceptively simple: it listened to conversations between doctors and patients and drafted the clinical notes that physicians would otherwise spend hours writing after their shifts. Within weeks, something unexpected happened. Patient satisfaction scores went up. Not because the AI was impressive—most patients never knew it was there—but because their doctors started making eye contact again.

That story is not exceptional. Across industries, in contexts ranging from the trading floors of global investment banks to the design studios of automotive manufacturers to the editorial rooms of streaming media companies, generative AI is doing something that no previous wave of enterprise technology has managed at this scale: it is returning human attention to where it matters most.

This is the central insight animating every page of this book. Generative AI is not primarily a story about machines doing things that humans used to do. It is a story about humans being freed to do things that only humans can do—to make judgments that require wisdom, to build relationships that require empathy, to create things that require imagination—while AI handles the cognitive labor that has always been necessary but rarely fulfilling.

But this insight, while true, is incomplete. Because generative AI is also a story about competitive advantage, market disruption, and the emergence of new business models that will be as difficult for laggards to replicate as the internet-native models of the 2000s proved to be for the incumbents of the 1990s. The organizations that understand both dimensions of this technology—the human and the strategic—are the ones building the capabilities that will define their industries for the next decade.

This book is for those organizations. And more specifically, it is for the leaders, architects, and domain experts within them who are responsible for turning the potential of generative AI into measurable, durable business value.

Why This Book and Why Now

The literature on artificial intelligence has never been richer—or more confusing. There are books about the mathematics of neural networks and books about the philosophy of machine consciousness. There are breathless predictions of AI-driven utopia and earnest warnings of existential catastrophe. There are technical manuals for machine learning engineers and management consulting reports on digital transformation.

What has been missing—and what this book is designed to provide—is a rigorous, industry-specific, implementation-focused guide for the leaders and practitioners who are making real decisions about generative AI right now: which use cases to prioritize, how to build the data foundations that AI requires, how to govern AI systems responsibly, how to bring organizations through the cultural transformation that genuine AI adoption demands, and how to measure whether any of it is actually working.

We wrote this book at a specific moment in the evolution of generative AI—a moment we believe is genuinely decisive. According to Gartner's 2023 Hype Cycle, generative AI sat at the peak of inflated expectations. By 2025, the technology moved into something more consequential: the period of productive deployment, where organizations that have built the right foundations are beginning to realize returns that justify the hype, while organizations that rushed to deploy without adequate preparation are managing the consequences.

This is the AI inflection point—wave 3 of the four-wave AI evolution framework we introduce in Chapter 1: the Emergence phase, where entirely new business models, value propositions, and market segments are being created with AI at their core. Organizations on the right side of this inflection point will enjoy compounding advantages—in data, in talent, in customer trust, in operational efficiency—that will be increasingly difficult for followers to overcome. Organizations on the wrong side risk becoming what Kodak became to photography, what Blockbuster became to video rental, and what countless pre-internet retailers became to commerce.

The urgency is real. But so is the complexity. And it is the combination of urgency and complexity that makes a book like this necessary.

Who This Book Is For

This book was written with four primary audiences in mind, each of whom will find different value in different parts of it.

Business Leaders and Executives

If you are a C-suite executive, a business unit leader, or a board member responsible for AI strategy, this book will give you the strategic frameworks, investment rationale, and industry-specific evidence you need to make confident decisions about where and how to deploy generative AI. You will find the ROI evidence, the competitive analysis, and the governance frameworks that allow you to lead AI transformation rather than simply respond to it.

Technology Leaders and Architects

If you are a CTO, CIO, Chief Data Officer, or solutions architect responsible for the technical implementation of AI at scale, this book will give you the reference architectures, deployment patterns, infrastructure considerations, and MLOps frameworks that translate AI strategy into production systems. Each industry chapter includes technical depth alongside business context, reflecting the reality that technology decisions in AI cannot be separated from the business problems they are designed to solve.

Domain Experts and Knowledge Workers

If you are a clinician, financial analyst, manufacturing engineer, creative professional, automotive specialist, or domain expert in any of the industries covered in this book, you will find practical guidance on how generative AI changes your work—not in the abstract, but in the specific workflows, tools, and professional practices that define your role. This book will help you understand which aspects of your expertise AI amplifies, which it challenges, and how to position yourself to thrive in an AI-augmented profession.

AI Practitioners and Researchers

If you are a data scientist, machine learning engineer, AI researcher, or technical practitioner working on generative AI systems, this book will give you the business and industry context that makes technical work meaningful and directs it toward high-value applications. Understanding why a healthcare system needs ambient AI scribes, why a financial institution needs explainable credit models, and why a manufacturer needs generative design tools will make you a more effective contributor to the teams building those systems.

What You Will Learn

This book is organized into three parts that build on each other deliberately.

Part 1 establishes the foundations—the conceptual, historical, and technical grounding that makes everything else in the book comprehensible and actionable. Part 2 applies those foundations to specific industries, examining in depth how generative AI is transforming healthcare, financial services, manufacturing, automotive, and media and entertainment. Part 3 addresses the cross-cutting capabilities—productivity, creativity, customer experience, and enterprise decision-making—that span every industry and every organization.

The following table summarizes what each chapter contributes to your understanding of generative AI for industries:

Chapter	Title	What You Will Learn
Chapter 1	**The AI Inflection Point: Why Generative AI Represents a Paradigm Shift**	You will learn why 2025 represents a genuine paradigm shift rather than an incremental improvement, how to think about the four waves of AI evolution, what distinguishes generative AI from all previous AI technologies, and how to assess your organization's position on the early-adopter to late-adopter spectrum.

(*continued*)

Chapter	Title	What You Will Learn
Chapter 2	**Foundations of Generative AI: The Evolution of AI Development and Deployment**	You will learn the mathematical and statistical principles that underpin generative models, how training methodologies including RLHF and constitutional AI shape model behavior, how to think about scaling laws and their implications for investment decisions, and the deployment patterns and production considerations that determine whether AI systems succeed in the real world.
Chapter 3	**Technical Underpinnings of Generative AI: Key Capabilities and Limitations of Current Systems**	You will learn how transformer architectures work and why they represent such a decisive advance over prior approaches, what large language models can and cannot do, where current systems genuinely excel and where they reliably fail, and how to set realistic expectations for AI capability that will survive contact with production environments.
Chapter 4	**Productivity Revolution: How Generative AI Redefines Knowledge Work**	You will learn how generative AI is redefining knowledge work across engineering, finance, healthcare, and every other domain that relies on expertise and contextual reasoning, how to distinguish AI copilots from AI agents and govern each appropriately, how to build an AI-ready organization through centers of excellence and structured enablement, and how to execute the 90-day adoption playbook that separates successful implementations from expensive experiments.

(*continued*)

Chapter	Title	What You Will Learn
Chapter 5	**Creative Industries in the Age of AI Co-creation**	You will learn how generative AI is transforming film, music, gaming, publishing, and advertising—not by replacing human creativity but by restructuring the creative process itself; how to navigate the intellectual property, bias, and authenticity challenges that AI co-creation introduces; and how leading creative organizations are positioning AI as a creative multiplier rather than a creative substitute.
Chapter 6	**Enterprise GenAI Decision Framework**	You will learn a structured framework for making build-vs.-buy decisions, sequencing AI use cases by impact and feasibility, establishing governance that enables rather than obstructs innovation, and aligning AI investment with measurable business outcomes at the enterprise level.
Chapter 7	**Customer Experience Transformation Through Personalization**	You will learn how the combination of traditional machine learning and generative AI creates personalization capabilities that were previously impossible at scale, the technical architecture required to deliver sub-100-millisecond personalized experiences across millions of customers, how to build responsible personalization that earns customer trust rather than eroding it, and the measurement frameworks that connect personalization investment to business outcomes.

(*continued*)

Chapter	Title	What You Will Learn
Chapter 8	**Healthcare: From Diagnosis to Drug Discovery**	You will learn how ambient AI scribes are returning thousands of clinician hours to patient care; how generative models are transforming diagnostic imaging, drug discovery, and clinical trial design; how to navigate the regulatory, privacy, and safety requirements that make healthcare AI uniquely complex; and how different healthcare settings—academic medical centers, community hospitals, and integrated health systems—require different implementation approaches.
Chapter 9	**Financial Services: Risk Assessment, Fraud Detection, and Personalized Banking**	You will learn how AI is transforming credit decisioning, fraud detection, and customer personalization in financial services; how leading institutions including NatWest, Travelers, Nasdaq, S&P Global, and Mitsubishi UFJ Bank have achieved measurable business outcomes from generative AI; how to build AI governance frameworks that satisfy regulators while enabling innovation; and how the rise of agentic AI is beginning to reshape lending, underwriting, and claims processing.
Chapter 10	**GenAI in Manufacturing: Design Optimization and Supply Chain Intelligence CAD Software**	You will learn how generative design is replacing traditional CAD workflows with AI-driven multi-objective optimization, how foundation models are transforming demand forecasting and supply chain planning, how digital twins powered by generative AI are enabling predictive maintenance and virtual commissioning, and how conversational AI assistants are changing the experience of work on the shop floor.

(*continued*)

Chapter	Title	What You Will Learn
Chapter 11	**Automotive Industry: Personalization at Scale**	You will learn how generative AI is reshaping the automotive value chain from R&D and manufacturing through sales, in-vehicle experience, and ownership lifecycle; how Software-Defined Vehicles and agentic AI are converging to create AI-defined vehicles; how to architect personalization platforms that scale across millions of vehicles while meeting GDPR, CCPA, and automotive safety standards; and how leading OEMs are treating personalization as a core digital product rather than a feature.
Chapter 12	**Media and Entertainment: Content Creation and Audience Engagement**	You will learn how generative AI is transforming every stage of the media production pipeline from concept development through post-production and distribution; how streaming platforms, sports broadcasters, gaming studios, and news organizations are leveraging AI for hyper-personalization and operational efficiency; how to navigate the copyright, authenticity, and creative labor questions that AI co-creation raises; and how to build the organizational capabilities that allow creative professionals to lead AI adoption rather than be displaced by it.

How to Read This Book

This book is designed to be read in sequence, but it is also designed to be useful in any order, depending on your role and your most pressing priorities.

If You Are Reading As a Business Leader or Executive

Begin with Chapters 1 and 6. Chapter 1 will give you the strategic framing—the inflection point, the competitive stakes, the early-adopter advantage—that makes everything else urgent and concrete. Chapter 6 will give you the enterprise decision framework that translates strategic intent into investment sequencing and governance design. From there, read the industry chapters most relevant to your sector, then return to Chapter 4 for the organizational transformation playbook.

If You Are Reading As a Technology Leader or Architect

Begin with Chapters 2 and 3, which provide the technical foundations you need to evaluate AI capabilities honestly and set realistic expectations for your stakeholders. Then work through the industry chapters most relevant to your deployment context, paying particular attention to the reference architectures, deployment patterns, and MLOps considerations in each. Chapter 7 provides particularly detailed technical architecture guidance for personalization systems that applies across industries.

If You Are Reading As a Domain Expert

Go directly to the chapter covering your industry, then read Chapter 4 for the workforce transformation and organizational readiness frameworks that apply to every knowledge-intensive profession. Chapters 5 and 7 are also valuable regardless of your specific domain, as they address the creative and customer experience dimensions of AI that touch every industry.

If You Are Reading As an AI Practitioner

Read Chapters 2 and 3 for technical depth, then use the industry chapters as a map of the highest-value application domains. Each industry chapter includes implementation patterns, architectural guidance, and code examples that will orient your technical work toward problems where it will have the most impact.

The Principles That Guided This Book

Every book reflects choices—about what to include and what to leave out, about what to argue and what to leave open. We want to be transparent about the principles that shaped ours.

AI As Amplifier, Not Replacement

We believe the most important thing to understand about generative AI is that it creates its greatest value by amplifying human capability rather than replacing human judgment. This is not wishful thinking or a hedge against a technology we find threatening. It is what the evidence consistently shows. Every mature, high-value AI implementation examined in this book preserves a meaningful role for human expertise at the point where the stakes are highest. We have written this book accordingly, and we are skeptical of framings—whether utopian or dystopian—that treat AI as a substitute for human intelligence rather than a collaborator with it.

Implementation over Theory

There is no shortage of books about what AI might eventually do. This book is about what AI is doing now, in real organizations facing real constraints. Every strategic claim we make is grounded in evidence from actual deployments. Every framework we offer has been tested against the messy reality of enterprise implementation. We have tried to be honest about what is working, what is not, and where the evidence is genuinely uncertain.

Responsibility As a Competitive Advantage

We believe that ethical AI—AI that is transparent, fair, privacy-preserving, and accountable—is not in tension with effective AI. It is a prerequisite for it. Organizations that treat governance, bias mitigation, and explainability as obstacles to be minimized will eventually face the regulatory, reputational, and customer trust consequences of that choice. Organizations that build responsibility into their AI programs from the start will find that it enables them to move faster, scale further, and earn the kind of customer trust that no marketing budget can purchase.

Industry Depth over Breadth

We made the deliberate choice to go deep on a specific set of industries rather than attempting to survey the entire landscape of generative AI applications. Healthcare, financial services, manufacturing, automotive, and media and entertainment were chosen because they represent a diverse cross-section of AI maturity, regulatory environment, data characteristics, and workforce impact and because the depth of coverage possible within each allowed us to provide genuinely useful implementation guidance rather than high-altitude observation.

A Note on Pace

Generative AI is moving faster than any book can track. By the time you read these words, new models will have been released, new capabilities will have emerged, and some of the specific tools and platforms referenced in individual chapters will have been updated, superseded, or discontinued.

We have tried to write a book that ages well despite this reality. The strategic frameworks—the force multiplier principle, the five patterns of successful adoption, the enterprise decision framework, and the governance imperatives—are grounded in principles that do not change with each new model release. The industry analyses are structured around business problems and organizational dynamics that evolve slowly, even as the technology changes rapidly. The implementation guidance is expressed in patterns and principles rather than version-specific tool configurations wherever possible.

What will not change is the fundamental dynamic this book describes: the organizations that build the data foundations, governance structures, talent capabilities, and cultural conditions for sustained AI advantage now will find those advantages compounding over time. The organizations that wait for the technology to stabilize before investing will find themselves perpetually behind a moving target.

The field is moving fast. This book is designed to help you move purposefully.

An Invitation

Writing this book required us to look carefully at what is actually happening with generative AI in the industries we cover—not what is being claimed in press releases or promised in pitch decks, but what is working in production, what is failing in deployment, and what the organizations achieving genuine results are doing differently from those that are not.

What we found was simultaneously more encouraging and more demanding than the mainstream AI narrative suggests. More encouraging because the value being created by well-implemented generative AI is real, measurable, and in many cases transformative—not for some distant future version of the technology, but for the systems being deployed today. More demanding because the path to that value is not the simple plug-and-play that AI vendors often imply. It requires investment in foundations that take time to build, governance that requires organizational will to sustain, and talent development that does not happen overnight.

We wrote this book because we believe that the leaders who understand both the opportunity and the demands—who approach generative AI with strategic clarity, implementation discipline, and a genuine commitment to responsible deployment—will be the ones who look back on this period as the moment they established an enduring advantage.

We invite you to be one of those leaders.

Welcome to *Building Generative AI Solutions for Industries with AWS.*

CHAPTER 1

The AI Inflection Point

1.1 Introduction

Generative AI poses a challenge to the human mind in terms of uniqueness and creativity. It is designed to think, process, imagine, create, and generate like the human mind. It is based on human neural networks and large language models (LLMs), which demonstrate remarkable capabilities in generating diverse content, triggering heated debates over authorship, copyright infringement, and the very nature of intelligence.

Generative AI algorithms are trained on massive datasets that can generate new data similar to the input data they were trained on, and they can be improved through continuous learning. Generative AI can produce unique results, with far-reaching applications across a variety of businesses. It opens the horizon of artificial intelligence, not just to analyze or predict, but also to generate results, expanding opportunities across various sectors.

1.1.1 Why Generative AI Matters for Business?

Generative AI matters for businesses because of its market positioning, high ROI, cost reduction, and competitive advantage.

- GenAI adds 15–40% incremental economic value compared to other AI and analytics.
- Work productivity increased by 35–70% by the implementation of GenAI automation.
- Generative AI helps organizations in marketing by generating high-quality creative and personalized content that leads to cost reduction by 5–15%.

N. Sendas et al., *Building Generative AI Solutions for Industries with AWS*,
https://doi.org/10.1007/979-8-8688-2830-0_1

- Generative AI shows immersive potential in R&D, manufacturing, customer care, marketing, and sales that saves time and money.
- Early adopters of generative AI are implementing industry-specific solutions to gain long-term leadership and showcase their value potential by offering differentiated products.

1.1.2 The AI Inflection Point: Why Generative AI Represents a Paradigm Shift

Generative AI is fast evolving, ushering in a paradigm shift for both businesses and everyday consumers across practically every industry. AI success stories can be built within organizations by increasing competitiveness and adaptability; otherwise, these rapidly developing technologies have immense disruptive potential and an unexpected threat. Employees also need to adapt to the developing generative AI technologies so that they do not risk their jobs.

According to Gartner, generative artificial intelligence (AI) is positioned at the peak of the hype cycle for emerging technologies in 2023 and is anticipated to have a significant revolutionary impact within two to five years. Generative AI opens new avenues for innovation and opportunities for businesses, employees, and customers.

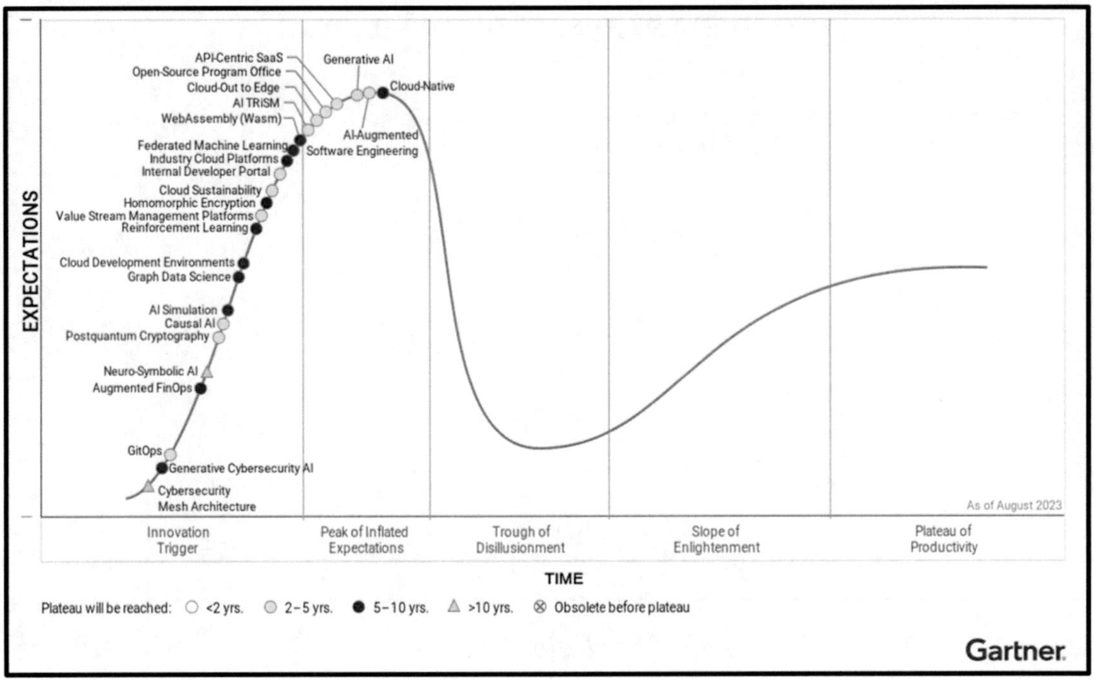

Figure 1-1. *Hype Cycle for Emerging Technologies, 2023*

When Did the Shift Happen?

To understand the inflection point and when the actual shift happens, we divide AI evolution into four waves. Let's understand them in detail.

Wave 1: Efficiency (2020+)

In wave 1, organizations mostly focus on cost reduction and the automation of iterative tasks and on eliminating human errors by deploying narrow AI applications.

Wave 2: Excellence (2023+)

In wave 2, organizations focus on consistently enhancing the quality and performance of existing processes and products. Rather than just automating what humans do, wave 2 technologies boost human capabilities and enable previously unattainable levels of performance.

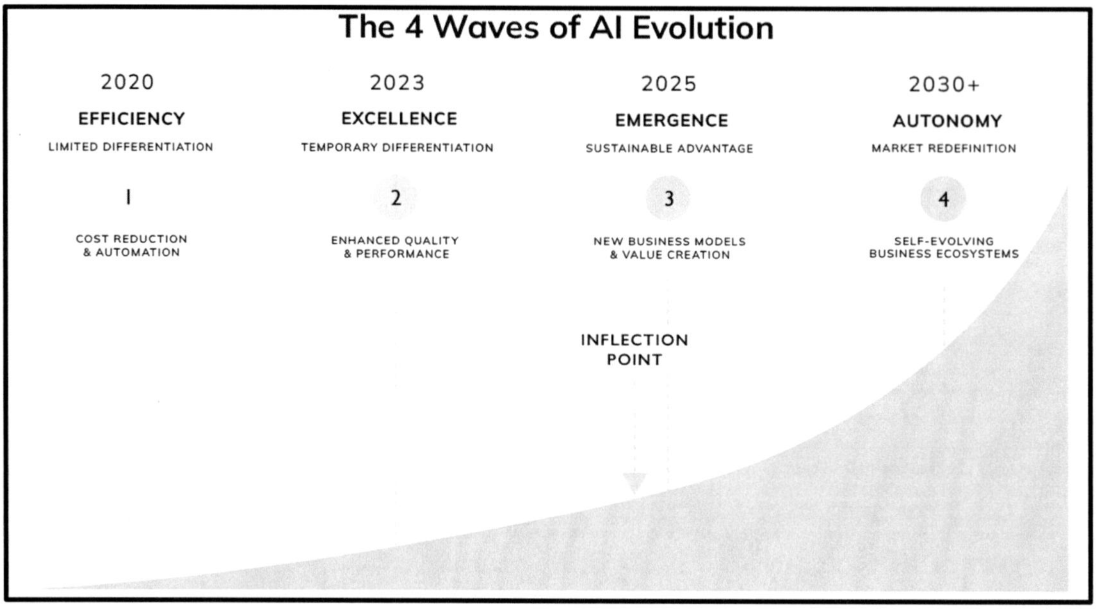

Figure 1-2. *The Four Waves of AI Evolution*

Wave 3: Emergence (2025+)

Wave 3 focuses on developing entirely new business models, value propositions, and market segments with AI at their core.

Wave 3 is the critical inflection point.

The AI revolution has reached a critical inflection point in 2025–2027, dividing businesses into market leaders who will enjoy massive profits and followers who risk becoming obsolete.

The inflection point is complex, messy, and urgent for business success with AI. It requires parallel experimentation to learn faster and adapt to rapidly evolving AI capabilities, which can be possible with AI specialists. The AI ecosystem needs to be set up to access specialized AI capabilities and transform the data assets into generative capabilities.

Wave 4: Autonomy (2030+)

Wave 4 portrays the future, which emphasizes self-evolving corporate ecosystems with minimal human intervention. To address complicated problems, AI systems will not only execute but also choose strategies, redesign themselves regularly, and communicate with one another.

Why Does AI Inflection Point Matter to Leaders and Organizations?

The AI inflection point conveys to leaders and organizations that GenAI is no longer an experimental or an add-on technology. It is becoming a core driver of competitiveness, innovation, and long-term survival. Organizations that have invested early in AI, data foundations, and scalable platforms will be in a leading position during the critical inflection point. Those who delay this investment will fall behind as new business models, innovations, and technologies will not survive without GenAI.

For employees, continuous upskilling is essential to stay relevant, and for industries, an early move to adopt GenAI technology is beneficial in many ways for long-term business benefits.

Here is a business view framework for early adopters vs. late adopters

Table 1-1. *Early adopters vs. late adopters*

Dimension	Early Adopters	Late Adopters
Market Share Implications	First-mover advantage, strong brand association with GenAI innovation, and expanding market share through differentiated and faster offerings.	Loose first mover opportunities, compete for niche positioning and pricing, and struggle to displace incumbents.
Competitive Moat Opportunities	Establish an ecosystem, proprietary data assets, models, and integrated AI platforms that are difficult for competitors to replicate.	Dependent on third-party AI tools and platforms, creating weak differentiation.
Customer Expectations Evaluations	Establish the brand as a leader and elevate consumer expectations around proactive, intelligent, and personalized experiences.	Forced to respond rather than innovate to meet customer expectations set by market leaders.

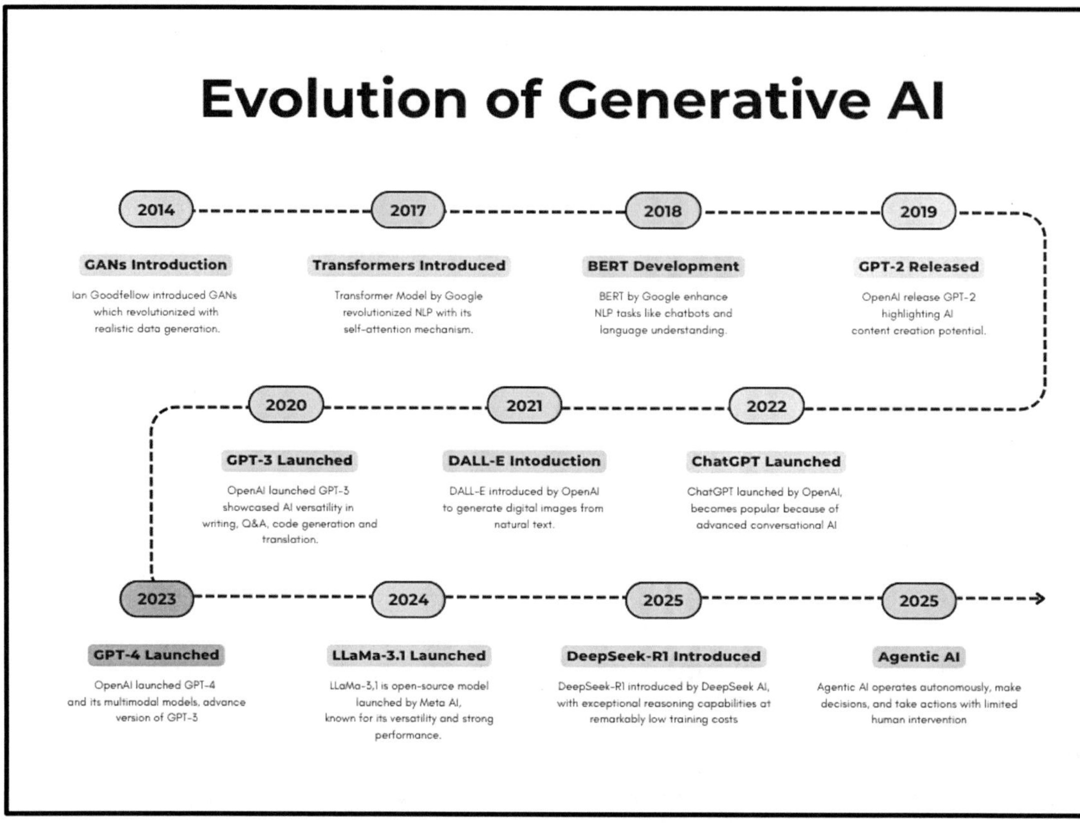

Figure 1-3. *The Evolution of Generative AI over the Years*

Generative AI got a key breakthrough in 2014 with the invention of Generative Adversarial Networks (GANs) by Ian Goodfellow, enabling AI to generate realistic images, which accelerated progress in computer vision and art generation.

In 2017, Google researchers introduced the "Transformer" that revolutionized natural language processing with its self-attention mechanism, which led to BERT by Google that introduced an advanced humanlike conversation system, like chatbots.

OpenAI launched GPT-2 in 2019, followed by GPT-3 in 2020, which has the potential to enable large-scale text generation into mainstream use, followed by DALL-E in 2021.

In 2022, ChatGPT, based on GPT-3.5, became popular with its advanced conversational AI, even for common users without any technical knowledge. Later, in 2023, GPT-4 and its multimodal AI came to global attention for its broader context window.

Open source innovation expanded with Meta AI's LLaMA models in 2024, and in 2025, DeepSeek AI introduced DeepSeek-R1, a low-cost, high-reasoning model.

Today, in 2025, generative AI stands at an inflection point with agentic AI, which are smart and empowered AI systems designed to operate autonomously with limited human intervention. Agentic AI solves multi-step complex problems with sophisticated reasoning, decision-making, and iterative planning, thus enhancing productivity and operations across industries.

Multimodal AI and Agentic AI

Multimodal AI refers to an advanced AI system capable of simultaneously processing and understanding multiple types of data, such as text, audio, images, and video, for richer insights.

Agentic AI takes the AI system a step further by being proactive rather than reactive and acting autonomously and making decisions according to the user's requirements without human intervention.

Multimodal AI and agentic AI combine to form **Multimodal Agentic AI,** which understands the various forms of input and acts independently to assist the user. With multimodal agentic AI, personalized customer service, and AI-powered digital human agents, real-time interactions with different types of customers are possible, enabling them to solve queries and issues directly with a personalized touch, like humans.

Multimodal Agentic AI shows highly evolved AI capabilities with increased human–AI interaction. It makes AI more intuitive and can be seamlessly integrated into people's daily lives with applications in healthcare, smart homes, AI education, and customer assistance services.

How Does Multimodal and Agentic AI Impact Businesses?

Multimodal and agentic AI helps the business thrive by automating the routine tasks and helps the organization in many ways:

- High efficiency
- Time-saving
- Cost reduction
- Quick decision-making
- Improved customer experience

- Generating new revenue streams
- Personalized digital agents

1.1.3 Historical Context: From Rule-Based Systems to Generative Models

The evolution from rule-based systems to the advent of machine learning in the 1980s is a revolution that reflects a significant shift in scale and improvement over time. The transition from a rule-based approach to generative models is a transformative and fascinating journey.

The evolution of machine learning was followed by the expansion of neural networks and deep learning in the 2000s, fueled by advancements in computational power, including higher processing speeds and the ability to handle massive data, which led to breakthroughs in image recognition, natural language processing, and autonomous systems. Currently, AI is being driven by transformative technologies such as large-scale pre-trained models and generative AI, which are changing industries ranging from healthcare to creative arts.

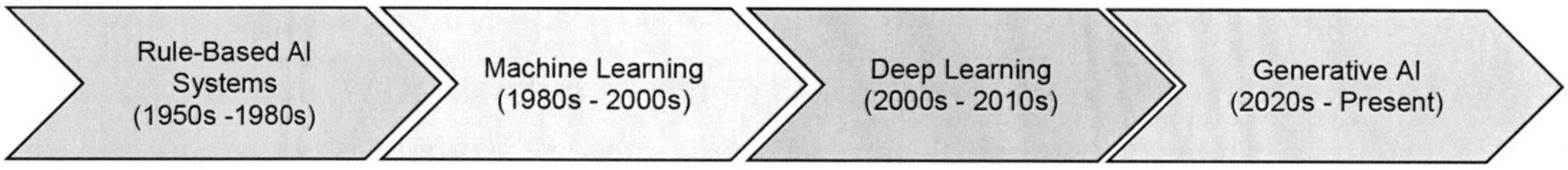

Figure 1-4. *The Four Waves of AI Evolution*

Rules-Based AI Systems: The Birth of AI

The first era of AI, often referred to as symbolic AI, was based on replicating human reasoning by encoding. The encoding of human intelligence was first done through logical rules and complex relationships in computers. The expert problem-solving systems were developed by implementing a wide range of "if-then" rules that mimic human decision-making in specific domains.

Key Milestones of Rule-Based AI Systems

1. Alan Turing and the Turing Test (1950)

   Alan Turing, a British mathematician, developed the Turing Test in 1950 to assess a machine's capacity to demonstrate intelligent behavior comparable to that of a human.

2. Dartmouth Conference (1956)

   The term artificial intelligence was coined at the Dartmouth Conference in 1956, and that time is officially considered the "birth of AI." It was announced at the conference that any facet of learning or other feature of intelligence can be precisely characterized so that a machine can replicate it.

3. Formal Logic and Problem-Solving Development

   Early AI researchers focused heavily on formalizing human reasoning through logic and problem-solving techniques, which laid the groundwork for later AI developments.

Challenges and Limitations of Rule-Based AI Systems

In the 1950s, rule-based systems were a huge success, but with time, they faced many challenges and limitations in critical ways:

1. Flexibility Issues

   Rule-based AI systems follow predefined rules and handle a fixed set of inputs and situations, making them inflexible in the face of unseen situations.

2. Scalability Issues

   As the scope of problems increased, the number of rules required to represent knowledge accurately grew exponentially, making these systems cumbersome and difficult to manage.

3. Brittleness

   Rule-based AI is highly brittle in real-world applications, as it cannot handle uncertain input that does not exactly match the rules.

4. Adaptability Issues

   Rule-based AI systems struggled to adapt to the complexity of human intelligence despite making significant strides in problem-solving.

Machine Learning: Predictive AI

The 1980s to 2000s were the era of machine learning (ML), a subset of AI, marked by a pivotal shift in the development of artificial intelligence. Over time, researchers have recognized the limitations of rule-based systems, and they have pursued new approaches that focus on learning from data rather than relying solely on predefined rules.

Key Milestones of Machine Learning

1. Supervised Learning

   Supervised learning is one of the foundational techniques of machine learning, where a model is trained on a labeled dataset to make predictions for new, unseen data. This method is used for fraud detection, customer retention, churn prediction, forecasting, and more.

2. Unsupervised Learning

   In unsupervised learning, models are trained on a dataset without labeled outputs. This method is instrumental in tasks such as customer segmentation, recommendation systems, and meaningful compression, among others.

3. Reinforcement Learning (RL)

   Reinforcement learning (RL) involves model training through a trial-and-error process in which an agent continuously receives feedback and learns to make decisions with it. RL was relatively niche at the time, but it paved the way for eventual advances in autonomous systems and robotics.

4. The Support Vector Machine (SVM)

   SVMs were developed in the 1990s and have become a powerful tool for classification tasks, allowing machines to separate data into distinct categories by finding the optimal hyperplane. This approach has proven useful across a range of real-world applications, including image recognition and bioinformatics.

5. Ensemble Methods

   Ensemble methods such as Gradient Boosting, Random Forests, and AdaBoost gained prominence in the 1990s and 2000s. These ensemble methods combine multiple models to improve the model's prediction accuracy and overcome individual model limitations.

Challenges and Limitations

While machine learning has substantially enhanced AI, there have been certain challenges:

1. Data Limitations

   Early ML algorithms necessitated huge volumes of labeled data for supervised learning, which was difficult to obtain, particularly in specialized disciplines such as health and science.

2. Computational Constraints

   Machine learning algorithms were computationally intensive, and existing hardware couldn't always provide the required processing power, limiting the range of possible applications.

3. Overfitting

   One common issue with machine learning models is overfitting, where a model performs well on training data but poorly on new, untested data. Excessive model complexity or overfitting to the training data can impair generalizability.

Neural Networks and Deep Learning: Breakthrough in AI

Neural networks are inspired by the neural structure of the human brain and were introduced in the 1950s and 1960s. But, due to computational and data constraints, it was not widely used till the 2000s. There were two breakthroughs in the 2000s: Graphical Processing Units and Big Data, which enhanced the deep learning models.

Key Milestones of Deep Learning

Let's discuss the key milestones of the deep learning journey:

1. Transfer Learning

   Transfer learning became a key strategy for deep learning in the 2010s, enabling a model trained on one task to be adapted for a different, but related task. This technique enabled deep learning models to perform well on tasks with limited data by leveraging pre-trained models, such as those trained on large datasets like ImageNet, across a variety of applications.

2. Convolutional Neural Network (CNN)

   CNN is a deep learning model that revolutionized the way machines process image and video data. With CNNs, image classification, object detection, and facial recognition have achieved high accuracy levels previously thought unattainable. CNN has had a significant impact on the surveillance, automotive, and entertainment industries.

3. AlexNet

   AlexNet is a convolutional neural network (CNN) that revolutionized the field of image recognition. In 2012, it won the ImageNet Large Scale Visual Recognition Challenge (ILSVRC), significantly outperforming other models at the time and demonstrating the power of deep learning.

4. Recurrent Neural Networks (RNNs)

   A recurrent neural network is designed for sequential data, such as time series data or text data. LSTMs are an upgraded version of RNNs that analyze sequences of data in memory, making them especially suitable for tasks such as language modeling, speech recognition, and machine translation.

5. Natural Language Processing (NLP)

   NLP has seen significant advances in understanding human language with deep learning models like LSTMs, attention mechanisms in 2014, and transformer models in 2017. The development of Google's BERT model in 2018 has given new heights to NLP tasks, including question answering, machine translation, and sentiment analysis.

6. Generative Adversarial Networks (GANs)

   For the first time, Generative Adversarial Networks (GANs) were introduced by Ian Goodfellow in 2014, which consist of two neural networks: the generator and the discriminator that work against each other to improve the quality of generated data, such as images, audio, or text. GANs demonstrated great success in producing realistic visuals, and they have since been applied in fields such as art creation, data augmentation, and drug discovery.

Challenges and Limitations

Deep learning models reached heights of success, but faced various challenges and limitations in the 2000s and 2010s:

1. Computation and Data Requirements

   Training deep learning models requires a large amount of cleaned, labeled data and substantial computational resources, which is a concern.

2. Time Consumption

   Deep learning models are time-consuming and computationally expensive to train.

3. Ethical Issues

   As deep learning systems became increasingly prevalent, concerns about bias, privacy, and the ethical application of AI developed.

4. Black-Box Nature

   Deep learning models follow a "black-box" approach, which makes them opaque and difficult to interpret. This creates issues regarding openness, accountability, and fairness in decision-making systems, especially in sensitive sectors such as healthcare and criminal justice.

Generative AI and Large Language Models (LLMs): Rise of a New Era

Generative AI is the most sensational technological advancement, widely used in day-to-day activities. The main models behind today's generative AI are large language models (LLMs) and Generative Adversarial Networks (GANs), which are capable of generating humanlike content. These models are trained on massive databases of text from books, websites, art, music, and other sources, enabling them to capture intricate patterns and expertise.

Key Milestones of Generative AI

Major key milestones achieved by generative AI are as follows:

1. Autonomous Systems

   The development of self-driving cars, drones, and robots remains a prominent trend in artificial intelligence. These systems are based on deep learning, computer vision, and reinforcement learning to navigate complicated surroundings and complete tasks with minimum human intervention.

2. Healthcare

   AI's contribution to healthcare is quickly expanding, with advances in diagnostics, medication development, personalized treatment, and patient care. AI is also playing a role in predictive medicine by forecasting illness progression and suggesting preventive treatments.

3. AI in Creativity

   AI is gaining popularity in the creative field, such as creating art, music, literature, stories, and other forms of content. AI is increasingly seen as a co-creator, enhancing human creativity and enabling new forms of artistic expression.

4. Customer Services

   AI offered enhanced customer services, like AI-powered chatbots and virtual assistants, in sectors such as retail, finance, and telecommunications. These systems can answer consumer questions, process transactions, and make personalized recommendations, improving user experience and lowering the operating expenses.

Challenges and Limitations

Key challenges and limitations faced by today's generation of AI are as follows:

1. Privacy and Data Security

   Too much data is available on online social platforms, and AI relies largely on this big data, much of which contains personally identifiable and sensitive information that raises serious privacy and data security concerns. Personal data must be collected, stored, and used with caution to avoid misuse, breaches, or unauthorized access.

2. Liability and Accountability

   The progress of generative AI has made AI more independent and capable of making decisions. If something goes wrong, who will be liable and accountable for that? AI, a developer, or an organization that makes the system.

3. Economic Impact

   Artificial intelligence and automation are altering industries and labor markets, generating concerns about job loss and economic inequality. As AI systems become more capable of performing tasks previously performed by people, there is concern that many jobs may be lost, resulting in unemployment and societal instability.

4. Overreliance on AI

   Relying on AI to make critical decisions may result in the loss of human judgment and knowledge. The healthcare sector and criminal justice are two such sectors that need human judgment for accurate judgment, rather than relying completely on AI.

5. Safety and Security Concerns

   Highly autonomous AI systems pose new security and safety hazards such as cyberattacks, adversarial attacks, commit fraud, and engage in other undesirable actions like autonomous weapon attacks.

1.1.4 Defining the Scope: What Makes Generative AI Different from Previous Technologies

Generative AI made a sensation with the most widely used generative AI app, ChatGPT, in 2022. Earlier, traditional AI had significantly influenced various business domains.

Understanding Generative AI

Generative AI is a subset of artificial intelligence that focuses on generating new content based on already existing data, such as text, photos, music, audio, video, and 3D models. Generative AI is one of the AI implementations that uses large language models (LLMs). LLMs are trained over huge datasets, and they learn and discover patterns from the existing data and generate something new which is similar to the original. Sometimes, it is so similar that it is difficult to distinguish between original and generated content.

In contrast to existing AI systems that have humanlike intelligence, which are designed to perform certain tasks, generative AI can generate whole new content or new data without explicit instructions.

Understanding Traditional AI

Traditional AI employs predefined rules and logic to emulate the human mind's learning and problem-solving capabilities. It employs rules created by people to evaluate huge databases, interpret, and predict outputs as per the data problem.

There are several fields of Traditional AI, such as machine learning, deep learning, natural language processing (NLP), and computer vision, which work significantly in the real world.

Difference Between Generative AI and Traditional AI

Let's compare generative AI and traditional AI in a tabular format.

Table 1-2. *Generative AI and traditional AI: a comparison*

Category	Traditional AI	Generative AI
Aim	A rule-based problem-solving approach works on labelled data for data modeling and prediction.	A creative approach for generating new data based on human creativity and instinct.
Data Requirements	Demands large volumes of structured and labeled data.	It operates on huge volumes of unlabeled data, which is diverse.
Models used	• Regression and classification models • Artificial neural networks (ANN) • Recurrent neural network (RNN) • Convolutional neural network (CNN) • Natural language processing (NLP)	• GANs (Generative Adversarial Networks) • VAEs (Variational Autoencoders) • RNNs (recurrent neural networks) • Transformer models • Diffusion models
Strengths	• It can rapidly handle and analyze massive amounts of data while producing reliable results. • It solves problems with precision and high efficiency.	• It can generate new content like text, audio, music, code, video, images, and 3D models. • It offers a high level of creativity and adaptability.
Limitations	• Traditional AI cannot handle tasks that require creativity. • It is not able to adapt to new and unforeseen circumstances.	• GenAI fails to overcome potential biases in training data. • The creation of GenAI models needs high computational resources, time, and expertise.
Applications	Used widely in various sectors like banking, healthcare, retail, ecommerce, etc., for predictions, decision-making, and process automation.	Used for creative content creation and artistic expression, such as art, music, code, videos, images, documents, etc., for various domains.

Various Generative AI Models

There are various types of generative AI models. Let's discuss widely used models here:

1. GANs (Generative Adversarial Networks)

   Generative Adversarial Networks are a combination of two neural networks: a generator and a discriminator, which compete against each other to generate data. It was the first model for generative AI introduced in 2014 by Ian Goodfellow, and it became a revolution in the field of AI. The adversarial process generates very realistic outputs, making GANs effective in producing photorealistic images, voice, and motions. DALL-E 2 and Style GAN are popular and widely used GAN models.

2. VAEs (Variational Autoencoders)

   Variational Autoencoders are based on an encoder-decoder architecture where they implement probabilistic models that compress incoming data before decoding it to produce new, equivalent material. Some of the examples of VAEs are NVAE and convolutional VAE.

3. Autoregressive Models

   Autoregressive models generate output sequentially, by predicting the next token of an element in a series based on previous elements. They excel in creating coherent sequences of text, music, and other sequenced data. GPT-3 and GPT-4 are the popular autoregressive models.

4. Transformer Models

   Transformer models have made enormous advances across various natural language processing tasks and complex sequence generation. Transformers use self-attention, resulting in significant advances in language understanding and generation. BERT and GPT-3 are based on a transformer model.

5. Diffusion Models

 Diffusion models generate data by gradually transforming random noise into coherent outputs using a series of learning steps. They've become popular for producing high-quality photos. Famous examples are DALL-E 2 and Stable Diffusion.

The Technical-Business Translation

For any organization, generative AI adoption requires both technical and business readiness, and they need to work hand-in-hand. Technical teams must be skilled in AI, data readiness, and scalable infrastructure. At the same time, business leaders must establish data governance, invest in training, accept calculated risks, and define realistic ROI expectations. Sustainable GenAI success happens only when technology capability and business strategy mature together.

AI projects become stagnant if technical systems are robust but business alignment is weak. Projects fail when business ambitions are high but technical foundations are weak.

Let's take an example of deploying an AI agent for supply chain planning:

To deploy an AI agent for supply chain planning, the technical team builds a generative AI agent that can automate multi-step workflows with ERP, CRM, and analytics systems. From the business perspective, AI agents execute the routine planning, reporting, and coordination tasks at a faster speed, with fewer errors and minimal human effort.

GenAI capabilities, combined with real business values, minimize effort, make quick operational decisions, and achieve practical outcomes.

Future of Generative AI

The future of generative AI has immense potential across various industries, and with the emergence of multimodal AI and agentic AI, its accessibility has been enhanced. With the evolution of generative AI, cybersecurity threat also increases, and organizations are developing strategies and implementing ethical measures to integrate generative AI into their security frameworks to stay ahead of evolving threats.

In the future, with the advent of generative AI, it will be necessary to strike a balance between technical and business perspectives by increasing innovation, generation, and productivity with secure, ethical, and responsible deployment of these technologies.

1.2 References

- https://arxiv.org/html/2504.07936v1
- https://arxiv.org/html/2411.05902v1
- https://www.mckinsey.com/capabilities/tech-and-ai/our-insights/the-economic-potential-of-generative-ai-the-next-productivity-frontier
- https://www.gartner.com/en/newsroom/press-releases/2023-08-16-gartner-places-generative-ai-on-the-peak-of-inflated-expectations-on-the-2023-hype-cycle-for-emerging-technologies
- https://www.linkedin.com/pulse/ai-inflection-point-why-2025-separate-market-leaders-from-axel-unger-i5zmf/
- https://lanternstudios.com/insights/blog/the-history-of-ai-from-rules-based-algorithms-to-generative-models/
- https://www.researchgate.net/publication/388035967_The_Evolution_of_AI_From_Rule-Based_Systems_to_Data-Driven_Intelligence
- https://www.linkedin.com/pulse/what-makes-generative-ai-different-from-other-anthony-bartolo/
- https://medium.com/@byanalytixlabs/generative-ai-vs-traditional-ai-understand-key-differences-ca2d3e37c45d

CHAPTER 2

Foundations of Generative AI: The Evolution of AI Development and Deployment

In the introduction chapter, we have understood the basic difference between traditional AI and generative AI. Additionally, we have discussed AI evolution from rule-based models to generative models. Generative AI is considered the AI inflection point where a paradigm shift actually happens. Now, it's time to deep dive into the foundations of generative AI. In this chapter, we will cover the following foundational topics in detail:

1. Mathematical and statistical foundations
2. Architecture evolution and technical details
3. Training methodologies and optimization
4. Scaling laws and computational considerations
5. Data engineering for GenAI
6. Deployment patterns and production considerations

2.1 Mathematical and Statistical Foundations

The mathematical and statistical foundations behind generative AI are divided into probabilistic foundations and core mathematical concepts.

N. Sendas et al., *Building Generative AI Solutions for Industries with AWS*,
https://doi.org/10.1007/979-8-8688-2830-0_2

2.1.1 Probabilistic Foundations

- Maximum Likelihood Estimation in Generative Modeling

  Generative modeling aims to learn the underlying probability distribution of data so that it can generate new, similar kinds of data. A key statistical method used in training generative models is **Maximum Likelihood Estimation (MLE),** which is used to estimate the parameters of a probability distribution by maximizing the likelihood function of the observed data.

Generative Models that use Maximum Likelihood Estimation (MLE) are Variational Autoencoders (VAEs), diffusion models, Gaussian Mixture Models (GMMs), and Hidden Markov Models (HMMs).

  Business Implications of Maximum Likelihood Estimation: It helps in producing better quality model results for loyal users and more revenue.

- Variational Inference (VI) and the Evidence Lower Bound (ELBO)

  Variational inference, from its core, has a Bayesian perspective that aims to find a simpler, tractable distribution that closely approximates the true, often complex, posterior distribution (the distribution of hidden variables given observed data). It uses the Evidence Lower Bound (ELBO), which provides a lower bound for the intractable log-likelihood data, and by maximizing the ELBO effectively gives a good approximation of the true posterior distribution and a well-performing model.

  Variational inference works well in cases where you have little data or uncertain data.

Variational Autoencoders (VAEs) utilize variational inference and ELBO in generative modeling.

Business Implications of Variational Inference: VI helps in generating a profitable growth engine at low cost.

- Information Theory Concepts: Entropy, KL Divergence, and Mutual Information

  Information theory has three key concepts: Entropy, KL divergence, and mutual information.

  Entropy

  Entropy measures the unpredictability and randomness in the dataset. A dataset with high entropy means a higher level of randomness, making it more difficult to make predictions from, while a dataset with low entropy is easier to classify and more predictable. Entropy is commonly employed in decision tree algorithms to discover the feature that best separates the dataset.

  Business Implications of Entropy: Businesses prefer a dataset with low entropy for consistent performance and faster deployment, which helps in reducing failure rates.

  KL Divergence

  KL Divergence (Kullback-Leibler Divergence) is an information theory concept that measures how much one probability distribution differs from another distribution. It helps in assessing how well a learned probability distribution approximates the true distribution of the data.

KL Divergence is used in VAE training, generative model comparison, and evaluation.

Business Implications of KL Divergence: Models with lower KL divergence typically need less fine-tuning and reduce deployment costs by 30–50%. Businesses can clarify KL divergence metrics from various vendors on tasks similar to theirs while evaluating and making decisions.

Mutual Information

Mutual information measures the amount of information revealed by one random variable about another random variable. It helps in identifying features that give the most information about the target variable, thus helping in feature selection, as well as in understanding the relationship between different features.

Business Implications of Mutual Information: Mutual information helps in improving targeting results with higher conversion rates at reduced cost and faster model training.

- Bayesian Approaches to Generative Modeling

In the Bayesian approach toward generative models, prior knowledge and data likelihood are utilized to compute the posterior probability, which serves as an updated probability after observing new data. The Bayesian approach in generative modeling helps in a better understanding of uncertainty and variability in data.

Bayesian Neural Networks, Generative Adversarial Networks (GANs), and Variational Diffusion Models are based on the Bayesian approach of generative modeling.

Business Implications of the Bayesian Approach: The Bayesian approach helps in reducing risks by taking fewer bad decisions.

2.1.2 Core Mathematical Concepts

- Backpropagation Through Time and Gradient Flow

Backpropagation through time (BPTT) is a technique for training recurrent neural networks (RNNs) that involves propagating errors backward in time. In RNNs, there are connections between nodes in distinct time steps, i.e., the output of the network at one time step depends on both the input at that time step and the prior time steps.

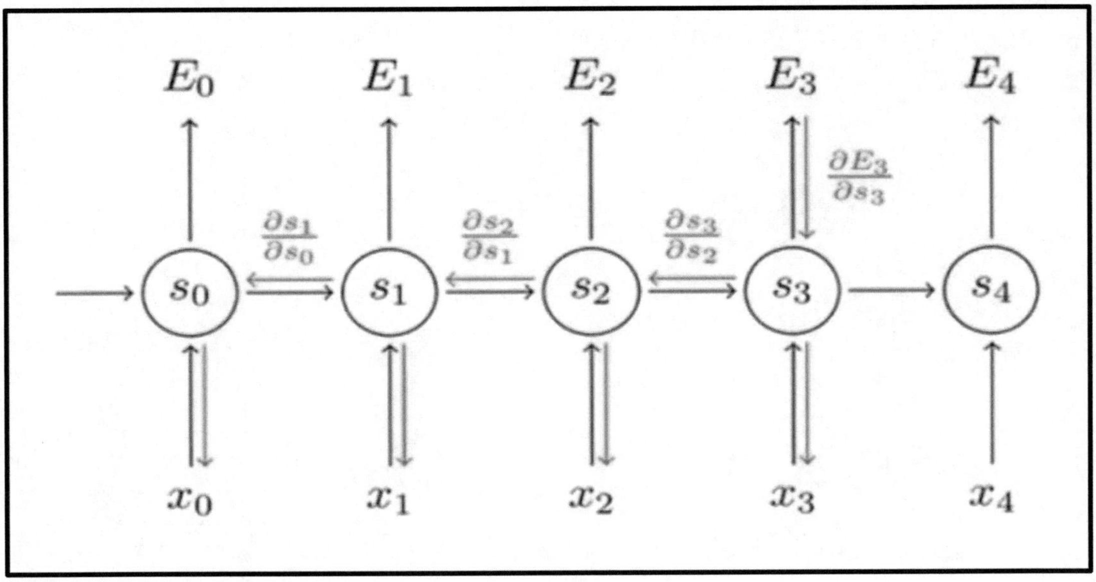

Figure 2-1. *Backpropagation Through Time*

During training, the partial derivative of the error is computed with respect to weights and backpropagated through the unfolded network, and weights are updated using gradient descent. Backpropagation through time allows the RNN to learn to predict the output at each time step based on the input at that time step as well as the previous time steps. The error gradient propagates backward through the network during training, and this path is known as gradient flow.

- Attention Mechanisms: Scaled Dot-Product and Multi-Head Attention

  Scaled Dot-Product and Multi-Head Attention are attention mechanisms that are core components of the Transformer architecture.

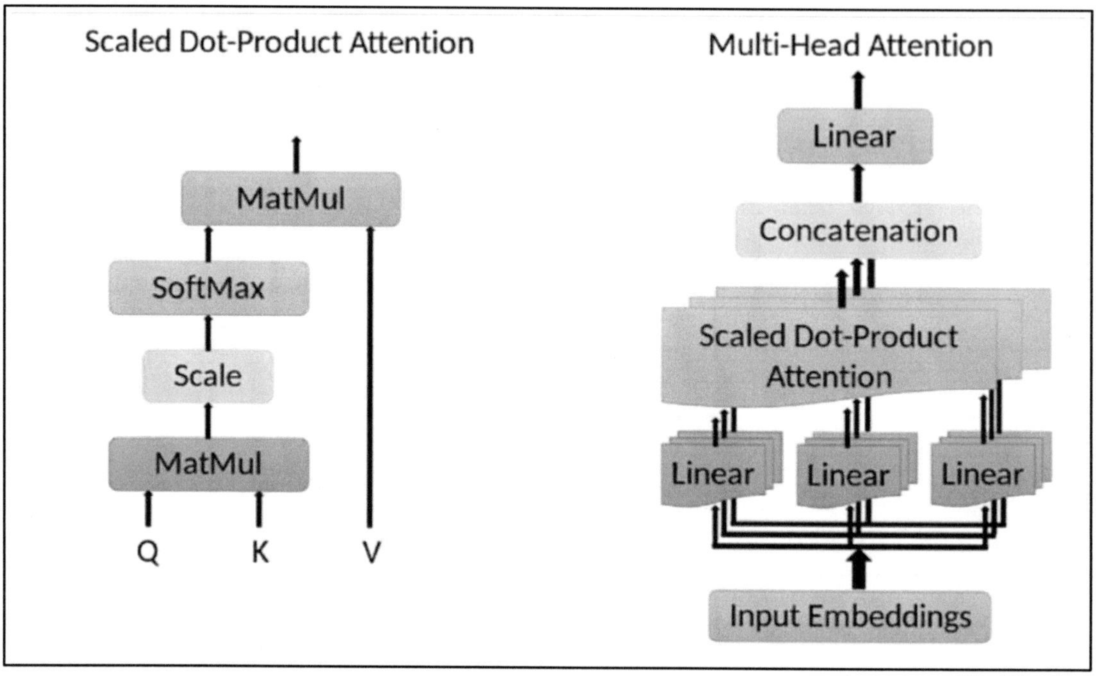

Figure 2-2. *Scaled Dot-Product Attention vs. Multi-head Attention*

In Scaled-Dot Product, attention scores are obtained by calculating the dot product of the query, key, and value vectors. The dot product is then scaled by the square root of the critical vector dimensions to stabilize the training process, and finally, the softmax function is applied.

Multi-head Attention is an advanced version of the scaled-dot attention mechanism, where the scaled-dot product runs in parallel multiple times. Each attention sequence learns different patterns and captures unique aspects of the relationship between input elements. These individual attention outputs are concatenated and then linearly processed to obtain the predicted dimension.

- Positional Encodings and Sequence Modeling

  As we know, in the English language, the order of words matters, which is why in sequential data analysis, the order of elements is crucial. Transformers cannot understand word order since they process several elements at the same time. As a result, positional encoding saves the day by allowing transformers to understand sequences.

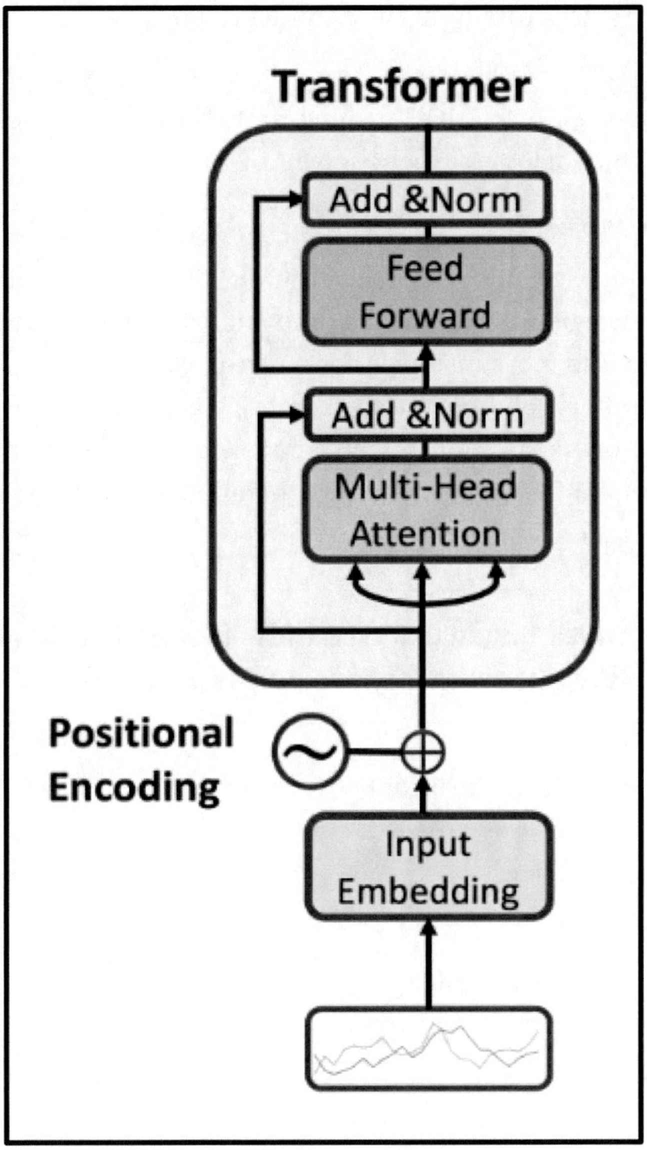

Figure 2-3. *Transformer with Positional Encoding*

The position information is encoded and transmitted directly to the transformer via the input embeddings. Transformers use two types of positional encoding: Absolute Positional Encoding and Rotary Position Embedding (RoPE).

- Loss Functions: Cross-Entropy, Contrastive Loss, and Adversarial Losses

  Cross-Entropy, Contrastive Learning, and Adversarial Losses are different types of losses in generative AI.

  Cross-Entropy Loss

  Cross-entropy loss, also called logarithmic loss or log loss, measures the difference between predicted probability distributions and actual distributions to measure the performance of classification tasks. To find the optimal solution, the cross-entropy loss function adjusts the weight of the machine learning model during training. It guides various generative tasks like image generation, music generation, code generation, and many more.

The cross-entropy loss function serves GANs (Generative Adversarial Networks), VAEs (Variational Autoencoders), and large language models.

  The goal is to reduce the error between actual and expected outcomes. Businesses' targets for lower cross-entropy values suggest higher performance.

  Contrastive Loss

  Contrastive loss is a metric-learning loss function that operates on pairs of embeddings received from the model. Based on ground truth, a similarity label is introduced, which states whether these two embeddings are "similar" or "dissimilar."

  A concept of "margin" is introduced by contrastive loss. A margin is the minimum distance "dissimilar" points need to keep, otherwise they are penalized, and "similar" points are penalized for being farther than the given margin.

Contrastive loss is used widely in Face Recognition and Face Verification tasks.

Adversarial Losses

Adversarial loss, in the context of Generative Adversarial Networks (GANs), is a type of loss function that measures how well a generator network can fool a discriminator network. In GAN, generators and discriminators are not trained simultaneously, so while training the generator, freeze the discriminator, and vice versa. The adversarial loss can be optimized by gradient descent in GANs.

Businesses look for well-optimized adversarial losses to balance output excellence with engineering complexity to ensure sustainable ROI.

2.2 Architecture Evolution and Technical Details

Let's deep dive into the architecture evolution of generative AI from RNNs to transformers, their limitations, challenges, and technical details, to understand the journey from where it all started and how we reached the level where we are today with generative AI.

2.2.1 From RNNs to Transformers

- LSTM/GRU Limitations and Vanishing Gradients

  The traditional recurrent neural network (RNN) faced the issue of vanishing gradients. During backpropagation, when weights are repeatedly multiplied by values less than 1, gradients shrink exponentially, a phenomenon called vanishing gradients.

  Thus, LSTM was developed in 1997 to address the vanishing gradient problem in sequential data. Gated Recurrent Unit (GRU) is a simpler variant of LSTM, which is faster to train but sometimes underperforms LSTM.

  LSTM/GRU limitations are as follows:

  1. They are computationally expensive.

2. Improved vanishing gradient problem, but does not eliminate them.

3. No parallel processing for sequential data makes them slow.

- Transformer Architecture Deep Dive: Self-Attention and Feed-Forward Layers

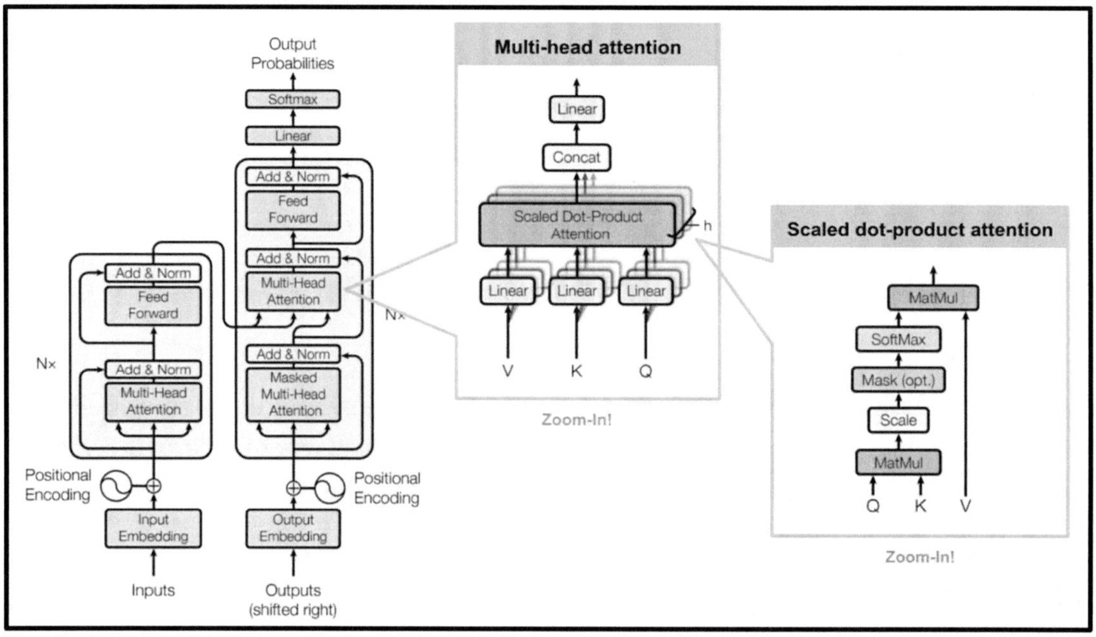

***Figure 2-4.** The Architecture of the Transformer Model*

The Transformer architecture was introduced in the 2017 paper "Attention Is All You Need," and it is designed to handle sequence-to-sequence tasks efficiently. Transformer architecture consists of an encoder and a decoder, which are built using stacked layers of self-attention and feed-forward neural networks.

The self-attention mechanism captures dependencies between all tokens of a sentence in sequence to understand the context of the input data. Following self-attention, each token embedding passes through a position-wise feed-forward network that processes features independently per position and adds non-linearity. The output of the feed-forward network was passed through a residual connection and layer normalization.

- Positional Encodings and Sequence Length Limitations

  Positional encodings are added to the input embedding to encode the position of each token in the sequence. Sinusoidal Positional Encodings or learned embeddings are used for each position. Even with the positional encodings and sequence length, transformers face a few limitations, like quadratic complexity, long sequences are computationally heavy and time-consuming, and there is a fixed sequence length, which can be handled by transformers.

- Architectural Variants: Encoder-Only, Decoder-Only, and Encoder-Decoder

  There are three architectural variants of transformers.

  Encoder-Only

  The encoder is the original transformer that takes a sequence of tokens, such as words in a sentence, understands, and extracts the relevant information from the input text. It learns contextual representation of text based on masked language models and is highly effective for text classification and semantic search tasks. BERT, RoBERTa, and DistilBERT are popular models that are based on an encoder-only architecture.

  Encoders are highly efficient and fast for understanding tasks like sentiment analysis, token classification, and embedding generation at a lower training cost.

  Decoder-Only

  The decoder only requires an explicit input sequence and generates text from left to right. It predicts the next word based on previous text; thus, it works well in text generation, document Q&A, and conversational AI. GPT-style and LLaMA are popular models that are based on a decoder-only architecture.

  Decoders are highly efficient for generative text but expensive at scale due to complex tasks and large datasets.

Encoder-Decoder

An encoder-decoder architecture consists of an encoder and a decoder. The encoder converts the input sequence into representations, and based on those representations, the decoder generates an output sequence. It is commonly used in sequence-to-sequence tasks like machine translation, question-answer, and text summarization. T5, BART, and MarianMT are popular models based on an encoder-decoder architecture.

Encoder-decoder works on the middle ground, is highly adaptable and efficient in inference, and can be expensive to train for complex tasks. Encoder-decoder is mainly used for translation and summarization tasks.

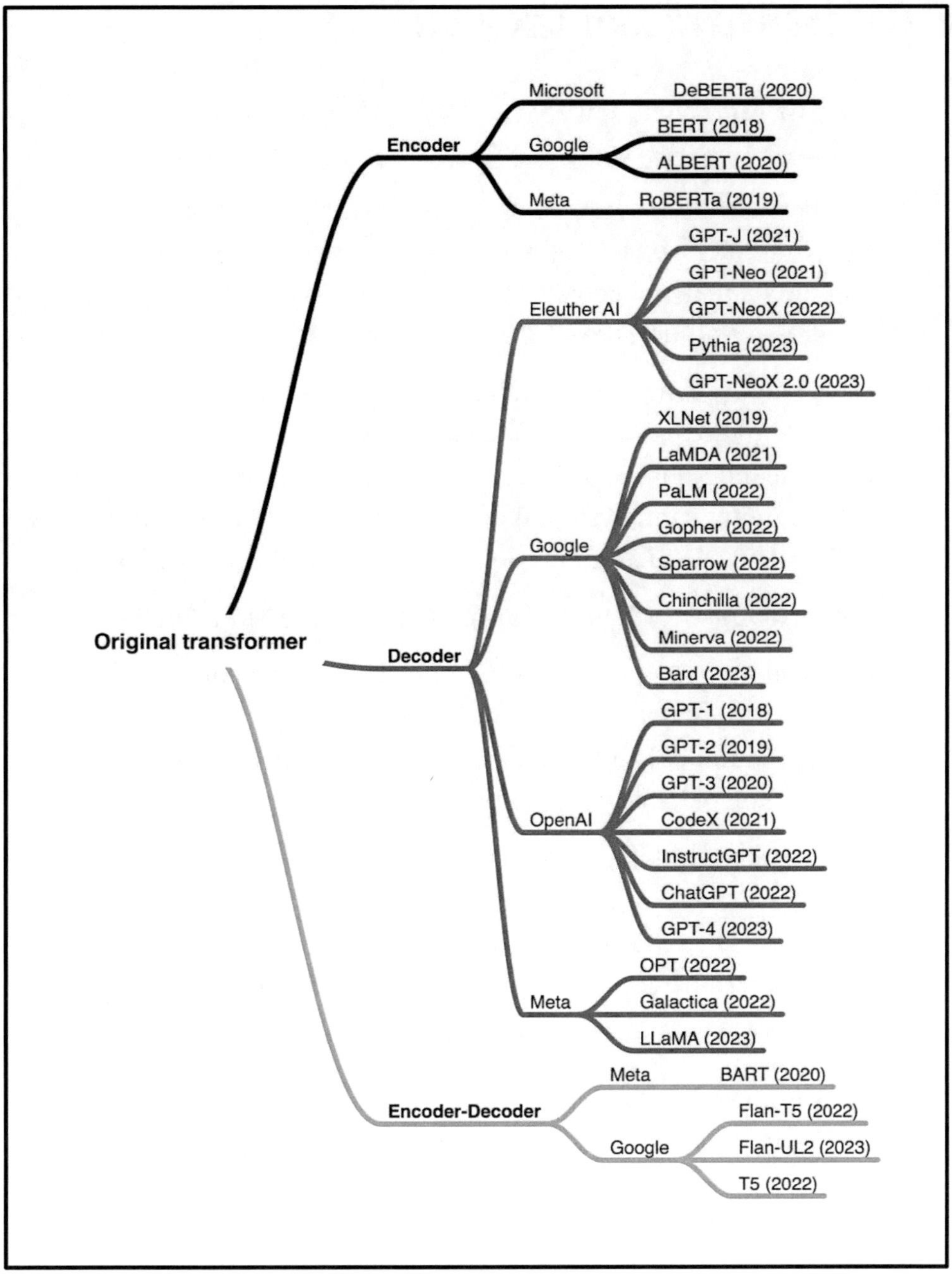

Figure 2-5. *Popular Models Based on Transformer Architecture*

2.2.2 Generative Model Taxonomies

- Autoregressive Models (GPTs) vs. Masked Language Models (BERT-Style)

  GPTs are based on autoregressive models, which are trained to predict the next token left to right from all previous tokens. These are unidirectional and good for text generation. Widely used autoregressive models are GPT-2, GPT-3, and GPT-4.

  Masked language models are trained by masking some tokens in the input and predicting them using context in the surrounding, both left to right and right to left. These work on bidirectional attention used for sentiment analysis and question-answer scenarios. BERT, RoBERTa, and DistilBERT are widely used masked language models.

- Variational Autoencoders (VAEs) and Latent Space Modeling

  Variational Autoencoder (VAE) is a type of generative model that encodes the input data into a latent space as probability distributions (mean and variance) and reconstructs data from this latent representation of data using sampling.

  In latent space modeling, data is compressed in a lower-dimensional hidden space that captures essential patterns, features, or hidden structures of data. This compressed data is used to generate new data, handling clustering problems and interpolation of data.

- Generative Adversarial Networks (GANs) and Adversarial Training

  GANs introduced in 2014 set up the road map for generative AI. GANs are generative models that are trained using neural networks, generators, and discriminators. Together, they try to optimize the adversarial loss. GANs are used for text generation, data augmentation, music generation, and many more.

  In adversarial training, the model is trained on clean data as well as data that has been intentionally perturbed (slightly tweaked) to fool the model. The idea is to train the model to defend against cyberattacks by exposing it to them during training. It is a reliable method for real-world scenarios like self-driving cars, healthcare, cybersecurity, and finance, although these are computationally expensive.

- Diffusion Models: Forward/Reverse Processes and Denoising Objectives

  Diffusion models are two-step processes: a forward process that gradually adds noise to data until it becomes pure noise and a reverse process where it gradually removes noise and generates new, clean samples effectively. Diffusion models are stable compared to GANs and state-of-the-art in text-to-image generation.

  The denoising objective is to minimize the difference between predicted denoised data and actual denoised data.

- Flow-Based Models and Invertible Transformations

  Flow-based models are also generative modes that map complex data distributions of images or audio into simple distributions, using a series of invertible transformations. Flow-based models provide exact likelihood estimation and efficient sampling, but are computationally heavy and less sharp in results compared to GANs.

2.3 Training Methodologies and Optimization

For generative AI, certain pre-training strategies should be followed to achieve better results. We will discuss pre-training strategies and some effective advanced training techniques for generative AI.

2.3.1 Pre-training Strategies

- Self-Supervised Learning Objectives: Next-Token Prediction and Masked Language Modeling

  Next-token prediction and masked language modeling are both popular NLP techniques for self-supervised learning. Next-token prediction predicts the next words of the sentence; it aims to generate language. It works from left to right, and famous models include GPT and LLaMa.

Masked language modeling predicts the missing/masked words of the sentence and aims to understand the language. It works bidirectionally, and famous models are BERT and RoBERTa.

- Curriculum Learning and Data Ordering Strategies

  Curriculum learning is a training strategy that mimics the human learning process by starting with the simpler concepts and then gradually moving toward complex concepts. This aims to facilitate a more natural and efficient learning process that works profoundly with LLM.

  Data ordering strategies are the strategies that design the curriculum for step-by-step learning based on either difficulty level, hierarchical curriculum, data-distribution strategies, or self-paced methods.

- Mixed Precision Training and Gradient Scaling

  Mixed-precision training is a deep learning optimization technique that utilizes both single-precision (float32) and half-precision (float16) floating-point representations for computations during model training. Its main aim is to accelerate the training process and reduce the computational resources usage, working very well with modern GPUs without sacrificing the model accuracy.

  Gradient scaling is a crucial technique employed in mixed-precision training to prevent gradient underflow. It scales up the loss before backpropagation, which ensures gradients don't vanish in FP16, thus resulting in stable model training and accuracy.

- Distributed Training: Data Parallelism, Model Parallelism, and Pipeline Parallelism

  Distributed training enables scaling across multiple GPUs to speed up training and handle bigger models like GPT and BERT with massive data in today's real-world scenarios.

Data Parallelism

This is the most common strategy used when the model easily fits in a single GPU's memory. In data parallelism, each GPU trains on a different subset of data with the full model. After computing gradients, all GPUs synchronize, and gradients are averaged before updating the weights.

Model Parallelism

Model parallelism is used when the model is too large for a single GPU. Different parts of the model (layers or parameters) are split across GPUs for training. GPUs require communication between them for forward and backward passes.

Pipeline Parallelism

In pipeline parallelism, different GPUs process different mini-batches simultaneously by dividing the model into stages to be processed by different GPUs. Parallel processing requires careful scheduling.

2.3.2 Advanced Training Techniques

- Reinforcement Learning from Human Feedback (RLHF)

  Reinforcement Learning from Human Feedback (RLHF) is widely implemented in LLM models, which involves reinforcement learning that considers human feedback. RLHF is widely used in generative AI for image generation, music generation, and voice assistants.

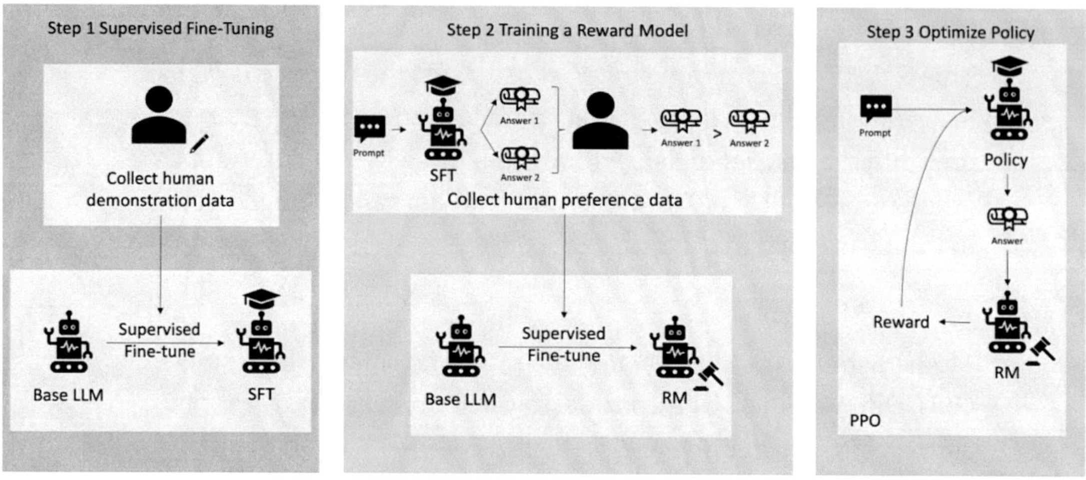

Figure 2-6. *Steps to Implement RLHF*

The steps to implement RLHF are as follows:

1. Supervised Fine-Tune (SFT), a language model (LM).
2. Collect human feedback data.
3. Training a reward model (RM) based on human feedback.
4. The reward model is used to optimize the language model with reinforcement learning (RL).

- Constitutional AI and Self-Supervised Alignment

  Constitutional AI (CAI) does not purely rely on human feedback, but follows a written "constitution" of rules and principles to evaluate and improve model outputs. The goal of self-supervision in CAI is to teach the model to self-critique and self-revise the output by referencing the constitution. The critiques and revisions are feedback that act as training signals, and output labels are produced by AI instead of humans, which is also called Reinforcement Learning from AI Feedback (RLAIF).

  This solution is more scalable, transparent, and free from human bias compared to RLHF.

- Instruction Tuning and Supervised Fine-Tuning

  Supervised fine-tuning (SFT) is training a pre-trained model on a labeled dataset for a specific task or domain. It aims to train a better model that follows the pattern of training data, where each input has a desired output. LLMs are a good example of supervised fine-tuning.

  Instruction tuning is a special type of SFT where the model is fine-tuned on instruction response pairs across many diverse tasks. It helps models to train flexibly to understand natural language instructions. ChatGPT is a good example of instruction tuning.

  Here is a consolidated comparison of advanced training techniques in generative AI from both business and technical perspectives.

Table 2-1. *Comparison of Advanced Training Techniques*

Approach	Business Trade-Offs	Cost and Timeline	Technical Requirements	Best-Fit Use Cases	Decision Guidance
RLHF (Reinforcement Learning from Human Feedback)	Highest output quality, strong, safe, and user satisfaction	$500K–$2M additional cost; 3–6 months	Human labeling pipeline (40+ hrs/week)	Consumer-facing, regulated, and safety-critical systems	Choose when brand risk, safety, and user trust are top priorities
Constitutional AI	More consistent behavior, lower operational cost, newer but riskier method	Low–medium cost; 1–3 months	Need well-defined ethical and operational principles	Transparent and compliance-heavy domains	Use when transparency, consistency, and predictability matter most
Supervised Fine-Tuning (SFT)	Fastest deployment, low cost, and lower quality	Low cost; weeks	Need high-quality labeled data; domain experts	Niche domain-specific applications	Select when strong labeled data already exists

- Parameter-Efficient Fine-Tuning: LoRA, Adapters, and Prompt Tuning

In large-scale pre-trained models, there are billions of parameters, and fine-tuning them is a task. So, parameter-efficient fine-tuning is used in such cases where a pre-trained model can adapt according to a new task by fine-tuning only a small fraction of the model's parameters. It requires less GPU memory, reduces computational resources cost, and provides better modeling performance.

LoRA

LoRA is Low Rank Adaptation, which doesn't fine-tune the full weight matrices but inserts low-rank matrix weights to capture task-specific updates. It is memory-efficient and works well for large-scale LLM fine-tuning like LLaMA-2.

Adapters

In adapters, a small trainable neural layers (adapter module) are added inside the frozen pre-trained model between transformation layers. In adapters, only adapter layers are trained, whereas base model weights stay the same.

Prompt Tuning

One method for fine-tuning is learning task-specific prompts, like prompt tuning or prefix tuning, instead of changing the model weights. This is the cheapest method, which works great for small task storage, but shows low performance on harder tasks.

2.4 Data Engineering for GenAI

Data engineering determines how reliably, securely, and cost-effectively an organization can operationalize generative AI. From a business perspective, this function directly influences time-to-market, model quality, regulatory risk, and long-term competitiveness. Leaders must decide whether to build proprietary pipelines, rely on managed platforms, or outsource capabilities based on strategic importance and scale.

Data engineering is the process of collecting, cleaning, organizing, and delivering data at scale specifically for training, fine-tuning, and serving generative AI models. We will discuss in detail how the dataset is curated and constructed for generative AI and the evaluation methodologies for curated data.

2.4.1 Dataset Construction and Curation

- Web Scraping at Scale and Data Deduplication

  Generative AI data engineering difficulties include web scraping and large-scale data deduplication. Whether to use third-party companies or develop extensive crawling and deduplication systems internally is up to the organizations. Long-term model reliability, data ownership, and infrastructure costs are all impacted by this decision.

  Generative AI models thrive on huge, diverse datasets, and most of them are scraps from the web that require careful engineering. Huge infrastructure is required with crawling tools for web scraping. Also, data quality needs to be maintained as real-time data is messy and disorganized. Another challenge is data storage and data versioning for reproducibility.

  Data deduplication is critical because LLMs memorize duplicated text, resulting in model overfitting, hallucinations, and bias reinforcement, and training on the same data repeatedly results in wasted compute resources and time. Hash-based, fuzzy string matching, and embedding-based semantic deduplication are some of the deduplication techniques.

- Data Quality Assessment and Filtering Pipelines

  Data quality pipelines are a choice for risk control and brand defense. Filtering and validation investments lower retraining expenses, reputational harm, and legal liability.

  Generative AI is based on LLM models, and LLMs memorize low-quality, biased, and duplicate data easily. As a result, data quality assessment is crucial to minimize data inaccuracies, hallucinations, toxic/biased reinforcement, poor generalization, and legal/compliance issues.

  Data quality for the generative AI process goes through a multi-stage filtering pipeline, which includes data ingestion and normalization, deduplication, quality heuristics, safety and compliance metrics, domain relevance filtering, human review, and final packaging to ensure secured, good-quality, diverse, and domain-appropriate data.

Figure 2-7. *Data Quality Flow for Generative AI*

- Tokenization Strategies and Vocabulary Construction

  Tokenization and vocabulary construction affect inference cost, multilingual performance, and domain adaptability. Businesses must determine whether standard tokenizers are sufficient or whether custom vocabularies provide a competitive advantage.

  Tokenization strategies and vocabulary construction are foundational units in building and fine-tuning generative AI models. Tokenization is done to extract the complete meaning by the model by breaking down raw text into smaller tokens. Subword Tokenization is the most common tokenization strategy used in LLMs. It creates a balance between word and character level of tokenization that splits rare words into smaller units, but keeps frequent words intact.

  Vocabulary is the set of tokens that covers all words, symbols, scripts, emojis, and code tokens that the model can recognize and embed. Various tokenization algorithms like BPE, WordPiece, SentencePiece, Byte-level BPE, etc., are used to build a vocabulary from a training corpus for generative AI modeling.

- Handling Multilingual and Multimodal Data

  Providing support for multilingual and multimodal data is a calculated move for market expansion. Investing in specialized architectures is necessary for organizations that target global or multi-channel users.

  Handling multilingual and multimodal data is a necessity for GenAI modeling, which can be achieved with the use of specialist architectures such as Multimodal Large Language Models (MLLMs) and agentic systems that combine varied information streams like text, image, audio, and video across multiple languages. Key strategies to handle multilingual and multimodal data include cross-lingual transfer learning, Agentic and Modular Systems, MLLMs, and instruction tuning to train and evaluate multilingual multimodal models.

2.4.2 Evaluation Methodologies

- Perplexity and Likelihood-Based Metrics

  Intrinsic metrics guide technical investment decisions and model selection strategies. Leaders use these indicators to balance performance gains against computing costs.

  There are some core intrinsic metrics like likelihood, cross-entropy, and perplexity, which are used for the evaluation of LLMs. These are used to compare models, track training progress, and estimate data quality. Low perplexity (PPL) means better language modeling.

- Human Evaluation Frameworks and Inter-annotator Agreement

  Human evaluation frameworks reflect organizational commitment to safety, ethics, and customer trust. It is a key operational decision whether to build internal annotation capability or outsource it.

  Generative AI models rely on a human evaluation framework to assess helpfulness, safety, quality, and accuracy of generated output. The human evaluation framework defines the criteria, rules, methods, and guidelines by which annotators judge GenAI outputs.

  Inter-annotator Agreement (IAA) measures consistency across different human annotators applying these frameworks, using metrics like Cohen's κ and Krippendorff's α. It covers structured, segmented, and multi-object annotation tasks, providing information on model performance limits and annotation quality.

- Automated Evaluation: BLEU, ROUGE, and BERT Score

  Automated metrics support rapid experimentation and cost-efficient benchmarking. Businesses must balance speed with accuracy when relying on automated scoring. There are some automated evaluation metrics like BLEU, Rouge, and BERT Score that are widely used in GenAI, especially for text generation tasks. These metrics cannot replace human judgment but support it.

BLEU

Bilingual Evaluation Understudy (BLEU) measures n-gram overlap between references and system output. It is best used for machine translation and summarization.

ROUGE

Recall-Oriented Understudy for Gisting Evaluation (ROUGE) measures overlap of n-grams, subsequences, or word pairs between system output and references. It is best used for summarization and text generation.

BERT Score

BERT Score uses contextual embeddings from a pre-trained model like BERT, RoBERTa, to compare the hypothesis vs. the reference. It captures semantic similarity and better correlates with human judgment compared to BLEU/ROUGE. It is best used for semantic text evaluation.

- Downstream Task Evaluation and Transfer Learning Assessment

  Downstream and transfer assessment indicates whether models can be reused across markets and domains and guides in platform scalability.

  Downstream task evaluation and transfer learning assessment are key methods for measuring the real-world utility of GenAI models beyond intrinsic metrics. Together, both become holistic and versatile frameworks across domains, languages, and real-world conditions.

  In downstream task evaluation, models are evaluated through full fine-tuning, zero-shot, or few-shot settings, and the focus is on the performance of pre-trained models compared to application-specific benchmarks. This provides insight into whether pre-training representations are practically useful and adaptable.

Transfer learning assessment investigates how knowledge gained in pre-training generalizes and adapts across tasks, domains, and modalities. This includes cross-task, cross-domain, cross-lingual, and cross-modal transfer. Evaluation involves measuring fine-tuning performance, few/zero-shot adaptability, data efficiency, and robustness against catastrophic forgetting.

2.5 Scaling Laws and Computational Considerations

The performance an organization can attain for every investment is determined by scaling laws and computational resources. From a business standpoint, this directs leadership choices about long-term platform competitiveness, sustainability goals, cloud spending, and capital allocation.

In production, the GenAI model is trained on a scale with an increase in parameters, data size, training time, and compute resources. Scaling laws help in improving a model's performance when trained on a scale. Computational considerations involve balancing accuracy with efficiency. It focuses on managing training costs, memory limits, parallelization, and energy use. Together, we will see in detail how scaling laws and compute strategies shape the trade-off between performance, cost, and sustainability in GenAI development.

2.5.1 Empirical Scaling Relationships

- Power Laws for Loss vs. Parameters, Data, and Compute

  Decisions about capacity planning and strategic budgeting are influenced by power laws. They are used by businesses to determine the extent to which higher training costs are justified by increased revenue or productivity.

  In GenAI, power laws describe how deep learning model training loss decreases as a function of model parameters, dataset size, and compute, which are the key variables. Power laws help in resource optimization, forecasting performance, preventing overfitting, and understanding various limitations like training data or parameter limitations.

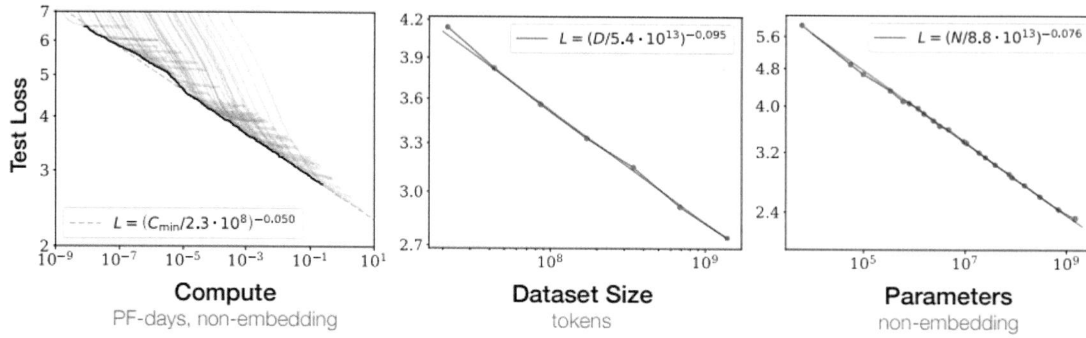

***Figure 2-8.** LLM Performance with an Increase in Model Size, Dataset Size, and Amount of Compute Used for Training*

The performance of a model has a power-law relationship with each of the three scale factors: number of parameters, dataset size, and compute size, given that it should not be bottlenecked by the other two factors.

- Chinchilla Optimal Training and Compute Allocation

  Chinchilla's optimal training promotes quicker commercialization and cost effectiveness. It assists businesses in determining whether to spend more money on larger hardware clusters or additional data pipelines.

  Chinchilla's optimal training method, introduced in 2022, can train with more parameters and 4× data with the same compute resources, and it also uses less compute for fine-tuning and inference, greatly facilitating downstream usage.

  Chinchilla's compute-optimal performance is obtained not just by increasing parameters, but also by training models on a larger set of tokens. Instead of blindly developing larger models, this puts the focus on data curation, quality, and longer training.

- Emergent Abilities and Phase Transitions

  Emergent abilities and phase transition open both strategic opportunities and governance risks, and organizations must prepare for sudden performance jumps that can disrupt markets.

Emergent abilities in large language models (LLMs) are suddenly highlighting new capabilities and gains, such as advanced reasoning, code generation, and in-context learning, that arise only beyond certain scale thresholds, showing abrupt, non-linear improvements in performance that resemble a phase transition.

Ultimately, it advocates for improved metrics, strong evaluation frameworks, greater mechanistic understanding, and proactive safety governance to handle unforeseen emergent features as LLMs scale.

- Sample Efficiency and Few-Shot Learning Capabilities

  Sample efficiency is how well a model uses its limited training data to learn, unlike traditional methods that require large datasets. It reduces dependency on large proprietary datasets and compliance costs, resulting in faster experimentation and market entry.

  In generative AI, LLMs are used with very limited data for fine-tuning or adaptation. There are a few techniques that help in improving efficiency, like transfer learning, parameter-efficient tuning (LoRA, adapters), active learning, and curriculum learning.

  As the name signifies, few-shot learning capacities mean the model can learn and perform new tasks with few examples given in a prompt and sometimes without any examples given in a prompt. This ability makes the model highly flexible and adaptable. Some domains lack large datasets, where GenAI showcases rapid prototyping and deployment.

2.5.2 Infrastructure and MLOps

- Model Checkpointing and Resumable Training

  Model checkpointing reduces financial risk by preventing loss of compute investments during failures, resulting in resilient project execution.

  There are some intermediate model states where we want to pause the training and save the model state, and wherever required, training can be resumed from that state. Such states in the model training process are called model checkpoints, and there can be many model checkpoints at regular intervals. From any model checkpoint, training can be resumed. These checkpoints come in handy whenever the machine crashes after hours of training or any other issue occurs in between; then, training can be resumed from a model checkpoint, saving time and compute resources.

As an interim model state from which to resume training, we must ensure that we save all of the information that a model uses throughout training, like model parameters, number of epochs, optimized parameters, and training metadata.

- Gradient Checkpointing and Memory Optimization

  Gradient checkpointing and memory optimization enable organizations to train larger models without major hardware upgrades, which extends infrastructure lifecycles and improves capital efficiency.

  Gradient optimization is a memory optimization technique that plays a very important role in making LLMs, deep neural networks, and generative AI models successful. Gradient checkpointing does not save every activation during the forward pass; it saves only a few key checkpoints after every $\sqrt{n}$ step (where n is the number of layers (depth) of the deep neural network), and during backpropagation, it recomputes the missing intermediate activations from these checkpoints instead of retrieving them from memory. Thus, it trades more computation for less memory usage, thus allowing for training a much larger model without running out of GPU memory with an extra 20–30% increase in fine-tuning time.

- Inference Optimization: Quantization, Pruning, and Distillation

  Inference optimization is necessary to improve the performance, efficiency, and characteristics of the LLM model. It directly impacts operating margins, customer experience, and pricing models at scale. Quantization, pruning, and distillation are key optimization techniques for LLM.

Quantization

Quantization works by decreasing the precision of the weights/activation parameters, which are typically 32-bit floating-point integers, to 16-bit. This leads to a smaller model size and faster inference.

Pruning

Pruning involves removing/pruning the parameters from a model that have only a little impact on its predictions. This helps in downsizing the model, resulting in faster inference.

Knowledge Distillation

Knowledge distillation conveys insights from a complex "teacher" model to a simpler "student" model, allowing performance to be maintained while requiring fewer processing resources. The main purpose of this technique is to minimize size, reduce cost, and achieve high computing speed.

- Serving Architectures: Batching, Caching, and Load Balancing

  Cloud spending, customer happiness, and system dependability are defined by serving architectures that are essential to achieve company performance commitments. Once a GenAI model has been trained, serving architecture is crucial for scaling inference. Three fundamental pillars for serving architecture are batching, caching, and load balancing.

  Batching

  In batching, multiple user requests are combined into a single forward pass, resulting in high throughput.

  Caching

  Caching saves previously computed results and resumes them, which reduces back-end load, lowers latency, improves response times, and saves compute and bandwidth usage.

Load Balancing

Load balancing distributes incoming traffic over numerous servers to avoid overloading, enhance fault tolerance, enhance scalability, and minimize latency.

2.6 Deployment Patterns and Production Considerations

The final stage for generative AI model development is deployment for production. From a business perspective, deployment decisions such as cloud-based APIs, on-premise hosting, hybrid setups, and edge deployment methods are made by determining long-term cost, scalability, efficiency, operational risk, data control, regulatory compliance, and vendor dependency while balancing speed-to-market.

Let's understand all deployment, production, security, and optimization pointers in detail.

2.6.1 Model Serving Architectures

- Synchronous vs. Asynchronous Inference

  In synchronous inference, the client sends an HTTP request to the ML server, which processes it immediately and sends the result in the same response. Synchronous inference is simpler to implement and has predictable latency.

  In asynchronous inference, the client sends the request to the ML server, which acknowledges the request and queues it for processing. The response is sent back to the client once it's ready, and the client does not wait for an immediate response. Asynchronous inference is complex to implement but has higher throughput and better GPU utilization.

  From a business standpoint, synchronous inference suits real-time, customer-facing applications where responsiveness impacts revenue and satisfaction. Asynchronous inference is better for high-volume, back-end, or analytics-driven workflows where efficiency and cost optimization are priorities.

- Batching Strategies and Throughput Optimization

  The majority of machine learning applications use a batching method (either static or dynamic batching) to provide numerous data samples to the model at the same time. In this situation, decreased latency can result in poorer throughput; conversely, higher latency correlates with higher throughput. Businesses must determine a balanced batch size and latency approach in generative AI models to maximize GPU efficiency and throughput optimization to reduce per-request costs.

- Model Versioning and A/B Testing Frameworks

  Model versioning and A/B testing frameworks in machine learning are critical for managing model lifecycles and maintaining peak performance in a production environment. Different iterations of models are saved as versions with complete metadata like parameters, number of echoes, and hyperparameters for reproducibility, traceability, and rollback capability.

  A/B testing frameworks provide a structured approach to compare the performance of several versions of models in a controlled production environment. Model versioning and A/B testing frameworks are frequently integrated into MLOps workflows. This interface enables the seamless deployment of new model versions, which are then validated in the real world through controlled A/B testing before full-scale deployment.

  Model versioning and A/B testing enable organizations to measure business impact before full rollout by reducing deployment risk and ensuring investments deliver measurable value.

- Cost Modeling and Resource Allocation

  Smart resource allocation is necessary for effective cost modeling for successfully deployed generative AI models in production. It allows executives to forecast operational expenses and prevent budget overruns. Various optimization techniques, like autoscaling, quantization, pruning, etc., are implemented to model the cost that comes from GPU hours, memory usage, network bandwidth, and storage.

2.6.2 Monitoring and Observability

- Model Drift Detection and Performance Degradation

  Model drift occurs when the performance of a deployed model degrades over time as the real-world environment in which it functions changes. A continuous monitoring and alerting system is necessary to detect model drift to avoid revenue loss, regulatory risk, and declining user trust in the business.

- Latency and Throughput Monitoring

  Latency and throughput monitoring involve measuring two interdependent performance indicators in a system: latency evaluates speed per request, while throughput quantifies the volume of requests handled successfully over time. Monitoring these indicators simultaneously with specialist tools helps in reaching GenAI systems with low latency and high throughput, while balancing performance and cost makes it easier for leaders to make capacity planning and service-level agreement (SLA) decisions.

- Output Quality Assessment in Production

  The quality of output of the generative AI model in production is assessed using a hybrid approach with automated evaluation, human-in-the-loop evaluation, and user-centric proxy metrics. This ensures that GenAI outputs are safe, dependable, and user-friendly in real-world environments while reducing future retraining costs.

- Feedback Loops and Continuous Learning Systems

  Feedback loops and continuous learning systems are what make GenAI models flexible and long-lasting in real-world use. Implicit or explicit feedback loops are mechanisms to capture signals from the system after deployment. ML architecture uses this feedback and adds new data to update models regularly without full retraining from scratch. This helps to improve output quality, alignment, and safety and reduce long-term maintenance costs.

2.6.3 Reliability and Fault Tolerance

- Checkpoint and Resume Strategies

  Generative AI inference workloads are latency-sensitive and often critical to failure. It is critical to ensure that the system is highly available despite many issues like hardware failures, network difficulties, or software flaws. It is necessary to periodically save models at checkpoints and resume long training jobs from the last checkpoint after failures, reducing wasted compute to reduce financial losses.

- Graceful Degradation and Failover Mechanisms

  Graceful degradation enables a system to retain essential functions when components fail, operating at a reduced capacity via shorter context, smaller model, etc., rather than completely failing, which protects consumer experience during an outage.

  Failover mechanisms provide a secondary, redundant system that takes over when the primary system fails, ensuring continuous, often seamless business operation.

- Disaster Recovery and Backup Procedures

  Disaster recovery is the pre-planning recovery method for resuming operations in case of any disaster, such as data corruption, system failure, network issue, hardware loss, or datacenter outages. It safeguards business assets and ensures regulatory compliance.

  Backup procedure is the practice of creating copies of data, like models, logs, and embedding, to be restored in case of failure. It reduces recovery time and protects critical intellectual property.

- Multi-region Deployment and Data Replication

  Multi-region deployment is the process of distributing an AI system's components across multiple geographic regions to enable high availability, disaster recovery, regional outages, and low-latency performance for worldwide users.

Data replication is a critical strategy for multi-region deployments, which involves creating and synchronizing data copies across these regions using methods such as log-based incremental replication, snapshot replication, or transactional replication to maintain data consistency and support uninterrupted operation during regional outages. This strategy improves the GenAI model's responsiveness, user experience, and overall system robustness.

- Incident Response and Escalation Procedures

  Incident response and escalation procedures are systematic methods for managing and resolving challenges by monitoring alerts and on-call rotation with the assigned ML engineers. An escalation policy specifies when and how to escalate important issues to the stakeholders and bring in more specialized teams to guarantee that issues are resolved efficiently on time with limited financial impact.

2.6.4 Security and Compliance

- Model Security: Adversarial Attacks and Data Poisoning Prevention

  Model security defends against all malicious acts like adversarial attacks and data poisoning, which can compromise model behavior, performance, and accuracy. In adversarial attacks, a malicious attempt is made to corrupt the model and generate misleading outputs through small, imperceptible changes to the input. When input data is poisoned by corrupted or biased data during model training, it is called data poisoning.

  Investing in model security preserves competitive advantage and lowers operational risk. It stops manipulation that might harm a company's reputation.

- Access Control and Authentication Systems

  Access control and authentication systems check a user's identity before granting or denying access to specified resources in accordance with predefined policies and responsibilities. Common access control approaches include Discretionary Access Control (DAC), Role-Based Access Control (RBAC), and Attribute-Based Access Control (ABAC), which provide varying levels of governance requirements and protect sensitive business assets.

- Data Privacy and PII Handling

  Data privacy is the proper acquisition, storage, and preservation of sensitive information, such as personally identifiable information (PII) of users, to ensure that it is only available to authorized persons. It helps in preventing misuse of personal information, meeting legal duties such as those outlined in GDPR, and strengthening consumers' confidence.

- Model Intellectual Property Protection

  Model intellectual property (IP) protection involves securing AI models, software, and creative works via legal procedures such as patents, copyrights, trademarks, and trade secrets. It preserves long-term competitive advantage and monetization opportunities.

- Regulatory Compliance (GDPR, AI Governance Frameworks)

  A well-structured AI governance framework ensures a secure system as AI models follow company rules, ethical values, and regulatory regulations. In contrast, compliance focuses on following external legal and industry norms, such as GDPR, which involves abiding by data minimization, user consent, and the right to explanation. They reduce legal uncertainty and enable sustainable AI adoption.

2.6.5 Cost Management and Optimization

- Resource Utilization Optimization and Rightsizing

  Resource utilization optimization and rightsizing are processes to assign resources like GPU compute, memory, networking, and other resources according to workload requirements to improve performance and efficiency of the system and allow businesses to reduce costs with a balanced optimization approach.

- Spot Instance Strategies and Preemptible Workloads

  Spot instance strategies and preemptible workloads utilize cloud resources that are interruptible and offer a discount; thus, GenAI expenses are reduced by up to 90%. They are best suited for non-critical or fault-tolerant jobs, requiring checkpointing, autoscaling, and diversification across regions or instance types to tolerate disruptions while maximizing efficiency and scalability in large-scale AI operations. Businesses must evaluate risk tolerance against potential cost savings.

- Training Cost Modeling and Budgeting

  GenAI expenses can be predicted and controlled by training cost modeling and budgeting, which projects computing, storage, and networking requirements. Techniques include FLOPs-based modeling, GPU-hour tracking, and budget alerts. Teams use transfer learning to save costs, minimize redundant runs, and leverage schedulers or quotas, assuring efficient expenditure while preserving model performance. It helps in prioritizing high-ROI projects and avoiding unplanned spending.

- Inference Cost Optimization and Capacity Planning

  In GenAI installations, inference cost optimization and capacity planning strike the right balance between performance and efficiency. Quantization, pruning, and distillation are used to reduce model size, while batching queries improves GPU efficiency and autoscaling clusters. Capacity planning allocates resources based on traffic projections and peak load simulations, resulting in cost-effective, reliable, and scalable inference during peak demand.

- Multi-cloud Strategies and Vendor Management

  Multi-cloud techniques help GenAI reduce lock-in, optimize costs, and increase resiliency. Organizations deploy workloads across various cloud providers like AWS, GCP, and Azure, replicate data globally, and use spot-market arbitrage. Contract negotiations, volume discounts, and portability via Kubernetes or Ray are all part of vendor management, which ensures long-term flexibility, cost savings, and high availability.

2.7 References

- https://en.wikipedia.org/wiki/Kullback%E2%80%93Leibler_divergence
- https://www.sciencedirect.com/topics/computer-science/cross-entropy-loss-functions
- https://arxiv.org/pdf/1406.2661
- https://medium.com/@lakshmi.pallempati22/backpropagation-through-time-bptt-7f32037a2699
- https://www.researchgate.net/figure/The-scaled-dot-product-attention-and-multi-head-self-attention_fig3_337683227
- https://arxiv.org/html/2502.12370v1
- https://medium.com/@anmoltalwar/types-of-nlp-transformers-409bb0ee7759
- https://lilianweng.github.io/posts/2023-01-27-the-transformer-family-v2/
- https://arxiv.org/pdf/1706.03762
- https://arxiv.org/pdf/2405.07490
- https://aws.amazon.com/what-is/reinforcement-learning-from-human-feedback/
- https://arxiv.org/pdf/2001.08361
- https://arxiv.org/pdf/2203.15556
- https://arxiv.org/pdf/2503.05788v2
- https://arxiv.org/html/2406.02290v1

CHAPTER 3

Technical Underpinnings of Generative AI: Key Capabilities and Limitations of Current Systems

3.1 Introduction

As we stand at the precipice of the AI revolution, understanding the technical foundations of generative artificial intelligence becomes crucial for both practitioners and decision-makers. While the previous chapters established the historical context and paradigm shift that generative AI represents, this chapter delves deep into the technical architecture, mechanisms, and operational principles that make these systems possible.

Generative AI's remarkable ability to create humanlike text, generate photorealistic images, compose music, and write functional code stems from sophisticated mathematical models and computational architectures that have evolved over decades. However, beneath the seemingly magical outputs lie complex neural networks, intricate training processes, and fundamental limitations that shape what these systems can and cannot accomplish.

The journey from simple rule-based systems to today's sophisticated generative models represents one of the most significant technological leaps in computing history. Unlike traditional software that follows explicit instructions, generative AI systems learn patterns from vast amounts of data and use these patterns to create entirely new

N. Sendas et al., *Building Generative AI Solutions for Industries with AWS*,
https://doi.org/10.1007/979-8-8688-2830-0_3

content. This fundamental shift from programmed logic to learned behavior has opened unprecedented possibilities while introducing new challenges and complexities.

This chapter provides a comprehensive examination of the technical underpinnings that power today's generative AI systems, exploring their core capabilities while honestly addressing their current limitations. Understanding these technical foundations is essential for anyone seeking to leverage generative AI effectively, whether for business applications, research endeavors, or strategic planning. We will explore how these systems work at the deepest level, what makes them so powerful, and where they still fall short of human-level intelligence.

3.2 Fundamental Architecture of Generative AI Systems

3.2.1 Neural Network Foundations

At the heart of every generative AI system lies a neural network—a computational model inspired by the human brain's structure and function. These networks represent a fundamental departure from traditional computing paradigms, moving away from explicit programming toward systems that can learn and adapt through experience. The concept of artificial neural networks dates back to the 1940s, but only recent advances in computational power and algorithmic sophistication have made today's generative AI possible.

Neural networks consist of interconnected nodes, called neurons or units, organized in layers that process information in a manner loosely analogous to biological neural systems. Each artificial neuron receives inputs from other neurons, applies a mathematical transformation to these inputs, and produces an output that can be passed to subsequent layers. This seemingly simple structure, when scaled to millions or billions of connections, creates systems capable of learning incredibly complex patterns and relationships in data. The fundamental principle behind neural networks in generative AI involves learning complex patterns from training data and using these patterns to generate new, similar content. Unlike traditional rule-based systems that require explicit programming for every possible scenario, neural networks develop their understanding through exposure to vast amounts of data, gradually adjusting internal parameters called weights and biases to minimize prediction errors.

The learning process in neural networks occurs through a method called backpropagation, where the network compares its outputs to desired results and adjusts its internal connections to reduce errors. This process is repeated millions of times across enormous datasets, allowing the network to develop increasingly sophisticated internal representations of the patterns it encounters. The beauty of this approach lies in its generality—the same basic architecture can learn to recognize images, understand language, or generate music, depending on the training data provided.

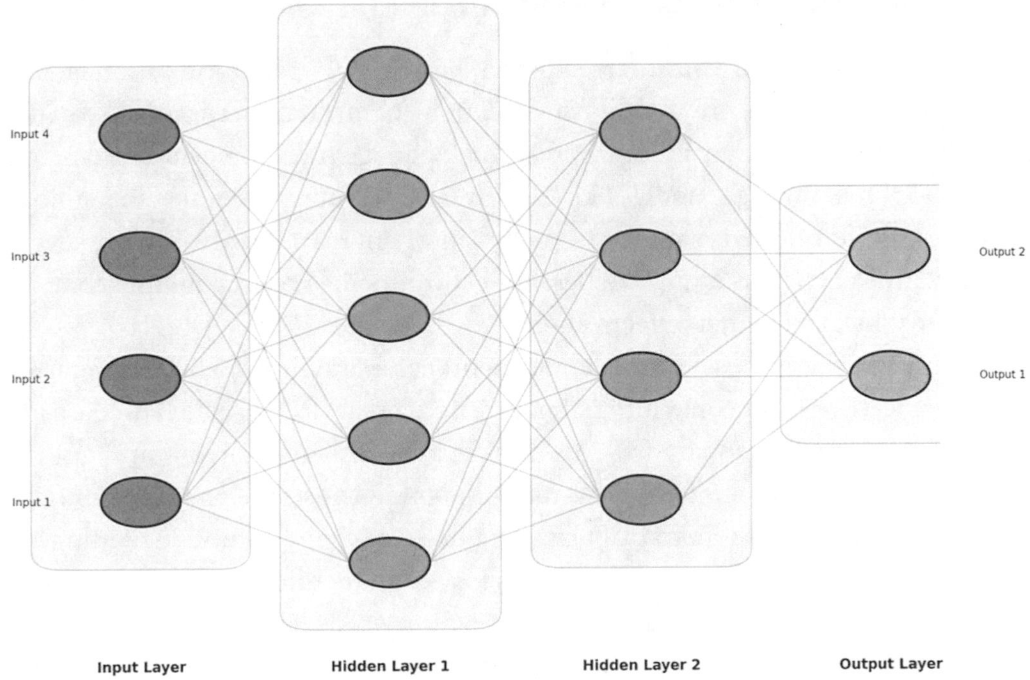

***Figure 3-1.** Basic neural network architecture illustrating input, hidden, and output layers with interconnected nodes*

Modern generative AI systems employ deep neural networks, meaning they often contain many layers of neurons, sometimes dozens to hundreds of layers deep. Each layer learns to recognize increasingly complex patterns, starting with simple features in early layers and building up to sophisticated concepts in deeper layers. For example, in a system trained on images, early layers might detect edges and colors, middle layers might recognize shapes and textures, and deep layers might identify specific objects or scenes.

3.2.2 The Transformer Revolution

The transformer architecture, introduced in the seminal 2017 paper "Attention Is All You Need" by Vaswani et al., represents the backbone of most modern generative AI systems. This architecture revolutionized natural language processing and became the foundation for breakthrough models like GPT, BERT, and countless others that followed. The transformer's introduction marked a pivotal moment in AI history, solving several critical limitations of previous approaches while introducing new capabilities that seemed almost magical in their effectiveness.

Before transformers, most natural language processing systems relied on recurrent neural networks (RNNs) or convolutional neural networks (CNNs), which processed text sequentially or through fixed-size windows. These approaches suffered from significant limitations, particularly in handling long-range dependencies—the ability to connect information that appears far apart in a text sequence. For example, understanding that a pronoun at the end of a paragraph refers to a noun mentioned at the beginning requires maintaining context across many intervening words. The transformer solved these problems through its revolutionary self-attention mechanism, which allows the model to weigh the importance of different parts of the input sequence when processing each element. This mechanism enables the model to directly connect any two positions in a sequence, regardless of their distance, making it exceptionally powerful for understanding context and relationships in language. For example, in the sentence "The cat that lived in the old house sat on the mat," the self-attention mechanism allows the model to directly connect "cat" with "sat," even though they're separated by several words.

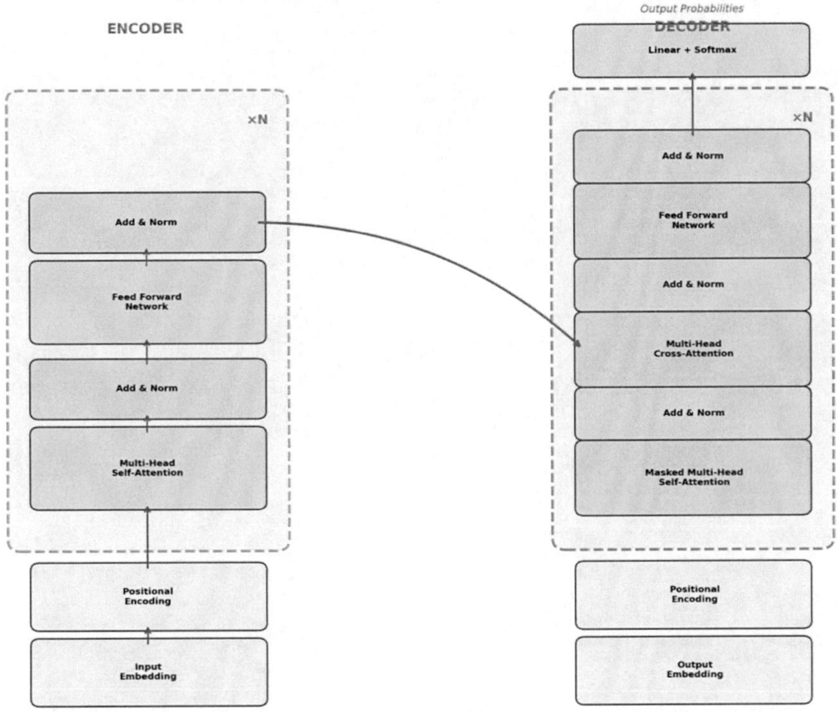

Figure 3-2. *High-level overview of the Transformer architecture showing Encoder and Decoder components with multi-head self-attention mechanisms*

The self-attention mechanism works by creating three different representations of each input token: queries, keys, and values. These representations are then used to compute attention scores that determine how much focus each token should receive when processing any given position. This process happens simultaneously for all positions in the sequence, making transformers highly parallelizable and efficient to train on modern hardware.

Multi-head attention represents another crucial innovation in the transformer architecture. Instead of using a single attention mechanism, transformers employ multiple attention "heads" that can focus on different types of relationships simultaneously. One head might focus on syntactic relationships between words, another on semantic similarities, and yet another on long-range dependencies. This parallel processing of different relationship types enables a richer and more nuanced understanding of language.

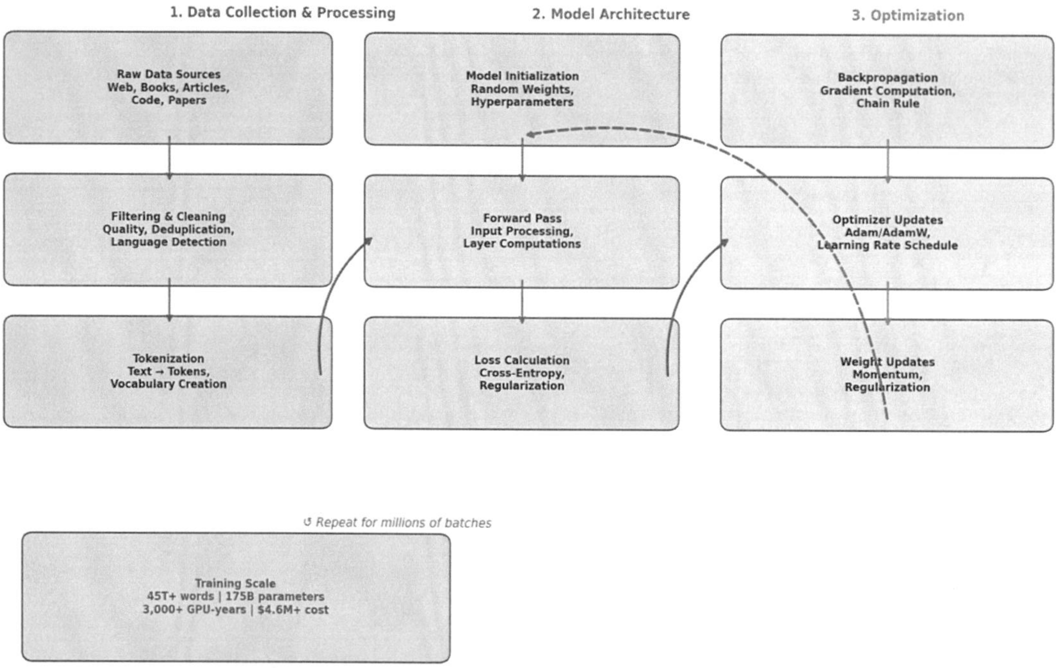

Figure 3-3. *Training pipeline for a large language model, from data collection and processing through tokenization, forward pass, loss calculation, and parameter optimization*

Positional encoding addresses a unique challenge in the transformer architecture. Since transformers process all positions in a sequence simultaneously rather than sequentially, they need a way to understand the order of words. Positional encodings are mathematical patterns added to the input embeddings that encode information about each token's position in the sequence. The original transformer architecture (Vaswani et al., 2017) used fixed sinusoidal functions that create unique patterns for each position while maintaining mathematical relationships that help the model understand relative positions. However, positional encoding techniques have evolved significantly since then. Many modern models use learned positional embeddings, where the model learns optimal position representations during training. More recently, approaches like Rotary Position Embeddings (RoPE), used in models such as LLaMA and PaLM, encode position by rotating the embedding vectors, which offers advantages in capturing relative positions and generalizing to sequence lengths not seen during training. Another notable approach is ALiBi (Attention with Linear Biases), which forgoes explicit positional encodings entirely and instead adds a linear bias directly to attention scores based on token distance.

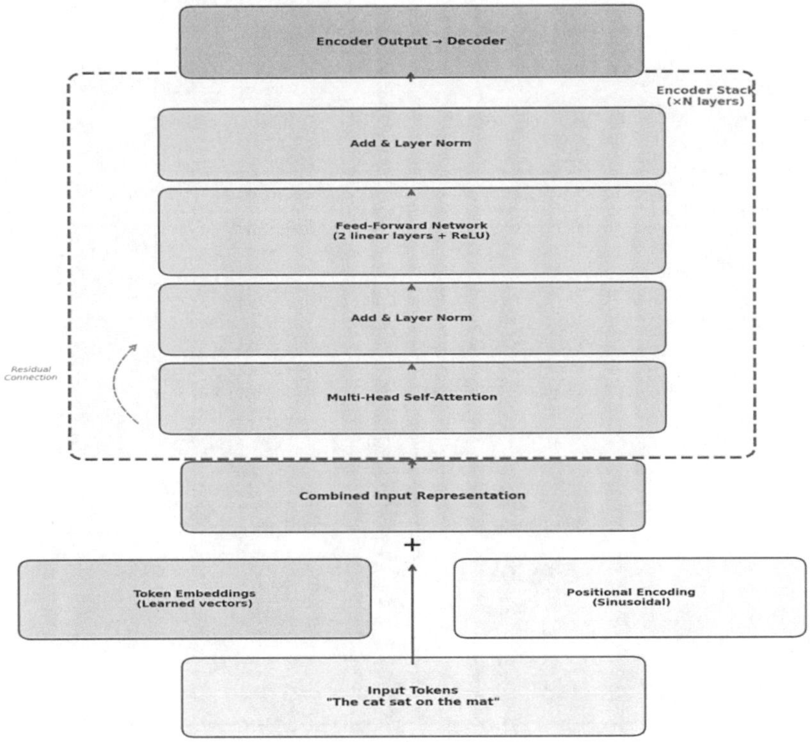

Figure 3-4. *Detailed Transformer model structure showing positional encoding, token embeddings, and the encoder stack with multi-head self-attention layers*

The feed-forward networks within each transformer layer provide the computational capacity for complex transformations. These networks apply learned transformations to the attention outputs, enabling the model to perform sophisticated reasoning and pattern recognition. The combination of attention mechanisms and feed-forward networks, repeated across multiple layers, creates systems capable of understanding and generating remarkably sophisticated language.

3.2.3 Large Language Models (LLMs) Architecture

Large language models represent the current pinnacle of generative AI for text-based applications, embodying the culmination of decades of research in natural language processing and machine learning. These models, exemplified by the GPT series, BERT, Claude, LLaMA, and numerous others, are built on transformer architectures but scaled to unprecedented sizes and trained on massive datasets that encompass much of human-written knowledge.

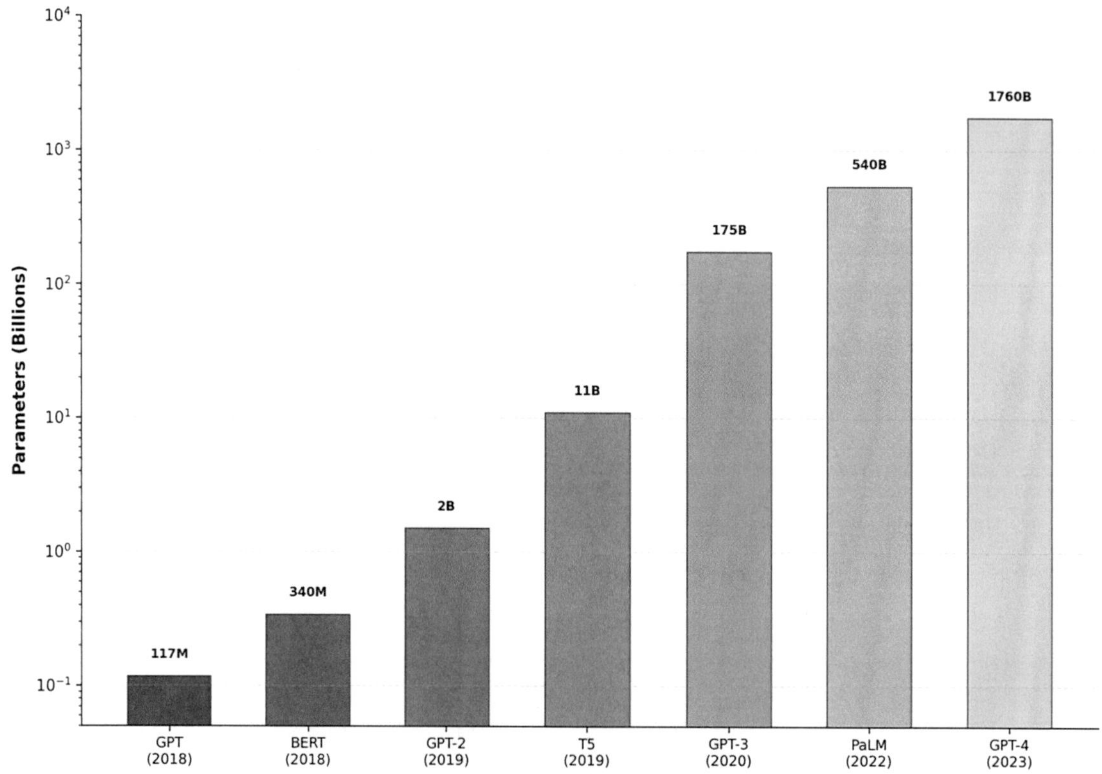

Figure 3-5. *Growth in language model parameters (in billions) from 2018 to 2023, showing the trend toward increasingly large models*

The architecture of modern LLMs involves several key innovations beyond the basic transformer design. The most obvious difference is scale—while early transformer models had millions of parameters, modern LLMs contain billions or even trillions of parameters. GPT-3 has 175 billion parameters, GPT-4 is estimated to have over a trillion parameters, and some recent models push even further into uncharted territory. This massive scale enables the models to capture incredibly nuanced patterns in language, from basic grammar and syntax to complex reasoning patterns and world knowledge. The training process for LLMs follows a sophisticated two-stage approach that has become the standard in the field. The first stage, called pre-training, involves training the model on massive text corpora to learn general language patterns, world knowledge, and reasoning capabilities. During this phase, the model learns to predict the next word in a sequence, a seemingly simple task that actually requires understanding grammar, semantics, factual knowledge, and even complex reasoning patterns.

Pre-training datasets for modern LLMs are truly staggering in scope. GPT-3 was trained on approximately 45 terabytes of text data, including books, articles, websites, and other textual content representing a significant portion of human-written knowledge. These datasets are carefully curated to include diverse sources while filtering out low-quality or harmful content. The breadth of this training data enables LLMs to develop knowledge across virtually every domain of human knowledge, from science and technology to arts and culture.

The second stage, fine-tuning, adapts the pre-trained model for specific tasks or aligns it with human preferences and values. This stage is crucial for creating AI systems that are not just knowledgeable but also helpful, harmless, and honest. Fine-tuning can involve supervised learning on high-quality examples, Reinforcement Learning from Human Feedback, or other specialized training techniques designed to shape the model's behavior.

Autoregressive generation represents the fundamental mechanism by which most LLMs produce text. The model generates text one token at a time, using all previously generated tokens as context for predicting the next token. This process continues iteratively, with each new token being added to the context for generating subsequent tokens. While this approach seems straightforward, it enables remarkably sophisticated behavior, as the model can plan ahead, maintain consistency across long passages, and even engage in complex reasoning chains.

The autoregressive nature of LLMs creates both their greatest strength and some of their most significant limitations. The strength lies in the model's ability to generate coherent, contextually appropriate text that can span thousands of words while maintaining consistency and relevance. The limitation arises from the sequential nature of generation, which can lead to compounding errors and makes it difficult for the model to revise or reconsider earlier decisions in light of later context.

3.3 Training Methodologies and Data Processing

3.3.1 The Training Process

Training generative AI models represents one of the most computationally intensive endeavors in modern computing, requiring enormous datasets, sophisticated algorithms, and unprecedented computational resources. The process involves exposing neural networks to vast amounts of data and iteratively adjusting billions of parameters to minimize prediction errors, a task that pushes the boundaries of what's technologically feasible.

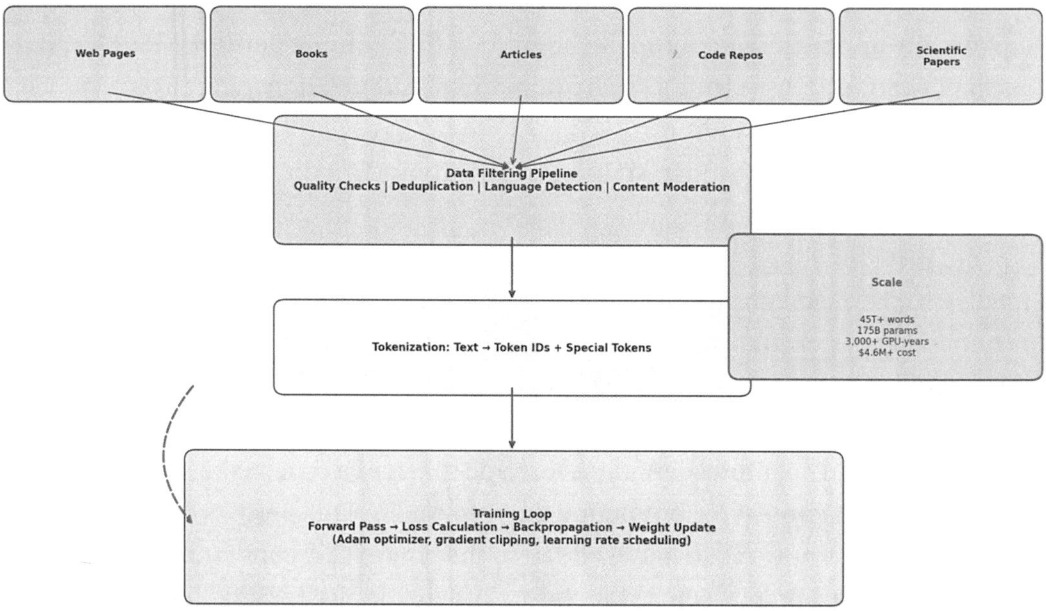

***Figure 3-6.** End-to-end training process for a large language model, covering data collection, model architecture configuration, and optimization procedures*

The scale of data required for training modern generative AI systems is truly staggering and represents a fundamental shift from earlier machine learning approaches. While traditional machine learning models might be trained on thousands or millions of examples, large language models require datasets containing hundreds of billions or even trillions of tokens. These datasets must be carefully curated, cleaned, and processed to ensure quality while maintaining the diversity necessary for robust performance across different domains and tasks. Data preprocessing represents a critical and often underappreciated aspect of training generative AI systems. Raw text data from the internet contains numerous quality issues, including duplicate content, low-quality writing, spam, and potentially harmful material. Sophisticated filtering pipelines are employed to address these issues, using both automated systems and human reviewers to ensure training data meets quality standards while maintaining the diversity necessary for robust performance.

The computational requirements for training large generative models are truly extraordinary and represent one of the most significant barriers to entry in the field. GPT-3's training required approximately 3,640 petaflop-days of computation, equivalent to running thousands of high-end GPUs continuously for months. The estimated cost for training GPT-3 was $4.6 million, and subsequent models have required even more resources. This computational intensity has led to the concentration of advanced AI capabilities among well-resourced organizations and has sparked important discussions about democratizing access to AI technology.

Modern training employs sophisticated distributed computing techniques to manage these enormous computational requirements. Training is typically distributed across thousands of GPUs or specialized AI chips, with careful coordination required to ensure that gradient updates are properly synchronized across all devices. This distributed approach introduces additional complexity, as communication between devices can become a bottleneck and failures in any part of the system can disrupt the entire training process.

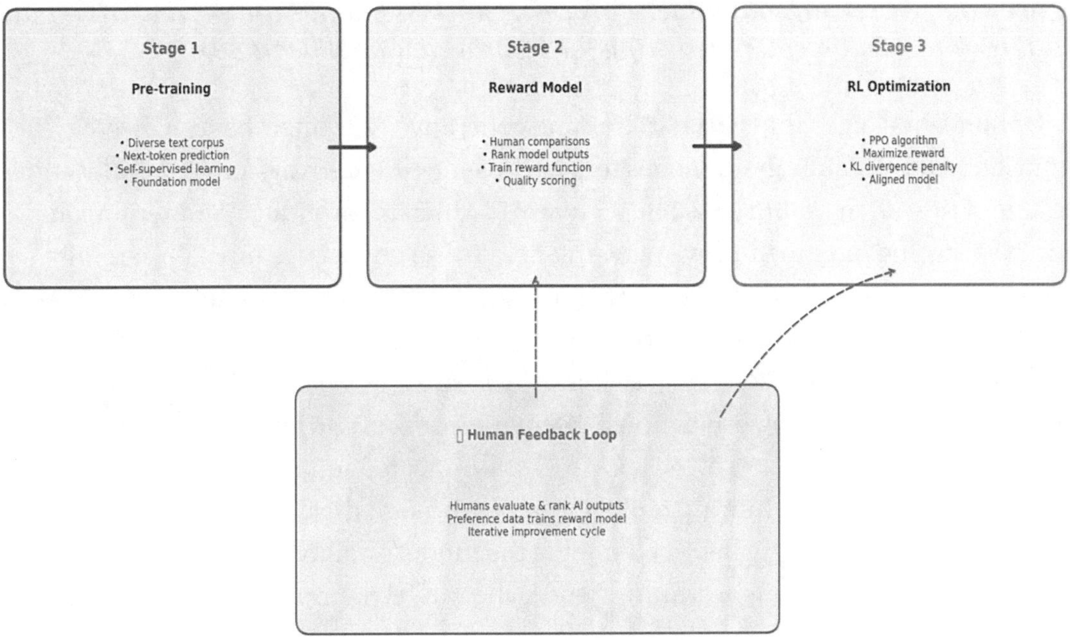

***Figure 3-7.** The three-stage Reinforcement Learning from Human Feedback (RLHF) pipeline: foundation model training, reward model learning, and policy optimization*

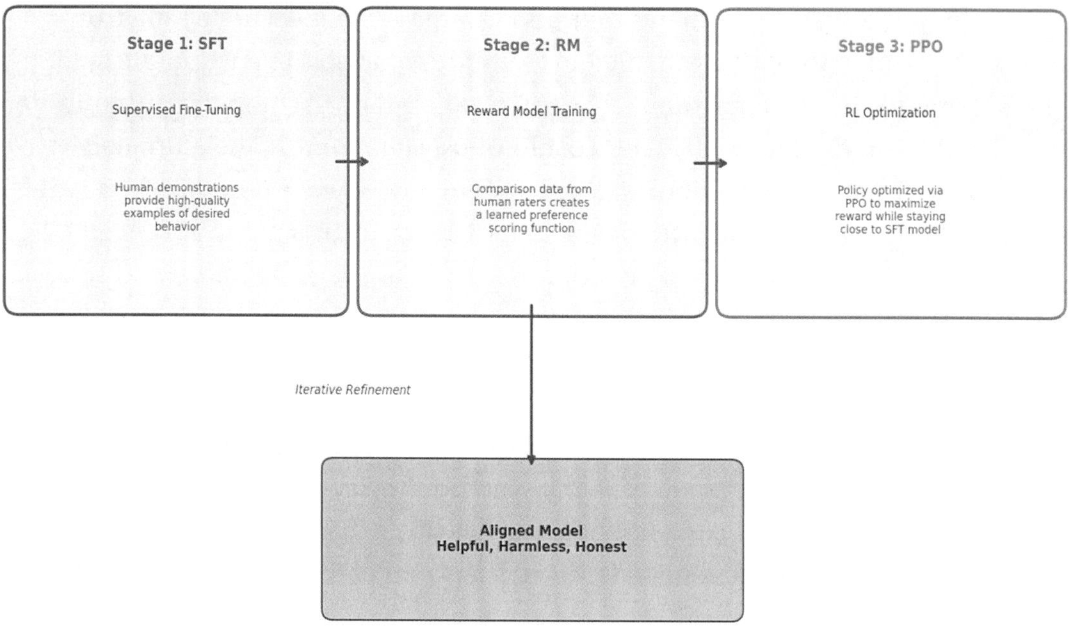

Figure 3-8. *Three-stage alignment process: supervised fine-tuning, reward model training, and reinforcement learning for improved model behavior*

Optimization algorithms used in training generative AI models have evolved significantly from simple gradient descent approaches. Modern systems typically employ variants of the Adam optimizer, such as AdamW, which incorporates momentum and adaptive learning rates to improve convergence. These optimizers must be carefully tuned with learning rate schedules that adjust the learning rate throughout training to balance fast initial learning with stable convergence.

The training process itself involves iteratively exposing the model to batches of training data, computing predictions, calculating errors, and adjusting model parameters to reduce those errors. This process is repeated millions of times across the entire dataset, often requiring multiple passes through the data to achieve optimal performance. The challenge lies in balancing the model's ability to learn from the training data while avoiding overfitting, where the model memorizes specific examples rather than learning generalizable patterns.

3.3.2 Reinforcement Learning from Human Feedback (RLHF)

Reinforcement Learning from Human Feedback represents one of the most significant recent advances in generative AI training, addressing critical challenges in aligning AI systems with human values and preferences. This technique, pioneered by OpenAI and subsequently adopted across the industry, has proven essential for creating AI systems that are not just capable but also helpful, harmless, and honest in their interactions with users.

The development of RLHF arose from a fundamental problem with traditional language model training. While models trained purely on internet text could generate fluent and knowledgeable responses, they often produced outputs that were unhelpful, potentially harmful, or misaligned with human intentions. Simply optimizing for predicting the next word in internet text doesn't necessarily lead to behavior that humans find valuable or safe. RLHF addresses this alignment problem through a sophisticated three-stage process that gradually shapes model behavior to better match human preferences and values. The first stage, supervised fine-tuning, involves training the model on high-quality human-generated examples of desired behavior. Human trainers create demonstrations of how the model should respond to various prompts, covering a wide range of tasks and scenarios. This stage helps the model learn appropriate response patterns and styles, moving beyond the sometimes chaotic patterns found in raw internet text.

The second stage focuses on training a reward model that can predict human preferences. Rather than requiring humans to write perfect responses for every possible input, this approach leverages human comparative judgments, which are often easier and more reliable to obtain. Human evaluators are presented with multiple model responses to the same prompt and asked to rank them according to quality, helpfulness, and alignment with human values. This comparative data is used to train a separate neural network that learns to predict human preferences, essentially creating an automated system for evaluating response quality.

The third and final stage uses reinforcement learning to optimize the language model's behavior according to the learned reward model. The model generates responses and receives rewards based on the reward model's predictions of human preferences. Through techniques like Proximal Policy Optimization (PPO), the model learns to generate responses that maximize these rewards while maintaining coherence and avoiding dramatic departures from its original capabilities.

The impact of RLHF on generative AI systems has been transformative. Models trained with RLHF demonstrate significantly improved helpfulness, reduced harmful outputs, and better alignment with human intentions. However, the process also introduces new challenges, including the potential for reward hacking, where models learn to exploit weaknesses in the reward model rather than genuinely improving their behavior. Additionally, the human preferences captured in RLHF may not represent universal values, raising important questions about whose preferences should guide AI behavior.

3.3.3 Emergent Abilities and Scaling Laws

One of the most fascinating and somewhat mysterious aspects of large generative models is the emergence of capabilities that weren't explicitly programmed or directly trained. As models scale beyond certain parameter thresholds, they begin to exhibit new abilities that seem to arise spontaneously from the complex interactions of their neural networks. This phenomenon has profound implications for our understanding of artificial intelligence and suggests that continued scaling may unlock even more sophisticated capabilities.

The concept of emergent abilities in AI systems challenges traditional notions of how complex behaviors arise from simple components. In smaller models, capabilities tend to scale smoothly with model size—a larger model might be slightly better at language tasks than a smaller one, but the improvement is gradual and predictable. However, at certain scale thresholds, entirely new capabilities can appear suddenly and dramatically, often surprising even the researchers who trained the models.

Few-shot learning represents one of the most striking examples of emergent abilities in large language models. While smaller models require extensive fine-tuning on task-specific data to perform new tasks, sufficiently large models can learn to perform new tasks from just a few examples provided in their input context. This capability wasn't explicitly trained—the models were simply trained to predict the next word in text sequences—yet the ability to recognize patterns and apply them to new situations emerged naturally from the learning process.

Chain-of-thought reasoning represents another remarkable emergent capability that has transformed how we think about AI reasoning. Large models can break down complex problems into step-by-step reasoning processes, showing their work and arriving at correct answers through logical chains of inference. This capability enables models to solve mathematical problems, logical puzzles, and complex analytical tasks that would be impossible through simple pattern matching.

The emergence of code generation capabilities in models trained primarily on natural language text demonstrates the surprising generalizability of large-scale learning. Models like GPT-3 and its successors can generate functional code in multiple programming languages, debug existing code, and even create complete applications from natural language descriptions. This capability emerged despite the models being trained primarily on natural language text, suggesting that the underlying patterns of logic and structure are shared across different domains.

Research into scaling laws has provided important insights into how model performance improves with increased parameters, training data, and computational resources. These empirical laws, first systematically studied by researchers at OpenAI and DeepMind, reveal predictable relationships between model scale and performance across a wide range of tasks. The laws suggest that performance improvements follow power-law relationships with scale, meaning that consistent improvements require exponential increases in resources.

The implications of scaling laws are both encouraging and sobering. On one hand, they suggest that continued scaling will yield further capability improvements, potentially leading to even more sophisticated AI systems. On the other hand, they reveal diminishing returns, meaning that each new capability breakthrough requires increasingly massive investments in computational resources and training data.

Understanding emergent abilities and scaling laws has become crucial for AI research and development planning. Organizations must balance the potential benefits of larger models against the enormous costs and technical challenges involved in training them. Additionally, the unpredictable nature of emergent abilities makes it difficult to anticipate what new capabilities might arise from future scaling efforts, creating both exciting possibilities and potential risks.

3.4 Core Capabilities of Current Generative AI Systems

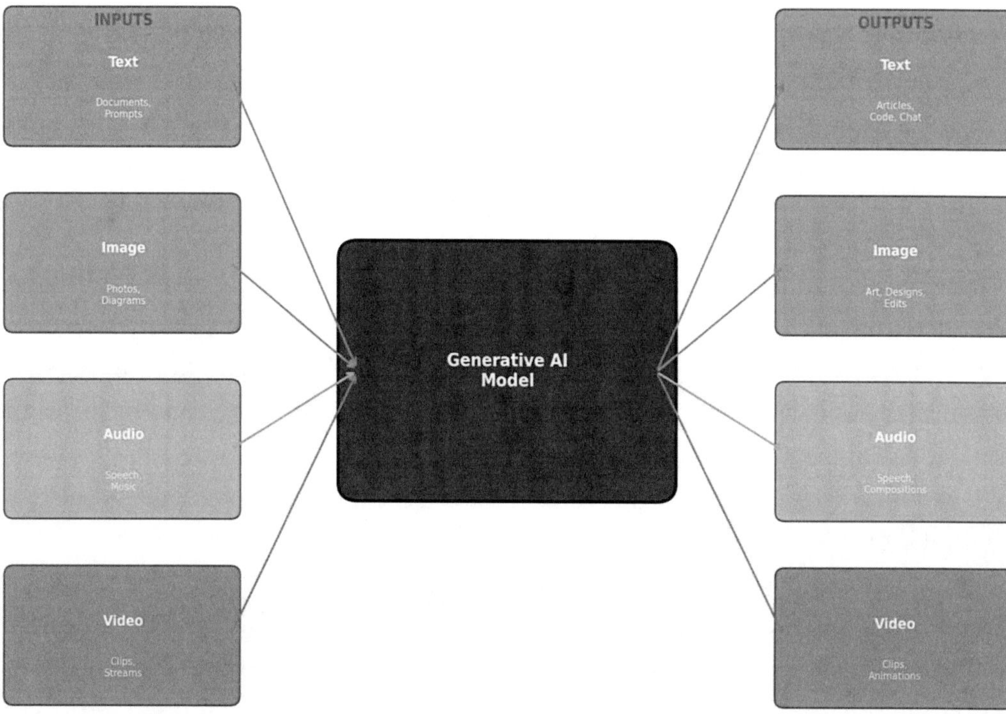

Figure 3-9. *Multimodal generative AI capabilities showing text, image, audio, and video inputs and outputs processed by a central model*

3.4.1 Natural Language Processing and Generation

Modern generative AI systems have achieved unprecedented proficiency in understanding and generating human language, representing a quantum leap from earlier natural language processing approaches. These systems demonstrate sophisticated linguistic capabilities that span multiple dimensions of language understanding, from basic grammar and syntax to complex semantic relationships and pragmatic reasoning. The depth and breadth of these capabilities have transformed how we interact with computers and opened new possibilities for human–AI collaboration.

Text generation represents perhaps the most visible and impressive capability of current generative AI systems. These models can produce coherent, contextually appropriate text across an enormous range of styles, genres, and domains. Whether writing technical documentation, creative fiction, academic essays, or casual conversation, modern AI systems can adapt their writing style, tone, and content to match the requirements of the task and the preferences of the user. The quality of generated text often rivals or exceeds human-produced content in terms of grammatical correctness, coherence, and even creativity.

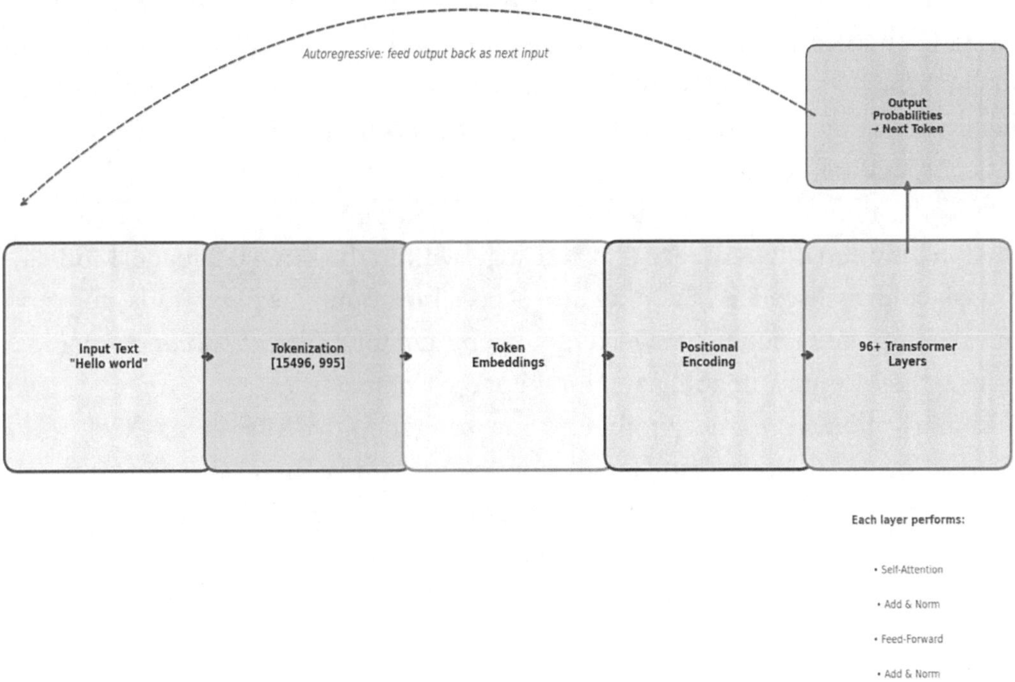

Figure 3-10. *Internal processing pipeline of a Transformer-based language model, from input tokenization and positional encoding through multi-layer processing to output generation*

The sophistication of modern text generation goes far beyond simple template filling or phrase recombination. These systems demonstrate a genuine understanding of context, maintaining consistency across long passages while adapting to changing circumstances within the text. They can maintain character voices in creative writing, follow complex argumentative structures in analytical pieces, and even incorporate subtle stylistic elements that make their writing engaging and natural.

Language translation capabilities in modern generative AI systems have surpassed traditional machine translation approaches by capturing nuance, context, and cultural references that were previously impossible for automated systems to handle. Rather than relying on word-by-word substitution or phrase-based translation, these systems understand the meaning and intent behind text and can express that meaning naturally in the target language. This approach enables more accurate translation of idiomatic expressions, cultural references, and context-dependent meanings.

The translation capabilities extend beyond simple language pairs to include translation between different registers and styles within the same language. Models can translate formal academic writing into accessible popular explanations, convert technical jargon into plain language, or adapt content for different audiences while preserving the essential meaning and intent of the original text.

Summarization represents another area where generative AI systems excel, demonstrating the ability to distill lengthy documents into concise summaries while preserving key information and maintaining coherence. These systems can identify the most important points in complex documents, understand relationships between different sections, and present information in a logical, accessible format. The sophistication of modern summarization goes beyond simple extraction of key sentences to include genuine synthesis and reorganization of information.

The summarization capabilities of current systems extend to different types of summaries for different purposes. They can create executive summaries that focus on key decisions and outcomes, technical abstracts that preserve important methodological details, or popular summaries that make complex topics accessible to general audiences. This flexibility demonstrates a deep understanding of how information needs vary across different contexts and audiences.

Question answering capabilities in modern generative AI systems represent a significant advance over earlier information retrieval approaches. Rather than simply finding documents that contain relevant keywords, these systems can synthesize information from their training data to provide comprehensive, accurate answers to complex questions. They can handle questions that require reasoning across multiple pieces of information, questions that involve counterfactual scenarios, and questions that require explanation and justification of their answers.

The question answering capabilities extend to different types of reasoning, including factual recall, logical inference, causal reasoning, and even creative problem-solving. Models can answer questions about historical events, explain scientific concepts, solve mathematical problems, and provide advice on practical matters. The depth and accuracy of these responses often rival those of human experts, though with important limitations that we will explore later in this chapter.

3.4.2 Multimodal Capabilities

Recent advances in generative AI have extended beyond text to encompass multiple modalities, creating systems that can work with images, audio, video, and code in addition to natural language. These multimodal capabilities represent a significant step toward more general artificial intelligence and have opened new possibilities for creative expression, technical problem-solving, and human–computer interaction.

Text-to-image generation has emerged as one of the most striking and publicly visible capabilities of modern generative AI systems. Models like DALL-E, Midjourney, Stable Diffusion, and others can create photorealistic or artistic images from textual descriptions, revolutionizing creative workflows and visual content creation. These systems demonstrate a sophisticated understanding of visual concepts, artistic styles, composition principles, and the relationships between textual descriptions and visual representations.

The sophistication of text-to-image generation extends far beyond simple object recognition and placement. These systems can understand complex spatial relationships, lighting conditions, artistic styles, and even abstract concepts that must be translated into visual form. They can create images that combine multiple objects in realistic ways, apply specific artistic techniques, and even generate images in the style of particular artists or artistic movements.

The impact of text-to-image generation on creative industries has been profound, enabling rapid prototyping of visual concepts, democratizing access to high-quality visual content creation, and inspiring new forms of artistic expression. However, these capabilities have also raised important questions about copyright, artistic authenticity, and the economic impact on professional artists and designers.

Image-to-text generation represents the complementary capability, allowing AI systems to describe images, answer questions about visual content, and extract text from images with high accuracy. These vision-language models can provide detailed descriptions of scenes, identify objects and their relationships, and even interpret the emotional content or artistic qualities of images. The accuracy and sophistication of these descriptions often rival those of human observers.

The applications of image-to-text generation extend beyond simple description to include accessibility tools for visually impaired users, content moderation systems that can identify inappropriate visual content, and analytical tools that can extract information from charts, diagrams, and other visual data representations. These capabilities have made visual content more accessible and have enabled new forms of automated content analysis.

Code generation represents another remarkable multimodal capability that has transformed software development practices. AI systems can generate functional code in multiple programming languages from natural language descriptions, debug existing code, explain code functionality, and even create complete applications from high-level specifications. This capability bridges the gap between human intentions expressed in natural language and the precise formal requirements of computer programming.

The sophistication of code generation capabilities extends to understanding programming paradigms, following coding conventions, optimizing for performance, and even incorporating security best practices. Models can generate code that follows specific architectural patterns, uses appropriate libraries and frameworks, and includes proper error handling and documentation. The quality of generated code often meets professional standards and can significantly accelerate software development processes.

Audio and music generation capabilities have also advanced significantly, with AI systems now able to compose music in various styles, generate speech in different voices, and create complex audio content from textual descriptions. These systems can understand musical theory, compose coherent melodies and harmonies, and even generate lyrics that match musical content. The quality of generated audio content has reached levels that are often indistinguishable from human-created content.

3.4.3 Reasoning and Problem-Solving

Current generative AI systems demonstrate sophisticated reasoning capabilities that extend far beyond simple pattern matching or information retrieval. These systems can engage in logical reasoning, solve complex problems, and even exhibit forms of creativity and insight that were previously thought to be uniquely human capabilities. The depth and sophistication of these reasoning abilities represent one of the most significant advances in artificial intelligence.

Logical reasoning capabilities in modern AI systems encompass various forms of inference, from basic deductive reasoning to more complex forms of analogical and causal reasoning. These systems can follow logical chains of reasoning, identify fallacies in arguments, construct valid proofs, and even engage in sophisticated philosophical reasoning. The ability to maintain logical consistency across complex arguments while considering multiple perspectives demonstrates a level of reasoning sophistication that approaches human-level performance in many domains.

The logical reasoning capabilities extend to understanding and applying formal logical systems, including propositional logic, predicate logic, and even more specialized logical frameworks. Models can work with logical formulas, apply inference rules correctly, and identify when arguments are valid or invalid. This capability has important applications in fields like law, philosophy, and computer science, where formal reasoning is essential.

Mathematical problem-solving represents another area where current AI systems excel, demonstrating the ability to solve complex mathematical problems across various domains, from basic arithmetic to advanced calculus, linear algebra, and even proof construction. These systems can understand mathematical notation, apply appropriate solution strategies, and explain their reasoning in ways that are helpful for human learners.

The mathematical capabilities extend beyond mere calculation to include understanding mathematical concepts, recognizing patterns, and applying mathematical reasoning to real-world problems. Models can solve word problems that require translating natural language descriptions into mathematical formulations, optimize complex functions, and even discover new mathematical relationships or proofs.

Scientific reasoning capabilities enable AI systems to analyze scientific problems, propose hypotheses, design experiments, and interpret results. These systems can understand scientific methodology, apply domain-specific knowledge, and even generate novel research ideas. The sophistication of scientific reasoning in current AI systems has led to their use in various research contexts, from drug discovery to materials science.

The scientific reasoning capabilities include understanding experimental design principles, statistical analysis methods, and the relationships between theoretical predictions and empirical observations. Models can critique scientific arguments, identify potential confounding variables, and suggest improvements to experimental protocols. This capability has significant implications for accelerating scientific discovery and improving research quality.

Creative problem-solving represents perhaps the most intriguing aspect of current AI reasoning capabilities. These systems can approach problems from novel angles, generate creative solutions that humans might not consider, and even exhibit forms of insight and intuition that lead to breakthrough solutions. The creative problem-solving capabilities extend across domains, from engineering and design to artistic expression and strategic planning.

The creative aspects of AI reasoning challenge traditional notions of creativity and intelligence, suggesting that sophisticated pattern recognition and recombination can lead to genuinely novel and valuable insights. However, questions remain about whether these systems truly understand the problems they're solving or are simply very sophisticated at pattern matching and recombination.

3.5 Fundamental Limitations of Current Systems

3.5.1 Knowledge and Factual Accuracy Limitations

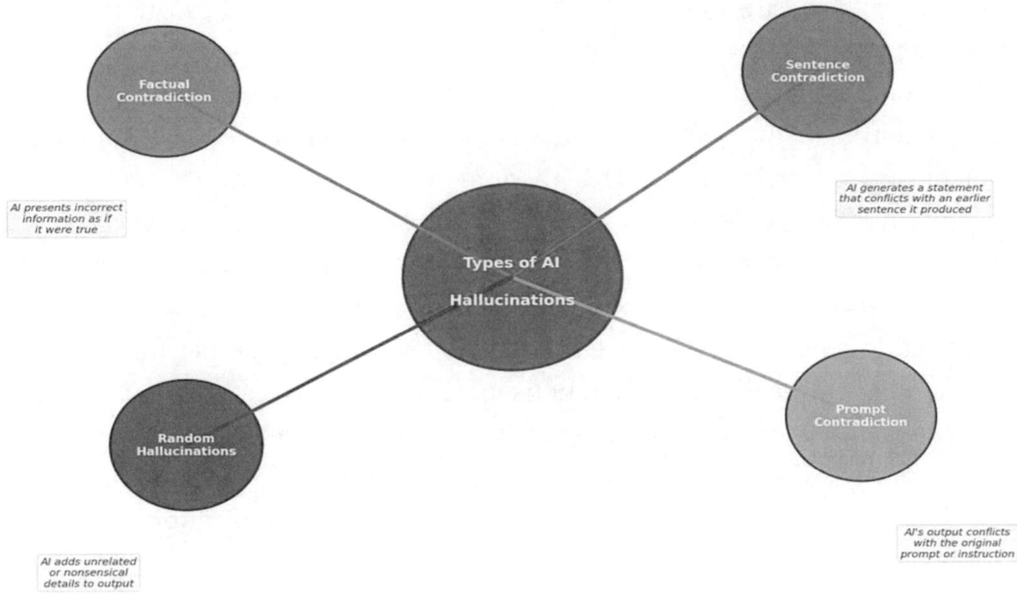

Figure 3-11. *Taxonomy of AI hallucination types: sentence contradiction, prompt contradiction, factual contradiction, and nonsensical or irrelevant generation*

Despite their impressive capabilities, current generative AI systems face several fundamental limitations that significantly impact their reliability and usefulness in many applications. These limitations stem from the underlying architecture and training methodologies of these systems and represent some of the most significant challenges facing the field of artificial intelligence today.

Knowledge cutoffs represent one of the most obvious and practically significant limitations of current generative AI systems. Most models are trained on data up to a specific point in time, creating knowledge gaps about recent events, developments, and discoveries. This limitation is particularly problematic in rapidly evolving fields like technology, medicine, and current events, where information can become outdated quickly. Users must be aware of these knowledge cutoffs when relying on AI systems for information about recent developments.

The knowledge cutoff problem is exacerbated by the enormous computational costs and technical complexity involved in retraining large models. Unlike traditional databases that can be updated continuously, large language models require complete retraining to incorporate new information effectively. This creates a fundamental tension between the desire for current information and the practical constraints of model training and deployment.

Hallucination represents perhaps the most serious limitation of current generative AI systems, referring to the tendency of these models to generate plausible-sounding but factually incorrect information. This phenomenon occurs because models optimize for coherence and plausibility rather than factual accuracy, leading them to confidently present false information when they lack knowledge about a topic or when their training data contained errors. The hallucination problem is particularly insidious because the false information generated by AI systems often appears highly credible and well-reasoned. Models can generate fake citations that look authentic, create detailed but entirely fictional historical accounts, or present incorrect scientific information with apparent authority. This makes it difficult for users to identify false information without extensive fact-checking, limiting the reliability of AI systems in applications where accuracy is critical.

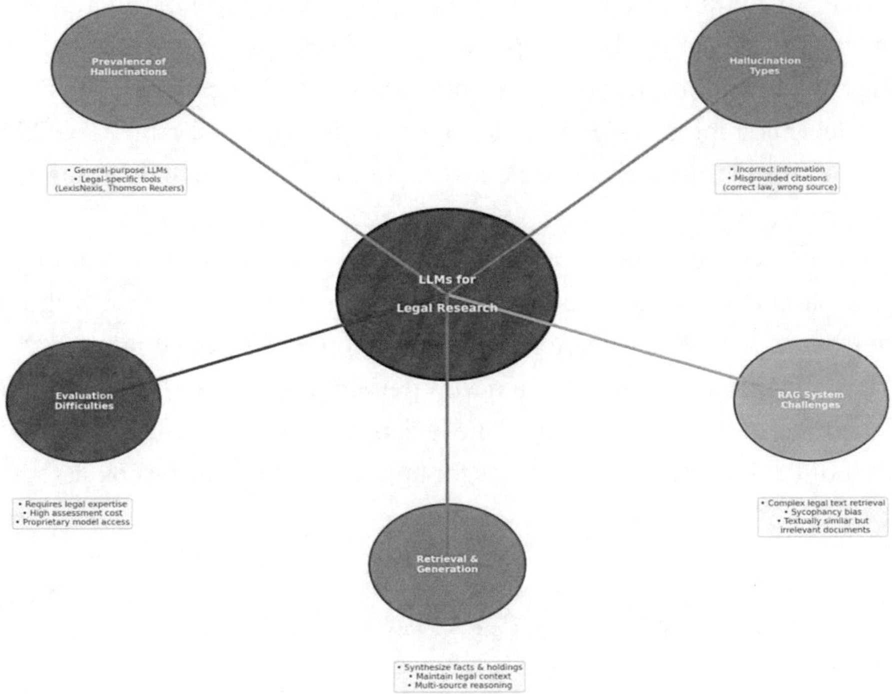

Figure 3-12. *Key challenges of using large language models for legal research, including hallucination types, RAG system difficulties, and evaluation complexity*

Source attribution represents another significant limitation of current generative AI systems. These models struggle to provide reliable citations or trace their outputs back to specific sources in their training data. When asked for sources, models often generate plausible-looking but entirely fictional citations, creating a false impression of scholarly rigor. This limitation makes it difficult to verify information provided by AI systems and raises important questions about intellectual property and attribution. **Retrieval-Augmented Generation (RAG)** has emerged as a practical approach to mitigate this limitation. RAG systems supplement the generative model by first retrieving relevant documents from a defined knowledge base, then grounding the model's response in that retrieved content. This allows the system to cite specific sources for its outputs, improving both attribution and factual accuracy. However, RAG is not a complete solution—the model can still hallucinate information not present in the retrieved documents, misinterpret retrieved content, or fail to retrieve the most relevant sources. Attribution quality ultimately depends on the retrieval system's accuracy and the model's faithfulness to the retrieved material.

The source attribution problem stems from the way these models are trained and operate. During training, models learn patterns from vast amounts of text without maintaining explicit links between learned information and its sources. The compressed nature of the learned representations makes it nearly impossible to trace specific outputs back to their origins in the training data, creating fundamental challenges for verification and attribution.

Factual inconsistency represents another troubling limitation, where models may provide contradictory information across different conversations or even within the same conversation. This inconsistency can occur when models encounter conflicting information in their training data or when they generate responses based on different aspects of their learned representations. The lack of a consistent, coherent knowledge base makes it difficult to rely on AI systems for applications requiring consistent factual accuracy.

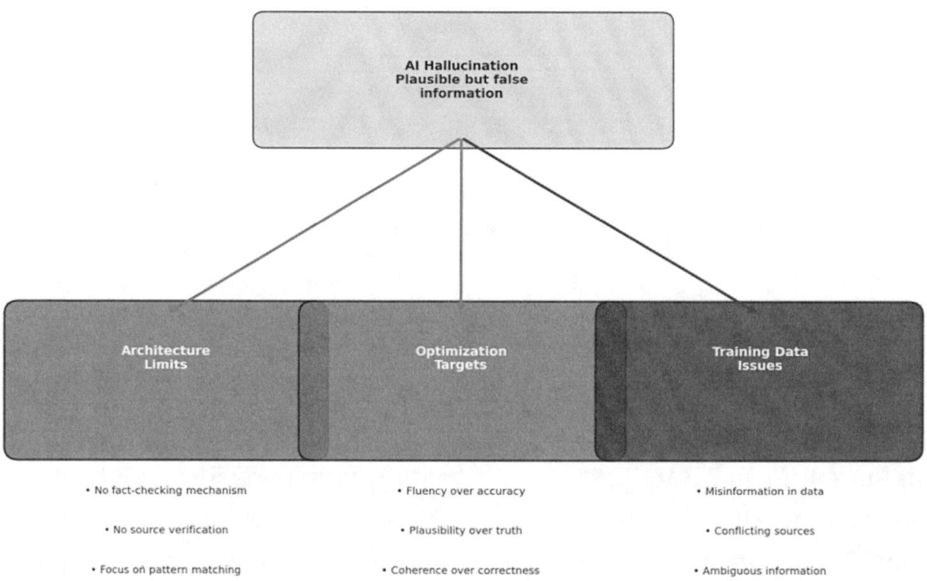

Figure 3-13. *Root causes of AI hallucination: architecture limits, optimization targets prioritizing fluency over accuracy, and training data issues*

3.5.2 Reasoning and Logic Limitations

While generative AI demonstrates impressive reasoning capabilities in many contexts, significant limitations remain in formal reasoning, logical consistency, and systematic problem-solving. These limitations often become apparent when models are pushed beyond their comfort zones or when they encounter problems that require strict adherence to logical rules rather than pattern-based reasoning.

Formal logic represents one area where current AI systems struggle despite their apparent sophistication. While models can often solve logical problems correctly, they may do so through pattern recognition rather than genuine logical reasoning. When faced with novel logical problems that don't match patterns from their training data, these systems may make errors that reveal their lack of true logical understanding.

The formal logic limitations become particularly apparent in complex scenarios requiring multiple steps of logical inference or when dealing with edge cases that require careful attention to logical rules. Models may correctly apply logical principles in straightforward cases but fail when problems require creative application of logical rules or when multiple logical systems interact in complex ways.

Causal reasoning presents another significant challenge for current AI systems. While models can often identify correlations and associations in data, understanding true cause-and-effect relationships requires a deeper understanding of mechanisms and counterfactual reasoning that current systems often lack. This limitation can lead to incorrect conclusions about causation and inappropriate recommendations for interventions or policy decisions.

The causal reasoning limitations are particularly problematic in scientific and policy contexts, where understanding causal relationships is essential for making accurate predictions and effective decisions. Models may confuse correlation with causation, fail to account for confounding variables, or make incorrect predictions about the effects of interventions based on observational data patterns.

Mathematical accuracy, while generally impressive, still shows significant limitations in current AI systems. Models may make computational errors, apply incorrect formulas, or fail to recognize when their mathematical reasoning has gone astray. These errors can be particularly problematic because they're often embedded within otherwise coherent and convincing explanations, making them difficult to detect without careful verification.

Long-term planning and multi-step reasoning over extended contexts represent fundamental challenges for current AI architectures. While models can engage in sophisticated reasoning within their context windows, they struggle with tasks requiring extensive long-term planning, maintaining consistency across very long reasoning chains, or coordinating multiple complex sub-goals over extended periods.

3.5.3 Context and Memory Limitations

Context window constraints represent one of the most fundamental architectural limitations of current generative AI systems. Most models have limited context windows, typically ranging from 4,000 to 32,000 tokens, which restricts their ability to maintain coherence over very long conversations, process lengthy documents, or engage in extended reasoning chains that require maintaining large amounts of contextual information.

The context window limitation affects many practical applications of AI systems. Models may lose track of important information mentioned early in long conversations, fail to maintain consistency across lengthy documents, or be unable to process large datasets that exceed their context limits. This limitation becomes particularly problematic in applications requiring analysis of long documents, extended conversations, or complex multi-step tasks.

Memory persistence represents another significant limitation, as current systems lack persistent memory across conversations or sessions. Each interaction begins fresh, without access to previous conversations or learned preferences from past interactions. This limitation prevents AI systems from building long-term relationships with users, learning from past mistakes, or accumulating knowledge over time in the way humans do.

The lack of persistent memory affects the user experience and limits the potential for AI systems to serve as long-term assistants or collaborators. Users must repeatedly provide context and preferences, and systems cannot learn from past interactions to improve their performance over time. This limitation also prevents AI systems from building cumulative knowledge or expertise through experience.

Context degradation represents a more subtle but important limitation, where models may gradually lose track of earlier context as conversations become longer or as they process lengthy documents. Even within their context windows, models may give less attention to information that appears earlier in the sequence, leading to inconsistencies or forgotten information as interactions progress.

3.5.4 Bias and Fairness Issues

Training data bias represents one of the most serious and pervasive limitations of current generative AI systems. These models inherit and potentially amplify biases present in their training data, which often reflects societal biases related to gender, race, religion, culture, and other sensitive attributes. Since training data is typically drawn from internet sources and published texts, it inevitably contains the biases and prejudices present in human-generated content.

The bias problem is particularly insidious because it can be subtle and difficult to detect. Models may generate content that appears neutral and objective while actually reflecting underlying biases in ways that disadvantage certain groups or perpetuate harmful stereotypes. These biases can affect everything from job recommendations and educational content to creative outputs and factual information.

Representation gaps in training data create additional fairness challenges, as underrepresented groups may receive less accurate, less nuanced, or less appropriate responses from AI systems. If certain communities, languages, or perspectives are underrepresented in training data, the resulting models may perform poorly when serving these populations, potentially exacerbating existing inequalities.

Cultural bias represents another dimension of the fairness problem, as models trained primarily on English-language Western content may not adequately represent global perspectives, cultural nuances, or non-Western ways of thinking. This limitation can lead to culturally inappropriate responses, misunderstanding of cultural contexts, or the imposition of Western perspectives on global audiences.

Amplification effects represent a particularly concerning aspect of AI bias, where models may not just reflect existing biases but actually amplify them, making them more pronounced in generated content than they were in the original training data. This amplification can occur through the model's optimization process, which may inadvertently strengthen certain patterns while weakening others.

3.6 Technical Challenges and Ongoing Research

3.6.1 Computational Efficiency and Sustainability

The massive computational requirements of current generative AI systems present significant challenges that extend far beyond mere technical considerations to encompass environmental, economic, and social implications. The scale of computation required for training and deploying these systems has grown exponentially, creating urgent needs for more efficient approaches and raising important questions about the sustainability of current AI development trajectories.

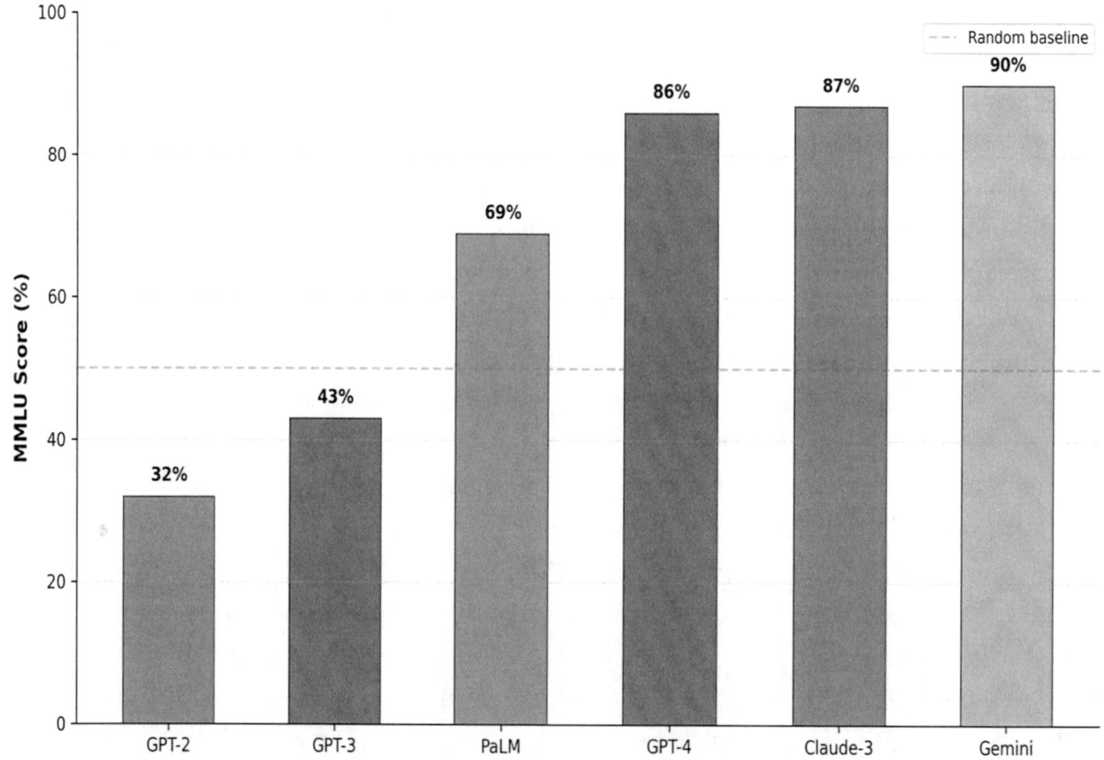

Figure 3-14. *Benchmark comparison of AI model performance (MMLU scores) across GPT-2, GPT-3, PaLM, GPT-4, Claude-3, and Gemini*

Energy consumption represents one of the most pressing concerns associated with large-scale AI systems. Training a single large language model like GPT-3 requires enormous amounts of electricity, with estimates suggesting that the training process consumed approximately 1,287 megawatt-hours of electricity, equivalent to the annual electricity consumption of about 120 average American homes. The carbon footprint of such training runs can be substantial, particularly when powered by electricity grids that rely heavily on fossil fuels.

The energy consumption problem extends beyond training to include inference costs, as running large models for real-time applications requires significant computational resources. Popular AI services may handle millions of queries per day, each requiring substantial computational resources to generate responses. The cumulative energy consumption of inference across all deployed AI systems represents a growing environmental concern that will only increase as these systems become more widely adopted. Hardware requirements for training and running large generative models create significant barriers to entry and contribute to the concentration of AI capabilities among well-resourced organizations. Training state-of-the-art models requires access to thousands of high-end GPUs or specialized AI chips, infrastructure that costs millions of dollars and is available to only a small number of organizations worldwide. This hardware concentration raises important questions about the democratization of AI technology and equitable access to advanced AI capabilities.

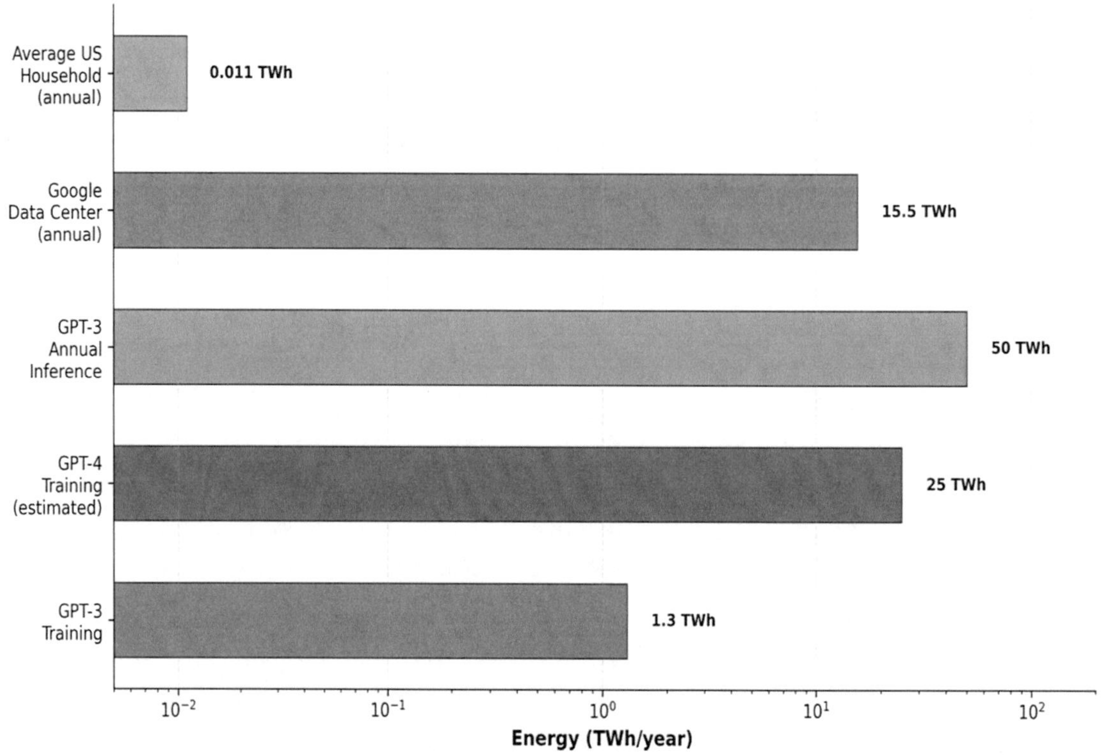

Figure 3-15. *Energy consumption comparison across AI model training and inference workloads, highlighting the computational sustainability challenge*

The specialized nature of AI hardware also creates supply chain vulnerabilities and dependencies that can affect the entire AI ecosystem. The limited number of manufacturers capable of producing cutting-edge AI chips, combined with the enormous demand for these components, has led to supply shortages and price increases that further limit access to AI technology.

Inference costs represent an ongoing operational challenge that affects the practical deployment of large AI models. Running large models for real-time applications requires significant computational resources, making it expensive to provide AI services at scale. These costs can limit the accessibility of AI technology and create economic barriers that prevent widespread adoption of beneficial AI applications.

Model compression research focuses on creating smaller, more efficient models that maintain performance while reducing computational requirements. Techniques like knowledge distillation, pruning, and quantization aim to create models that capture the essential capabilities of large models while requiring significantly less computational resources. These approaches show promise for making AI technology more accessible and sustainable.

The development of more efficient architectures represents another important research direction, with researchers exploring alternatives to the transformer architecture that might provide similar capabilities with lower computational requirements. Approaches like mixture of experts, sparse attention mechanisms, and novel architectural designs aim to improve the efficiency of AI systems while maintaining or improving their capabilities.

3.6.2 Alignment and Safety Research

Ensuring that AI systems behave in alignment with human values and intentions represents one of the most critical challenges facing the AI research community. As AI systems become more capable and autonomous, the importance of alignment research has grown dramatically, with researchers working to develop methods for creating AI systems that are not just powerful but also safe, beneficial, and aligned with human interests.

Value alignment represents a fundamental challenge in AI safety, involving the complex task of defining and implementing human values in artificial systems. This challenge is complicated by the diversity of human values across cultures, individuals, and contexts, making it difficult to specify universal values that should guide AI behavior. Researchers are exploring various approaches to value alignment, including learning values from human behavior, democratic processes for value specification, and philosophical frameworks for ethical AI.

The value alignment problem is further complicated by the dynamic nature of human values, which can change over time and vary across different situations. AI systems must be able to adapt to changing values while maintaining consistency and avoiding harmful behaviors. This requires sophisticated approaches to value learning and updating that can handle uncertainty and conflicting preferences.

Robustness research focuses on ensuring that AI systems perform reliably across diverse scenarios, edge cases, and adversarial conditions. Current AI systems often fail when confronted with inputs that differ significantly from their training data or when faced with adversarial attacks designed to exploit their weaknesses. Developing robust AI systems requires advances in training methodologies, evaluation techniques, and architectural designs that can handle unexpected situations gracefully.

The robustness challenge extends beyond technical considerations to include social and economic robustness, ensuring that AI systems continue to function appropriately as they interact with human societies and economic systems. This includes considerations of how AI systems might affect employment, social structures, and power dynamics and how to design systems that promote beneficial outcomes for society as a whole.

Interpretability research aims to make AI systems more transparent and understandable, addressing the "black box" nature of current large models. Understanding how AI systems make decisions is crucial for building trust, identifying potential problems, and ensuring that systems behave as intended. However, the complexity of large neural networks makes interpretability extremely challenging, requiring new techniques and frameworks for understanding complex AI behavior.

The interpretability challenge is particularly acute for large language models, where the decision-making process involves millions or billions of parameters interacting in complex ways. Researchers are developing various approaches to interpretability, including attention visualization, activation analysis, and causal intervention techniques, but significant challenges remain in making these systems truly understandable.

Control and oversight represent critical aspects of AI safety, involving the development of mechanisms for maintaining appropriate human control over AI systems as they become more capable and autonomous. This includes technical approaches for ensuring that humans can intervene in AI decision-making, as well as institutional and regulatory frameworks for governing AI development and deployment.

The control problem becomes increasingly complex as AI systems become more capable, potentially reaching points where they can modify themselves or create other AI systems. Ensuring that such systems remain under human control and aligned with human values requires careful design of control mechanisms and governance structures that can adapt to rapidly evolving AI capabilities.

3.6.3 Emerging Architectural Innovations

The field of AI architecture continues to evolve rapidly, with researchers exploring new approaches that could address current limitations while unlocking new capabilities. These architectural innovations represent the cutting edge of AI research and may define the next generation of AI systems.

Mixture of Experts (MoE) architectures represent a promising approach to scaling AI systems more efficiently by activating only relevant parts of large models for specific tasks. Rather than using all parameters for every computation, MoE models route inputs to specialized expert networks that are most relevant for the particular task or domain. This approach can dramatically improve efficiency while maintaining or even improving performance compared to traditional dense models.

The MoE approach addresses several limitations of current architectures, including computational efficiency and the ability to handle diverse tasks within a single model. By specializing different parts of the model for different types of tasks or domains, MoE architectures can achieve better performance while using computational resources more efficiently. This approach also enables models to scale to much larger sizes without proportional increases in computational costs.

Retrieval-Augmented Generation (RAG) represents another important architectural innovation that combines generative models with external knowledge bases to improve factual accuracy and provide source attribution. RAG systems can query external databases or document collections to retrieve relevant information, which is then used to inform the generation process. This approach addresses some of the key limitations of current systems, including hallucination and lack of source attribution. RAG systems offer several advantages over traditional language models, including the ability to access up-to-date information, provide verifiable sources for their claims, and adapt to new information without requiring retraining. These systems can be particularly valuable in domains where accuracy and source attribution are critical, such as scientific research, legal analysis, and factual question answering.

Constitutional AI represents an innovative approach to training AI systems that embed specific principles and constraints directly into model behavior. Rather than relying solely on human feedback, constitutional AI uses a set of written principles or "constitution" to guide model training and behavior. This approach can help ensure that AI systems behave consistently according to specified values and principles, even in novel situations.

The constitutional AI approach offers several potential advantages, including greater transparency in value specification, more consistent behavior across different contexts, and the ability to update or modify guiding principles without complete retraining. However, challenges remain in defining appropriate constitutional principles and ensuring that they are properly implemented in model behavior.

Multimodal integration represents another important area of architectural innovation, focusing on developing more sophisticated ways to combine different types of input and output modalities. Current multimodal systems often treat different modalities separately, but future architectures may integrate them more deeply, enabling richer understanding and more sophisticated reasoning across different types of information.

Advanced multimodal architectures could enable AI systems that can seamlessly work with text, images, audio, video, and other data types in integrated ways, leading to more natural and powerful human–AI interactions. These systems could understand complex scenes, generate rich multimedia content, and engage in sophisticated reasoning that spans multiple modalities.

3.7 Performance Metrics and Evaluation

3.7.1 Traditional Metrics

Evaluating the performance of generative AI systems presents unique challenges that go far beyond traditional machine learning evaluation approaches. The subjective nature of many generative tasks, combined with the open-ended possibilities for outputs, makes it difficult to develop comprehensive and meaningful evaluation frameworks. Nevertheless, researchers have developed various metrics and evaluation approaches that provide insights into different aspects of generative AI performance.

Perplexity represents one of the most fundamental metrics for evaluating language models, measuring how well a model predicts text by calculating the average uncertainty in predicting the next word in a sequence. Lower perplexity scores indicate that the model is better at predicting the training data, suggesting a better understanding of language patterns. However, perplexity has limitations as an evaluation metric, as it may not correlate well with human judgments of text quality or usefulness.

The relationship between perplexity and actual performance on downstream tasks is complex and sometimes counterintuitive. Models with lower perplexity don't always perform better on practical tasks, and the metric can be misleading when comparing models trained on different datasets or with different architectures. Despite these limitations, perplexity remains valuable as a basic measure of model performance and as a tool for comparing different training approaches.

BLEU (Bilingual Evaluation Understudy) scores evaluate the quality of generated text by comparing it to reference texts, measuring the overlap of n-grams between generated and reference texts. Originally developed for machine translation evaluation, BLEU has been adapted for various text generation tasks. The metric provides a quantitative measure of similarity between generated and reference texts, but it has significant limitations in capturing semantic meaning, creativity, and overall quality.

BLEU scores can be particularly problematic for creative or open-ended generation tasks, where there may be many valid outputs that differ significantly from any specific reference text. The metric also tends to favor shorter outputs and may not adequately capture the fluency or coherence of generated text. Despite these limitations, BLEU remains widely used due to its simplicity and the availability of reference implementations.

ROUGE (Recall-Oriented Understudy for Gisting Evaluation) scores assess the quality of summaries by measuring overlap with reference summaries, focusing on recall rather than precision. ROUGE includes several variants that measure different types of overlap, including word-level, phrase-level, and longest common subsequence measures. Like BLEU, ROUGE provides quantitative evaluation but may not capture all aspects of summary quality.

The limitations of ROUGE are similar to those of BLEU, including difficulty in handling multiple valid summaries and potential bias toward specific writing styles or approaches. However, ROUGE remains valuable for comparing different summarization approaches and tracking improvements in summarization systems over time.

Human evaluation remains crucial for assessing qualities that automated metrics cannot capture, including coherence, creativity, appropriateness, and overall usefulness. Human evaluators can assess whether generated content meets user needs, follows instructions correctly, and demonstrates appropriate understanding of context and intent. However, human evaluation is expensive, time-consuming, and can be inconsistent across different evaluators.

The challenges of human evaluation include ensuring consistency across evaluators, defining clear evaluation criteria, and scaling evaluation to cover the diverse range of tasks and outputs that generative AI systems can produce. Researchers have developed various frameworks for structured human evaluation, including comparative ranking approaches and detailed rubrics for specific aspects of performance.

3.7.2 Emerging Evaluation Frameworks

As generative AI capabilities have expanded and become more sophisticated, traditional evaluation metrics have proven insufficient for capturing the full range of abilities and limitations of these systems. This has led to the development of more comprehensive evaluation frameworks that attempt to assess AI systems across multiple dimensions and in more realistic contexts.

Capability benchmarks represent a significant advance in AI evaluation, providing comprehensive test suites that evaluate models across multiple domains and tasks simultaneously. Benchmarks like MMLU (Massive Multitask Language Understanding), SuperGLUE, and BIG-bench test models on hundreds or thousands of different tasks, providing a more holistic view of model capabilities than single-task evaluations. These comprehensive benchmarks reveal important patterns in AI development, showing how different models excel in different areas and how capabilities have evolved over time. They also help identify areas where current models still struggle, guiding future research directions and development priorities.

Safety evaluations have become increasingly important as AI systems become more capable and widely deployed. These assessments focus on measuring harmful content generation, bias in outputs, and alignment with human values. Safety evaluation frameworks test models' tendency to generate harmful, biased, or inappropriate content across various scenarios and contexts.

The development of safety evaluation frameworks represents a critical area of ongoing research, as traditional performance metrics often fail to capture important safety considerations. These frameworks must balance the need for comprehensive testing with practical constraints on evaluation time and resources while also addressing the evolving nature of safety concerns as AI capabilities advance.

Robustness testing evaluates model performance under adversarial conditions, edge cases, and distribution shifts that differ from training data. These evaluations are crucial for understanding how models behave when deployed in real-world conditions that may differ significantly from their training environments. Robustness testing includes adversarial attacks, out-of-distribution inputs, and stress testing under various challenging conditions.

The importance of robustness testing has grown as AI systems are deployed in increasingly critical applications where failure can have serious consequences. These evaluations help identify potential failure modes and guide the development of more reliable and robust AI systems.

Real-world performance evaluation represents perhaps the most important but also most challenging aspect of AI evaluation. Measuring how well models perform in actual deployment scenarios, with real users and real-world constraints, provides the most meaningful assessment of AI system value. However, real-world evaluation is complex, expensive, and difficult to standardize across different applications and contexts.

Real-world evaluation must consider factors like user satisfaction, task completion rates, error recovery, and long-term user engagement. These metrics provide insights into the practical value of AI systems that laboratory benchmarks may miss, but they require careful design to ensure meaningful and comparable results.

3.8 Future Directions and Technological Horizons

3.8.1 Scaling and Architecture Evolution

The future trajectory of generative AI development will likely be shaped by continued advances in scaling and architectural innovation, though the path forward is more complex and uncertain than simple extrapolation from current trends might suggest. While scaling has been the primary driver of capability improvements in recent years, emerging research suggests that the relationship between scale and capability is more nuanced than initially understood.

Parameter scaling continues to be an active area of research and development, with some models already reaching trillions of parameters and future models potentially scaling even further. However, the benefits of parameter scaling appear to follow diminishing returns, with each doubling of parameters providing smaller improvements in capability. This has led researchers to explore more sophisticated approaches to scaling that consider not just parameter count but also training data quality, computational efficiency, and architectural innovations.

The concept of compute-optimal scaling, popularized by research on scaling laws, suggests that optimal performance requires balanced scaling of model size, training data, and computational resources rather than simply maximizing any single dimension. This insight has important implications for future AI development, suggesting that continued progress will require advances across multiple dimensions simultaneously rather than focusing solely on building larger models.

Novel architectural approaches may emerge that are fundamentally more efficient or capable than current transformer-based models. Researchers are exploring various alternatives, including state-space models, retrieval-augmented architectures, and hybrid approaches that combine different architectural paradigms. These innovations could potentially achieve better performance with lower computational requirements or unlock entirely new capabilities.

The development of specialized models optimized for specific domains or tasks represents another important trend in AI architecture evolution. Rather than pursuing ever-larger general-purpose models, some researchers are focusing on creating highly optimized models for specific applications, such as scientific reasoning, code generation, or creative tasks. These specialized models may achieve superior performance in their target domains while requiring fewer resources than general-purpose alternatives.

3.8.2 Integration and Ecosystem Development

The future of generative AI will likely involve deeper integration into broader technological ecosystems, moving beyond standalone applications to become integral components of complex software systems and workflows. This integration will require advances in API design, tool integration, and system architecture that enable seamless incorporation of AI capabilities into existing technological infrastructure.

API and tool integration represents a critical area for future development, as AI capabilities become more widely adopted across different applications and industries. Future AI systems will need to integrate seamlessly with existing software tools, databases, and workflows, requiring sophisticated interfaces and integration frameworks that can handle the complexity and variability of real-world systems.

Multi-agent systems represent an emerging paradigm where multiple AI agents collaborate to accomplish complex tasks that exceed the capabilities of individual systems. These systems could coordinate different specialized AI models, combine different types of expertise, and handle complex workflows that require multiple types of reasoning and action. The development of effective multi-agent systems will require advances in coordination protocols, communication frameworks, and distributed reasoning approaches.

Human–AI collaboration represents perhaps the most important area for future development, focusing on creating interfaces and workflows that optimize the partnership between humans and AI systems rather than replacing human capabilities entirely. This approach recognizes that humans and AI systems have complementary strengths and that the most effective applications often involve close collaboration between human intelligence and artificial intelligence.

Edge deployment represents another important trend, bringing generative AI capabilities to edge devices and local environments rather than relying entirely on cloud-based systems. This approach offers advantages in terms of privacy, latency, and accessibility, but requires significant advances in model compression, efficient architectures, and specialized hardware designed for AI inference at the edge.

3.8.3 Addressing Current Limitations

Future research and development efforts will necessarily focus on addressing the fundamental limitations identified in current generative AI systems. Progress in these areas will be crucial for enabling broader adoption and more reliable deployment of AI technology across critical applications.

Improving factual accuracy and reducing hallucination represents one of the most important challenges for future AI development. Researchers are exploring various approaches, including Retrieval-Augmented Generation, fact-checking systems, uncertainty quantification, and improved training methodologies that emphasize accuracy over fluency. These approaches show promise but require significant additional development to achieve reliable factual accuracy across diverse domains.

Developing systems with persistent memory and context retention across extended interactions represents another critical area for improvement. Future AI systems may incorporate various forms of memory architectures, from simple conversation history to sophisticated episodic and semantic memory systems that can accumulate knowledge and experience over time. These advances could enable AI systems to serve as long-term assistants and collaborators rather than stateless tools.

Enhancing reasoning capabilities and reducing logical errors will require advances in both architectural design and training methodologies. Researchers are exploring approaches like chain-of-thought training, formal reasoning integration, and hybrid systems that combine neural networks with symbolic reasoning systems. These approaches aim to create AI systems that can engage in more reliable and systematic reasoning while maintaining the flexibility and generality of current neural approaches.

Bias mitigation and fairness improvement represent ongoing challenges that will require continued research and development. Future approaches may include more sophisticated bias detection and mitigation techniques, diverse training data curation, and evaluation frameworks that can identify and address various forms of bias and unfairness. These efforts will be crucial for ensuring that AI systems serve all users fairly and equitably.

3.9 Conclusion

The technical underpinnings of generative AI represent a remarkable convergence of decades of research in machine learning, neural networks, computational linguistics, and cognitive science. From the foundational concepts of artificial neural networks to the sophisticated transformer architectures that power today's most advanced systems, the technical evolution has been both rapid and revolutionary, transforming our understanding of what artificial intelligence can achieve.

The journey from simple perceptrons to today's large language models with hundreds of billions of parameters illustrates the power of scaling combined with architectural innovation. The transformer architecture, with its self-attention mechanisms and parallel processing capabilities, has proven to be a remarkably flexible and powerful foundation for generative AI systems. The addition of techniques like Reinforcement Learning from Human Feedback has enabled these systems to be aligned with human values and preferences in ways that seemed impossible just a few years ago.

Current generative AI systems demonstrate unprecedented capabilities across a wide range of tasks, from natural language understanding and generation to multimodal content creation and complex reasoning. These systems can engage in sophisticated conversations, generate creative content, solve complex problems, and even exhibit forms of emergent intelligence that surprise their creators. The breadth and depth of these capabilities have opened new possibilities for human–AI collaboration and have begun to transform industries and workflows across the economy.

However, significant limitations remain that constrain the reliability and applicability of current systems. Issues with factual accuracy, reasoning consistency, bias, and computational efficiency represent fundamental challenges that must be addressed as the technology matures. The hallucination problem, context limitations, and enormous computational requirements represent constraints that affect both the practical deployment and the broader accessibility of these powerful technologies.

The technical challenges facing generative AI are matched by equally significant opportunities for innovation and improvement. Emerging architectural approaches like mixture of experts, Retrieval-Augmented Generation, and constitutional AI offer promising directions for creating more reliable, efficient, and aligned systems. Research into scaling laws, emergent abilities, and novel training methodologies continues to reveal new insights about how these systems work and how they might be improved.

Understanding these technical foundations is crucial for anyone working with or planning to implement generative AI systems. The capabilities are impressive and continue to expand rapidly, but awareness of the limitations is equally important for responsible deployment and realistic expectation setting. The field is moving quickly, with new developments and breakthroughs occurring regularly, making it essential to stay informed about both advances and limitations.

As we stand at this technological inflection point, the technical underpinnings of generative AI continue to evolve at an unprecedented pace. The next few years will likely bring significant advances in addressing current limitations while unlocking new capabilities that we can barely imagine today. The combination of continued scaling, architectural innovation, and improved training methodologies promises to deliver even more sophisticated and capable AI systems.

The implications of these technical advances extend far beyond the laboratory or the technology sector. As generative AI systems become more capable and widely deployed, they will increasingly shape how we work, learn, create, and interact with information and each other. Understanding the technical foundations of these systems is therefore not just important for technologists but for anyone who wants to understand and navigate the rapidly changing landscape of human–AI interaction.

The future of generative AI lies in addressing current limitations while continuing to push the boundaries of what artificial intelligence can achieve. The technical foundations laid by current research provide a solid base for continued innovation, but significant challenges remain in creating systems that are not just powerful but also reliable, fair, and aligned with human values and interests.

As we move forward, the technical evolution of generative AI will continue to be driven by the interplay between scaling, architectural innovation, and improved understanding of how these complex systems work. The journey from today's impressive but limited systems to the more capable and reliable AI systems of the future will require continued research, innovation, and careful attention to the technical details that make these remarkable systems possible.

The technical underpinnings explored in this chapter provide the foundation for understanding not just how current generative AI systems work, but also how they might evolve and improve in the years to come. As we continue to push the boundaries of artificial intelligence, these technical foundations will remain crucial for creating systems that are not just powerful but also beneficial, safe, and aligned with human values and aspirations.

3.10 References

1. Vaswani, A., et al. (2017). "Attention Is All You Need." *Advances in Neural Information Processing Systems*, 30. `https://arxiv.org/abs/1706.03762`

2. Brown, T., et al. (2020). "Language Models are Few-Shot Learners." *Advances in Neural Information Processing Systems*, 33. `https://arxiv.org/abs/2005.14165`

3. Ouyang, L., et al. (2022). "Training language models to follow instructions with human feedback." *Advances in Neural Information Processing Systems*, 35. `https://arxiv.org/abs/2203.02155`

4. Wei, J., et al. (2022). "Emergent Abilities of Large Language Models." *Transactions on Machine Learning Research*. `https://arxiv.org/abs/2206.07682`

5. Hoffmann, J., et al. (2022). "Training Compute-Optimal Large Language Models." *arXiv preprint* arXiv:2203.15556. `https://arxiv.org/abs/2203.15556`

6. Goodfellow, I., et al. (2014). "Generative Adversarial Nets." *Advances in Neural Information Processing Systems*, 27. `https://arxiv.org/abs/1406.2661`

7. Radford, A., et al. (2019). "Language Models are Unsupervised Multitask Learners." *OpenAI Blog*. `https://openai.com/research/better-language-models`

8. Devlin, J., et al. (2018). "BERT: Pre-training of Deep Bidirectional Transformers for Language Understanding." *arXiv preprint* arXiv:1810.04805. `https://arxiv.org/abs/1810.04805`

9. Ramesh, A., et al. (2021). "Zero-Shot Text-to-Image Generation." *International Conference on Machine Learning*. `https://arxiv.org/abs/2102.12092`

10. Anthropic. (2022). "Constitutional AI: Harmlessness from AI Feedback." *arXiv preprint* arXiv:2212.08073. `https://arxiv.org/abs/2212.08073`

11. OpenAI. (2023). "GPT-4 Technical Report." *arXiv preprint* arXiv:2303.08774. `https://arxiv.org/abs/2303.08774`

12. Touvron, H., et al. (2023). "LLaMA: Open and Efficient Foundation Language Models." *arXiv preprint* arXiv:2302.13971. `https://arxiv.org/abs/2302.13971`

13. Kaplan, J., et al. (2020). "Scaling Laws for Neural Language Models." *arXiv preprint* arXiv:2001.08361. `https://arxiv.org/abs/2001.08361`

14. Hendrycks, D., et al. (2020). "Measuring Massive Multitask Language Understanding." *International Conference on Learning Representations*. `https://arxiv.org/abs/2009.03300`

15. Strubell, E., et al. (2019). "Energy and Policy Considerations for Deep Learning in NLP." *Proceedings of the 57th Annual Meeting of the Association for Computational Linguistics*. `https://arxiv.org/abs/1906.02243`

16. Lewis, P., et al. (2020). "Retrieval-Augmented Generation for Knowledge-Intensive NLP Tasks." *Advances in Neural Information Processing Systems*, 33. `https://arxiv.org/abs/2005.11401`

17. Fedus, W., et al. (2022). "Switch Transformer: Scaling to Trillion Parameter Models with Simple and Efficient Sparsity." *Journal of Machine Learning Research*, 23. `https://arxiv.org/abs/2101.03961`

18. Bai, Y., et al. (2022). "Constitutional AI: Harmlessness from AI Feedback." *Anthropic.* `https://arxiv.org/abs/2212.08073`
19. Papineni, K., et al. (2002). "BLEU: a Method for Automatic Evaluation of Machine Translation." *Proceedings of the 40th Annual Meeting of the Association for Computational Linguistics.* `https://aclanthology.org/P02-1040/`
20. Lin, C. Y. (2004). "ROUGE: A Package for Automatic Evaluation of Summaries." *Text Summarization Branches Out.* `https://aclanthology.org/W04-1013/`

CHAPTER 4

Productivity Revolution: How Generative AI Redefines Knowledge Work

***Figure 4-1.** A Cross-Functional Team Using AI-Powered Tools Together, Representing the Shift to Human–AI Collaboration in Knowledge Work*

N. Sendas et al., *Building Generative AI Solutions for Industries with AWS*,
https://doi.org/10.1007/979-8-8688-2830-0_4

4.1 Waves of Disruption

There is a new wave of productivity transformation underway, one not driven by hardware, mobility, or cloud computing, but by generative artificial intelligence (GenAI). Just as the Industrial Revolution redefined labor and the internet transformed communication, generative AI is redefining how knowledge work is created, managed, and scaled.

While previous advances focused on optimizing existing workflows, generative AI introduces a fundamental shift where machines can now generate content, ideas, and even make decisions. In knowledge work, defined by tasks that rely on expertise, creativity, and contextual reasoning, this has profound implications.

Early adoption across industries illustrates the breadth and depth of this disruption. In a controlled lab study, GitHub Copilot, powered by OpenAI's Codex, demonstrated a 55.8% increase in task completion speed among software developers compared to non-users, providing results that, while striking, may not fully reflect the variability of real-world development environments (Peng et al., 2023). In financial services, Morgan Stanley launched an internal GPT-4-based knowledge assistant to support over 16,000 advisors with client communication and portfolio insights (OpenAI, 2023). In healthcare, GE HealthCare partnered with Amazon Web Services to develop foundation models that accelerate both clinical diagnostics and operational decision-making (GE HealthCare, 2024).

Leaders, subject matter experts, and engineering teams must now ask: How will this change not just how we work, but what we prioritize, build, and scale? This chapter provides a look at how generative AI is catalyzing a productivity revolution—where human expertise is no longer the ceiling, but the starting point.

4.2 The Anatomy of Knowledge Work

Figure 4-2. *The Knowledge Work Lifecycle Showing Where Generative AI Augments Data Intake, Reasoning, and Insight Generation*

Knowledge workers are individuals whose core contributions stem from their capacity to interpret complex information, apply contextual understanding, and articulate insights that shape organizational decisions. Spanning domains such as engineering, finance, healthcare, marketing, operations, law, and design, their work is distinguished by cognitive effort rather than manual execution. As noted by IBM (2023), knowledge workers create value through a combination of subject matter expertise, analytical reasoning, and effective communication. These skills are essential in today's data-rich, decision-driven world.

The defining inputs of knowledge work include structured and unstructured data, situational context, and cognitive effort. Outputs range from code, strategy documents, reports, and analyses to customer interactions and product designs. While the specific nature of tasks varies by domain, certain systemic challenges are consistent across roles.

4.2.1 Common Bottlenecks in Knowledge Work

Despite the proliferation of digital tools, knowledge work continues to suffer from structural inefficiencies:

- **Context Switching:** The average knowledge worker toggles between 8 and 12 applications daily (RingCentral, 2018), with each switch requiring an estimated 23–25 minutes to fully regain focus (Mark et al., 2008). This fragmentation contributes to cognitive fatigue and loss of productivity.
- **Documentation Debt:** Organizational knowledge is often siloed across disparate systems. In many cases, critical information exists only in the tacit knowledge of individuals, resulting in retrieval delays, redundant work, and inconsistent decision-making.
- **Time-Intensive Analysis:** A significant proportion of time, estimated between 30% and 40%, is spent extracting actionable insights from unstructured sources such as emails, PDFs, support tickets, and meeting transcripts. In engineering, developers spend more time understanding code bases and debugging than writing new code (Stripe & Harris Poll, 2018). In healthcare, physicians spend about as much time interfacing with electronic health records as they do with patients (Tai-Seale et al., 2017).

While digital tools and the advent of the internet have offered incremental improvements, they have not resolved the underlying friction, and in some cases, they introduce additional layers of complexity and tool sprawl. This is where the opportunity to leverage GenAI comes in. GenAI can meaningfully reduce cognitive load at the most demanding points in the clinical workflow, offloading high-effort tasks like real-time documentation, patient history summarization, and pattern recognition in radiology and pathology. The opportunity is not to replace clinical judgment, but to protect the cognitive bandwidth needed to exercise it well.

4.2.2 Domain-Specific Impact of Generative AI

Although generative AI can benefit all forms of knowledge work, its impact is shaped by the nature of the task and domain-specific constraints. Three broad categories illustrate this variation:

- **Creative Work (e.g., marketing, design, content creation):** GenAI tools like DALL-E and Midjourney accelerate the ideation phase by generating visual or textual drafts. However, human oversight remains essential to preserve originality, brand integrity, and emotional nuance. A meta-analysis of 28 peer-reviewed studies comprising over 8,000 participants found that human–AI collaboration yielded superior creative performance compared to humans working alone, with a moderate effect size ($g \approx 0.27$) (arXiv, 2025).
- **Analytical Work (e.g., data analysis, financial modeling, academic research):** GenAI excels at parsing large datasets and identifying latent patterns. Bloomberg CTO reported that internal AI tools could streamline analyst workloads by up to 80%, enabling faster turnaround of financial insights and market intelligence (FNLondon, 2025). Nevertheless, formulating hypotheses, validating assumptions, and contextualizing results still rely heavily on human judgment.
- **Technical and Procedural Work (e.g., software development, DevOps, IT operations):** This category represents some of the clearest and best-documented productivity gains from GenAI. In experimental studies, GitHub Copilot users completed programming tasks 55.8% faster on average (Peng et al., 2023), and field deployments have demonstrated a 26% increase in completed tasks per developer (Cui et al., 2025). The hybrid nature of this work, which blends logic, syntax, and creativity, makes it well suited to GenAI augmentation.

These domain-specific effects underscore the necessity of designing tailored implementation strategies. Rather than attempting to automate knowledge work wholesale, organizations should focus on strategic augmentation to enhance the cognitive leverage of professionals while preserving the uniquely human dimensions of creativity, judgment, and empathy.

4.3 Amplification, Not Automation: AI As a Force Multiplier

Generative AI should be understood not as a tool for replacing knowledge workers, but as a force multiplier that amplifies their capabilities. Rather than automating entire roles, it enhances productivity by accelerating routine tasks, improving quality, and expanding cognitive reach. Studies show GenAI tools like GitHub Copilot reduce task completion time while lowering cognitive load (Peng et al., 2023). This enables professionals to reallocate effort toward higher-value activities such as strategy, creativity, and innovation. So while GenAI should not be seen as a substitute for human work, it should be leveraged as a partner in scaling its impact.

4.4 AI Copilots vs. Agents

Generative AI tools can be categorized as either copilots or agents. AI copilots, such as GitHub Copilot and Microsoft 365 Copilot, function as embedded assistants that enhance user productivity while keeping humans firmly in control. Where copilots stay within defined boundaries, AI agents operate more independently, executing multi-step tasks through frameworks like AutoGPT or LangChain, yet they still require significant human supervision to ensure outputs remain accurate, safe, and aligned with intended goals. The distinction is critical: copilots augment cognition within existing workflows, whereas agents introduce a layer of automation that demands its own framework for oversight, governance, and compliance.

4.5 Enhancing Speed and Cognitive Reach

Generative AI enables knowledge workers to offload cognitively intensive yet routine tasks. This substantially reduces both time expenditure and mental load. Rather than starting from a blank slate, users can draw on AI-generated suggestions, summaries, or drafts, accelerating ideation, synthesis, and execution. This is not merely a matter of efficiency, but an expansion of capability. When a 30-minute task can be completed in 10 minutes, the reclaimed time can be redirected toward higher-value contributions such as strategy development, experimentation, or decision-making.

Even modest task automation can generate significant gains at scale. If generative AI absorbs just 10–20% of repetitive tasks, teams can shift their focus toward critical thinking, innovation, and oversight. This expanded cognitive reach is most visible in software engineering through a methodology known as *vibe coding*, popularized by OpenAI co-founder Andrej Karpathy in 2025.

Vibe coding is a prompt-driven, conversational approach where developers guide large language models (LLMs) through natural language instructions to generate and refine code. Rather than manually producing every line, developers act as reviewers, testers, and curators of AI-generated outputs. According to AWS VP Deepak Singh, tools like Amazon Q Developer have evolved from autocomplete aids into full-fledged collaborative "pair programmers" (Silicon Angle, 2024), and real-world adoption reinforces this claim.

At National Australia Bank, roughly 40% of production code originates from AI-generated suggestions, still validated through acceptance testing. Y Combinator CEO Garry Tan further asserts that with this style of development, small engineering teams of ten can match the output of traditional teams five to ten times larger (Slashdot Developers, 2025).

The transformation extends beyond pure productivity metrics. Shopify CEO Tobi Lütke reported dramatic efficiency gains, stating stating, "I shipped more code in the last 3 weeks than the decade before" using AI agents like Anthropic's Claude[1].

Outside of developers, in analytics, generative AI can summarize customer feedback, identify trends, and accelerate reporting cycles. In customer support, AI agents analyze prior cases and internal documentation to recommend resolution paths, significantly reducing time to closure. These applications facilitate the reallocation of human cognition away from repetitive or mechanical work and toward strategic functions such as decision-making, innovation, and creative leadership.

In short, generative AI does not merely enhance task speed; it expands what knowledge workers can achieve within the same time constraints, fundamentally increasing the limits of individual and team productivity.

[1] https://www.cnhinews.com/news/article_4f38e8ee-e708-5d97-822f-c384a748453c.html

4.6 Multimodal Capabilities: Unlocking New Domains

A defining advancement of next-generation generative AI models is their multimodal capability, which is the ability to process and generate not only text but also images, audio, video, and code. This expands the applicability of AI far beyond text-based tasks, enabling broader productivity gains across diverse fields.

For example, in design, tools like Midjourney and DALL-E allow professionals to produce visual assets from textual prompts, streamlining creative processes. Advanced models such as Google's Gemini and Anthropic's Claude 3 support input combinations of text and images, opening new use cases in customer onboarding, education, and product documentation.

These multimodal capabilities are particularly valuable in domains that integrate diverse data types. In clinical settings, patient information often spans structured fields (vital signs), unstructured notes, diagnostic imagery, and machine-generated signals. Multimodal AI can synthesize these inputs through a single interface, transforming interaction with complex datasets into a conversational, intuitive process that reduces friction and accelerates insights.

As generative AI becomes increasingly multimodal, its potential to support knowledge work across industries expands in both scope and depth.

The expansion of AI capabilities across multiple modalities from text to images, audio, and code fundamentally changes how knowledge workers interact with information systems. Rather than switching between specialized tools for different data types, professionals can now engage in unified, conversational workflows that mirror the iterative nature of knowledge work itself. This convergence of multimodal capabilities with the inherently cyclical processes of knowledge work creates powerful feedback mechanisms that continuously refine both human expertise and AI performance.

4.7 Knowledge Work As a Feedback Loop

Unlike linear or repetitive tasks in traditional industries, knowledge work is inherently iterative. It requires ongoing refinement, decision-making, and contextual adaptation. Generative AI aligns well with this dynamic by acting as a collaborative partner rather than a static tool.

Each interaction with a generative AI model, whether through refining prompts, editing outputs, or rejecting irrelevant responses, constitutes a feedback loop. These loops not only improve the user's prompt engineering skills but also enhance model performance over time. Techniques such as Reinforcement Learning from Human Feedback (RLHF) and domain-specific fine-tuning allow models to become more context-aware, accurate, and aligned with organizational norms and language.

Importantly, generative AI is not a fixed deployment; it evolves with use. As individuals and teams interact with the system, it becomes more attuned to their goals, processes, and vocabulary—transforming AI into a responsive, co-evolving asset that mirrors the adaptive nature of knowledge work itself.

4.8 Creating an AI-Ready Organization

Figure 4-3. *Generative AI Adoption Across Healthcare, Finance, Software Engineering, and Creative Industries*

As generative AI reshapes how knowledge work is conducted, AI literacy is becoming a foundational competency across roles. According to Microsoft's 2024 Work Trend Index, 66% of business leaders report they would not hire candidates without AI skills, yet only 39% of workers using AI have received formal training. This gap underscores the urgent need for structured organizational enablement (Microsoft, 2024).

To become truly AI-ready, organizations must move beyond ad hoc experimentation. They must assess how generative AI can be embedded across functions to enhance productivity, decision accuracy, and innovation. A 2023 BCG study found that consultants using generative AI completed 12% more tasks and delivered outputs rated 40% higher in quality, especially for ideation and synthesis (Dell'Acqua et al., 2023). These results indicate not only faster delivery but also elevated intellectual output, which are key indicators of knowledge work transformation.

4.8.1 Operationalizing the AI Center of Excellence (CoE)

From a technical leadership perspective, an effective AI Center of Excellence (CoE) functions as a centralized capability hub responsible for model development, infrastructure reliability, and architectural consistency. In mature organizations, this core team typically consists of five to eight dedicated roles:

Core Team (5–8 FTEs)

- **ML Engineering Lead**: Owns model selection, fine-tuning strategies, and production deployment standards
- **MLOps Engineer**: Manages CI/CD pipelines, monitoring, observability, and model lifecycle automation
- **Data Engineer**: Ensures high-quality data pipelines, feature stores, and data validation
- **Research Scientist**: Tracks emerging model capabilities, benchmarks performance, and evaluates new techniques
- **Solutions Architect**: Defines integration patterns across enterprise systems and cloud environments

In addition to the core team, additional roles must be considered such as Security and Compliance and UX / Product Design. These roles can sometimes be leveraged or shared between teams and are part of an overarching group for the organization.

While the investment in this technical team structure may appear substantial, it is modest relative to the downstream productivity gains and risk reduction achieved through centralized standards, shared tooling, and reusable architectures.

For business and executive leaders, the AI CoE must also function as a governance and prioritization body. This is commonly formalized through a cross-functional steering committee that meets monthly and owns investment decisions, risk management, and value realization.

Steering Committee Composition

- CTO or CIO (technical direction and platform strategy)
- CFO or Finance Leader (capital allocation and ROI oversight)
- Chief Risk or Compliance Officer (regulatory and reputational risk)
- Business Unit Leaders (use case prioritization)
- HR or People Leader (workforce enablement and change management)

The core responsibilities of this team would be to approve and sequence AI use cases, allocate annual budgets, define governance policies and acceptable use standards, and review progress and remove organizational blockers.

Mature organizations utilizing these models define success metrics early, which, for example, can include

- **Use Cases in Production**: 3–5 in Year 1
- **Measured Productivity Gains**: 15–25%
- **User Adoption**: ≥60% within six months
- **Incident Rate**: <1% of outputs requiring escalation

This dual structure ensures technical rigor while maintaining executive accountability, which is a balance consistently observed in successful large-scale AI transformations.

4.8.2 Strategic Implementation Framework

Establishing an AI-ready culture requires executive alignment and deliberate planning. Leaders must rethink organizational design, hiring strategies, and training programs. As with the enterprise transition from on-premise to cloud, generative AI adoption must be led by cross-functional collaboration, not just isolated innovation labs. C-suite support is essential to ensure AI efforts align with core business goals, workforce capabilities, and compliance standards.

The transformation begins by identifying high-leverage opportunities, such as accelerating R&D, improving customer support response times, or enhancing strategic decision-making through better data analysis. As an example, Morgan Stanley's deployment of GPT-4-powered assistants for 16,000 financial advisors involved months of design work to scope use cases, ensure compliance, and define guardrails (OpenAI, 2023).

Following this, organizations should establish cross-functional Centers of Excellence (CoEs) that include product owners, ML engineers, data scientists, legal teams, compliance officers, and business unit leaders. These CoEs develop and enforce enterprise-wide AI standards, ranging from prompt engineering guidelines and tool selection to data governance and bias mitigation protocols.

4.8.3 Training and Workforce Development

Training is central to effective adoption. Providing access to tools like Amazon Q, Microsoft Copilot, and ChatGPT is not enough, as employees must understand prompt design, failure modes, hallucination risk, and regulatory implications. According to Microsoft, while 75% of knowledge workers are already using generative AI, most lack the structured support to use it effectively (Microsoft, 2024).

Finally, deployment must include robust monitoring and governance. Organizations must implement role-based access controls, audit trails, and acceptable use policies, particularly in industries handling sensitive data. Intellectual property concerns, compliance risks, and transparency mandates all require clear operational boundaries.

As adoption scales, continuous feedback and measurement become essential. Leaders should evaluate metrics such as output quality, time savings, and reduction in redundant work. These insights ensure AI investments yield measurable, repeatable value while reinforcing trust and accountability across the enterprise.

4.8.4 Learning from AI Implementation Challenges

Starbucks' difficulties with automated inventory management illustrate how even well-resourced organizations can struggle with AI implementation when foundational systems and processes aren't adequately prepared. The coffee giant partnered with o9 Solutions on an "automated ordering" program that used machine learning to continually refine predictions of upcoming store sales, aiming to reduce out-of-stocks. The system was designed to analyze historical sales data and seasonal patterns to predict optimal inventory levels for each store location [2].

In practice, though, it tended to recommend too few products, contributing to shortages and customer dissatisfaction—problems compounded by inconsistent data from Starbucks' scattered supplier network. Under new leadership in 2024, the company scaled back much of the automation, acknowledging that the technology had been deployed before fundamental data-quality and integration issues were resolved. This case illustrates that successful AI implementation requires not just sophisticated algorithms, but also robust data governance, modernized infrastructure, and careful attention to the operational context in which AI systems must function.

The 90-Day AI Adoption Playbook

Successful AI adoption is rarely constrained by model capability; instead, it is limited by an organization's ability to align infrastructure, governance, and workforce readiness in a coordinated way. In the first 30 days, effective organizations focus on establishing a shared foundation rather than deploying technology prematurely. This period is characterized by parallel technical and business activity: engineering teams assess data readiness, infrastructure capacity, and tool viability, while business leaders align stakeholders, approve funding, and define risk boundaries. Jointly, these efforts converge on a small set of high-leverage pilot use cases with clearly defined success metrics and governance guardrails. The objective of this initial phase is not speed, but clarity, ensuring that experimentation occurs within a controlled, well-understood operating context.

The second and third months shift from preparation to evidence-based execution and decision-making. Between days 30 and 60, organizations launch limited pilots to real users, integrating models into existing workflows, monitoring performance, and collecting feedback. This phase often surfaces organizational friction such as training gaps, workflow misalignment, or data quality issues which are invisible during planning. The final 30 days focus on translating pilot outcomes into executive decisions. Technical teams analyze performance, cost, and scalability, while business leaders evaluate return

[2] https://www.businesstimes.com.sg/companies-markets/consumer-healthcare/inside-starbucks-supply-struggles-ai-glitches-scattered-suppliers-and-sandwich-shortages

on investment, adoption patterns, and risk exposure. By day 90, organizations are positioned to make an informed choice to scale, pivot, or discontinue each initiative, supported by data and results, rather than intuition. This disciplined cadence transforms AI adoption from exploratory experimentation into a repeatable, governable capability.

4.9 Conclusion

Generative AI is fundamentally reshaping knowledge work by amplifying human capability. From software development to healthcare, AI reduces routine tasks and enables professionals to focus on strategy, creativity, and judgment. As multimodal systems mature and feedback loops evolve, organizations that invest in AI literacy, structured governance, and cross-functional integration will unlock significant productivity and innovation gains.

However, the path to successful AI transformation extends far beyond technology adoption. Research reveals that **70–85% of AI projects fail to deliver expected value**, with **95% of businesses seeing no return on their AI investments** [3]. The distinction between success and failure lies not in the sophistication of AI tools, but in the organizational foundations that support their implementation.

Critical success factors include

> **Robust Data Infrastructure:** Organizations must address data quality, governance, and integration challenges before deploying AI systems. The Starbucks "automated ordering" initiative's failure due to fragmented supplier data and outdated infrastructure demonstrates that sophisticated algorithms cannot compensate for poor data foundations.

[3] MIT NANDA (2025). The GenAI Divide: State of AI in Business 2025. MIT Media Lab.

Comprehensive Change Management: Successful implementations require structured training programs (40+ hours rather than brief introductions), clear communication about AI's role as augmentation rather than replacement, and active engagement with employees who may resist technological change. Organizations that treat AI adoption as a simple tool deployment rather than an organizational transformation consistently underperform.

Realistic Scope and Expectations: The most successful deployments begin with targeted, high-value use cases rather than attempting wholesale automation. Starting with 10–20% task automation allows organizations to build competency, refine processes, and demonstrate value before scaling.

Governance and Standards: Clear guidelines for tool selection, prompt engineering, quality control, and intellectual property protection are essential. Organizations lacking standardized approaches face inconsistent outputs, security risks, and compliance challenges.

Executive Sponsorship and Cross-Functional Collaboration: AI initiatives require sustained leadership commitment and coordination across departments. Centers of Excellence that include technical, legal, compliance, and business stakeholders are more likely to navigate implementation challenges successfully.

Competitive advantage will not stem from AI adoption alone, but from how effectively it is embedded into workflows while addressing these foundational requirements. AI must be integrated thoughtfully, balancing technological capability with organizational readiness and preserving human expertise while scaling cognitive capacity. Organizations that learn from both successes and failures, approaching AI transformation with strategic patience rather than tactical urgency, will ultimately realize the transformative potential that generative AI promises for knowledge work.

In the next chapter, we will dive deep into the creative industries and how they are leveraging generative AI for content co-creation, a domain where the collaboration between human creativity and artificial intelligence is producing entirely new forms of artistic expression and commercial value.

4.10 References

- Cui, Z., Demirer, M., Jaffe, S., Musolff, L., Peng, S., & Salz, T. (2025). *"The Effects of Generative AI on High-Skilled Work." Management Science.* `https://papers.ssrn.com/sol3/papers.cfm?abstract_id=4945566`
- OpenAI (2023). *"How Morgan Stanley is using GPT-4 for wealth management."* `https://openai.com/customers/morgan-stanley`
- GE HealthCare (2024). *"GE HealthCare and AWS announce strategic collaboration to accelerate healthcare transformation with generative AI."* `https://www.gehealthcare.com/about/newsroom/press-releases/ge-healthcare-and-aws-announce-strategic-collaboration-to-accelerate-healthcare-transformation-with-generative-ai`
- IBM (2023). *"What is a knowledge worker and what do they do?"* `https://www.ibm.com/think/topics/knowledge-worker`
- Stripe & Harris Poll (2018). *The Developer Coefficient.* `https://stripe.com/reports/developer-coefficient-2021`
- Tai-Seale, M., et al. (2017). *"Electronic Health Record Logs Indicate That Physicians Split Time Evenly Between Seeing Patients and Desktop Medicine." Health Affairs,* 36(4), 655–662. `https://doi.org/10.1377/hlthaff.2016.0811`
- RingCentral (2018). *"From Workplace Chaos to Zen."* `https://netstorage.ringcentral.com/documents/connected_workplace.pdf`
- Mark, G., Gudith, D., & Klocke, U. (2008). "The Cost of Interrupted Work: More Speed and Stress." Proceedings of CHI 2008. ArXiv (2025). *"Generative AI and Creativity: A Systematic Literature Review and Meta-Analysis."* `https://arxiv.org/abs/2505.17241`

- FNLondon (2025). *"Bloomberg tech chief says AI could streamline 80% of analyst workload."* https://www.fnlondon.com/articles/bloomberg-tech-chief-says-ai-could-streamline-80-of-analyst-workload-48649cc1
- Peng, S., Kalliamvakou, E., Cihon, P., & Demirer, M. (2023). *"The Impact of AI on Developer Productivity: Evidence from GitHub Copilot."* https://arxiv.org/abs/2302.06590
- Silicon Angle (2024). *"Revolutionizing software development: Deepak Singh on gen AI, AWS Q Developer and the future of coding."* https://siliconangle.com/2024/11/27/revolutionizing-software-development-deepak-singh-gen-ai-aws-q-developer-future-coding/
- Slashdot Developers (2025). *"'Vibe Coding' is Letting 10 Engineers Do the Work of a Team of 50 To 100, Says YC CEO."* https://developers.slashdot.org/story/25/03/18/1428226/vibe-coding-is-letting-10-engineers-do-the-work-of-a-team-of-50-to-100-says-yc-ceo
- Dell'Acqua, F., et al. (2023). "*Navigating the Jagged Technological Frontier*. HBS Working Paper 24-013.
- Microsoft Work Trend (2024). *"AI at Work Is Here. Now Comes the Hard Part."* https://www.microsoft.com/en-us/worklab/work-trend-index/ai-at-work-is-here-now-comes-the-hard-part
- https://news.microsoft.com/source/2024/05/08/microsoft-and-linkedin-release-the-2024-work-trend-index-on-the-state-of-ai-at-work/

CHAPTER 5

Creative Industries in the Age of AI Co-creation

5.1 Introduction: Setting the Scene

Figure 5-1. *The Evolution of Creative Industries from Traditional Tools to AI-Powered Co-creation*

N. Sendas et al., *Building Generative AI Solutions for Industries with AWS*,
https://doi.org/10.1007/979-8-8688-2830-0_5

The creative industries have always existed at the crossroads of imagination and technology. From the first images brushed onto cave walls to the editing suites of modern film studios, creators have drawn on the tools of their time to tell stories, shape culture, and capture emotion. In each era, the available technology has not only influenced *what* could be made but also *how* it was made and *who* had the means to make it.

While GenAI was once confined to research labs and science fiction, it is now embedded in the everyday workflows of writers, designers, musicians, filmmakers, and game developers. These systems are no longer simply assisting with routine tasks, but instead are increasingly *co-creating*: writing scripts, composing music, sketching visual concepts, and iterating alongside human partners in real time.

This shift is subtle, but profound. Earlier creative tools, from the typewriter to digital cameras, were largely passive. This means they responded to the human operator's commands without contributing ideas of their own. In contrast, modern generative models can suggest, adapt, and even surprise with things the creator never dreamed of. For example, a filmmaker might feed an AI a description of a city at dawn, only to receive a cinematic storyboard that reveals angles and lighting choices she hadn't imagined. A musician might hum a tune into a laptop and hear it returned as a fully orchestrated piece. The line between tool and collaborator is beginning to blur.

To understand the scale of this change, it's useful to recall how previous creative revolutions unfolded. When photography emerged in the 19th century, painters feared for their livelihood; yet photography opened new artistic movements, while painting evolved in directions that no longer sought to replicate reality. Digital editing was once viewed as a threat to the integrity of film, yet it has become an inseparable part of cinematic storytelling. In each case, the technology didn't simply replace an old skill; instead, it reframed the possibilities of the medium itself.

AI co-creation may prove to be the most radical shift yet, because it touches not just the tools, but the *process* and the *authorship*. In an AI-augmented workflow, the human creator is no longer the sole originator of every idea. Instead, creativity becomes a dialogue, a back-and-forth where the AI's output sparks new directions, challenges assumptions, and accelerates iteration cycles. For some, this partnership is exciting, but for others, it raises uneasy questions about originality, ownership, and the role of human taste.

The creative industries are vast, varied, and span advertising agencies, game studios, film production houses, music labels, publishing companies, fashion brands, and more. Each sector is struggling with its own version of the same questions: How should we integrate these systems? What skills will remain essential? What new skills will be needed? And perhaps most importantly, how do we preserve the human touch that gives creative work its cultural and emotional resonance?

In the chapters that follow, we will explore the historical precedents that can guide us, define what AI co-creation truly means, and examine its manifestations across different industries. We will look at the opportunities and risks, the economic and workforce implications, and the futures we might anticipate or help to shape.

The goal is not to romanticize or demonize this technology, but to understand it. Co-creation with AI is not a distant prospect; it is already here, shaping the pitches, prototypes, and productions of the present day. The decisions made now by individual creators, by companies, and by entire industries will determine whether this transformation enriches the creative landscape or erodes it.

5.2 Historical Context: Technology's Role in Creativity

The relationship between creativity and technology stretches back to humanity's earliest forms of expression. Each major leap in creative possibility has come from an advance in tools, from primitive pigments created with berries and chisels to modern digital platforms. Although the tools themselves change, the pattern is familiar: new inventions disrupt established practices, expand the boundaries of art, and invite new ways of creating.

5.2.1 The Printing Press and the Rise of Mass Communication

In the 15th century, Johannes Gutenberg's printing press transformed the speed and scale of sharing ideas. Before movable type, books were laboriously copied by hand, making them rare and expensive. Printing made it possible to reproduce text quickly, which increased literacy and expanded the reach of authorship. Political ideas, scientific discoveries, and creative works could now circulate widely, shaping entire cultures.

5.2.2 Photography and the Democratization of Imagery

Four centuries later, photography introduced another profound change. Painters had long been responsible for producing accurate images of people and places. A camera could achieve this in seconds, something that once required years of training and skill. Some feared this would end painting altogether. Instead, painting evolved in new directions such as Impressionism and Cubism, no longer tied to realism. Photography did not replace the visual arts but changed their purpose.

5.2.3 Recorded Sound and Film Editing

The 20th century brought tools that expanded creative reach in both sound and vision. Sound recording preserved performances that were once only able to be experienced live. Film editing enabled directors to shape time and space, opening possibilities far beyond the stage. Entirely new genres emerged, from radio drama to music videos to experimental cinema. These tools not only improved efficiency but also created artistic possibilities that had not existed before.

5.2.4 The Digital Turn

In the late 20th century, creative production entered the digital era. Non-linear editing software replaced the physical splicing of film. Desktop publishing enabled the design of entire magazines without traditional typesetting. Musicians could compose and mix from home using digital audio workstations. These changes lowered costs, reduced barriers to entry, and welcomed a wider diversity of creators. Industries saw new voices emerge that had been excluded when production was expensive and inaccessible.

5.2.5 From Automation to Co-creation

Until recently, creative tools primarily automated mechanical steps while humans retained control of conceptual and artistic decisions. A paintbrush might create a smoother line, a camera could capture an image more quickly, and editing software could speed up assembly, but the human guided the creative vision.

Generative AI alters this relationship. It can now contribute to the earliest stages of creation, proposing ideas, generating variations, and interpreting instructions. In this way, it operates less like a passive instrument and more like a collaborator. A filmmaker might describe a scene and receive an AI-generated storyboard that suggests camera angles they had not considered. A musician might hum a melody into a computer's microphone and hear it returned as a full orchestration. These exchanges can open unexpected creative directions.

5.2.6 A Timeline of Transformation

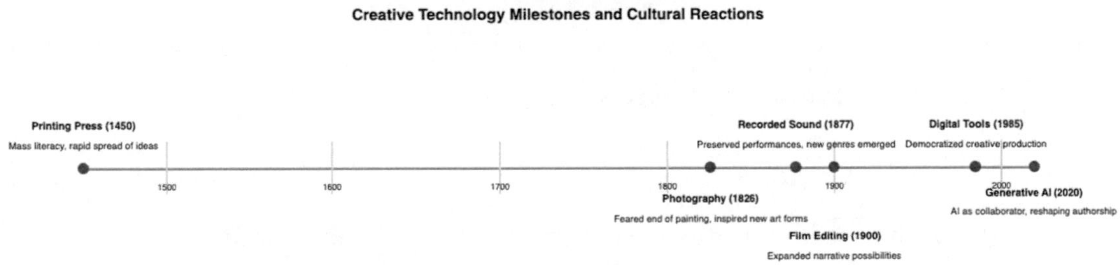

Figure 5-2. *Timeline of Major Technological Milestones in Creative Industries, from the Printing Press to Generative AI*

5.2.7 Lessons from the Past

Looking back, each technological leap in creativity has followed a familiar sequence. Initial resistance often comes from those most skilled in the previously established methods. This is followed by a period of exploration, as early adopters test the limits of the new tool. Eventually, the technology becomes part of everyday practice. The creative movements that endure are the ones that adapt the tool to complement and serve artistic intent, rather than allowing the tool to dictate the art.

For painters after the arrival of photography, this meant embracing abstraction and subjective vision. For filmmakers, after the arrival of digital editing, it meant reimagining storytelling in ways that were impossible with physical film. Today, the creative industries face a similar choice. AI co-creation can be dismissed as a novelty, resisted as a threat, or embraced as a new medium with its own strengths and weaknesses. The record of history suggests that those who adapt without losing their creative purpose will shape the most compelling future.

5.3 Defining AI Co-creation

The term *AI co-creation* refers to a creative process in which artificial intelligence participates as an active partner rather than a passive tool. This distinguishes it from earlier forms of automation, where technology simply executed predefined instructions. In co-creation, AI generates ideas, interprets prompts, and offers variations that can influence the direction of a project.

5.3.1 Types of AI Co-creation

1. **Generative Creation**

   Generative creation is the most visible form, producing entirely new material such as text, images, music, or 3D models. These systems are typically based on large neural networks trained on vast datasets. Language models like GPT-series tools (openai.com) generate written narratives, dialogue, and copywriting. Image models such as Stable Diffusion (stability.ai) and DALL-E (openai.com) synthesize visuals from text prompts. Music-focused models can output melodies, harmonies, and full arrangements in response to a user's specifications.

2. **Collaborative Assistance**

   In collaborative assistance, the AI operates like a creative partner that builds on human input. A screenwriter might outline a scene, and the AI fills in dialogue options with variations in tone. A designer might sketch a logo concept, and the AI produces alternative colors or layouts. This back-and-forth mirrors a conversation between two human collaborators, with each influencing the other's choices.

3. **Curatorial Intelligence**

   In this mode, AI does not create from scratch but acts as an intelligent filter, sorting through large datasets or media libraries to find, rank, and recommend material based on style, mood, or thematic relevance. For example, an editor assembling a documentary might ask an AI to locate all archival clips matching a specific tone or visual motif. Or in sports broadcasting where an editor can ask an AI to find highlights of a sports player to build a montage of achievements. Recommendation engines in streaming platforms already employ elements of this approach (netflixtechblog.com).

5.3.2 Technical Enablers

Modern AI co-creation relies on advances in model architecture, training techniques, and computational infrastructure.

Transformer Models

Introduced in 2017 by Vaswani et al., the transformer architecture enables AI to process and generate sequences with remarkable contextual awareness (arxiv.org). This design powers most state-of-the-art language and multimodal models, allowing them to produce coherent and contextually relevant outputs.

Multimodal Systems

Multimodal models can process and generate across different input types—such as combining text, images, audio, and video—enabling richer forms of co-creation. For instance, a model might generate a storyboard complete with visual frames and dialogue captions, drawing on both visual and linguistic capabilities (openai.com).

Diffusion Models

In image generation, diffusion models work by learning to reverse a denoising process, trained to progressively recover structure from noise by approximating the underlying statistical patterns of the data they were trained on. This mechanism, more stable and controllable than earlier generative approaches, underlies tools like Stable Diffusion and Midjourney, producing high-quality visuals that respond to nuanced prompt descriptions (Huggingface.co).

Prompt Engineering and Iteration

In AI co-creation, prompts are not one-off commands but evolving instructions. Creators refine inputs based on outputs, shaping the AI's results toward the desired style or concept. This iterative loop mirrors how human collaborators exchange drafts and feedback.

5.3.3 The Human–AI Creative Loop

A defining feature of AI co-creation is the *feedback cycle* between human and machine:

1. **Human initiates** with a concept or prompt.
2. **AI generates** a first draft or set of options.
3. **Human evaluates** the output, selecting or refining ideas.
4. **AI responds** with revisions or new variations.
5. The cycle repeats until the final creative work emerges.

This loop accelerates the ideation stage while allowing the human creator to retain editorial control. In practice, the process can produce results in minutes that might otherwise take hours or days.

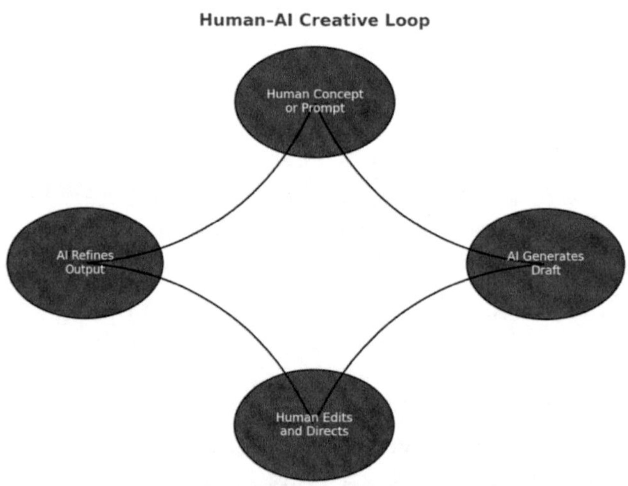

Figure 5-3. *The Iterative Human–AI Creative Loop Showing Prompt, Generation, Evaluation, and Refinement Stages*

5.3.4 Why This Is Different from Past Tools

Earlier creative technologies, from the printing press to desktop publishing, as discussed above, were merely amplifiers of human execution speed. They did not introduce new concepts into the process without human initiation. Generative AI systems, by contrast, can propose unexpected ideas and challenge the creator's assumptions. This blurring of authorship is why the term "co-creation" has gained traction in both academic and industry discussions (springer.com).

5.3.5 Ethical and Legal Boundaries

The emerging field of AI co-creation presents complex ethical and legal challenges that require careful navigation. As humans and AI systems collaborate to produce creative works, questions arise about intellectual property rights, attribution, and ownership.

Defining AI co-creation also means defining the limits of responsibility and authorship:

- **Intellectual Property:** Laws in many jurisdictions currently grant copyright only to works created by humans (copyright.gov).
- **Bias and Representation:** Models trained on biased datasets may unintentionally reinforce stereotypes.
- **Transparency:** Creators and platforms face growing pressure to disclose when AI has contributed to a work.

Traditional copyright frameworks struggle to accommodate works where authorship is distributed between human and machine. Ethically, concerns emerge around transparency and whether consumers should know when content is AI-assisted. Additionally, liability issues become complicated when harmful or infringing content results from human–AI collaboration.

As this technology evolves, legal systems worldwide are working to develop frameworks that balance innovation with appropriate protections, while ethical guidelines increasingly emphasize informed consent, proper attribution, and responsible deployment of AI co-creation tools. The boundary between human and machine contribution continues to blur, necessitating ongoing dialogue between technologists, legal experts, ethicists, and creative professionals.

5.3.6 Conclusion: From Concept to Collaboration

AI co-creation is more than a new tool in the creative toolkit; it represents a shift in how ideas take shape. For the first time, widely accessible technology can contribute at the conceptual level, suggesting directions that a human creator might never have considered alone. This shift blurs the boundary between ideation and execution, making the creative process faster, more iterative, and often more surprising.

As with every past transformation in creative history, the real value of AI co-creation will be determined not by the technology itself but by how humans choose to integrate it. When guided by strong editorial vision, these systems can amplify originality and push the limits of form. Without that vision, the risk is creative homogenization and overreliance on machine defaults.

The next step and the upcoming section is to move from theory into practice. By examining how AI co-creation is already shaping industries like film, music, publishing, and design, we can see both the possibilities and the challenges in real-world contexts. These examples will reveal not only the potential of AI as a collaborator but also the boundaries that still need to be defined.

5.3.7 Technology–Business Integration in AI Co-creation

As AI co-creation moves from experimentation into professional creative workflows, its impact can no longer be evaluated through technology alone. Each creative domain now sits at the intersection of three forces: what AI systems are technically capable of, how those capabilities reshape economic models, and the organizational constraints that govern quality, legality, and brand identity.

To examine this intersection clearly, the sections that follow apply a consistent analytical structure across creative domains. For each industry, we assess (1) the current technical capabilities and limitations of AI systems, (2) the resulting shifts in production economics and revenue models, and (3) the integration challenges organizations must resolve to deploy AI responsibly at scale. This framing reveals not only where AI delivers value today but also where human expertise remains indispensable and where strategic decisions, rather than technical ones, determine success.

5.4 Case Studies by Industry

Across creative industries, the impact of AI co-creation is shaped by the same underlying dynamic: technical capability enables new forms of creation, economic forces determine which uses scale, and organizational constraints govern how responsibly these systems are deployed. In practice, AI adoption succeeds not where models are most advanced, but where technical outputs can be integrated into existing workflows, priced sustainably, and governed within legal and brand boundaries. The following industry examples illustrate this interaction in context. They show where AI accelerates production, where human judgment remains essential, and where strategic decisions, rather than model performance, ultimately define creative and commercial outcomes.

5.4.1 Film and Television

In film and television production, AI is starting to influence everything from pre-production concept art to post-production editing. Visual concept models can generate entire storyboards from a single scene description, giving directors a rapid way to explore stylistic choices before committing to a costly shoot. For example, tools like Midjourney and Stable Diffusion have been used by independent filmmakers to prototype scenes and experiment with lighting styles without building full sets (stability.ai).

Scriptwriting is also evolving. AI language models can produce dialogue variations for a given scene, allowing writers' rooms to evaluate alternative character interactions in minutes. This is not about replacing screenwriters, but about widening the range of creative options available early in the process.

***Figure 5-4.** An AI-Generated Storyboard Illustrating How Filmmakers Use Generative Models for Visual Pre-production*

5.4.2 Music

Musicians and producers are using AI for both inspiration and execution. Platforms like AIVA generate melodies, chord progressions, or full arrangements based on a few style inputs (aiva.ai). In practice, many artists feed AI-generated parts into digital audio workstations, then layer human performance and mixing on top.

One particularly interesting application is in personalized soundtracks. Game developers and streaming platforms are experimenting with adaptive scores that change in real time based on a player's actions or a viewer's emotional engagement. AI systems handle the continuous generation, while composers define the sonic palette and thematic motifs (`https://www.audiocipher.com/post/adaptive-music-machine-learning`).

While these tools dramatically reduce production time and cost, their effectiveness varies by genre and requires human oversight for quality, rights management, and stylistic consistency. This shifts the composer's role from sole creator to that of curator of AI-generated material.

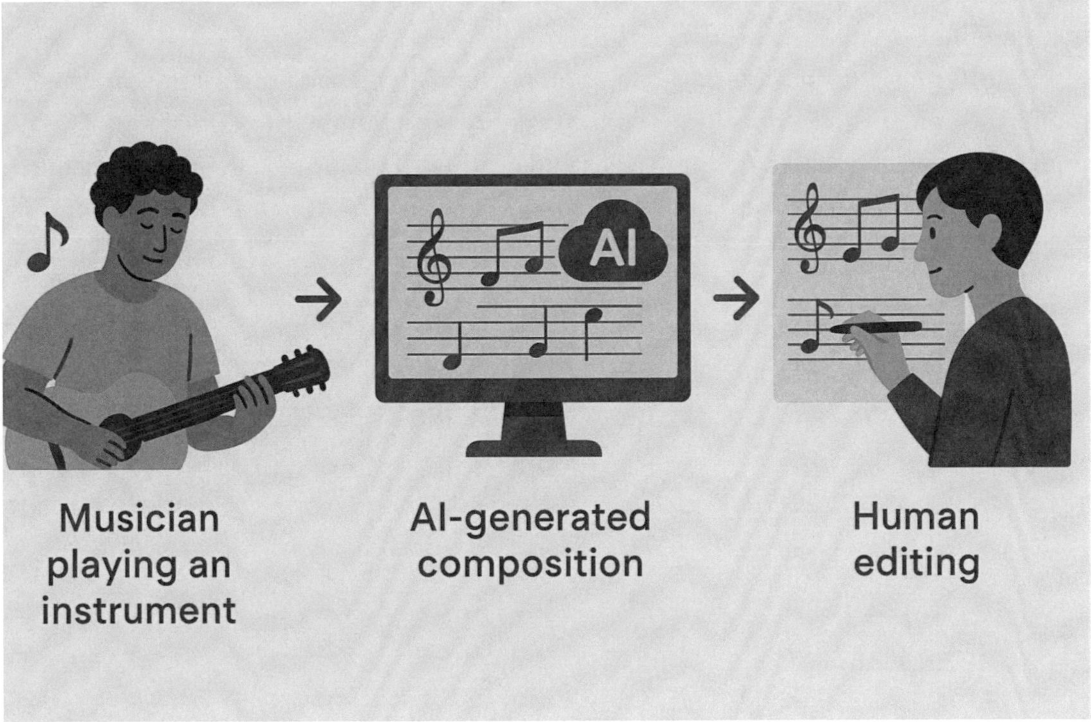

***Figure 5-5.** AI-Assisted Music Production, from Melody Generation to Adaptive Real-Time Scoring*

5.4.3 Gaming

AI's role in gaming goes beyond asset generation. Design teams can use AI to generate dialogue trees for non-player characters (NPCs), enabling richer interactions without hand-writing every possible exchange.

In 2025, Ubisoft unveiled an experimental generative AI system called "Teammates," featuring AI companions Pablo and Sofia in a first-person shooter environment. These NPCs listen to natural speech, adapt to player tactics in real time, and maintain coherent personalities throughout live missions. This represents one of the first playable demonstrations of dynamic AI dialogue from a major studio, though still an experiment in closed testing, moving beyond pre-scripted conversation trees to truly adaptive character interactions (`https://builtin.com/articles/collaborative-ai-games-model`).

From a business perspective, this capability reduces content authoring costs and enables richer player experiences, but it also introduces challenges around narrative coherence, real-time latency, and the governance of emergent AI behavior in live environments.

In world-building, procedural generation powered by AI can create landscapes, architecture, and even local cultures with backstory. The human role shifts from handcrafting every detail to defining rules and aesthetic constraints, then curating the AI's output for consistency and quality.

Figure 5-6. *AI-Driven Game Development Including Procedural World-Building and Dynamic NPC Dialogue*

5.4.4 Publishing

In publishing, AI is being applied to everything from editorial support to book marketing. Authors can use AI to draft sections of text based on an outline, then refine the "voice" and "nuance." Non-fiction authors often use AI as a research assistant, using it to generate summaries or identify relevant sources from large, disparate sources.

Economically, AI-assisted drafting and personalization can compress editorial timelines and lower production costs, though these gains must be weighed against real cost drivers including GPU inference at scale, the review labor still required to validate outputs, and the integration overhead of embedding AI into existing workflows. Broader questions remain around authorship, disclosure, and the long-term valuation of human voice in a market increasingly saturated with machine-generated text.

In marketing, AI systems can produce variant cover designs or targeted promotional copy for different reader segments. This personalization can extend to interactive stories, where readers influence plot direction and the AI adjusts the narrative accordingly.

Figure 5-7. *AI-Powered Publishing Workflows Spanning Editorial Drafting, Cover Design, and Targeted Marketing*

5.4.5 Advertising and Design

The advertising industry has been the quickest to adopt AI for campaign ideation. Creative teams can input a brand's mood, audience profile, and campaign goals into AI systems, which then generate hundreds of headline and visual combinations in minutes. Creative professionals then select, adapt, and combine these outputs to create final campaigns.

AI-powered design tools also make it possible to localize ads across markets without starting from scratch. For example, an AI might generate culturally relevant imagery and adjust copy tone for different regions, while brand managers ensure alignment with overall messaging (adobe.com).

This shift transforms creative economics by favoring speed and scale, forcing agencies to reconsider pricing models, client disclosure practices, and brand positioning in a landscape where AI-generated variations are inexpensive but differentiation remains human-led.

Figure 5-8. *AI-Generated Advertising Concepts Showing Rapid Campaign Ideation and Cross-Market Localization*

5.4.6 Patterns Across Industries

As generative AI technologies mature, organizations across these industries are discovering powerful new approaches to innovation, creativity, and problem-solving. From healthcare to entertainment, manufacturing to financial services, AI tools are fundamentally reshaping how professionals conceptualize and execute their work. Across these industries, though, several consistent themes emerge:

1. **Acceleration of Ideation**: AI shortens the time from concept to prototype, enabling more iterations before production.
2. **Expanded Creative Range**: By generating multiple options, AI encourages exploration beyond the creator's initial instincts.
3. **Evolving Human Roles**: Creators spend less time on repetitive execution and more on high-level direction, curation, and integration.
4. **Integration Challenges**: Issues of style consistency, bias mitigation, and intellectual property remain significant hurdles.

5.4.7 From Experiment to Standard Practice

These case studies show that AI co-creation is not confined to experimental art projects. It is already embedded in the daily work of film crews, composers, game designers, authors, and advertising teams. The technology's greatest strength lies in its ability to widen the creative space while keeping human judgment at the center of decision-making.

The industries that succeed with AI co-creation are not the ones that hand over the reins entirely. Instead, they are the ones that use AI as a creative multiplier, integrating it into workflows in ways that respect both artistic vision and ethical boundaries.

The next section will explore **opportunities and risks**, looking beyond adoption patterns to the broader implications of this shift for creative quality, cultural diversity, and the economics of creative work.

5.5 Opportunities and Risks

The integration of AI into creative workflows presents a complex landscape of possibilities and challenges. As with any transformative technology, the potential benefits come with corresponding risks that must be carefully navigated.

5.5.1 Democratization of Creativity

Perhaps the most significant opportunity of AI co-creation is the lowering of technical barriers that have historically limited creative expression. Tools that once required years of specialized training are being reimagined with AI interfaces that respond to natural language instructions.

A graphic designer with decades of experience in Adobe Photoshop might spend hours achieving a specific visual effect. Now, a student with no formal training can describe that same effect to an AI and receive results in seconds. This shift is particularly powerful in domains where technical skill has been a gatekeeper to creative participation.

In filmmaking, technologies like Runway ML (runwayml.com) allow creators to generate visual effects that would previously have required specialized teams and substantial budgets. Independent filmmakers can now produce science fiction narratives or period pieces without the prohibitive costs of practical effects or location shooting.

Music production, traditionally dependent on access to instruments and recording equipment, is similarly being transformed. Tools like AIVA and Soundraw enable composers to orchestrate complex arrangements without mastering every instrument (soundraw.io). This democratization extends the creative palette available to musicians regardless of their formal training.

However, this democratization is not without complications. As barriers lower, markets may become saturated with AI-assisted content, potentially making it harder for creators to stand out. The question becomes not whether someone can create, but whether their creation will find an audience in an increasingly crowded landscape.

5.5.2 Hyper-personalization of Content

AI co-creation enables unprecedented levels of content personalization. Rather than producing a single version of a creative work, creators can generate variations tailored to different audiences, contexts, or individual preferences.

In publishing, this might mean books that adapt their language complexity to the reader's vocabulary level or interactive narratives that reshape themselves based on reader engagement patterns. Educational content could adjust examples to align with a student's interests or learning style, potentially increasing engagement and retention.

Entertainment platforms are already experimenting with adaptive content. Netflix's "Bandersnatch" interactive film demonstrated early possibilities, but AI co-creation could take this further, with stories that continuously adapt rather than following pre-scripted branches (netflix.com).

The marketing implications are equally significant. Brands can generate thousands of ad variations targeted to specific demographic segments, testing effectiveness in real time. This capability, demonstrated by platforms like Persado (persado.com), allows messages to be optimized for different cultural contexts or consumer preferences.

The risk in this hyper-personalization is the potential fragmentation of shared cultural experiences. When content adapts to individual preferences, we may lose the common reference points that have traditionally united audiences. There are also privacy concerns, as effective personalization requires increasingly detailed data about consumer preferences and behaviors.

5.5.3 Productivity and Iteration Speed

The acceleration of creative workflows represents another substantial opportunity. Tasks that once took days can now be completed in hours or minutes, allowing for more iterations and refinement within the same production timeline.

A marketing team that might have produced three campaign concepts in a week can now generate dozens, increasing the chances of finding truly innovative approaches. Game developers can rapidly prototype level designs or character models, getting immediate visual feedback rather than waiting for rendering processes.

This speed enables a more experimental approach to creativity. When iteration costs drop, creators can take greater risks, knowing they can quickly pivot if an approach isn't working. The result is often more innovative work that might not have emerged from more cautious, resource-constrained processes.

However, this acceleration brings its own challenges. Faster production doesn't necessarily mean better quality, and there's a risk that quantity may be prioritized over depth. Creative work often benefits from incubation periods—time for ideas to mature and develop. When AI tools make instant generation possible, this valuable reflection time may be sacrificed.

5.5.4 Intellectual Property Challenges

As AI becomes an active participant in the creative process, traditional notions of authorship and ownership grow increasingly complex. Current copyright frameworks were designed for human creators, leaving significant questions about works produced through human-AI collaboration.

When an AI system trained on millions of existing works generates something new, who holds the rights to that creation? The human who provided the prompt? The AI's developers? The creators whose work formed the training data? These questions remain largely unresolved in legal systems worldwide.

Some jurisdictions, including the United States Copyright Office, have taken the position that AI-generated works without human creative input cannot be copyrighted (copyright.gov). However, the reality of AI co-creation is more nuanced, with human and machine contributions often deeply intertwined.

For creative professionals, this uncertainty creates both risks and defensive strategies. Some are carefully documenting their creative process to demonstrate the human judgment involved. Others are exploring blockchain-based provenance systems that track the evolution of creative works from concept to completion.

5.5.5 Bias and Cultural Homogenization

AI systems learn from existing data, which means they can amplify biases present in their training sets. In creative contexts, this can lead to the perpetuation of stereotypes or the marginalization of underrepresented perspectives.

Image generation systems have demonstrated biases in how they represent different genders and ethnicities (arxiv.org). Language models may reproduce patterns of representation from their training data, potentially reinforcing rather than challenging cultural assumptions.

Beyond explicit bias, there's a subtler risk of homogenization. When creators worldwide use the same AI tools trained on similar datasets, a kind of aesthetic convergence can emerge. The unique cultural and regional variations that have historically enriched creative expression may be flattened in favor of styles that perform well in the AI system.

This risk is particularly acute for cultures whose creative traditions are underrepresented in training data. As AI co-creation becomes more prevalent, preserving diverse creative voices will require intentional effort and careful curation of training datasets.

5.5.6 Creative Deskilling and Overreliance

As AI systems become more capable, there's a risk that certain creative skills may atrophy. If AI can generate competent prose or pleasing melodies on demand, will creators still develop these foundational skills themselves?

Historical precedent offers some perspective. When calculators became widespread, there were concerns about mathematical deskilling. In practice, basic calculation skills declined somewhat, but higher-level mathematical thinking remained essential. Similarly, AI may automate certain creative tasks while placing greater emphasis on conceptual thinking, curation, and direction.

The greater risk may be overreliance—creators becoming dependent on AI suggestions rather than developing their own aesthetic judgment. This could lead to a form of creative learned helplessness, where professionals struggle to work without AI assistance.

5.5.7 Ethical Frameworks and Governance

As these opportunities and risks unfold, the need for ethical frameworks and governance structures becomes increasingly apparent. Industry standards around transparency, attribution, and data usage are beginning to emerge, though they remain inconsistent across sectors and regions.

Some creative platforms now require disclosure when AI has contributed to a work. Getty Images, for instance, prohibits AI-generated submissions to its creative library (gettyimages.com). This transparency allows consumers to make informed choices about the media they consume.

Professional organizations in design, film, and writing are developing guidelines for ethical AI use, addressing questions of attribution, compensation, and creative integrity. These efforts represent an important step toward responsible integration of AI co-creation into established industries.

The most effective governance approaches will likely balance innovation with protection, allowing creative exploration while establishing guardrails around issues like consent, representation, and fair compensation. As with previous technological shifts, the most sustainable paths forward will emerge from dialogue between creators, technologists, policymakers, and the public.

5.6 Economic and Workforce Implications

The integration of AI co-creation tools into creative industries is reshaping not only how creative work is produced but also who produces it and how they are compensated. These changes present both opportunities and challenges for the creative workforce.

5.6.1 Shifting Labor Demand

As AI systems take on more execution-oriented tasks, human creative labor is shifting toward higher-level functions. Rather than spending hours on technical execution, professionals increasingly focus on direction, curation, and conceptual development.

A graphic designer who once spent days manually creating variations of a logo might now generate dozens of options with AI in minutes, then apply their expertise to select and refine the most promising concepts. Their value shifts from technical execution to aesthetic judgment and client communication.

This pattern repeats across industries. Writers may spend less time drafting and more time editing AI-generated content to match their voice. Musicians might focus on selecting and combining AI-generated phrases rather than composing every note. Film editors might use AI to assemble rough cuts based on emotional beats, then refine these assemblies with their human sensibility.

Research by the World Economic Forum suggests that creative roles are among those least likely to be fully automated, but most likely to be significantly transformed by AI augmentation (weforum.org). This transformation typically involves a shift from production to direction—from making to choosing.

5.6.2 Emerging Job Roles

As creative workflows evolve, entirely new job roles are emerging at the intersection of creativity and technology. These hybrid positions require both artistic sensibility and technical understanding of AI systems.

Prompt engineers specialize in crafting the instructions that guide AI creative systems. This role requires understanding both the capabilities of AI models and the nuances of language that produce the best results. A skilled prompt engineer can save hours of iteration by framing requests in ways that align with the AI's strengths.

AI art directors oversee the integration of AI-generated elements into larger creative projects. They develop style guides that maintain consistency across human and AI contributions, and they identify which aspects of a project are best handled by each type of contributor.

Synthetic content auditors evaluate AI-generated material for quality, bias, and potential legal issues. This role combines technical knowledge with ethical judgment, ensuring that AI outputs meet both creative standards and regulatory requirements.

These emerging roles often command premium compensation, as they require rare combinations of technical and creative skills. Educational institutions are beginning to develop specialized programs to prepare students for these hybrid careers, though much of the current workforce is developing these skills through self-directed learning and on-the-job experience.

5.6.3 Displacement and Adaptation

While new opportunities are emerging, certain existing roles face disruption. Entry-level positions that have traditionally focused on technical execution—junior designers, production assistants, and copywriters—may see reduced demand as these functions become partially automated.

A 2023 Goldman Sachs report estimated that approximately 300 million jobs worldwide could be affected by AI automation, with creative industries experiencing significant transformation (goldmansachs.com). However, the report also noted that historically, technological disruption has ultimately created more jobs than it eliminated, though often in different sectors or requiring different skills.

For individual creative professionals, adaptation is becoming essential. This means not only learning to use AI tools effectively but also identifying which aspects of their expertise remain distinctively human. Those who position themselves as AI-complementary rather than AI-replaceable are finding the most sustainable career paths.

Retraining programs are emerging to support this transition. The Adobe Digital Academy offers courses for creative professionals looking to integrate AI into their workflows (adobe.com). Industry associations and unions are also developing resources to help members navigate changing skill requirements.

5.6.4 Economic Models in Transition

Beyond individual careers, entire economic models within creative industries are evolving. The economics of content creation, traditionally based on scarcity and craft, must adapt to a world where certain types of content can be generated at unprecedented scale and speed.

Subscription models are becoming more prevalent, with creators offering ongoing access to their expertise rather than charging per project. Platforms like Patreon (patreon.com) enable direct support from audiences, potentially reducing dependence on intermediaries.

Value is increasingly derived from curation and context rather than production alone. When AI can generate endless variations, the ability to select the right option and place it in a meaningful context becomes the scarce resource. This shift favors those with deep domain knowledge and refined taste within their creative field.

Intellectual property frameworks are struggling to keep pace with these changes. Traditional copyright models assume identifiable human authors, while AI co-creation introduces more distributed forms of authorship. Some creators are exploring alternative approaches, including Creative Commons licensing or blockchain-based systems for tracking attribution and compensation.

5.6.5 Inequality and Access

The economic impacts of AI co-creation are not evenly distributed. Those with early access to advanced tools and the skills to use them effectively gain significant advantages. This creates the potential for widening inequality within creative industries.

Geographic disparities are particularly concerning. Creators in regions with reliable high-speed internet and access to cutting-edge technology can leverage AI co-creation more effectively than those in areas with limited infrastructure. Similarly, language barriers may disadvantage creators working in languages less well-supported by current AI systems.

Addressing these disparities requires intentional effort from technology developers, educational institutions, and policymakers. Open source AI initiatives, localized training programs, and infrastructure investments can help ensure that the benefits of AI co-creation are widely shared rather than concentrated among already-privileged creators.

5.7 Looking Ahead: The Future of Creative AI Collaboration

As AI co-creation tools mature and become more deeply integrated into creative workflows, several emerging trends point toward the future of human-machine collaboration in creative industries. These developments suggest not only technical evolution but also cultural and artistic transformation.

5.7.1 Integration with Immersive Technologies

The convergence of AI co-creation with virtual reality (VR), augmented reality (AR), and mixed reality (MR) presents particularly exciting possibilities. These technologies are moving beyond separate domains to form interconnected creative ecosystems.

Imagine a filmmaker using natural language to describe a scene, which an AI instantly visualizes in three-dimensional space. The director can then step into this virtual environment using VR, make adjustments through gesture and voice, and see the changes rendered in real time. This kind of immersive co-creation collapses the distance between conception and experience.

Companies like Meta and Microsoft are already exploring these intersections. Meta's Reality Labs has demonstrated AI systems that can generate or modify virtual environments based on verbal instructions within VR (meta.com). Microsoft Mesh combined AI with mixed reality to enable collaborative creation in shared virtual spaces until its retirement in late 2025 (microsoft.com).

For architects and environmental designers, these technologies enable clients to experience and modify proposed spaces before construction begins. For game developers, they allow narrative environments to be generated and refined through direct interaction rather than through code or external tools.

As these technologies mature, the boundary between creator and audience may blur further. Immersive experiences could adapt in real time to viewer engagement, with AI systems generating content responsive to emotional reactions or expressed preferences.

5.7.2 Evolution of Creative Agents

Current AI co-creation tools generally respond to specific prompts without maintaining long-term creative context. The next generation of systems is likely to develop more persistent creative memory and agency.

Creative agents with longer-term memory could maintain stylistic consistency across projects, learn a creator's preferences over time, and develop distinctive creative "personalities" that complement their human collaborators. Rather than starting fresh with each interaction, these systems would build on previous collaborations.

Some researchers are exploring fully autonomous creative agents capable of initiating projects based on observed trends or identified opportunities. These systems might propose concepts unprompted, drawing connections between disparate influences or identifying unexplored creative territory.

The relationship between human creators and these more autonomous systems will require careful negotiation. The most productive approaches will likely involve clear frameworks for human oversight and intervention, ensuring that AI autonomy serves rather than supplants human creative vision.

5.7.3 The Cultural Question: Human Taste As Ultimate Filter

As AI systems become more sophisticated in generating content across media, a fundamental question emerges: Will human aesthetic judgment remain the ultimate arbiter of creative value?

There are compelling reasons to believe it will. Creative work derives its significance not just from its formal qualities but from its cultural context and human meaning. An AI might generate technically impressive music, but humans determine whether that music resonates emotionally or culturally.

However, this relationship may become more complex as AI systems develop the ability to predict human preferences with increasing accuracy. When an AI can reliably generate content that audiences find appealing, the role of human curators may shift from selection to direction—specifying which human preferences should be prioritized.

Some creative communities are already establishing principles that preserve human centrality in the creative process. These include transparency about AI involvement, prioritization of human creative intent, and recognition that technical capability must be guided by human values and meaning.

The most likely future is not one where AI replaces human creativity, but one where the definition of creativity itself evolves. The creative act may increasingly involve collaboration between human vision and machine capability, with each contributing what they do best to a shared creative outcome.

Across creative domains, the same pattern emerges. AI co-creation consistently accelerates ideation and reduces execution costs, but value creation depends on how well organizations integrate these tools into human-led workflows. Where AI is treated as a replacement, creative quality and trust often erode. Where it is positioned as an augmentative layer governed by clear quality controls, economic intent, and ethical boundaries, it becomes a multiplier of human creativity rather than a substitute for it. The competitive advantage lies not in access to AI tools, but in the organizational ability to integrate them responsibly and strategically.

5.8 Conclusion

The integration of AI into creative workflows represents more than a technological shift; it marks a fundamental reimagining of the creative process itself. Throughout human history, creativity has evolved alongside our tools—from cave paintings to printing presses to digital design software. Each transition has sparked both concern and excitement, ultimately expanding rather than diminishing the scope of human expression.

AI co-creation stands apart from previous transitions in its ability to contribute at the conceptual level. For the first time, widely accessible technology can suggest ideas, generate variations, and respond to creative direction with a degree of autonomy previously unimagined. This shift challenges traditional notions of authorship and creativity while opening new possibilities for collaboration.

For creative leaders navigating this transformation, the path forward requires both experimentation and ethical foresight. Those who approach AI as a creative partner rather than a mere tool will discover new modes of expression and efficiency. Those who establish thoughtful boundaries around AI use will preserve the human values and perspectives that give creative work its meaning.

The most successful integrations will be those that enhance rather than replace human creativity, amplifying vision, removing technical barriers, and freeing creators to focus on the aspects of their work that are most distinctively human. In this evolving relationship, technology serves as both a mirror and a window, reflecting our creative impulses while opening views onto previously unimagined possibilities.

As we move forward, the enduring value of human creativity lies not in technical execution alone, but in the uniquely human capacity to find meaning, to connect disparate ideas, and to create work that resonates with shared human experience. In partnership with increasingly sophisticated AI, these human qualities become not less but more essential to the creative future we are building together.

Next, we will look into how generative AI is transforming the field of decision intelligence and the decision-making process across multiple other industries.

CHAPTER 6

Enterprise GenAI Decision Framework

In the previous chapter, we discussed how GenAI is influencing the creative industries. In this chapter, we will discuss how GenAI is transforming the field of decision intelligence. Generative AI-driven decision intelligence is a cutting-edge approach that enhances decision-making capabilities across multiple domains, including health, law, retail, education, manufacturing, finance, and entertainment, by integrating generative AI with an intelligent decision-making approach. Generative AI generates synthetic data and simulates multiple future scenarios by analyzing business situations and forecasting outcomes, enabling more precise, faster decision-making at optimal cost.

Generative AI-driven decision intelligence transforms the traditional decision-making process by adding simulation, analysis, reasoning, and adaptive learning capabilities, making decision-making more agile, precise, and scalable at the enterprise level.

6.1 The New Era of AI-Driven Strategic Decision-Making

A new era of AI-driven strategic decision-making has emerged in which AI augments human decision-making, ethics, and judgment and navigates technological advancement in industry by continuously analyzing signals across markets, operations, supply chains, demands, and customer behavior.

Businesses are growing and evolving with the advancement of generative AI, which generates different scenarios and simulates them with speed, depth, and high accuracy that is difficult to achieve using a manual process. In business operations, AI copilots are incorporated to create, validate, and implement quicker, adaptable strategies.

N. Sendas et al., *Building Generative AI Solutions for Industries with AWS*,
https://doi.org/10.1007/979-8-8688-2830-0_6

6.1.1 Rise of Generative AI Intelligence

Generative AI is poised to revolutionize strategic activities by enhancing the strategist's work, such as analysis and insight generation, while addressing the challenges posed by human biases and the social aspects of strategy.

- Why Strategic Planning Is Becoming Harder: Complexity, Volatility, and Data Overload

  Global markets, supply chain, product demand, time-to-market, and customer expectations are changing faster and have become more complex and volatile than the traditional method can keep up with. Data volumes have grown exponentially, creating analysis bottlenecks and making it harder for leaders to do strategic planning and extract meaningful insights without AI augmentation. Three key factors make strategic planning harder.

  1. Complexity

     GenAI systems are complex in nature because of their technical implementation, ethics, and regulations. The highly interconnected and rapidly changing environment makes strategic planning more complex and difficult to implement. The black box nature of models, governance frameworks, regulatory shifts, and competitive dynamics creates system-level complexity where small changes can have outsized impacts.

  2. Volatility

     The rapid advancement and use of GenAI technology increases market volatility. Real-time adaptation to market instability is required since GenAI faces intense competition, uncertainty, and quick changes, and in such scenarios, traditional static planning cycles won't work.

  3. Data Overload

     GenAI faces data-related difficulties, and the information extracted from this data is overloaded. Large volumes of pertinent, high-quality data are essential because using biased or poor-quality data produces unreliable and erroneous results.

In addition, handling this data presents serious privacy, security, and intellectual property (IP) issues that need to be resolved to guarantee compliance and foster confidence.

- The Rise Of Generative Intelligence As a Strategic Partner

  Generative AI becomes a collaborative strategic partner capable of ideation, planning, analysis, refinement, and decision exploration before execution. Generative AI models interact with complex data to generate hypotheses, simulating various situations, and producing probabilistic results. Researcher, interpreter, thought partner, simulator, and communicator are five roles for GenAI that come into play at various steps across different phases of strategy development, like designing the strategy, mobilizing the organization, executing, monitoring, and reviewing.

- How GenAI Changes the Decision-Making Paradigm

  Generative AI transforms the linear decision-making paradigm from hindsight-driven to a continuous foresight-driven intelligence system. With multi-scenario analysis, simulation, and reasoning, it provides real-time insights and suggests tactics to help executives navigate business uncertainties confidently. The future of decision-making will be collaborative human–AI models that augment human capabilities with GenAI insights and predictive powers. Key shift GenAI brings in a decision-making paradigm, from Opaque black box models to Explainable models and from Solo to Augmented Intelligence of the human–AI co-pilot model.

6.1.2 Role of AI Copilots

AI Copilots act as intelligent data-driven partners by predicting insights, automating routine tasks, and enhancing real-time strategic decision-making.

- The Role of AI Copilots in Executive and Operational Planning

  In executive and operational planning, AI copilots act as real pilots who can analyze real-time complex data, synthesize it, act as scenario planners, make decisions, and guide leaders through strategic choices. They bridge the gap between data and decision-making by providing context-aware insights and recommendations.

AI Copilots acts as a strategic thinker in executive planning to perform tasks like relevant information retrieval, data analysis, strategy formation, insights prediction, and enhanced decision-making. In operational planning, AI copilots automate the task, help in resource allocation, workflow optimization, and real-time monitoring and response accordingly.

- Human–AI Collaboration Models in Strategic Decision Cycles

  In human-overseen scenarios, AI copilots propose collaborative decision-making frameworks to validate and develop GenAI models. Human–AI collaborating models combine computer precision with human intuition, enabling hybrid intelligence systems that improve strategic alignment, minimize biases, and shorten decision cycles while maintaining accountability and human oversight.

  Human–AI collaboration works in various models as follows:

  1. AI acts as an assistant, and humans are the primary decision-makers.
  2. AI as an autonomous agent with minimum human intervention
  3. A balanced partnership between AI and humans.

6.1.3 Benefits of Generative AI-Driven Decision-Making for Business

Generative AI-driven decision-making offers various benefits for businesses by speeding up the analysis and insights from complex data, enhancing prediction with better strategy, giving companies a competitive edge while automating tasks, and cutting costs. We have listed six such benefits below:

1. Precise prediction and forecasting
2. Cost and time reduction
3. Faster data-driven decisions

4. Augment and automate
5. Improved efficiency and productivity
6. Contextualized communication

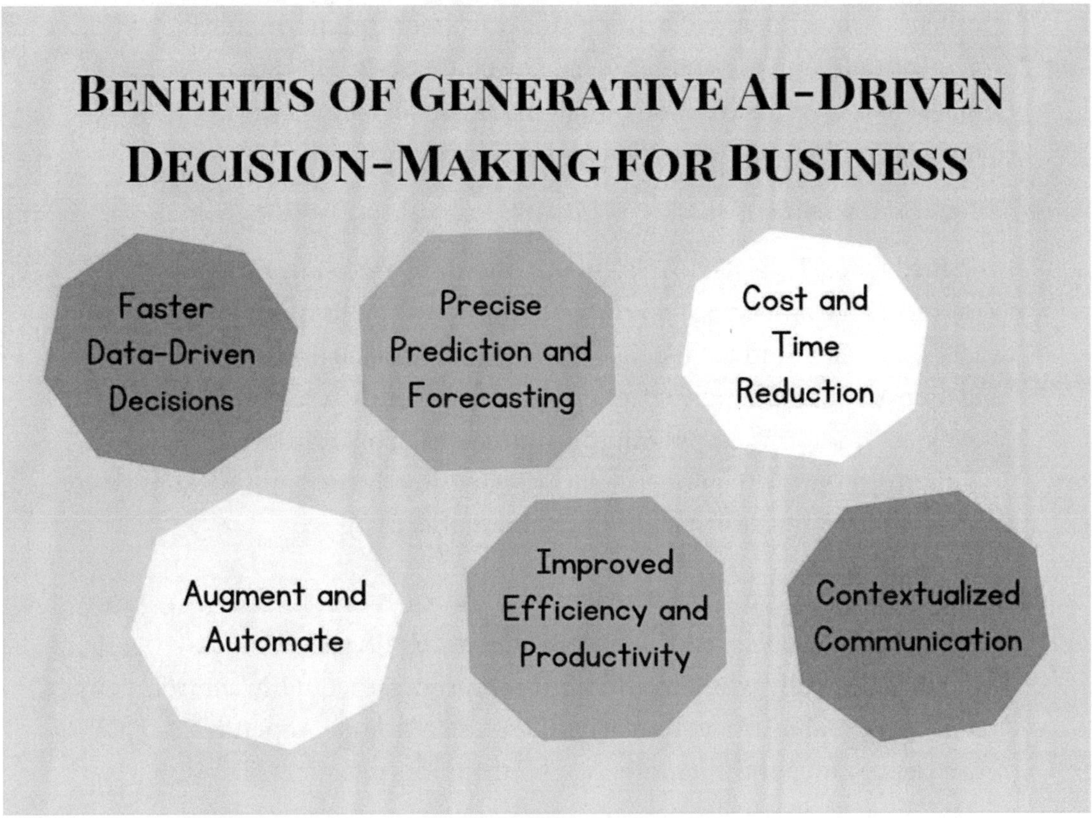

Figure 6-1. *Benefits of Generative AI Decision-Making*

6.1.4 How GenAI Influences Decision-Making Across Organizational Roles?

Generative AI is embedded in enterprise workflows and reshaping how different organizational roles approach decision-making. GenAI does not completely replace human judgment because it is critical for decision-making, but it augments insights and simulations at each level. A combination of human intuition with AI-driven analysis and automation shifts decision-making from hierarchical to decentralized, leading to faster, data-driven, and innovative choices. Let's discuss how GenAI supports different decision types:

- Strategic Decisions

  At the executive level, AI acts as a strategic intelligence engine, synthesizing market trends, competitive dynamics, and scenario forecasts. Leaders use these insights via simulation models and executive dashboards to explore strategic assumptions, mergers, acquisitions, and consolidations, to evaluate trade-offs. Final decisions are still based on human intelligence, considering long-term accountability, vision, and governance.

- Tactical Decisions

  At the tactical level, GenAI improves planning precision, performance analytics, and resource optimization for the VPs and Directors. Generative business analytics and forecasting tools help leaders understand performance patterns, identify bottlenecks, and evaluate trade-offs across multiple initiatives. It also assists leaders with project prioritization, scenario evaluation, hiring, and budget allocation to translate insights into actionable plans.

- Operational Decisions

  At the operational level of decision-making, GenAI is embedded directly into daily workflows to optimize processes, quality control, detect anomalies, suggest next actions, and automate repetitive analysis. Managers and individual contributors use tools like AI Copilot to provide contextual knowledge to raise exceptions, escalations, and adaptive process changes.

- Automated Decisions

  At the automated decision-making level, AI agents automate workflows for routine high-frequency, low-risk decisions that require consistency and quick action. AI agents operate continuously within defined governance boundaries and escalate exceptions to humans when needed to be handled.

GenAI enables organizations to scale decision-making effectively by combining human strategic judgment with GenAI-driven intelligence and automation across every level.

6.2 Foundations of Generative Decision Intelligence

Generative Decision Intelligence integrates enterprise structured and unstructured data, reasoning engines, and generative models to analyze data, understand business models, make strategic choices, and generate high-stakes decision workflows. Unlike classic analytics, it not only interprets historical data but also creates strategic options, simulates scenarios, adapts in real time, and proposes actions. It creates an intelligent layer that enhances operational strategy and executive thinking in complex environments to make more precise and adaptable business decisions.

6.2.1 What Is Generative Decision Intelligence?

Generative Decision Intelligence is the combination of generative AI and decision intelligence for fast, accurate, and creative decision-making by operating data and AI in a closed collaboration.

- Combining Generative Models, Reasoning, and Enterprise Context

  Generative AI framework blends LLMs, knowledge graphs, RAG pipelines, and structured enterprise systems (ERP, MES, CRM) for decision intelligence. Reasoning engines enable GenAI to generate grounded insights by evaluating limitations, goals, and business logic. This fusion enables domain-aware judgements customized to actual operational, financial, and market circumstances.

- Differences from Predictive Analytics, BI Dashboards, and Optimization Tools

  Predictive analytics forecasts outcomes, BI dashboards visualize data, and optimization tools identify mathematical optima. By combining insights, suggesting solutions, outlining trade-offs, and creating decision narratives, Generative Decision Intelligence goes one step further. Leaders can investigate "what-if" scenarios in natural language without exclusively depending on numerical analysis, thanks to its support for ambiguous, multi-variable decisions.

6.2.2 How GenAI Understands, Synthesizes, and Generates Insights

- Natural Language Interfaces for Decision Workflows

  GenAI interprets executive prompts, their context, language, queries, and strategic objectives expressed in natural language. It turns ambiguous enquiries into structured analytical tasks, enabling executives to connect with complicated data sources conversationally. This democratizes access to enterprise intelligence across non-technical roles and reduces technological barriers.

- RAG and Domain Grounding

  Retrieval-Augmented Generation (RAG) anchors current responses to enterprise knowledge by integrating real-time contextual data with historical data, operating procedures, and technical documents. It ensures adaptive dynamic workflows with factual accuracy and domain fidelity for complex task management. By domain grounding, generative AI reasons with verified organizations, enabling reliable AI-driven recommendations aligned with internal constraints and market realities.

- Multi-step Reasoning, Agentic Planning, and Tool Orchestration

  Advanced GenAI implements a multi-step reasoning system to evaluate circumstances, divide the procedure into small tasks, and plan action items accordingly. Agentic AI helps in tools orchestration, forecasting engines, algorithm optimization, and model simulation to create detailed and composite insights. Consequently, the AI transforms from a passive assistant to an autonomous analytical agent that facilitates end-to-end decision cycles.

6.3 Capability Areas: Where GenAI Improves Decision Quality

Generative AI improves decision quality by integrating deep reasoning, contextual awareness, and synthetic insight generation across strategic, operational, and knowledge-intensive workflows. It improves forecasting, accelerates process optimization, and transforms enterprise knowledge into actionable intelligence. GenAI empowers organizations to produce faster, more accurate, and more resilient decisions with greater transparency and confidence by generating various scenarios and diagnosing inefficiencies with reasoning.

6.3.1 Strategic Foresight and Scenario Planning

Scenario planning is a tool for strategic foresight planning, which helps organizations to overcome uncertainty and helps in developing robust strategic thinking, which is the need of today's dynamic and complex business environment. Generative AI revolutionizes enterprises by enhancing scenario planning at scale with a fraction of the cost and time.

- Market Simulations

  GenAI generates various demands, pricing, and customer response scenarios using historical patterns and real-time signals and simulates a dynamic market. GenAI models are able to explore non-linear relationships, any emerging disruptions, and work on strategic alternatives, unlike static econometric models.

- Long-Term Trend Forecasting

  GenAI models analyze various economic indicators, the evolution process, technological progress, and social behavioral patterns to forecast long-term trends. They analyze unstructured and structured data to forecast, which helps in strategic planning, expansion decisions, and market timing information for continuous upgrade and growth.

- Sensitivity and What-If Analyses

  GenAI rapidly generates what-if scenarios by permutation and combination of various operational, financial, or market variables and evaluating ripple effects across the enterprise. This generates reasoning models that are sensitive toward change in cost, demand, supply, and competition, resulting in robust scenarios, comparable outcomes with thorough analysis.

- Competitive Landscape Interpretation

  It is easy to interpret the competitive landscape using GenAI by synthesizing news, price surge, product launches, technical advancement, etc. It helps in identifying competitive strategy, innovative themes, and emerging threats and produces scenarios for proactive market strategy adjustments.

6.3.2 Operational Optimization and Process Acceleration

GenAI significantly enhances operational optimization and process acceleration by automating the design process, workflow diagnostics, and improving decision routing across various business functions.

- Workflow Diagnostics

  GenAI evaluates the operation workflows by analyzing logs, KPIs, and process mapping to identify inefficiencies, delays, and root causes and then optimizes them. GenAI augments traditional Six Sigma diagnostic methods to identify hidden bottlenecks and recommends targeted improvements.

- Automated Process Redesign

  GenAI helps in redesigning and optimizing automated process flows for acceleration, cost, compliance, and resource allocation. It helps in designing workflow blueprints and procedural drafts by evaluating data, restrictions, and all variations. In an enterprise setting, AI-driven redesign accelerates transformative tasks like labor-equipment planning, supply chain reengineering, and digitalization.

- Decision Routing (Triage, Prioritization, Exception Management)

  GenAI helps in decision routing and automates the triage process based on priority, urgency, risk, and impact of the process. It prioritizes the task based on context and routes it to the right teams. GenAI can autonomously handle exceptions, thus improving efficiency and saving a lot of time compared to manual exception handling.

  A hybrid human–AI decision system is developed to enhance responsiveness and alertness in planning, supply chain, maintenance, monitoring, quality checks, and customer support.

6.3.3 Knowledge Acceleration and Expert Augmentation

GenAI accelerates knowledge and augments experts by providing access to data and extracting relevant information and handles routine tasks efficiently, allowing the enterprise to focus on high-level analysis and decision-making.

- Synthetic Data and Hypothetical Scenarios

  The GenAI model produces synthetic data and generates hypothetical scenarios to enrich the training, simulation, and forecasting experience at the enterprise level. It is helpful in case of sparse historical data and enables AI systems to learn and industries to explore the unknown scenarios and learn from them.

- Summarization of Policies, Reports, and Historical Decisions

  GenAI automatically processes huge amounts of engineering documentation, policies, audits, and decision logs and generates clear summaries and insights. By highlighting trends, inconsistencies, and lost opportunities, it builds an institutional memory layer that enhances governance and accelerates the onboarding of leaders and operators.

- Turning Implicit Expert Knowledge into Explicit, Reusable Reasoning

  GenAI conducts expert interviews, examines expert knowledge from emails, chats, and technical notes, and converts it into decision trees, best-practice manuals, and structured reasoning frameworks. This reduces dependency on human expertise and mitigates the skill shortage by sharing and scaling tacit knowledge.

6.3.4 Technical Architecture for Decision Systems

For technical leaders and architects, it is extremely important to understand the technical architecture of GenAI to design reliable, scalable, and trustworthy GenAI-driven decision systems. Each layer of GenAI technical architecture contributes to improving decision quality and better architecture patterns.

1. Data Layer

   The data layer provides the model with real-time, relevant, high-quality, and secure data. It connects the GenAI system to enterprise data sources, performs semantic search, and feeds contextual information into the prompt pipeline to improve decisions and better architectural patterns.

2. Model Layer

   The model layer consists of LLMs, foundation models, and ML pipelines that perform reasoning, prediction, generation, and planning. The technical team evolves independently by modularizing GenAI capabilities to handle various tasks. It helps architects to optimize models based on cost, latency, performance, and governance requirements.

3. Business Logic

   The business logic layer integrates GenAI model outputs into enterprise systems via RAG workflows, prompts, API calls, orchestration frameworks, and agentic workflows. The business logic layer ensures that architects and developers make context-aware decisions and helps align AI-generated recommendations with real-world scenarios to construct an actionable plan.

4. Human Interface

   In a human-in-the-loop (HITL) design, the technical team works on the AI-generated recommendations. Experts can review, approve, override, and refine through feedback loops, interfaces, alerts, and decision dashboards. This layer enhances trust and reliability by combining machine reasoning with human domain expertise and continuously improves the model and decisions by implementing a feedback loop.

5. Audit Trail

   Audit trail layer provides logs of queries, pipelines, data, prompts, model responses, decision outcomes, and user interactions. This layer ensures compliance, security, traceability, and explainability via monitoring through a logging framework and observability tools. For technical architects, this layer ensures that GenAI systems are governable and accountable, providing post-decision analysis, risk management, debugging, and regulatory compliance.

6.3.5 Business Process Integration

Generative AI offers very powerful AI capabilities to business leaders to improve decisions, accelerate innovations, and manage organizational changes effectively. Businesses adopted AI to strengthen change management and governance, but it is important to understand how GenAI is integrated into these existing business processes.

GenAI Integration in Change Management

GenAI is integrated into change management through a structured approach focused on augmenting, not replacing, employees.

- Introduction of AI into Existing Workflows

  GenAI enables organizations to gradually integrate AI into existing workflows, rather than replace them entirely. Businesses can embed AI copilots into dashboards, platforms, and workflow pipelines to elevate decision-making with smooth adaptation.

- Training Requirements by Role

  AI training must be given according to the employee's role in the organization to ensure effective use of AI. Managers learn to interpret AI recommendations for operational decisions, executives learn to apply AI insights for strategic planning, and individual contributors learn to work in collaboration with AI tools.

- Resistance Handling

  Organizations need to address and communicate the positioning of AI as an augmentation tool, not a human expertise replacement. Transparent communication helps in building trust and encourages adoption across teams.

- Success Measurement

  Leadership should showcase the benefits of AI efforts and continuously improve implementation techniques by keeping an eye on decision speed, forecast accuracy, operational efficiency, and staff productivity.

GenAI Integration in Governance

GenAI is integrated into the governance step-by-step approach to reduce risks and ensure alignment with ethical standards.

- Decision Rights (Who Can Override AI?)

  Clear governance is needed to distinguish the situations where AI can act autonomously and when human approval is required. Establishing decision rights ensures that high-risk decisions remain under human authority while allowing AI to automate routine processes.

- Escalation Paths

  Organizations must set up escalation paths for situations when AI recommendations are ambiguous, conflicting, or outside predefined thresholds to ensure sensitive and complex decisions are reviewed by experts.

- Audit Requirements

  Organizations can examine how results were produced by keeping track of AI inputs, suggestions, and decisions through audit trails. This openness promotes internal responsibility, legal compliance, and continuous improvement of AI system development.

- Risk Management

  GenAI governance frameworks include safeguards, including decision thresholds, data privacy measures, and bias detection. These systems assist companies in reducing risks while guaranteeing that AI-driven aligns with ethical, legal, and business standards.

6.4 Industry Applications

Generative AI supports high-value decisions across industries like financial services, healthcare, and media while balancing model intelligence, governance, and system integration. We will discuss a few reference design architectures to understand how technical, business, and integration teams implement GenAI in their respective industries.

6.4.1 Financial Services → Credit Decisions

GenAI-assisted credit decisions in financial services combine predictive models, generative reasoning, risk management, regulatory compliance, and explainability to support lending decisions.

- Technical Perspective

  Technical teams design a hybrid model architecture combining traditional credit risk models with generative AI RAG architectures. Key components of the hybrid model structure include feature engineering from financial histories, credit scores, income patterns, transaction behavior, and alternative data sources, predictive risk models, GenAI explainability for approvals or denials, and bias monitoring to ensure compliance with lending regulations.

- Business Perspective

  Business teams define the approval workflows, risk management, and regulatory compliance constraints. Executives define approval workflows by implementing human-in-the-loop systems to determine whether AI recommendations require human review. They need to explain every adverse action and portfolio risk management to maintain acceptable default rates. Businesses also focus on optimizing the customer experience by reducing loan approval times with GenAI.

- Integrated Approach

  The integration team implements GenAI across multiple steps, such as borrower information, business, and industry analysis, financial analysis, collateral evaluation, and the risk profile in the credit decision process, as described in the image below.

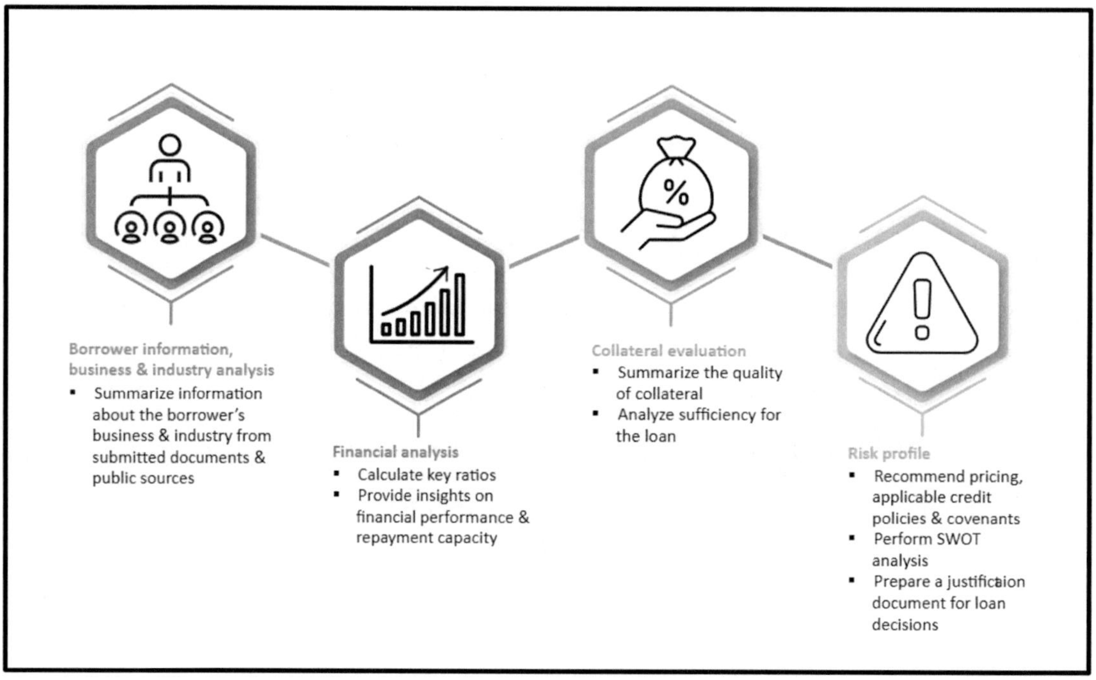

Figure 6-2. *GenAI for Automating Credit Decision Process*

6.4.2 Healthcare → Treatment Recommendations

GenAI is being implemented for treatment recommendations to provide accurate clinical insights that are trusted by physicians and patients. These recommendations must be compliant with healthcare regulations and seamlessly embedded into clinical workflows.

- Technical Perspective

  The technical team designs the GenAI architecture using RAG for treatment recommendations by integrating multiple clinical data sources and synthesizing the patient data. It recommends treatment options, highlights potential risks, and generates explanations and traceability to ensure physicians understand how recommendations were generated.

- Business Perspective

  Healthcare business leaders focus on ensuring that AI systems support clinical practice without replacing physician judgment. Successful adoption requires physician trust, clinical validation, and clear governance policies. Business teams also evaluate patient safety, regulatory compliance, and ethical standards, ensuring the AI system aligns with healthcare regulations and clinical best practices.

- Integrated Approach

  The integration team implements GenAI across multiple areas in the healthcare industry to meet technical and business perspectives, as described in the image below.

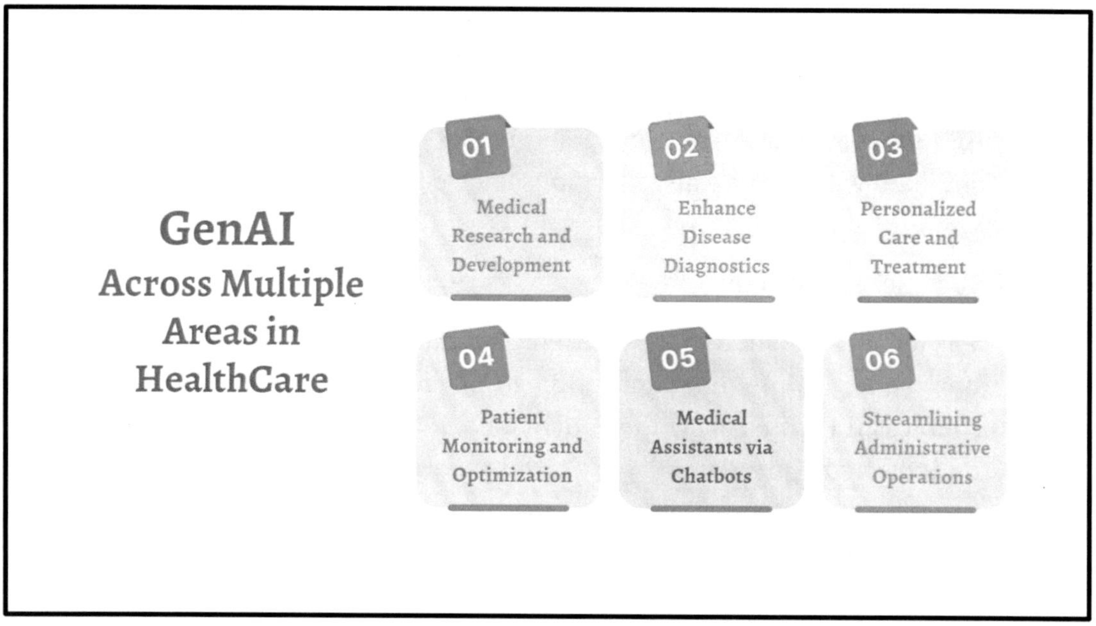

Figure 6-3. *Generative AI Across Healthcare*

6.4.3 Media → Content Recommendations

Generative AI is implemented for content recommendation using the RAG architecture that understands context and personalized algorithms to improve audience engagement at reduced cost while fitting seamlessly into existing media production and distribution systems.

- Technical Perspective

  The technical team designs the GenAI architecture that generates automated personalized content by leveraging user behavior data, viewing history, demographics, and engagement signals. In order to ensure consistent and contextually appropriate outputs, these models often make use of retrieval-based architectures to refer to current editorial guidelines, brand voice documents, and historical content archives.

- Business Perspective

  Business teams focus on maximizing audience engagement while controlling production costs. With GenAI, large volumes of content, including marketing materials, social media posts, and article drafts, can be created in less time based on defined editorial policies, brand guidelines, and quality standards, which are typically reviewed by human editors.

- Integrated Approach

  The integration team implements GenAI across multiple areas in the media and entertainment industry to create consistent and scalable content, as described in the image below.

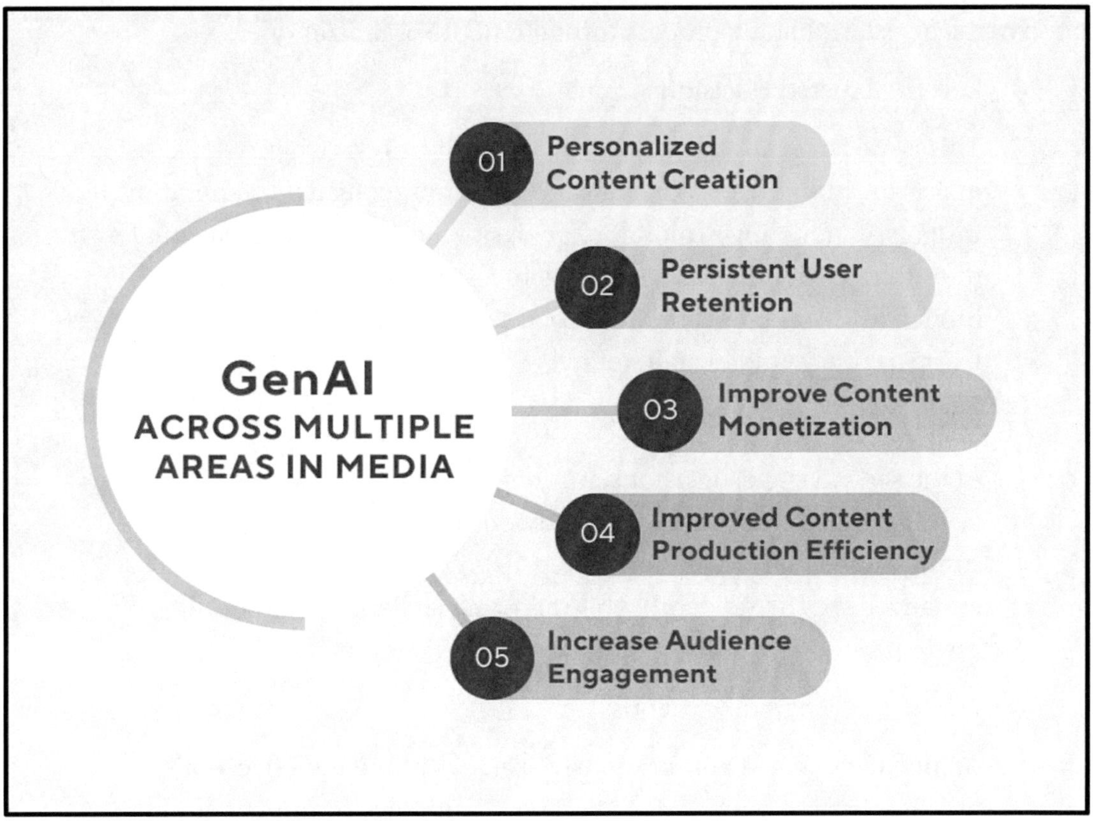

Figure 6-4. *Generative AI Across Media*

6.5 Strategic Patterns for Enterprise Adoption

Strategic patterns for enterprise adoption define how enterprises adopt GenAI from experimentation to an autonomous decision system at scale. GenAI models are deployed using deployment parameters, following governance rules to achieve faster decisions with better consistency and sustained value. Some factors, like regulatory compliance, human oversight, and perseverance, need to be taken into consideration while adopting GenAI copilots into workflows and allowing operational agents to work on strategic patterns.

6.5.1 The Maturity Model for GenAI in Decision Support

The maturity model for GenAI in decision support provides businesses with an organized path from early testing to complete, strategic integration, where AI highly improves the decision-making process throughout the organization.

- Level 1: Assisted Decisions

  This is the foundational stage of the maturity model where GenAI assists the human decision-makers by summarizing data, generating insights, conducting exploratory analysis, and answering contextual questions. GenAI acts as an intelligent assistant, which does not influence the outcome, reduces cognitive load, and also accounts for trust, accuracy, and explainability.

- Level 2: Augmented Decisions

  At the second stage, decisions are augmented by generative AI, keeping humans accountable. GenAI starts recommending options, simulating scenarios, planning, forecasting, and risk analysis with enhanced speed and depth while allowing leaders to validate all assumptions and apply judgment before execution.

- Level 3: Automated Decisions

  At this stage, GenAI autonomously executes predefined decisions within governed boundaries. Workflow routing, exception handling, pricing modifications, inventory restocking, and other decisions are made without human input. In order to ensure alignment with risk tolerance, legal standards, and business objectives, human control shifts to monitoring and policy definition.

- Level 4: Autonomous Planning Systems

  At this stage, GenAI becomes an autonomous planning system that generates, evaluates, and adapts multi-horizon plans continuously. Humans only supervise outcomes, not the processes. GenAI systems integrate forecasting, optimization, and reasoning engines to plan production, capital allocation, or portfolio strategies autonomously. This level represents a shift from decision support to machine-driven strategic orchestration.

6.5.2 Common Enterprise Deployment Patterns

Common enterprise deployment patterns are executive strategic approaches for introducing Copilot for strategy and planning, operational processes, and intelligent agents for operations with high availability and minimum risk. These deployment patterns cover a range of code deployment techniques, full or controlled rollout with phased releases.

- Executive Strategy Copilots

  Executive strategy copilots compile enterprise-wide data, including financial information, market signals, risks, and performance measures for strategic decision-making and work across silos. They produce strategic narratives, scenario analyses, and board-ready insights, and leaders can assess long-term strategy, capital allocation, and growth plans in real time.

- Line-of-Business Process Copilots

  Line-of-business copilots integrate GenAI straight into operational processes, including manufacturing, supply chain, finance, procurement, and human resources. They help in prioritizing decisions, planning, and handling exceptions. They expedite operational choices while adhering to company norms and KPIs by functioning inside domain-specific settings.

- Operational Intelligence Agents

  Operational intelligence agents continuously keep an eye on systems, spot irregularities, and make choices or suggestions instantly. To respond to deviations on their own, they integrate with MES, ERP, IoT platforms, and monitoring tools. These agents perform exceptionally well in settings like factories, logistics networks, and IT processes that demand speed, size, and consistency.

- AI-Driven PMO and Planning Hubs

  GenAI-powered PMOs manage enterprise initiatives by anticipating delivery risks, allocating resources optimally, and monitoring program dependencies. These planning hubs enable proactive oversight and quicker implementation of transformation projects by offering predictive information regarding budget overruns, timetable slippage, and strategic alignment.

6.5.3 Build Your Decision Framework

To successfully deploy generative AI in real-world scenarios, organizations need to build a joint decision framework where technical teams (architects, data scientists, engineers) and business stakeholders (leaders, managers, domain experts) collaborate to provide the solution that aligns with business goals while meeting technical feasibility, governance, and risk requirements. Follow the steps below to build the decision framework with measurable outcomes.

Step 1: Decision Type Classification

The first step is understanding the nature of the decision type and its classification, frequency, stakes, and reversibility.

- Classify whether the decision is strategic, tactical, or operational, as strategic and tactical decisions need to involve human expertise and others can be automated via AI.
- The next step is to identify the frequency of decision-making, as continuous decisions can be automated without any human intervention.

- Evaluate the stakes of incorrect decisions: high, medium, or low, as high-stakes decisions may require human oversight
- Determine whether the decision is easily reversible or difficult, as irreversible decisions typically require stronger governance and human approval.

Step 2: Technical Requirements

Technical teams assess whether the AI solution can support the decision in real-world scenarios or not.

- Determine whether the data source for structured and unstructured data is relevant and reliable or not.
- Define the latency requirement of the decision, as some decisions can tolerate batch processing, while others require real-time AI inference.
- Define acceptable accuracy thresholds for AI outputs, as high-impact decisions demand higher model accuracy.
- Identifying the expandability needs of the AI decisions for compliance, auditing, or user trust also influences model selection and system design.

Step 3: Business Requirements

Business stakeholders define organizational constraints and acceptance considerations.

- Evaluate the team's level of comfort with the adoption of AI-driven insights and provide the necessary training and pilot programs for the adoption.
- Industries must comply with governance regulations regarding data usage, fairness, and explainability.
- Determine the risk tolerance of autonomy AI systems, as high-risk environments require stronger governance and oversight.
- Assess the organizational change requirement to integrate AI into existing workflows and decision processes.

Step 4: Hybrid Decision Design

Most of the enterprise decisions involve hybrid human–AI collaboration rather than full automation.

- AI roles must be defined, such as data analysis, generating recommendations, detecting patterns, or automating routine decisions and operational tasks.
- Human roles must be defined, such as approving critical decisions, handling exceptions, and defining strategic objectives.
- Define how AI and humans will interact, such as AI copilots, dashboards, workflow tools, or automated alerts.
- Define clear rules for when humans can override AI recommendations, particularly in cases involving anomalies, ambiguity, uncertainty, or ethical considerations.

After completing the above steps, the organization will be able to produce actionable outcomes:

- A recommended technical architecture that includes data pipelines, AI models, integration layers, and governance controls
- An implementable road map outlining pilot programs, testing, scaling, and operational deployment
- A risk mitigation plan that has defined governance policies, human oversight mechanisms, and monitoring tools to manage AI-related risks
- Well-defined success metrics such as decision speed, accuracy improvements, operational efficiency, and user adoption rates

6.6 Architectural Considerations for GenAI-Based Decision Systems

GenAI-based decision systems require modular, scalable architectures that combine foundation models, enterprise data, and reasoning layers. Key considerations include integrating structured and unstructured data, grounding outputs through RAG, enabling agent-based orchestration, and implementing feedback loops for continuous learning. Robust governance, security, auditability, and human-in-the-loop controls are essential to ensure trustworthy, compliant, and resilient decision-making at enterprise scale.

- Essential Building Blocks (LLMs, Vector Stores, RAG, Agents)

  Essential building blocks for GenAI decision systems are LLMs, vector databases, Retrieval-Augmented Generation (RAG), and agent frameworks.

  LLMs manage reasoning and generation, while vector databases provide semantic retrieval. RAG grounds outputs in enterprise knowledge, and agents coordinate multi-step decision workflows across tools and systems.

- Integrating Structured + Unstructured Data

  Effective decision intelligence requires a combination of structured (ERP, CRM, spreadsheets, financials) and unstructured data (images, documents, emails, logs, reports, social media data). GenAI can reason holistically across operational, financial, and contextual information via modern architectures that integrate diverse data types through embeddings, metadata enrichment, and schema alignment.

- Feedback Loops and Continuous Learning

  The GenAI decision system is a continuous learning process through closed-loop feedback mechanisms that capture performance, outcomes, and corrections. Prompt tuning, retrieval optimization, policy improvement, and model retraining are all influenced by these feedback loops. Decisions continue to evolve in response to shifts in market dynamics, business situations, and regulatory needs.

- Safety, Governance, Auditability, and Risk Controls

  Guardrails such as content filters, policy engines, access restrictions, and decision boundaries are integrated into enterprise structures. Audit logs, explainability layers, and traceable data lineage ensure compliance and accountability. Governance frameworks specify where automation is permitted, how risks are reduced, and how decisions made by GenAI can be examined and contested.

- Human-in-the-Loop Systems for Critical Decisions

  GenAI architectures implement a human-in-the-loop control system for critical decisions. This works in a hybrid model where AI proposes actions and humans approve, override, or refine the outcomes to balance scale and speed. This approach works in domains like finance, healthcare, and safety-critical operations where trust, ethical judgment, and regulatory compliance are essential.

6.7 Organizational Transformation for AI-Driven Strategy

Organization transformation is the critical enabler to extract maximum benefits from the GenAI-driven strategy. This involves not only technological changes but also learning new skills, redesigning roles, adopting hybrid operating models, and incorporating governance rules to embed GenAI into everyday decision-making.

The teams of the organizations need to evolve from traditional analysts to AI strategists who can supervise, contextualize, and validate AI-generated insights. To meet the corporate objectives and to implement autonomous decision-making workflows and models, new positions in teams like AI planners, prompt engineers, and agent designers need to be fulfilled.

Most organizations implement hybrid operating models that combine AI governance and a Center of Excellence across business units for better productivity. Decision-centric KPI frameworks, ROI, training, and organizational change ensure accelerating and sustainable adoption and measuring various value parameters.

6.7.1 What Teams Need to Change

For the implementation of GenAI, teams need to proactively change from a traditional approach to an AI-driven approach and develop the skills and train for the new roles.

- From Analysts to "AI-Enabled Strategists"

  Organizational teams must shift from traditional analysts working with Excel and dashboards reporting to a supervisor for validation to AI-enabled strategists. AI-enabled strategists use AI literacy with domain expertise for framing the right questions, simulating multi-scenario outputs, and translating GenAI suggestions into strategic actions.

- New Roles: AI Planners, Prompt Engineers, and Agent Designers

  As the industry grows and adopts new technology, new skills and new roles need to be defined, and training is needed to produce reliable and goal-aligned decisions at scale. For operationalizing GenAI in enterprises, specialized roles are introduced, like AI planners, Prompt engineers, and agent designers. AI planners plan and align models with business objectives. Prompt engineers optimize quality reasoning and interaction, and agent designers build autonomous workflows using tools and applications.

6.7.2 Operating Models for GenAI Deployment

The three main operating models for GenAI deployment are centralized, decentralized, and federated, which are implemented to balance agility, governance, and compliance, to achieve a Center of Excellence for decision intelligence.

- Centralized vs. Federated AI Teams

  There are two approaches for teams to work on operating models for GenAI deployments: centralized teams or federated AI teams. Centralized teams ensure efficiency and consistency and follow governance effectively, while federated AI teams empower various business units to innovate and act quickly. Many enterprises work on a hybrid approach where core platforms and governance are handled by centralized teams while federated domain teams work on local decision-making workflows to customize copilots and agents.

- Centers of Excellence for Decision Intelligence

  Centers of Excellence (COEs) for decision intelligence define standards, evaluation metrics, reusable components, and best practices to adopt GenAI to achieve excellence. It accelerates enterprise scaling by sharing architecture, governance models, and use cases while preventing duplicative or fragmented AI implementations.

- AI Governance, Guardrails, and Compliance Frameworks

  Strong AI governance frameworks set decision boundaries, thresholds for risk-taking, accountability, and auditability. Guardrails ensure that rules, regulations, moral principles, and all data policies are followed. Scaling GenAI in regulated, high-impact strategic and operational decision environments requires these controls.

6.7.3 Measuring Value and Accelerating Adoption

Measuring the value of generative AI and accelerating its adoption requires a holistic, strategic framework that moves beyond immediate productivity metrics to encompass long-term transformation, strategic KPIs, improvement planning, customer value, and responsible change management.

- KPI Frameworks

  Enterprises must track both operational and strategic KPIs like forecast accuracy, plan stability, exception rates, decision cycle times, and adoption metrics. Tracking these KPIs quantifies how GenAI improves the enterprise performance, efficiency, ROI, sales, decision quality, time-to-market, adaptability to change, and consistency across domains and supply chains.

- ROI for Planning Improvements

  The practical results of ROI measurement for improvement in planning include shorter planning times, better resource allocation, decreased risk exposure, and quicker reaction to market shifts. Leaders can verify the business impact of AI-driven planning by comparing it to baseline traditional methods using scenario simulation and can make a quick decision.

- Playbooks, Training Paths, and Change Management

  Role-based training, organized playbooks, and ongoing change management all accelerate the GenAI adoption process. To guarantee that teams trust and utilize GenAI-powered decision systems efficiently, organizations must make investments in AI literacy, practical experimentation, and cultural alignment.

6.8 Future Vision: AI As the Enterprise's Strategic Brain

GenAI is evolving from enterprise decision-making to a strategic brain that continuously senses signals, context, updates, reasoning, and accordingly coordinates actions across the organization. AI will simulate strategies, optimize results in real time, and align execution across departments using the power of generative models, agents, and digital twins. Humans and AI will work in collaborative mode to establish self-optimized enterprises that are more intelligent, adaptive, and resilient. While AI manages scale, speed, and complexity, humans will establish intent, ethics, and restrictions, and together they will focus on long-term value creation.

- Self-Optimizing Enterprises

  Businesses will function as self-optimizing systems in the future, with GenAI continuously sensing external and internal signals, simulating results, and making near-real-time strategy adjustments. These companies improve resilience, efficiency, and competitive responsiveness while lowering human latency through dynamic rebalancing of resources, pricing, supply chains, and operations.

- AI Planning Agents Coordinating Across Departments

  AI planning agents will function as independent coordinators in the areas of sales, operations, supply chain, finance, and human resources. These agents use the shared company environment to mediate disputes, negotiate trade-offs, and match local choices with global goals. Humans take on supervisory responsibilities, confirming objectives, limitations, and moral limits.

- Enterprise Digital Twins Folding into GenAI Reasoning

  GenAI reasoning loops will directly incorporate enterprise digital twins, which reflect assets, organizational structures, and processes. This increases decision confidence by allowing AI to evaluate strategies in simulated situations before execution. Digital twins develop into living knowledge substrates that use feedback from the actual world to continuously upgrade GenAI models.

- Regulatory, Ethical, and Societal Implications

  As AI develops into a strategic decision-maker, accountability, transparency, and governance become critical. Businesses need to handle sovereignty, explainability, bias, and regulatory compliance. To preserve trust, avoid unforeseen effects, and match AI-driven decisions with organizational and societal ideals, ethical frameworks and human oversight will be crucial.

6.9 Summary and Closing Reflections

- Key Takeaways

  Generative AI-driven decision-making is transforming how enterprises analyze complex scenarios, understand context with reasoning, incorporate changes and trends, and execute plans as a true decision partner.

  GenAI helps in forecasting, accelerates performance, augments experts' knowledge, and delivers value in various sectors like finance, healthcare, banking, manufacturing, automotive, media, and entertainment. Strategic planning, robust architecture, mature deployment, and organizational transformation are all necessary for successful AI-driven decision-making.

- The Path Forward for Enterprises

  GenAI operates in a hybrid mode and has now become central to enterprise decision-making, focusing on scalability, expandability, and innovation across industries. Below are some facts and the path forward for GenAI-powered decision intelligence platforms across industries.

  - According to the AIM Media House report, in the finance sector, currently 47% of GenAI has been adopted and 53% is planned for adoption within the next year.

- Approximately 50% of organizations have built GenAI-powered platforms in-house, and approximately 37% still depend on the traditional dashboard-based decision-making system.
- About 33% of the enterprises' supply chain functions are currently using GenAI platforms, with 67% planning to adopt GenAI to scale at inventory planning and risk analytics.
- Major roadblocks for GenAI scalability at enterprises are data silos, an inconsistent data landscape, and tech maturity.
- GenAI is also starting to be adopted for customer service, operations, and sales by organizations, and many more advancements are yet to be implemented in the years to come.

6.10 References

1. The Executive Guide to Artificial Intelligence for Strategic Leadership and Innovation. `http://oxfordcentre.uk/resources/artificial-intelligence/the-executive-guide-to-artificial-intelligence-for-strategic-leadership-and-innovation/`
2. How AI is transforming strategy development. `https://www.mckinsey.com/capabilities/strategy-and-corporate-finance/our-insights/how-ai-is-transforming-strategy-development`
3. Generative AI for decision-making: A multidisciplinary perspective. `https://www.sciencedirect.com/science/article/pii/S2444569X25000964`
4. Agentic Retrieval-Augmented Generation. `https://arxiv.org/pdf/2501.09136`
5. Generative AI in Health Systems. `https://www.nature.com/collections/gebbdegeje`

6. Harnessing gen AI in financial services. https://www.deloitte.com/us/en/insights/industry/financial-services/generative-ai-financial-services-pioneers.html

7. AWS for Manufacturing. https://aws.amazon.com/manufacturing/

8. Redefining Auto Innovation With AI and Digitalization. https://www.nvidia.com/en-in/industries/automotive/

9. Generative AI for the media and entertainment industry. https://www.pwc.com/us/en/technology/alliances/library/microsoft-gen-ai-media-entertainment.html

10. AIM Media House Report. https://aimmediahouse.com/generative-ai/report-assessing-the-need-of-genai-powered-decision-intelligence-platforms

11. Why financial institutions must adopt GenAI in commercial lending. https://www.tcs.com/what-we-do/industries/banking/white-paper/adopting-generative-ai-commercial-lending

12. Generative AI (Gen AI) in Healthcare. https://www.latentview.com/blog/generative-ai-in-healthcare/

13. How Generative AI in Media Is Transforming Monetization Strategies? https://www.tredence.com/blog/generative-ai-in-media

CHAPTER 7

Customer Experience Transformation Through Personalization

The evolution of customer experience has reached an inflection point where generative AI enables unprecedented levels of personalization at scale. Organizations across industries are discovering that the combination of traditional machine learning techniques with generative AI capabilities creates transformative opportunities to understand, predict, and respond to individual customer needs in real time. This chapter explores how businesses are leveraging these technologies to fundamentally reimagine customer interactions, moving beyond segment-based approaches to truly individualized experiences that drive both customer satisfaction and business outcomes.

The promise of personalization is not new. For decades, companies have attempted to tailor experiences to individual preferences, from simple product recommendations to customized marketing messages. However, previous approaches were constrained by technological limitations, data silos, and the inability to process and act on information at the speed and scale required for meaningful personalization. Generative AI, combined with advances in real-time data processing and machine learning, has removed these constraints, enabling a new paradigm where every customer interaction can be uniquely crafted to maximize value for both the customer and the organization.

This transformation extends far beyond marketing and sales. Personalization powered by generative AI is reshaping product development, customer service, pricing strategies, and even the fundamental business models of leading organizations. Companies that master these capabilities are creating sustainable competitive advantages, while those that lag risk becoming commoditized in markets where customers increasingly expect experiences tailored to their specific needs, contexts, and preferences.

N. Sendas et al., *Building Generative AI Solutions for Industries with AWS*,
https://doi.org/10.1007/979-8-8688-2830-0_7

7.1 The Business Case for AI-Driven Personalization

The economic imperative for personalization has never been stronger. Research across industries demonstrates that personalized experiences drive measurable improvements in key business metrics. In retail, personalized product recommendations can increase conversion rates by 20–30% while reducing customer acquisition costs by up to 50%. Financial services institutions implementing personalized advisory services report 15–25% increases in assets under management and significant improvements in customer lifetime value. Healthcare organizations using personalized patient engagement strategies see 30–40% improvements in treatment adherence and patient satisfaction scores.

These improvements stem from fundamental shifts in how customers interact with organizations. Personalization reduces friction in the customer journey by anticipating needs, streamlining decision-making, and presenting relevant options at the right time. This efficiency translates directly to business value through increased conversion rates, higher average order values, and improved customer retention. In automotive, personalized vehicle configuration and financing recommendations increase purchase completion rates by 25–35% while reducing the time from initial interest to purchase decision.

Beyond immediate transaction metrics, personalization creates compounding value through enhanced customer relationships. Customers who experience consistently relevant, personalized interactions develop stronger brand affinity and become advocates, driving organic growth through referrals and positive word-of-mouth. Manufacturing companies using personalized B2B portals report 40–50% increases in repeat purchase rates and significant expansion of wallet share as customers consolidate suppliers in favor of those providing superior personalized experiences.

The cost structure of personalization has fundamentally changed with generative AI. Traditional personalization required extensive manual segmentation, content creation, and campaign management, limiting its application to high-value customer segments or specific touchpoints. Generative AI enables automated creation of personalized content, recommendations, and interactions at marginal cost, making comprehensive personalization economically viable across entire customer bases. This democratization of personalization capabilities is particularly transformative for mid-market companies that previously lacked resources to compete with larger competitors on customer experience.

However, realizing these benefits requires more than technology deployment. Organizations must develop new capabilities in data management, algorithm development, content operations, and organizational alignment. The most successful implementations treat personalization as a strategic capability requiring sustained investment and continuous optimization rather than a one-time technology project. Companies that approach personalization with this mindset consistently outperform competitors, achieving 2–3× higher returns on their customer experience investments.

7.2 Machine Learning Foundations for Personalization

Effective personalization systems rely on multiple machine learning techniques working in concert to understand customer behavior, predict preferences, and generate appropriate responses. Collaborative filtering remains foundational, identifying patterns across customer populations to recommend products, content, or actions based on similarities between users. In retail, collaborative filtering powers product recommendation engines that analyze purchase histories and browsing behaviors across millions of customers to identify relevant suggestions. Financial services firms use collaborative filtering to recommend investment products and banking services based on patterns observed in customers with similar financial profiles and goals.

Content-based filtering complements collaborative approaches by analyzing the attributes of items and matching them to customer preferences. This technique proves particularly valuable in domains with rich item metadata, such as automotive configurations where vehicles can be characterized across hundreds of dimensions including performance specifications, features, styling elements, and price points. Healthcare applications use content-based filtering to match patients with relevant educational content, treatment options, and care providers based on detailed medical histories and condition-specific attributes.

Deep learning architectures have dramatically expanded the sophistication of personalization systems. Recurrent neural networks and transformer models capture sequential patterns in customer behavior, enabling the prediction of next actions, optimal timing for interventions, and likely responses to different engagement strategies. Manufacturing companies use these models to predict equipment maintenance needs and automatically personalize service recommendations based on usage patterns, operating conditions, and historical maintenance data. The ability to process long sequences of interactions enables these systems to identify subtle patterns that simpler models miss.

Reinforcement learning represents a paradigm shift in how personalization systems learn and optimize. Rather than training on historical data alone, reinforcement learning agents continuously experiment with different personalization strategies and learn from the outcomes. This approach proves particularly powerful in dynamic environments where customer preferences evolve rapidly or where the optimal strategy depends on complex contextual factors. Retail applications use reinforcement learning to optimize promotional strategies, learning which offers to present to which customers at which times to maximize both short-term conversion and long-term customer value.

Generative AI adds a new dimension to these foundational techniques by enabling the creation of personalized content, recommendations, and interactions that go beyond selecting from predefined options. Large language models can generate personalized product descriptions, email content, and conversational responses tailored to individual customer preferences, communication styles, and contexts. In financial services, generative models create personalized investment summaries and market commentary that explain complex information in terms relevant to each customer's portfolio, risk tolerance, and financial goals. This capability to generate rather than merely select personalized content dramatically expands the scope and sophistication of personalization strategies.

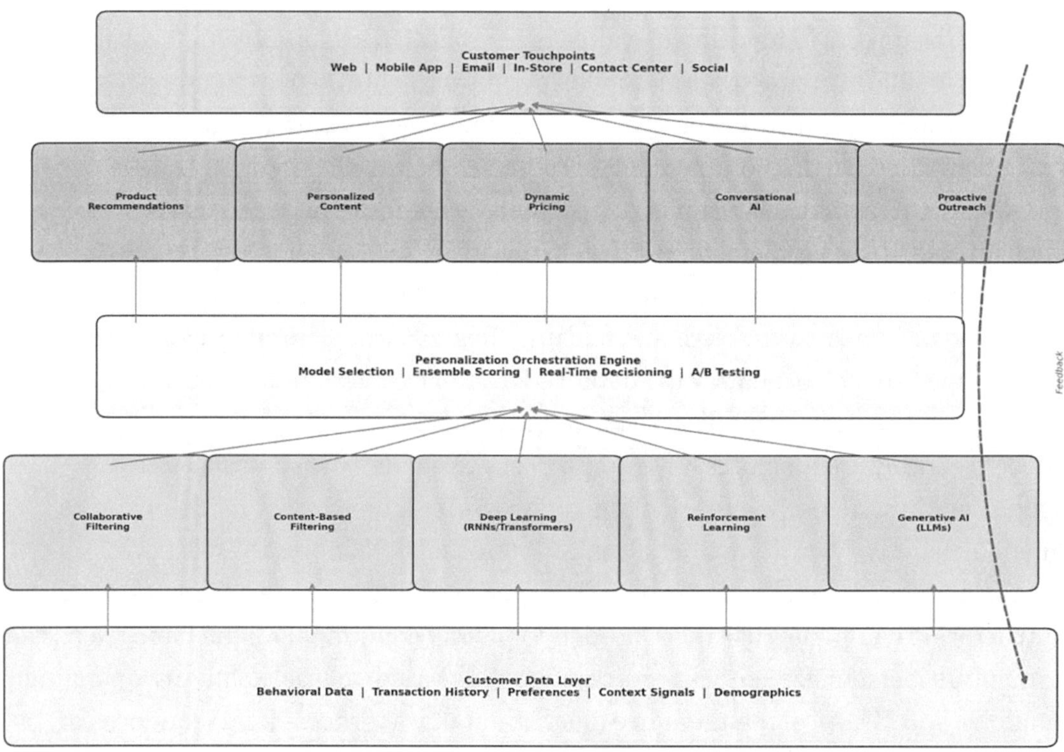

Figure 7-1. *Integrated AI personalization system architecture showing the integration of collaborative filtering, content-based filtering, deep learning, reinforcement learning, and generative AI with data flows between components*

7.3 Real-Time Personalization Systems Architecture

Implementing personalization at scale requires sophisticated technical architectures capable of processing vast amounts of data, executing complex models, and delivering personalized experiences with minimal latency. Modern personalization systems typically employ a multi-tier architecture that separates data ingestion, feature engineering, model serving, and experience delivery into specialized components optimized for their specific functions.

The data ingestion layer captures customer interactions across all touchpoints in real time, streaming events from web applications, mobile apps, point-of-sale systems, customer service platforms, and IoT devices into a unified data pipeline. In retail, this might include browsing behavior, search queries, product views, cart additions, purchases, and customer service interactions. Automotive manufacturers capture vehicle telemetry, service appointments, dealer interactions, and digital engagement across owned and third-party platforms. Healthcare systems integrate electronic health records, patient portal interactions, appointment scheduling, and remote monitoring data.

Feature engineering transforms raw event streams into meaningful signals that personalization models can consume. This layer performs real-time aggregations, calculates derived metrics, and maintains customer state representations that capture both historical patterns and current context. Advanced implementations use feature stores that provide consistent feature definitions across training and serving environments while enabling efficient feature computation and retrieval. Manufacturing B2B platforms maintain features representing customer ordering patterns, inventory levels, production schedules, and supply chain status to enable personalized recommendations for reordering, alternative products, and delivery options.

The model serving layer hosts trained machine learning models and provides low-latency inference capabilities. Modern architectures employ model serving platforms that support multiple model types, enable A/B testing and gradual rollouts, and provide monitoring and observability. Financial services implementations often maintain dozens or hundreds of specialized models for different personalization tasks, customer segments, and product categories, requiring sophisticated orchestration to determine which models to invoke for each customer interaction and how to combine their outputs into coherent personalization decisions.

Experience delivery systems consume model predictions and generate personalized user interfaces, content, and interactions. This layer integrates with content management systems, recommendation engines, and customer engagement platforms to render personalized experiences across channels. Generative AI components in this layer create dynamic content, personalized messaging, and conversational interactions that adapt to individual customer needs. Healthcare patient portals use this architecture to generate personalized health dashboards, educational content, and care recommendations that update in real time as new data becomes available.

Latency requirements drive critical architectural decisions. Many personalization use cases require sub-100 millisecond response times to avoid degrading user experience. Achieving this performance at scale requires careful optimization of data access patterns, model complexity, and infrastructure deployment. Edge computing and content delivery networks enable personalization decisions to be made closer to end users, reducing network latency. Model optimization techniques including quantization, pruning, and knowledge distillation reduce inference time while maintaining prediction quality. Caching strategies balance personalization freshness with computational efficiency.

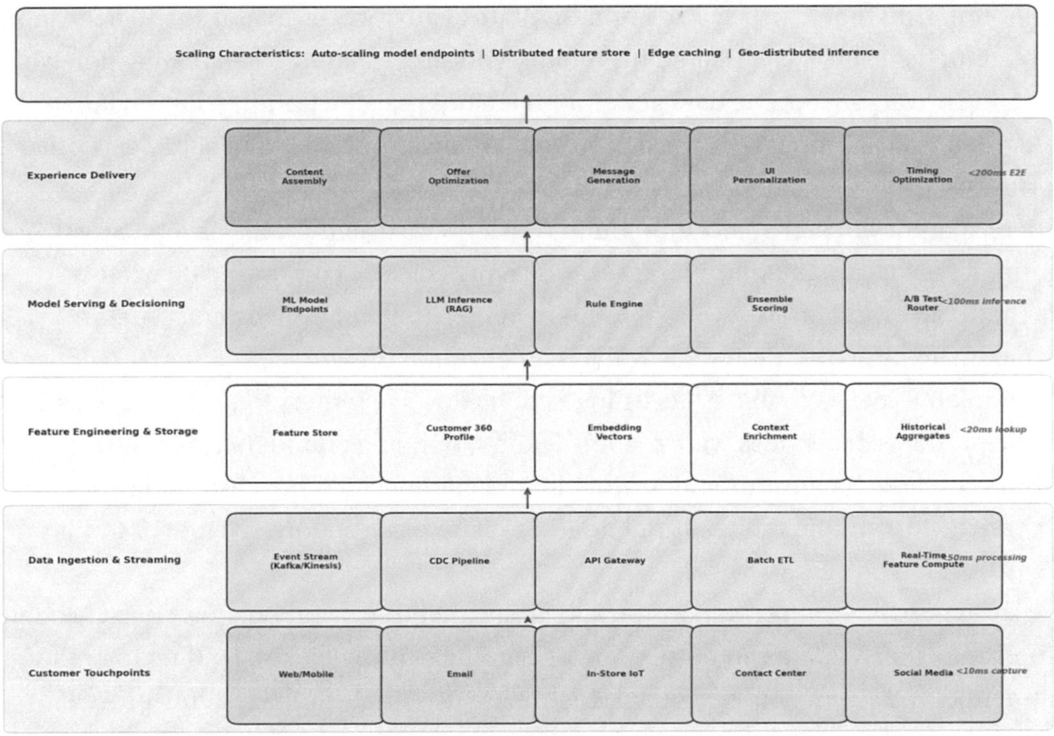

***Figure 7-2.** Real-time personalization systems architecture showing data flow from customer touchpoints through ingestion, feature engineering, model serving, and experience delivery layers with latency requirements*

7.4 Privacy, Ethics, and Responsible Personalization

The power of AI-driven personalization brings significant responsibilities regarding customer privacy, data protection, and ethical use of personal information. Organizations must navigate complex regulatory requirements while building customer trust through transparent and responsible personalization practices. The regulatory landscape continues to evolve, with frameworks like GDPR in Europe, CCPA in California, and sector-specific regulations in healthcare and financial services establishing strict requirements for data collection, processing, and use.

Privacy-preserving personalization techniques enable organizations to deliver relevant experiences while minimizing data collection and retention. Federated learning allows models to be trained on distributed data without centralizing sensitive information, particularly valuable in healthcare where patient data privacy is paramount. Differential privacy adds mathematical guarantees that individual customer data cannot be reverse-engineered from model outputs, enabling personalization while protecting privacy. Synthetic data generation creates realistic training datasets that preserve statistical properties of real customer data without exposing actual customer information.

Transparency in personalization builds customer trust and satisfies regulatory requirements for explainability. Organizations must clearly communicate what data they collect and how they use it for personalization and provide customers meaningful control over their data and personalization preferences. Financial services firms implement explainable AI techniques that allow customers to understand why specific products or services were recommended, building confidence in AI-driven advisory services. Retail companies provide transparency into how browsing and purchase history influences recommendations, with clear options to reset or modify personalization profiles.

Bias in personalization systems poses significant ethical and business risks. Models trained on historical data can perpetuate or amplify existing biases, leading to unfair treatment of certain customer groups. Healthcare personalization systems must carefully monitor for biases that could result in disparate care recommendations across demographic groups. Financial services institutions implement rigorous bias testing to ensure lending recommendations and credit decisions don't discriminate based on protected characteristics. Automotive companies test personalization algorithms to verify they don't systematically disadvantage certain customer segments in pricing or product recommendations.

Consent management has become increasingly sophisticated as regulations require granular control over data use. Modern personalization platforms implement consent management systems that track customer preferences across multiple dimensions, including data collection, processing purposes, and sharing with third parties. These systems must operate in real time, immediately reflecting customer choices in personalization behavior. Manufacturing B2B platforms provide enterprise customers with detailed control over what operational data can be used for personalization vs. what must remain confidential for competitive reasons.

The right to be forgotten and data portability requirements necessitate careful data architecture and governance. Organizations must be able to completely remove customer data from personalization systems upon request while maintaining system functionality. Data portability requirements mean customers can export their personalization profiles and potentially transfer them to competitors. These capabilities require thoughtful system design that separates customer data from model parameters and maintains clear data lineage.

Ethical considerations extend beyond regulatory compliance to questions of manipulation and customer autonomy. Personalization systems optimized purely for business metrics might employ dark patterns or manipulative techniques that undermine customer agency. Leading organizations establish ethical guidelines for personalization that balance business objectives with customer welfare, avoiding practices that exploit psychological vulnerabilities or create harmful dependencies. Healthcare providers, in particular, must ensure personalization supports patient health outcomes rather than maximizing engagement metrics that might not align with patient well-being.

7.5 Organizational Transformation for Personalization Excellence

Successful personalization requires fundamental changes in organizational structure, processes, and culture. Traditional functional silos between marketing, product, technology, and customer service create barriers to delivering cohesive personalized experiences. Leading organizations restructure around customer journeys, creating cross-functional teams with shared accountability for personalization outcomes across touchpoints.

Data democratization enables personalization at scale by providing teams across the organization access to customer insights and personalization capabilities. Self-service analytics platforms allow marketers, product managers, and customer service representatives to understand customer behavior and test personalization strategies without depending on centralized data science teams. Retail organizations implement experimentation platforms that enable store operations teams to test localized personalization strategies while maintaining consistency with enterprise-wide approaches. Financial services firms provide relationship managers with AI-powered tools that surface personalized insights and recommendations during customer interactions.

Skill development represents a critical investment for personalization success. Organizations need talent that combines domain expertise with data literacy and AI understanding. Training programs help existing employees develop capabilities in data analysis, experimentation design, and AI-assisted decision-making. Manufacturing companies train sales and customer success teams to leverage personalization tools effectively, understanding both the technical capabilities and limitations of AI-driven recommendations. Healthcare organizations develop programs that help clinicians integrate personalized care recommendations into their practice while maintaining clinical judgment and patient relationships.

Governance frameworks balance innovation with risk management in personalization initiatives. Clear policies define acceptable uses of customer data, establish approval processes for new personalization use cases, and specify monitoring requirements for deployed systems. Cross-functional governance committees review personalization strategies for alignment with brand values, regulatory requirements, and ethical standards. Automotive manufacturers implement governance processes that ensure personalization in safety-critical systems like driver assistance features meets rigorous validation requirements.

Measurement and accountability systems align organizational incentives with personalization objectives. Traditional metrics focused on channel-specific performance often create conflicts between optimizing individual touchpoints and delivering cohesive customer experiences. Leading organizations implement customer-centric metrics that measure personalization effectiveness across the entire journey, with shared accountability across teams. Financial services institutions track metrics like personalized advice acceptance rates, customer financial outcomes, and relationship depth rather than just product sales in individual channels.

Change management proves critical as personalization transforms how organizations interact with customers. Employees accustomed to standardized processes and mass marketing approaches must adapt to dynamic, individualized customer engagement. Clear communication about personalization strategy, comprehensive training, and visible leadership support help organizations navigate this transition. Retail companies that successfully implement personalization at scale invest heavily in change management, ensuring store associates understand how personalization enhances rather than replaces their customer relationships.

Cultural transformation toward experimentation and continuous learning underpins sustainable personalization excellence. Organizations must embrace testing, accept that not all personalization strategies will succeed, and systematically learn from both successes and failures. This requires psychological safety where teams feel comfortable proposing and testing new approaches without fear of failure. Manufacturing companies foster experimentation cultures by celebrating learning from failed personalization tests as much as successful ones, recognizing that systematic experimentation drives long-term improvement.

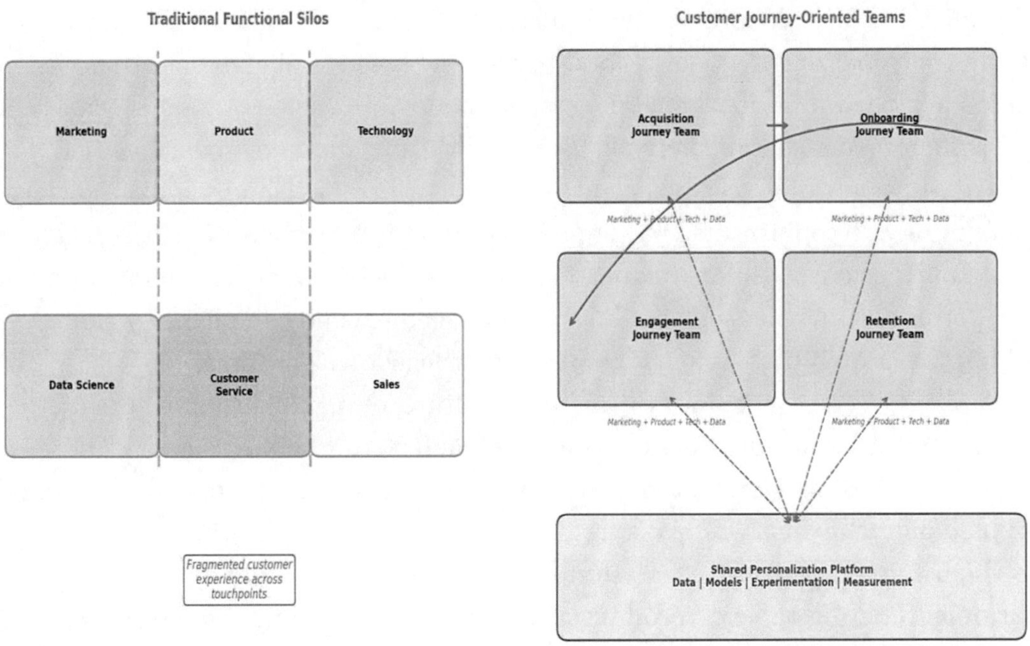

Figure 7-3. *Organizational structure comparison: traditional functional silos versus customer journey-oriented cross-functional teams enabling cohesive personalization*

7.6 Technology Stack and Platform Decisions

Building effective personalization capabilities requires assembling a technology stack that balances capability, integration, and total cost of ownership. Organizations face build-vs.-buy decisions across multiple layers of the personalization architecture, from data infrastructure through model development to experience delivery. These decisions significantly impact time-to-value, flexibility, and long-term scalability.

Customer data platforms (CDPs) have emerged as foundational infrastructure for personalization, providing unified customer profiles that integrate data from disparate sources. CDPs handle identity resolution, matching customer interactions across devices and channels to create comprehensive views of individual behavior. Retail implementations integrate point-of-sale data, ecommerce transactions, mobile app usage, and loyalty program activity into unified profiles that power personalization across all channels. Healthcare CDPs face additional complexity in integrating clinical data from electronic health records with patient engagement data from portals and mobile applications while maintaining HIPAA compliance.

Machine learning platforms provide infrastructure for developing, training, and deploying personalization models. Cloud-based ML platforms offer managed services for common personalization tasks including recommendation engines, propensity modeling, and customer segmentation. These platforms reduce infrastructure management overhead while providing scalability and integration with other cloud services. However, organizations with sophisticated requirements or unique personalization use cases may need to build custom ML infrastructure. Financial services firms often develop proprietary ML platforms that integrate with existing risk management and compliance systems while providing the flexibility to implement novel personalization algorithms.

Feature stores have become critical infrastructure for personalization at scale, providing consistent feature definitions and efficient feature serving across training and inference. Feature stores solve the training-serving skew problem where features computed differently in training vs. production lead to model performance degradation. Manufacturing companies use feature stores to maintain consistent representations of customer ordering patterns, product specifications, and supply chain status across multiple personalization models and applications.

Experimentation platforms enable systematic testing of personalization strategies through A/B testing and multi-armed bandit approaches. These platforms handle traffic allocation, statistical analysis, and result reporting while integrating with personalization systems to enable rapid iteration. Automotive manufacturers use experimentation platforms to test personalization strategies across digital channels, dealer interactions, and in-vehicle experiences, measuring impact on customer satisfaction and purchase behavior.

Real-time decisioning engines orchestrate personalization across touchpoints, determining what content, offers, or recommendations to present based on current context and customer state. These engines integrate with multiple data sources and ML models, applying business rules and constraints while optimizing for specified objectives. Retail decisioning engines balance multiple goals including revenue maximization, inventory management, and customer experience, making real-time trade-offs based on current business priorities.

Generative AI platforms provide capabilities for creating personalized content, conversational interactions, and dynamic experiences. Organizations must decide whether to use general-purpose large language models through APIs, fine-tune models on proprietary data, or develop specialized models for specific personalization tasks. Financial services firms often fine-tune models on historical customer communications and financial content to generate personalized investment commentary and advice that maintains appropriate tone and regulatory compliance.

Integration architecture determines how personalization capabilities connect with existing systems including CRM platforms, marketing automation tools, content management systems, and customer service applications. API-first architectures enable flexible integration while maintaining separation of concerns between personalization logic and channel-specific delivery. Healthcare organizations implement integration layers that enable personalization systems to interact with electronic health records, appointment scheduling systems, and patient communication platforms while maintaining appropriate security and privacy controls.

Observability and monitoring infrastructure provides visibility into personalization system performance, model behavior, and business impact. Comprehensive monitoring tracks technical metrics like latency and error rates alongside business metrics including conversion rates, customer satisfaction, and revenue impact. Anomaly detection identifies when personalization systems behave unexpectedly, triggering alerts and potentially automatic rollbacks. Manufacturing B2B platforms implement monitoring that tracks both system performance and business outcomes, enabling rapid identification and resolution of issues affecting customer experience.

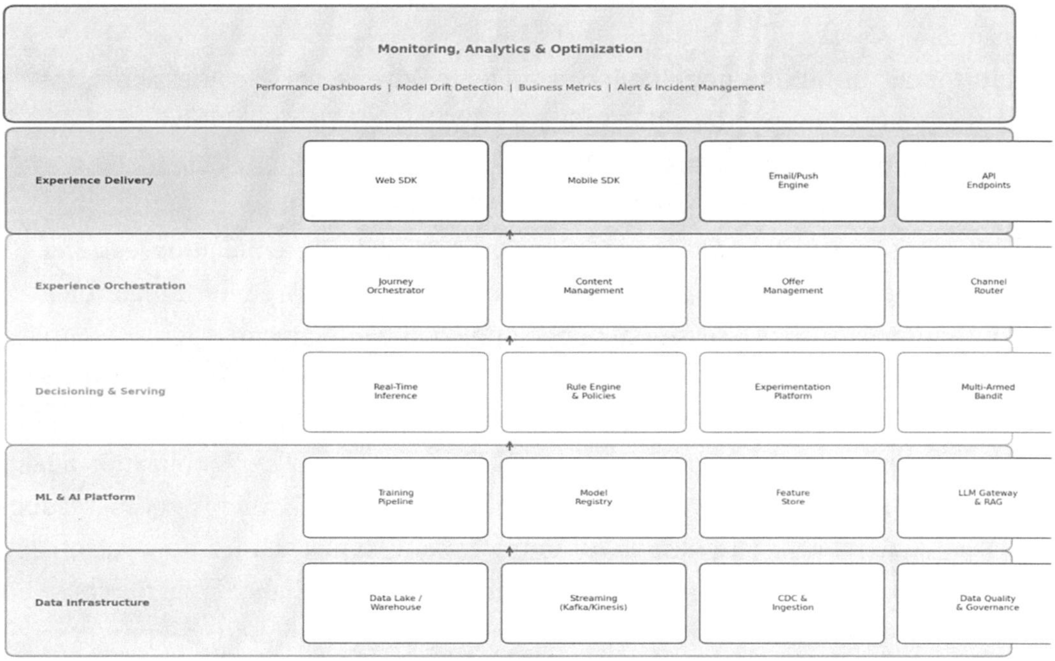

Figure 7-4. *Personalization technology stack showing layers from data infrastructure through ML platforms, feature stores, decisioning engines, and experience delivery with integration points*

7.7 Measurement, Optimization, and ROI

Demonstrating and maximizing return on investment from personalization requires sophisticated measurement frameworks that connect personalization activities to business outcomes. Traditional attribution models often fail to capture the full impact of personalization, which influences customer behavior across multiple touchpoints and time horizons. Organizations must develop measurement approaches that account for both immediate conversion impact and longer-term effects on customer relationships and lifetime value.

Incrementality testing provides rigorous measurement of personalization impact by comparing outcomes for customers receiving personalized experiences against control groups receiving non-personalized alternatives. Retail companies use incrementality testing to measure how personalized product recommendations affect not just immediate purchases but also subsequent shopping behavior, basket composition, and customer retention. These tests reveal that personalization often drives value through multiple mechanisms, including increased purchase frequency, higher average order values, and reduced churn, with total impact significantly exceeding immediate conversion lift.

Multi-touch attribution models allocate credit for customer outcomes across the various personalized interactions that influenced behavior. Financial services firms implement attribution models that recognize how personalized email campaigns, website experiences, and advisor interactions collectively contribute to product adoption and asset growth. Advanced attribution approaches use machine learning to learn contribution patterns from data rather than relying on predetermined rules, providing a more accurate assessment of personalization effectiveness across complex customer journeys.

Customer lifetime value (CLV) modeling connects personalization investments to long-term customer value creation. Organizations measure how personalization affects CLV through multiple pathways including increased retention, higher spending, reduced service costs, and referral generation. Automotive manufacturers track how personalized vehicle shopping experiences and ownership support affect not just initial purchase but also subsequent service revenue, accessory purchases, and likelihood of repurchase. CLV-based measurement justifies personalization investments that might not show immediate ROI but create substantial long-term value.

Experimentation velocity has emerged as a key performance indicator for personalization programs. Organizations that can rapidly test and learn from personalization strategies achieve better outcomes than those with slower iteration cycles. Leading retailers run hundreds of personalization experiments simultaneously, systematically testing hypotheses about customer preferences, optimal timing, and effective messaging. This high-velocity experimentation requires robust infrastructure, clear decision-making processes, and organizational commitment to data-driven optimization.

Segmentation analysis reveals how personalization effectiveness varies across customer groups, enabling targeted optimization and resource allocation. Healthcare organizations analyze personalization impact across patient populations, identifying which interventions work best for different conditions, demographics, and engagement levels. This analysis guides the development of specialized personalization strategies for high-value segments while identifying opportunities to improve effectiveness for underserved populations.

Cost-benefit analysis must account for the full economics of personalization including technology investments, operational costs, and opportunity costs of alternative investments. Comprehensive ROI models include infrastructure costs, data management expenses, model development and maintenance, content creation, and organizational change investments. Manufacturing companies evaluate personalization ROI against alternative customer experience investments, ensuring resources flow to the highest-impact initiatives.

Continuous optimization processes systematically improve personalization effectiveness over time. Organizations implement feedback loops that use performance data to refine models, update strategies, and identify new opportunities. Financial services firms use automated optimization systems that continuously adjust personalization parameters based on observed outcomes, gradually improving performance without manual intervention. These systems must balance exploration of new strategies with exploitation of known effective approaches, often using multi-armed bandit algorithms to manage this trade-off.

Leading indicators provide early signals of personalization effectiveness before lagging business metrics fully reflect the impact. Engagement metrics like click-through rates, time on site, and content consumption indicate whether personalization resonates with customers. Satisfaction metrics including Net Promoter Score and customer effort scores reveal how personalization affects overall experience quality. Monitoring these leading indicators enables rapid course correction when personalization strategies underperform.

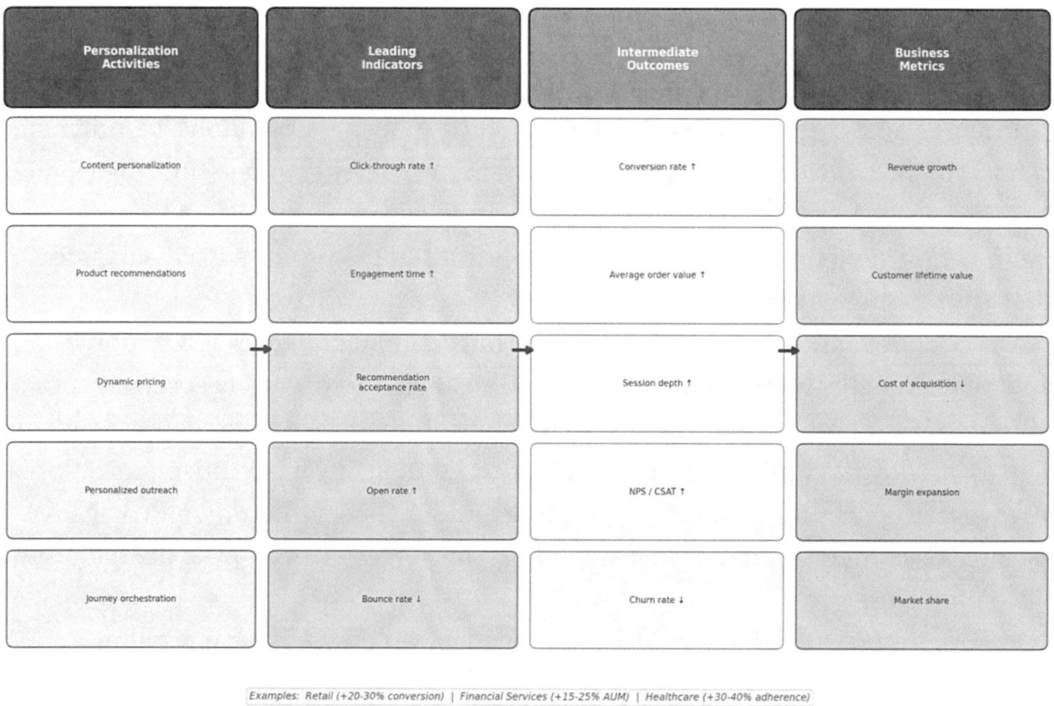

Figure 7-5. *Measurement framework showing causal relationships between personalization activities, leading indicators, intermediate outcomes, and ultimate business metrics*

7.8 Industry-Specific Personalization Strategies

While personalization principles apply across industries, effective implementation requires a deep understanding of industry-specific customer needs, regulatory constraints, and business models. Retail personalization focuses heavily on product discovery and purchase conversion, using browsing behavior, purchase history, and demographic data to recommend relevant products and optimize merchandising.

Advanced retail implementations personalize pricing, promotions, and inventory allocation based on individual customer price sensitivity, brand preferences, and purchase patterns. Omnichannel personalization connects online and offline experiences, enabling capabilities like personalized in-store recommendations based on online browsing and coordinated promotions across channels.

Automotive personalization spans the entire customer lifecycle from initial research through purchase, ownership, and eventual repurchase. During the shopping phase, personalization helps customers navigate complex vehicle configurations, recommending options based on stated preferences, budget constraints, and inferred priorities. Financing and insurance recommendations adapt to individual credit profiles and risk factors. Post-purchase personalization includes customized maintenance reminders, service recommendations based on vehicle usage patterns, and targeted offers for accessories and upgrades. Connected vehicle data enables increasingly sophisticated personalization of in-vehicle experiences including infotainment, navigation, and driver assistance features.

Manufacturing B2B personalization addresses the unique needs of business customers including complex procurement processes, multi-stakeholder decision-making, and ongoing relationship management. Personalized portals provide customized product catalogs, pricing, and inventory visibility based on customer contracts and purchasing patterns. Predictive analytics anticipate reordering needs and proactively recommend alternative products when preferred items face supply constraints. Technical documentation and support resources personalize based on customer equipment configurations and usage patterns. Account management teams receive AI-powered insights about customer needs, risks, and opportunities to guide relationship strategy.

Healthcare personalization must balance effectiveness with stringent privacy requirements and clinical safety considerations. Patient engagement platforms personalize educational content, care reminders, and wellness recommendations based on medical history, current conditions, and treatment plans. Personalization helps patients navigate complex healthcare systems by recommending appropriate providers, explaining insurance coverage, and coordinating care across multiple specialists. Clinical decision support systems provide personalized treatment recommendations to providers based on patient characteristics, the latest medical evidence, and institutional protocols. Population health management uses personalization to identify high-risk patients and target interventions most likely to improve outcomes.

Financial services personalization addresses diverse customer needs across banking, lending, investing, and insurance. Personalized financial advice adapts to individual goals, risk tolerance, life stage, and financial situation. Product recommendations consider not just immediate needs but also longer-term financial planning objectives. Personalized content explains complex financial concepts in terms relevant to each customer's situation. Fraud detection systems personalize based on individual transaction patterns, reducing false positives while maintaining security. Wealth management platforms provide personalized portfolio recommendations, market commentary, and rebalancing suggestions tailored to individual investment strategies.

Cross-industry patterns emerge despite these differences. Successful personalization in all industries requires comprehensive customer data, sophisticated analytics, real-time decisioning capabilities, and organizational alignment around customer-centric metrics. Privacy and trust considerations prove critical across sectors, with customers increasingly expecting transparency and control over personalization. The most effective implementations balance automation with human judgment, using AI to augment rather than replace human expertise in customer relationships.

7.9 Advanced Personalization Techniques and Emerging Capabilities

The frontier of personalization continues to advance as new AI capabilities and techniques emerge. Contextual bandits and reinforcement learning enable personalization systems to continuously learn and adapt based on customer responses, moving beyond static models trained on historical data. These approaches prove particularly valuable in dynamic environments where customer preferences evolve rapidly or where optimal strategies depend on complex contextual factors. Retail applications use contextual bandits to optimize promotional strategies, learning which offers to present to which customers at which times to maximize both short-term conversion and long-term customer value.

Causal inference techniques help personalization systems understand not just correlations but actual causal relationships between interventions and outcomes. This understanding enables more effective personalization by identifying which actions truly influence customer behavior vs. those that merely correlate with outcomes. Financial services firms use causal inference to determine which personalized communications actually drive product adoption vs. those that reach customers already inclined to purchase. This distinction enables more efficient resource allocation and more effective personalization strategies.

Multi-objective optimization addresses the reality that personalization must balance multiple goals including revenue, customer satisfaction, operational efficiency, and long-term relationship value. Advanced personalization systems explicitly model these trade-offs, finding Pareto-optimal solutions that maximize overall value rather than optimizing single metrics. Healthcare personalization systems balance patient engagement, clinical outcomes, and cost efficiency, recognizing that maximizing any single objective might compromise others.

Transfer learning enables personalization systems to leverage knowledge from related domains or customer segments to improve performance in data-sparse situations. New customer personalization benefits from patterns learned across existing customers, enabling relevant experiences even with limited individual history. Automotive manufacturers use transfer learning to personalize experiences for first-time buyers based on patterns observed in similar customers, gradually refining personalization as more individual data becomes available.

Federated learning allows personalization models to be trained across distributed data sources without centralizing sensitive information. This technique proves particularly valuable in healthcare where patient data privacy is paramount and in B2B manufacturing where customers may be unwilling to share detailed operational data. Federated learning enables collaborative model development that benefits all participants while maintaining data sovereignty and privacy.

Generative AI is transforming personalization by enabling the creation of truly unique content, recommendations, and experiences for each customer. Rather than selecting from predefined options, generative models can create personalized product descriptions, marketing messages, and conversational interactions tailored to individual preferences and contexts. Financial services firms use generative AI to create personalized investment summaries and market commentary that explain complex information in terms relevant to each customer's portfolio and goals. Healthcare applications generate personalized patient education materials that adapt to individual health literacy levels and learning preferences.

Multimodal personalization integrates signals from text, images, voice, and behavioral data to create a richer understanding of customer preferences and more sophisticated personalization strategies. Retail applications analyze product images that customers view and share to understand aesthetic preferences beyond what can be captured through text-based attributes. Automotive personalization systems integrate voice interactions, driving behavior, and infotainment usage to create comprehensive profiles that inform both in-vehicle experiences and broader customer engagement strategies.

Explainable AI techniques make personalization more transparent and trustworthy by providing clear explanations for recommendations and decisions. Customers increasingly expect to understand why they receive specific recommendations or offers. Financial services regulations often require explainability for credit and lending decisions. Explainable personalization builds customer confidence while enabling organizations to identify and correct biases or errors in personalization logic.

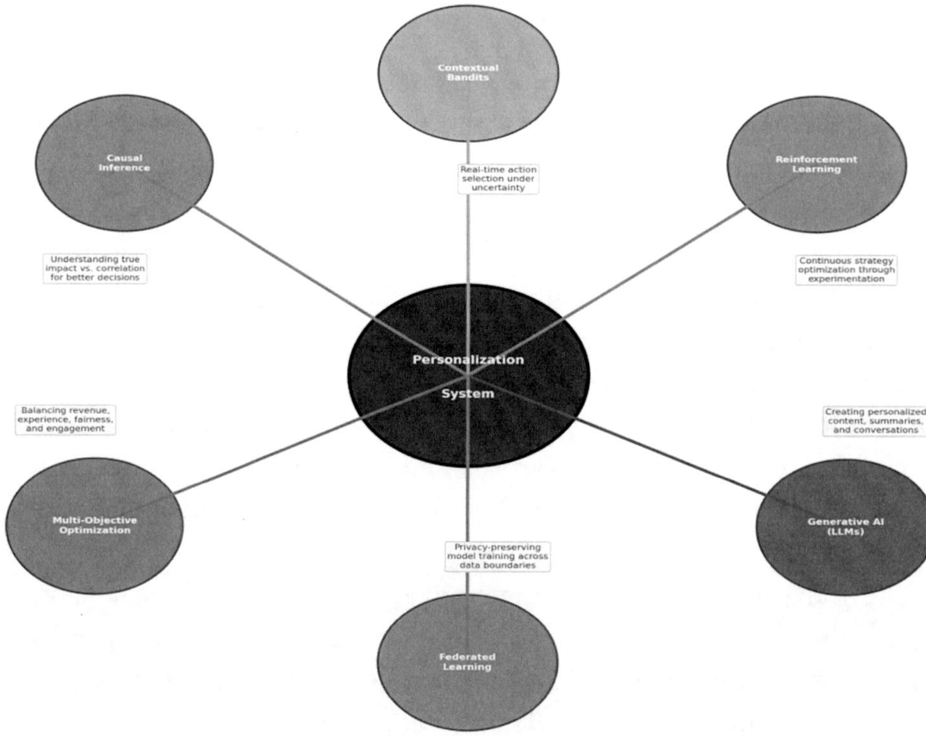

Figure 7-6. *Advanced techniques enhancing personalization: reinforcement learning, causal inference, multi-objective optimization, generative AI, contextual bandits, and federated learning*

7.10 Implementation Road Map and Best Practices

Organizations embarking on personalization transformation should follow a phased approach that builds capabilities incrementally while delivering value at each stage. Initial phases focus on foundational data infrastructure and basic personalization use cases that demonstrate value and build organizational support. Subsequent phases expand personalization scope, sophistication, and integration across touchpoints.

Phase one establishes data foundations including customer data platforms, identity resolution, and basic analytics capabilities. Organizations should prioritize high-impact, relatively simple personalization use cases that can demonstrate value quickly. Retail companies often start with personalized product recommendations on ecommerce sites, leveraging existing purchase and browsing data. Financial services firms might begin with personalized content recommendations in digital banking applications. These initial implementations prove the value of personalization while building technical capabilities and organizational experience.

Phase two expands personalization across additional touchpoints and customer journey stages. Organizations develop more sophisticated models incorporating broader data sources and advanced techniques. Integration between channels enables consistent personalization across customer touchpoints. Automotive manufacturers might expand from personalized digital marketing to include personalized vehicle configuration recommendations and financing options. Healthcare organizations extend from basic appointment reminders to comprehensive personalized care management programs.

Phase three implements real-time personalization capabilities, advanced AI techniques, and comprehensive optimization frameworks. Organizations develop capabilities for continuous learning and adaptation, moving beyond static models to dynamic systems that evolve with customer behavior. Manufacturing companies implement real-time personalization in customer portals that adapt recommendations based on current inventory, production schedules, and supply chain status. Financial services firms deploy real-time fraud detection and personalized financial advice that responds to market conditions and customer circumstances.

Phase four achieves personalization excellence through organizational transformation, advanced capabilities, and continuous innovation. Personalization becomes embedded in organizational culture and processes rather than a separate initiative. Organizations develop proprietary personalization capabilities that create sustainable competitive advantages. Leading retailers achieve this level of maturity, with personalization deeply integrated into merchandising, marketing, operations, and customer service.

Best practices span technical, organizational, and strategic dimensions. Technically, organizations should invest in robust data infrastructure before attempting sophisticated personalization, ensure models are regularly retrained and monitored, and implement comprehensive testing frameworks. Organizationally, cross-functional collaboration, clear governance, and continuous learning prove critical. Strategically, personalization should align with overall business objectives, focus on customer value creation, and balance short-term wins with long-term capability building.

Common pitfalls include underestimating data quality requirements, attempting overly ambitious initial implementations, neglecting privacy and ethical considerations, and failing to secure adequate organizational buy-in. Organizations should start with clear, measurable objectives, ensure executive sponsorship, invest in change management, and celebrate early wins to build momentum.

Success metrics should span technical performance, business outcomes, and customer experience. Technical metrics include model accuracy, system latency, and uptime. Business metrics encompass conversion rates, revenue impact, customer lifetime value, and ROI. Customer experience metrics include satisfaction scores, engagement levels, and qualitative feedback. Comprehensive measurement across these dimensions provides a complete picture of personalization effectiveness.

7.11 Future Directions and Strategic Implications

The trajectory of personalization technology points toward increasingly sophisticated, autonomous systems that anticipate customer needs and orchestrate experiences across expanding ecosystems of touchpoints and partners. Generative AI will enable personalization at unprecedented scale and granularity, creating truly unique experiences for each customer interaction. The boundary between personalization and product customization will blur as AI enables mass customization of physical products and services based on individual preferences.

Privacy-preserving techniques will become increasingly important as regulations tighten and customer expectations for data protection grow. Organizations that master privacy-preserving personalization will gain competitive advantages through enhanced customer trust. Federated learning, differential privacy, and synthetic data generation will evolve from research topics to standard practices in personalization implementations.

The integration of personalization across industry ecosystems will create new opportunities and challenges. Automotive personalization will extend beyond individual manufacturers to encompass charging networks, insurance providers, and mobility services. Healthcare personalization will integrate across providers, payers, pharmaceutical companies, and wellness platforms. These ecosystem-level personalization capabilities will require new forms of collaboration, data sharing, and governance.

Autonomous personalization systems will increasingly make decisions without human intervention, raising questions about accountability, transparency, and control. Organizations must develop frameworks for responsible automation that maintain appropriate human oversight while enabling the speed and scale advantages of AI-driven personalization. The balance between automation and human judgment will vary by industry and use case, with safety-critical applications maintaining higher levels of human involvement.

The competitive landscape will increasingly differentiate between organizations that master personalization and those that lag. Personalization capabilities will become table stakes in many industries, with customers expecting relevant, individualized experiences as standard. Organizations that fail to develop these capabilities risk commoditization and customer attrition. However, personalization alone will not guarantee success; it must be part of comprehensive customer experience strategies that deliver genuine value.

Strategic implications extend beyond customer-facing applications to internal operations and business models. Personalization techniques will optimize employee experiences, supply chain operations, and partner relationships. New business models will emerge based on personalization capabilities, including personalization-as-a-service offerings and data cooperatives that enable smaller organizations to achieve personalization at scale.

The organizations that thrive in this personalized future will be those that view personalization not as a technology project but as a fundamental capability requiring sustained investment, continuous innovation, and deep integration into strategy and operations. They will balance technological sophistication with ethical responsibility, business objectives with customer value creation, and automation with human judgment. Most importantly, they will recognize that personalization is not an end in itself but a means to build stronger, more valuable customer relationships that drive sustainable business success.

The transformation of customer experience through AI-driven personalization represents one of the most significant opportunities and challenges facing organizations today. Those that successfully navigate this transformation will create substantial competitive advantages, deeper customer relationships, and new sources of value creation. The journey requires vision, investment, and persistence, but the rewards for organizations that achieve personalization excellence are substantial and sustain competitive advantage in an increasingly personalized marketplace.

7.12 Conclusion: The Imperative of Personalization Excellence

Customer experience transformation through AI-driven personalization has evolved from a competitive advantage to a business imperative. Organizations across industries face customers who increasingly expect experiences tailored to their individual needs, preferences, and contexts. Meeting these expectations requires more than incremental improvements to existing approaches; it demands a fundamental transformation of how organizations understand customers, make decisions, and deliver experiences.

The technical foundations for personalization excellence are now accessible to organizations of all sizes. Cloud-based machine learning platforms, customer data platforms, and generative AI services democratize capabilities that were previously available only to technology giants with massive engineering resources. However, technology alone does not guarantee success. Organizations must develop complementary capabilities in data management, organizational alignment, ethical governance, and continuous optimization to realize the full potential of personalization.

The business case for personalization investment is compelling across industries. Retail organizations achieve 20–30% improvements in conversion rates and significant increases in customer lifetime value. Financial services firms report 15–25% growth in assets under management and deeper customer relationships. Healthcare providers see 30–40% improvements in treatment adherence and patient satisfaction. Manufacturing companies experience 40–50% increases in repeat purchase rates and wallet share expansion. These benefits compound over time as personalization systems learn and improve, creating sustainable competitive advantages.

Privacy and ethical considerations must be central to personalization strategies rather than afterthoughts. Organizations that build customer trust through transparent, responsible personalization practices will differentiate themselves in markets where data breaches and privacy violations erode confidence. Privacy-preserving techniques including federated learning and differential privacy enable effective personalization while protecting customer data. Explainable AI builds trust by helping customers understand personalization decisions. Bias monitoring and mitigation ensure fair treatment across customer populations.

Organizational transformation proves to be as important as technical implementation. Cross-functional collaboration, data democratization, and experimentation cultures enable personalization at scale. Organizations must develop new skills, restructure around customer journeys, and align incentives with customer-centric metrics. Change management investments help employees adapt to new ways of working where AI augments human judgment rather than replacing it. Leadership commitment and visible support prove critical to sustaining transformation through inevitable challenges.

The measurement frameworks organizations employ determine whether personalization investments deliver expected returns. Incrementality testing, multi-touch attribution, and customer lifetime value modeling provide a rigorous assessment of personalization impact. Leading indicators enable rapid course correction while lagging metrics confirm long-term value creation. Experimentation velocity emerges as a key performance indicator, with organizations that test and learn rapidly achieving superior outcomes.

Industry-specific considerations shape personalization implementation while cross-industry patterns provide valuable lessons. Retail personalization focuses on product discovery and purchase conversion. Automotive personalization spans the entire customer lifecycle from research through ownership. Manufacturing B2B personalization addresses complex procurement and relationship management. Healthcare personalization balances effectiveness with privacy and clinical safety. Financial services personalization provides tailored advice and product recommendations. Despite these differences, successful implementations share common characteristics including comprehensive data, sophisticated analytics, real-time decisioning, and customer-centric organizational alignment.

Advanced techniques including reinforcement learning, causal inference, multi-objective optimization, and generative AI push the boundaries of what personalization can achieve. These capabilities enable continuous learning, deeper understanding of cause and effect, balanced optimization across multiple objectives, and creation of truly unique experiences. Organizations that master these advanced techniques will establish leadership positions in their industries.

The implementation road map for personalization transformation follows a phased approach that builds capabilities incrementally while delivering value at each stage. Organizations should start with foundational data infrastructure and high-impact use cases, expand across touchpoints and journey stages, implement real-time capabilities and advanced techniques, and ultimately achieve personalization excellence through organizational transformation and continuous innovation. Best practices span technical, organizational, and strategic dimensions, with success requiring attention to all three.

Looking forward, personalization will become increasingly sophisticated, autonomous, and integrated across industry ecosystems. Generative AI will enable unprecedented scale and granularity of personalization. Privacy-preserving techniques will become standard practice as regulations tighten and customer expectations evolve. Ecosystem-level personalization will create new opportunities for collaboration and value creation. Autonomous systems will make more decisions without human intervention, requiring careful governance and oversight.

The strategic implications extend beyond customer-facing applications to internal operations and business models. Organizations will apply personalization techniques to employee experiences, supply chain optimization, and partner relationships. New business models will emerge based on personalization capabilities. The competitive landscape will increasingly differentiate between organizations that master personalization and those that lag, with personalization becoming table stakes in many industries.

Success in this personalized future requires viewing personalization not as a technology project but as a fundamental organizational capability. It demands sustained investment, continuous innovation, and deep integration into strategy and operations. Organizations must balance technological sophistication with ethical responsibility, business objectives with customer value creation, and automation with human judgment. Most importantly, they must recognize that personalization is a means to build stronger, more valuable customer relationships that drive sustainable business success.

The transformation of customer experience through AI-driven personalization represents both a tremendous opportunity and a significant challenge. Organizations that successfully navigate this transformation will create substantial competitive advantages, deeper customer relationships, and new sources of value creation. The journey requires vision, investment, and persistence, but the rewards are substantial and sustainable. As we move forward into an increasingly AI-powered future, personalization excellence will separate market leaders from followers, defining which organizations thrive and which struggle to remain relevant in markets where customers expect nothing less than experiences perfectly tailored to their individual needs.

CHAPTER 8

Healthcare: From Diagnosis to Drug Discovery

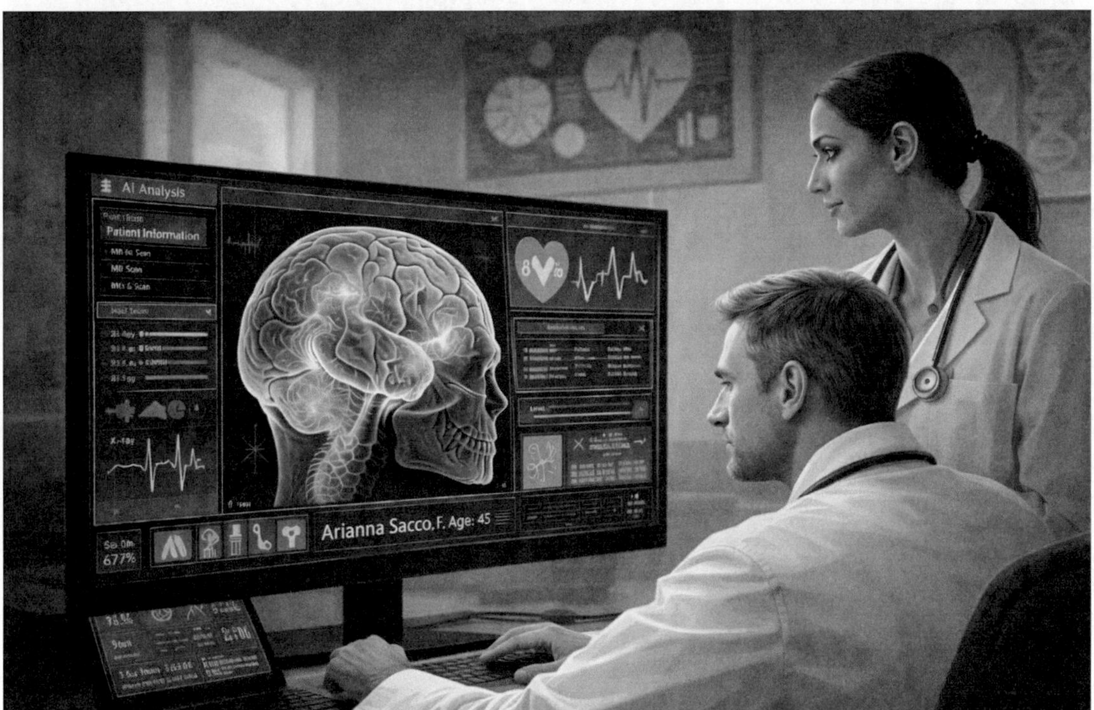

Figure 8-1. *Radiologists collaborating over a patient scan, representing AI's growing role in clinical imaging workflows*

N. Sendas et al., *Building Generative AI Solutions for Industries with AWS*,
https://doi.org/10.1007/979-8-8688-2830-0_8

8.1 Introduction: Setting the Scene

Healthcare has always been personal. A doctor listens to a patient describe their symptoms, asks follow-up questions, makes observations, and arrives at a diagnosis. NLP-based systems could already process and structure clinical language, a meaningful step forward, but generative AI goes further. It participates as an active contributor: listening in real time, interpreting clinical context, and generating coherent narrative notes that capture the texture of the encounter, the hesitations, the context, and the clinical judgment, not just its structured data points.

Picture a busy primary care clinic on a Monday morning. A physician moves from one exam room to the next, seeing patients with complaints ranging from persistent coughs to chronic pain management. In the past, they would have spent nearly as much time typing notes into the electronic health record as they did talking to patients. Now, an ambient AI system listens to each consultation, identifies who is speaking, extracts relevant medical terminology, and drafts structured clinical documentation automatically. The doctor reviews the draft, makes corrections where needed, and moves on. What once took hours of after-clinic documentation now takes minutes.

This isn't a pilot program at a single academic medical center. Ambient AI scribes are already handling thousands of medical conversations weekly across healthcare facilities. One multispecialty group reported saving 15,000 clinician hours after deploying AI scribes while also noting improvements in patient–physician interaction.[1] Companies like Suki have raised significant funding to build ambient AI assistants that integrate directly with electronic health record systems like Epic and Cerner.[2] The market is growing fast, with dozens of AI scribe products now competing for adoption.

The adoption curve is also not as steep as many predicted. Survey data suggests that roughly one in five general practitioners in the UK have already experimented with generative AI tools for documentation, brainstorming, and exploring treatment options.[3] What also surprised many observers is the learning curve for using these systems doesn't

[1] AMA, "AI scribes save 15,000 hours—and restore the human side of medicine," `https://www.amaassn.org/practice-management/digital/ai-scribes-save-15000-hours-and-restore-human-side-medicine`, Last Updated: 2024. Section: Drug Discovery News feature article.

[2] Reuters, "Healthcare startup Suki raises $70 million to build AI assistants for hospitals," Published: October 10, 2024.

[3] BMJ Health & Care Informatics, "Generative artificial intelligence in primary care: an online survey of UK general practitioners," `https://doi.org/10.1136/bmjhci-2024-101102`, Published: September 2024.

appear to correlate with age or years in practice. Some health systems report that older physicians are picking up the technology just as quickly as recent medical school graduates.

The impact goes beyond simple time savings. The real benefit may be reducing provider burnout, the cognitive exhaustion that comes from potentially spending evenings and weekends catching up on documentation. When clinicians can finish their notes before leaving the office, they get their personal time back, and in the office, when they're not distracted by typing during appointments, they can actually look patients in the eye and provide an elevated level of care.

This chapter explores generative AI's role across the full spectrum of healthcare, from the exam room to the research laboratory. We'll look at how these systems are changing clinical documentation, diagnostic imaging, drug discovery, and clinical trials. We'll examine the opportunities and the risks, and we'll consider what this means for the people who work in healthcare, as well as the patients they serve.

Healthcare is different from other industries where AI has made inroads. The stakes are higher. A mistake in a generated marketing headline is embarrassing. A mistake in a clinical note could affect patient safety. This reality shapes everything about how AI is being developed and deployed in medicine. Regulatory requirements are stricter. Validation processes are more rigorous, and the human-in-the-loop isn't optional—it's essential. Commentary in JAMA Health Forum has highlighted emerging risks such as overreliance and the difficulty physicians face in judging when to trust or override these systems when they fail in unexpected ways.[4]

At the same time, healthcare faces pressures that make AI adoption almost inevitable. Physician burnout has reached crisis levels. Administrative tasks consume time that could be spent with patients. Drug development takes over a decade and costs billions of dollars, with most candidates failing in clinical trials. These aren't problems that can be solved by hiring more people or working harder. They require new approaches.

Generative AI offers help not as a replacement for human judgment, but as a tool that handles the repetitive, time-consuming work, so clinicians and researchers can focus on what they do best. The question isn't whether AI will play a role in healthcare's future. It's already here. The question is how we shape that role to improve outcomes while maintaining the trust and safety that patients deserve.

---

[4] JAMA Health Forum, "Calibrating AI Reliance—A Physician's Superhuman Dilemma," DOI 10.1001/jamahealthforum.2025.0106, `https://jamanetwork.com/journals/jama-health-forum/fullarticle/2831560`, Published: March 21, 2025.

8.2 Historical Context: Medicine's Technological Evolution

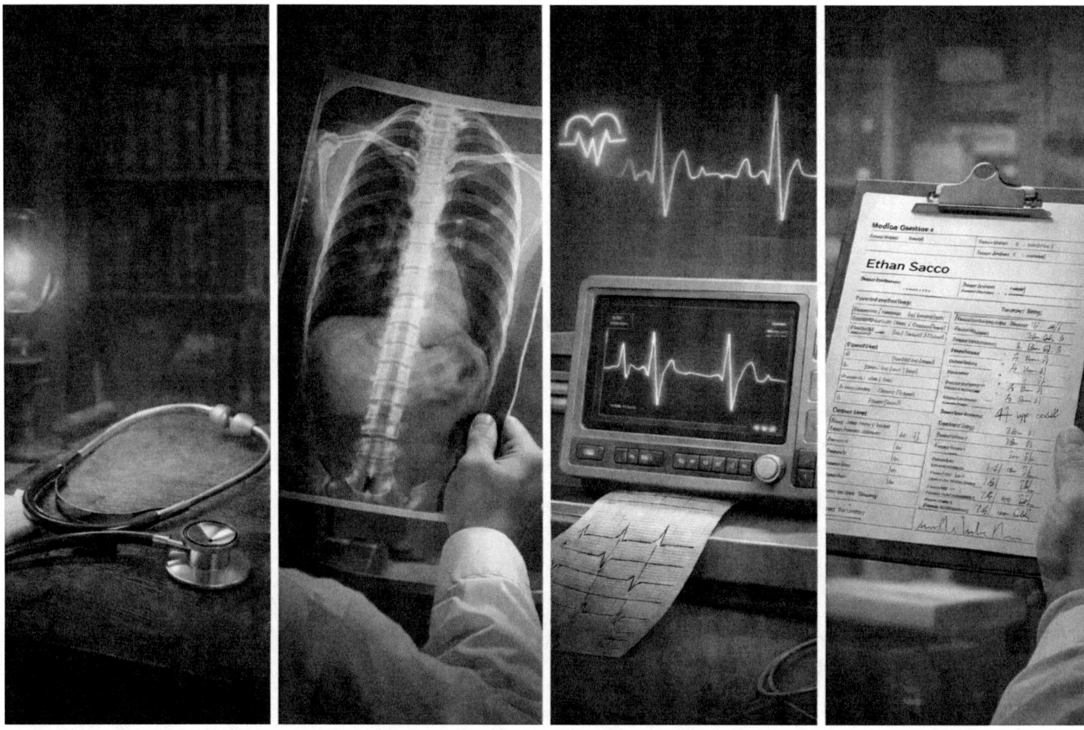

Figure 8-2. *Key milestones in healthcare technology from the stethoscope to generative AI*

The relationship between medicine and technology is older than most people realize. Every generation of physicians has had to adapt to new tools that changed how they practiced. The pattern has been roughly the same every time: initial skepticism, gradual adoption, and eventually a sense that the old way of doing things was unimaginable.

Consider the stethoscope. When René Laennec invented it in 1816, he was solving a practical problem. Placing an ear directly on a patient's chest was awkward and, in some cases, socially inappropriate. A wooden tube provided distance and, as it turned out, better acoustics. Many physicians resisted, though, arguing that the device created a barrier between doctor and patient and that it replaced skilled observation with mechanical dependence. Sound familiar? The same concerns appear almost word for word in today's debates about AI in clinical practice.

This pattern repeated with the X-ray. Wilhelm Röntgen's discovery in 1895 gave physicians the ability to see inside the body without cutting it open. Within a few years, X-ray machines appeared in hospitals across Europe and North America, but early adopters faced criticism. Some worried that the images were misleading, that physicians would trust shadows on a screen over their own clinical judgment. Others raised concerns about patient privacy. The idea that anyone could see through clothing and skin felt invasive, even voyeuristic. These debates faded as the technology proved its value, but they echo in current discussions about AI systems that can interpret medical images.

The 20th century brought a steady stream of diagnostic and therapeutic advances. Electrocardiograms gave cardiologists a window into heart function. CT scans and MRIs produced detailed cross-sectional images that X-rays couldn't match. Ultrasound allowed physicians to watch a fetus move in real time. Each technology expanded what medicine could see and do, and each required physicians to learn new skills, interpret new kinds of data, and trust machines to provide information that their own senses couldn't detect.

Then came the computer. The first clinical decision support systems appeared in the 1970s. MYCIN, developed at Stanford, could recommend antibiotics for bacterial infections based on patient symptoms and lab results. It performed well in tests, sometimes matching or exceeding the accuracy of infectious disease specialists but despite this, it never saw widespread clinical use. The technology was ahead of its time. Computers were expensive, interfaces were clunky, and physicians weren't ready to take advice from a machine.

The electronic health record changed the equation. Starting in the 1990s and accelerating after government incentive programs in the 2000s, hospitals and clinics shifted from paper charts to digital systems. The benefits were real—legible notes, accessible records, and easier coordination across providers—but so were the costs. Documentation burden exploded. Physicians found themselves spending more time typing than talking to patients. Studies began linking EHR use to burnout, job dissatisfaction, and even medical errors caused by alert fatigue.

This is the context in which generative AI enters healthcare. The technology arrives at a moment when physicians are overwhelmed by administrative work, when the promise of digital medicine has been partially offset by its burdens, and when the healthcare system is searching for ways to do more with limited resources.

What makes generative AI different from earlier clinical decision support? Previous systems were rule-based. They followed logic trees programmed by human experts. If the patient has symptom A and lab value B, recommend treatment C. These systems were brittle. They couldn't handle ambiguity or adapt to cases that fell outside their programmed rules.

Generative AI works differently. Large language models learn patterns from vast amounts of text. They can summarize, translate, draft, and respond to open-ended questions. They handle ambiguity better than rule-based systems because they're trained on the messy, inconsistent way humans actually communicate. This flexibility is what makes them useful for clinical documentation, where every patient encounter is slightly different and no two physicians describe the same finding in exactly the same words.

This flexibility comes with risks though; rule-based systems fail in predictable ways. When they don't know something, they say so. Generative models can produce confident sounding text that's partially or even entirely wrong. This is the trade-off that healthcare is now navigating: tools that are more capable and more adaptable, but also more opaque and harder to verify.

The physicians who adopted the stethoscope, the X-ray, and the EHR all faced versions of this challenge. New tools bring new capabilities and new risks. The question is always the same: How do we capture the benefits while managing the downsides? That same question is now being asked about generative AI.

8.3 Defining AI in Healthcare

To understand how generative AI is reshaping healthcare, it helps to be clear about what we're actually talking about. The term "reshaping" as it relates to generative AI in healthcare gets used loosely, and not every AI application in medicine works the same way.

At its core, generative AI refers to systems that can create new content rather than simply classify or predict based on existing data. In healthcare, this distinction matters. Traditional machine learning might look at a chest X-ray and flag it as "abnormal" or "normal." Generative AI can look at that same X-ray and write a draft radiology report describing what it sees. One gives you a label. The other gives you language.

This capability opens up applications across the entire healthcare spectrum, with clinical documentation being the most visible use case right now. Ambient AI systems can listen to patient–physician conversations and generate structured clinical notes in real time, identifying speakers, extracting medical terminology, and formatting the output to match electronic health record requirements.[1] The physician then reviews and edits the draft rather than creating it from scratch, eliminating administrative work and allowing them to fully focus on the patient.

Diagnostic support represents another major opportunity. Generative models can interpret medical images and produce draft reports for radiologists to review,[2] analyze pathology slides and generate findings, and even read electrocardiograms and summarize abnormalities. In each case, the AI produces content that a human expert then validates (human in the loop).

Drug discovery is interesting and pushes generative AI in a different direction entirely. Here, the systems design novel molecules, proteins, and antibodies. They propose chemical structures that might bind to a particular target, or they generate protein sequences with desired properties.[3] The output isn't text for humans to read. It's molecular blueprints for laboratories to synthesize and test.

Patient-facing applications form a fourth category. Chatbots and virtual assistants can answer health questions, help patients navigate care pathways, provide medication reminders, and offer basic triage guidance.[4] These systems generate conversational responses tailored to individual patient queries.

Figure 8-3. *The human-in-the-loop model for healthcare AI across documentation, diagnostics, and drug discovery*

What ties these applications together is the human–AI loop. Healthcare AI doesn't operate autonomously. A physician reviews the generated clinical note before signing it. A radiologist edits the draft report before it goes into the medical record. A medicinal chemist evaluates the proposed molecules before synthesis begins. The AI generates; the human validates.

This loop exists because healthcare demands it. The consequences of errors are too significant to accept unchecked AI output. Model deployments in healthcare need to be integrated into clinical workflows with appropriate human oversight. Model performance should be monitored after deployment, and the complexity of health data makes ongoing monitoring especially important.

The technical foundations of healthcare AI draw on the same architectures used elsewhere. Large language models power clinical documentation and text summarization. Diffusion models and other generative architectures support medical imaging applications. Specialized models trained on molecular data enable drug discovery. What differs is the regulatory environment, the validation requirements, and the integration challenges.

One of the greatest of these challenges is that healthcare data comes in many forms. Electronic health records contain structured fields and unstructured clinical notes. Radiology systems store medical images in standardized formats, laboratory systems produce test results, genomic sequencing generates massive datasets, and wearable devices stream continuous physiological measurements, to name a few. All of this to say, modern healthcare data strategy must support the collection and use of data from many disparate sources.

All isn't lost, as interoperability standards help connect these systems. Health Level Seven (HL7), Fast Healthcare Interoperability Resources (FHIR), and Digital Imaging and Communications in Medicine (DICOM) provide frameworks for exchanging health data between systems. Generative AI applications need to work within these standards, reading data from source systems and writing outputs back in compatible formats.

The regulatory landscape adds another layer of complexity. In the United States, the FDA oversees AI-based medical devices, while HIPAA governs the privacy and security of protected health information. Similar regulations exist in other jurisdictions, so healthcare AI must always be built with these requirements in mind from the start, not bolted on afterward.

8.4 Case Studies by Domain

Generative AI is already at work across healthcare, though the maturity and scale of adoption varies considerably by domain. Some applications have even moved into routine clinical use, while others remain experimental. Looking at specific examples helps illustrate both what's possible today and what challenges remain.

8.4.1 Clinical Documentation and Patient Care

The documentation burden on clinicians has been building for decades. Electronic health records promised efficiency but delivered the opposite for many physicians. Studies consistently show that doctors spend as much time on administrative tasks as they do on direct patient care. Generative AI offers a way to shift that balance. In practice, deploying clinical decision support systems, such as those used for early sepsis detection, requires careful integration with EHR workflows, validation to minimize alert fatigue, and alignment with regulatory expectations for clinical safety and accountability.

Ambient AI scribes represent the most mature application in this space. These systems use speech recognition and large language models to convert patient-physician conversations into structured clinical notes.[1] The technology has moved beyond pilot programs into production deployments at health systems of various sizes.

This workflow is straightforward, too. The AI listens to the clinical encounter, identifies the speakers, extracts relevant medical information, and generates a draft note formatted for the electronic health record. The physician reviews the draft, makes corrections, and signs off. What once required 10–15 minutes of typing after each visit now takes a quick review.

Figure 8-4. *A clinician engaging directly with a patient while ambient AI handles real-time documentation*

The benefits extend beyond time savings. When physicians aren't focused on documentation during the visit, they can give patients their full attention. Eye contact improves. Conversations flow more naturally. The technology doesn't just make documentation faster. It changes the quality of the clinical encounter itself.

As with most things, the technology isn't perfect. AI-generated notes can contain errors. They might miss important details or include information that wasn't actually discussed.[2] This is why physicians need to review carefully rather than accepting drafts without scrutiny. The efficiency gains only materialize if the review process catches mistakes before they enter the permanent medical record.

Discharge summaries represent another documentation application. When patients leave the hospital, they need clear instructions about medications, follow-up appointments, and warning signs to watch for. Generating these summaries from multi-day hospital stays requires synthesizing information from numerous clinical notes, lab results, and imaging studies. Large language models can draft these summaries, pulling together information that would take a human considerable time to compile.[3]

8.4.2 Diagnostic Imaging and Radiology

Radiology departments face relentless volume pressure. The number of imaging studies grows year over year while the radiologist workforce struggles to keep pace. Generative AI offers a way to increase throughput without sacrificing quality.

The application here differs from ambient scribes. Instead of converting speech to text, these systems interpret medical images and generate draft reports.[4] A chest X-ray goes into the system, and then a draft report comes out describing the findings (noting any abnormalities) and suggesting follow-up if needed.

Radiologists then review these drafts rather than dictating reports from scratch. For straightforward cases, the AI draft might need only minor edits. For complex cases, the radiologist might substantially revise or rewrite the report. Either way, the AI handles the initial heavy lifting. Companies are already tackling this, with GE HealthCare and AWS having announced a strategic collaboration to accelerate healthcare transformation with generative AI.[5]

---

[5] GE HealthCare and AWS Announce Strategic Collaboration to Accelerate Healthcare Transformation with Generative AI," gehealthcare.com press release, Published: July 25, 2024.

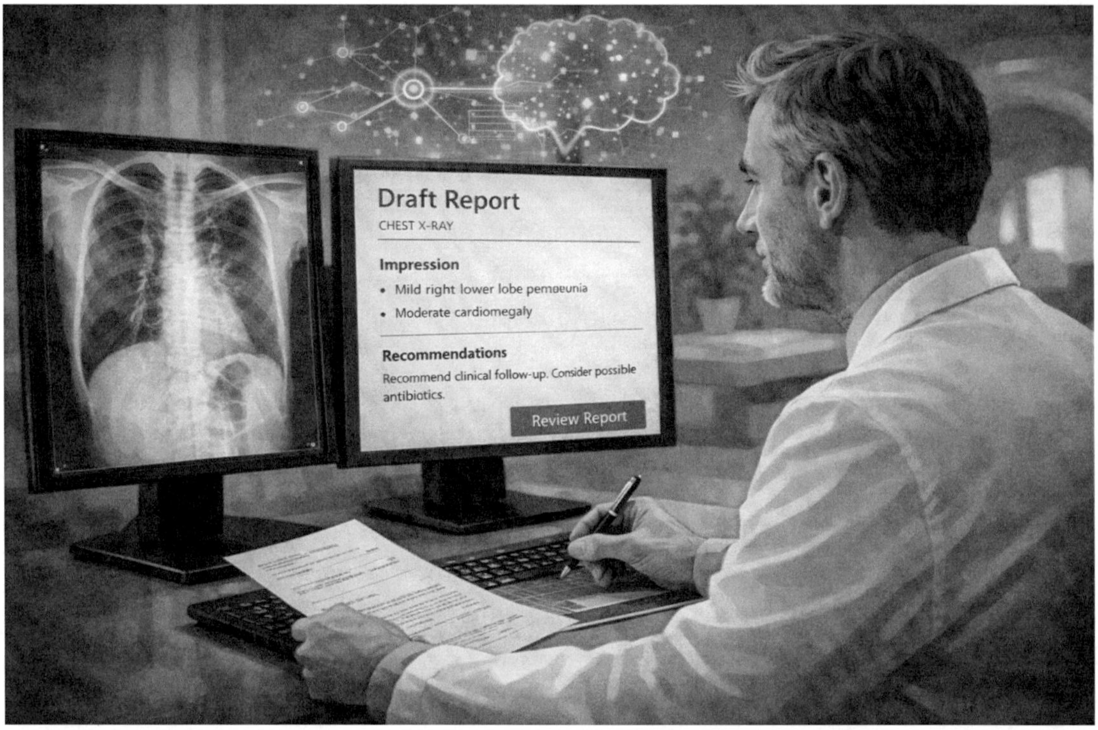

Figure 8-5. *A radiologist reviewing an AI-drafted report alongside a chest X-ray for validation*

Medical imaging innovation continues to advance. Systems now exist that convert low-dose CT acquisitions into high-resolution outputs, helping maintain diagnostic quality when paired with validated low-dose imaging protocols. Automated tools can also remove protected health information from medical images, enabling broader data sharing for research while protecting patient privacy.

The integration challenges are significant. Radiology AI needs to work within existing picture archiving and communication systems. It needs to handle the DICOM standard that governs medical image storage and transmission. And it needs to produce outputs that fit seamlessly into radiologist workflows. Understanding barriers to adoption remains an active area of research, particularly for applications like ultrasound reporting.[6]

[6] GE HealthCare, "Generative AI in Ultrasound Reporting: Understanding Barriers to Adoption," `https://www.gehealthcare.com/insights/article/generative-ai-in-ultrasound-reporting-understanding-barriers-toadoption`, Published: 2024.

8.4.3 Drug Discovery and Molecular Design

Drug discovery operates on a different timescale than clinical care. Developing a new medication can take a decade or more and costs billions of dollars, and even with that, most candidates fail somewhere along the way. Generative AI offers the possibility of shortening timelines and improving success rates.

The application here involves actually designing molecules, rather than generating text. Generative models can propose novel chemical structures predicted to bind to a particular biological target.[7] They can design proteins with desired properties and suggest modifications to existing compounds that might improve efficacy or reduce side effects.[8]

Like other use cases, this isn't about replacing medicinal chemists. It's about expanding the space of possibilities they can explore. A human scientist might consider dozens of molecular variations, while an AI system can evaluate millions. The human then focuses attention on the most promising candidates rather than exhaustively exploring every option.

The workflow typically involves a closed loop, where AI proposes candidates, laboratories synthesize and test them, and results are then fed back into the model, improving its predictions for the next round.[9] Each cycle narrows the search space and increases the likelihood of finding compounds worth advancing to clinical trials.

AI and generative models are reshaping the risk profile of drug pipelines by shortening timelines and reducing costs.[10] Startups founded by former researchers from leading AI labs are highlighting generative protein and molecule design as a key differentiator.[11]

---

[7] Briefings in Bioinformatics, "A survey of generative AI for de novo drug design: new frontiers in molecule and protein generation," `https://doi.org/10.1093/bib/bbae338`, Published: 2024.

[8] Frontiers in Pharmacology, "Generative artificial intelligence in drug discovery: basic framework, recent advances, challenges, and opportunities," `https://doi.org/10.3389/fphar.2024.1331062`, Published: February 2024.

[9] Nature Reviews Drug Discovery, `https://www.nature.com/nrd/`, Published: 2024.

[10] "How AI is transforming drug discovery," `https://www.drugdiscoverynews.com/`, Published: 2024.

[11] STAT News, "With $40 million, former DeepMind employees launch startup 'laser-focused' on AI protein design," `https://www.statnews.com/`, Published: February 12, 2025.

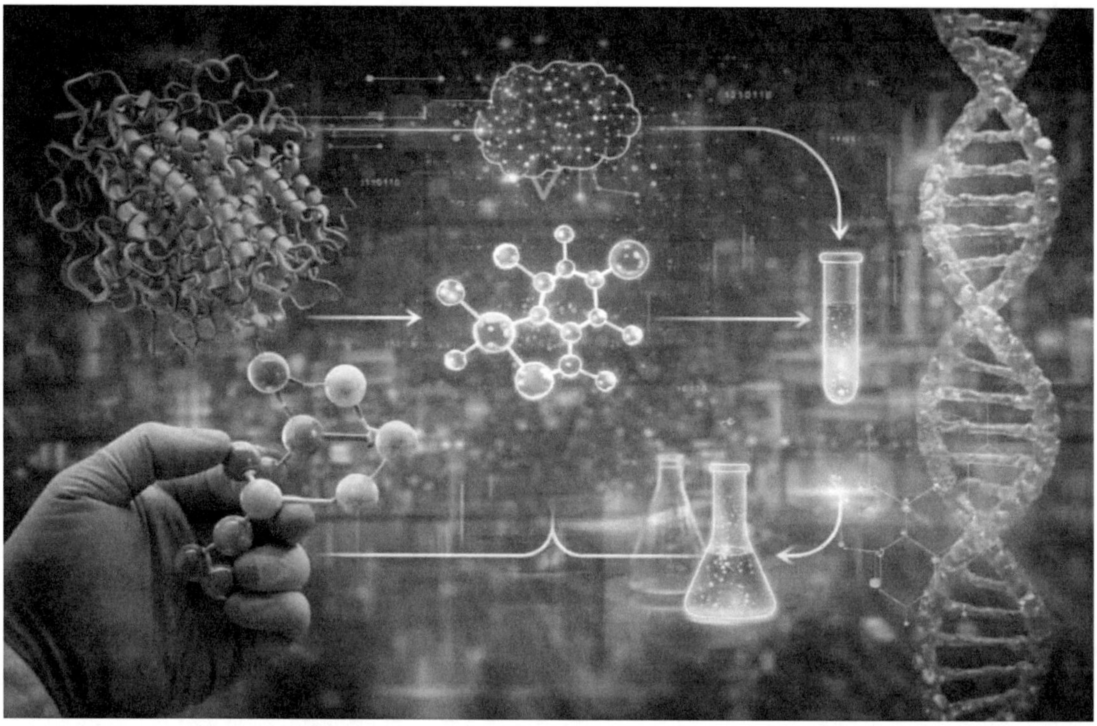

Figure 8-6. *The AI-driven drug discovery pipeline from molecular design through clinical trial optimization*

8.4.4 Clinical Trials and Decision Support

Continuing with the theme of drug discovery, we look to clinical trials, which are expensive, slow, and frequently fail. Patient recruitment alone can account for a third of trial timelines. Generative AI offers opportunities to improve efficiency at multiple stages.

Protocol design is one application where AI can help optimize eligibility criteria, balancing the need for a well-defined patient population against the practical challenges of recruitment.[12] Overly restrictive criteria might produce cleaner data but make it impossible to enroll enough patients. AI can simulate how different criteria would affect recruitment speed and suggest modifications.

[12] "Intelligent Clinical Trials: Using Generative AI to Fast-Track Drug Development," `https://www.weforum.org/whitepapers/`, Last Updated: 2024. Section: World Economic Forum policy and industry report.

Patient matching represents another opportunity. Finding patients who meet trial eligibility criteria requires searching through medical records and identifying candidates. This process has traditionally been manual and time-consuming. AI systems can automate that search, flagging potential matches for human review.[13]

The FDA has launched internal generative AI tools to summarize protocols, safety reports, and other documents, showing that regulators themselves are becoming AI users.[14]

Clinical decision support extends AI into routine patient care. In Chapter 6, we discussed clinical decision copilots, where these systems can surface drug interactions, flag potential safety issues, and suggest evidence-based treatment options.[15] Large language models add new capabilities here, handling the nuance and ambiguity that rule-based systems struggle with.

8.4.5 Administrative and Operational Applications

Healthcare generates enormous amounts of administrative work. Coding diagnoses and procedures for billing, processing insurance claims, obtaining prior authorizations, and managing revenue cycles. These tasks consume time and resources that could otherwise go to patient care.

Generative AI can automate many portions of this work, with systems that can read clinical notes and suggest appropriate billing codes.[16] They can draft prior authorization requests and identify claims likely to be denied, flagging them for review before submission.

Cleveland Clinic has deployed AI, including generative approaches, in revenue-cycle workflows to reduce delays and improve patient experience.[17] Multi-step AI agents are

---

[13] "UScienceDirect, "Optimizing Clinical Trial Eligibility Design Using Natural Language Processing Models and Real-World Data: Algorithm Development and Validation," Published: 2024.

[14] Reuters, "US FDA launches AI tool to reduce time taken for scientific reviews," `https://www.reuters.com/`, Published: June 2, 2025.

[15] Cell Reports Medicine, "Large language model as clinical decision support system augments medication safety in 16 clinical specialties," Published: 2025.

[16] AWS, "Generative AI enabled Medical Coding on AWS," `https://aws.amazon.com/blogs/industries/generative-ai-enabled-medical-coding-on-aws`, Published: 2024.

[17] Cleveland Clinic Consult QD, "AI Tools Boost Efficiency, Patient Experience," `https://consultqd.clevelandclinic.org/ai-tools-boost-efficiency-patient-experience`, Published: 2024.

being developed for prior authorization, denials management, and payment posting in health systems.[18]

The administrative applications may be less visible than clinical ones, but their impact on healthcare economics is substantial all the same. Every hour saved on paperwork is an hour that can go to patient care. Every denied claim caught before submission is revenue preserved. The cumulative effect across a health system can be significant.

8.5 Implementation Patterns by Healthcare Setting

While the core capabilities of generative AI are broadly applicable across healthcare, the path to implementation varies significantly by organizational setting. Academic medical centers, community hospitals, and multi-facility health systems operate under distinct technical, financial, and governance constraints, and AI initiatives that succeed in one context often fail when directly transferred to another.

Academic medical centers tend to approach generative AI through a research-first lens. These organizations typically operate complex electronic health record environments alongside homegrown systems, supported by strong data governance, institutional review boards, and dedicated research infrastructure. Decision-making is deliberate, with quality and safety prioritized over speed. Because of this, AI initiatives often begin as controlled research studies or pilot programs led by clinician scientists and only transition into clinical workflows after extensive validation. This approach favors long timelines (often measured in years rather than months) and budgets that are frequently supported by research grants rather than operational funds.

Community hospitals face a very different reality. Technical environments are usually simpler, centered on a single EHR vendor and supported by small or outsourced IT teams. Financial margins are thin, risk tolerance is low, and implementation speed matters. In these settings, generative AI adoption is most successful when it relies on vendor-provided solutions with clear return on investment, such as ambient documentation or revenue-cycle automation. Change management plays a critical role, as physician skepticism and workflow disruption can undermine adoption even when the technology performs well.

[18] Thoughtful.ai, "AI agents for prior authorization, denial management, and payment posting," `https://www.thoughtful.ai/healthcare`, Published: 2024.

Integrated health systems sit between these extremes. Standardized platforms and centralized data services enable scaling across facilities, while shared governance structures allow pilots at individual sites to expand network-wide. These organizations often balance internal development with vendor solutions, using Center-of-Excellence models to manage risk and reuse capabilities. Successful deployments typically follow a measured rollout pattern, validating performance at one location before extending AI-enabled workflows across the broader system.

Across all settings, the common determinant of success is alignment between technical feasibility, clinical workflow integration, and organizational readiness. Generative AI does not impose a single implementation model on healthcare; instead, it amplifies existing institutional strengths and weaknesses. Recognizing these contextual differences is essential for translating promising use cases into durable clinical and operational impact.

8.6 Opportunities and Risks

Figure 8-7. *Bedside patient care illustrating the balance between AI efficiency gains and safety risks*

Generative AI in healthcare presents a familiar pattern: significant potential benefits alongside meaningful risks. The technology could improve patient outcomes, reduce costs, and ease the burden on overworked clinicians. It could also introduce new failure modes, perpetuate biases, and create dependencies that prove difficult to manage. Both of these possibilities deserve serious consideration.

8.6.1 Opportunities

Expanding Access to Expertise

Healthcare expertise is unevenly distributed. Specialists cluster in urban academic medical centers, while rural communities struggle to attract physicians. Generative AI can help bridge this gap by making specialist-level capabilities more widely available.

A primary care physician in a rural clinic might use AI-assisted diagnostic tools to interpret imaging studies that would otherwise require referral to a distant specialist. A community hospital might deploy AI systems that help identify patients at risk for deterioration, catching problems earlier than would otherwise be possible. The technology doesn't replace specialists, but it can extend their reach.

This democratization extends to patients as well. AI-powered health assistants can help patients understand their conditions, navigate complex care pathways, and manage chronic diseases between clinical visits.[1] Connected care platforms can integrate data from wearables and medical devices, creating unified health data streams that flow directly into clinical workflows.

Reducing Clinician Burden

The administrative burden on healthcare workers has reached unsustainable levels. Physicians spend hours each day on documentation, coding, and other paperwork, with nurses facing similar pressures. This burden contributes to burnout, job dissatisfaction, and workforce attrition.

Generative AI directly addresses this problem. Ambient scribes, as discussed earlier in this chapter, reduce documentation time.[2] Automated coding systems speed up billing workflows, and AI-assisted prior authorization can cut through bureaucratic delays. Each application returns time to clinicians that can be spent on patient care.

The impact on workforce sustainability shouldn't be underestimated. Healthcare faces a growing shortage of physicians and nurses. Anything that makes existing workers more productive or reduces the factors driving them out of the profession has systemic value beyond the immediate efficiency gains.

Accelerating Discovery

Drug development timelines have stretched to the point where they threaten the economics of pharmaceutical research. Remember, bringing a new medication to market takes over a decade and costs billions of dollars, and most candidates fail along the way. Generative AI offers the possibility of compressing these timelines and improving success rates.[3]

AI can propose novel molecular candidates faster than traditional methods. It can help optimize clinical trial designs to reduce recruitment times.[4] It can analyze real-world evidence to identify promising therapeutic targets. Each application shaves time and cost from the development process.

The potential extends beyond pharmaceuticals. AI can accelerate research into rare diseases that have historically been neglected because patient populations are too small to support traditional drug development economics. It can enable personalized medicine approaches that tailor treatments to individual patient characteristics.

8.6.2 Risks

Patient Safety and Error Modes

Generative AI systems can produce confident-sounding outputs that are partially or entirely wrong. In healthcare, these errors can harm patients and take the form of a clinical note that omits a critical medication, a diagnostic report that misses an abnormality, or even a drug interaction that goes unflagged. Each represents a potential safety event.

The risk is compounded by the nature of generative AI errors. Traditional rule-based systems can fail too, but their failure modes tend to be more bounded. They break at the edges of what their rules cover, and those gaps can often be identified and addressed systematically. Generative models introduce a different class of risk: they can hallucinate plausible-sounding information with no indication that anything is amiss.[5] That is why it is crucial for clinicians to maintain appropriate skepticism, rather than blindly accepting AI outputs.

Healthcare AI models need integration into workflows with appropriate human oversight. Equally as important as clinicians reviewing generated outputs, model performance should be monitored after deployment. The complexity of health data makes ongoing monitoring all the more important.

Bias and Health Equity

AI systems learn from historical data, and historical data reflects historical inequities. Training datasets may underrepresent certain populations. Algorithms may perform differently across demographic groups. These biases can perpetuate or even amplify existing disparities in healthcare.

The concern is particularly acute for populations that have historically been underserved by the healthcare system. If AI tools work less well for these groups, the technology could widen rather than narrow health equity gaps. Addressing this risk requires careful attention to training data, ongoing monitoring of performance across populations, and willingness to adjust or withdraw systems that show problematic patterns.

Privacy and Data Governance

Healthcare AI requires access to sensitive patient information. Training models, validating performance, and deploying systems all involve handling protected health information. This creates privacy risks that must be carefully managed.

Regulations like HIPAA establish requirements for protecting patient data, but compliance alone doesn't eliminate risk. Data breaches can occur. De-identified data can sometimes be re-identified. AI models can potentially memorize and reproduce training data in unexpected ways. Healthcare organizations need robust data governance frameworks that go beyond minimum regulatory requirements.

Synthetic data generation offers one approach to privacy preservation, allowing researchers to work with datasets that preserve statistical properties while protecting individual patient information.[6]

Regulatory Uncertainty

The regulatory landscape for healthcare AI continues to evolve. Agencies such as the FDA are developing frameworks for overseeing AI-based medical devices, but many questions remain unresolved.[7] How should continuously learning systems be regulated? Who bears liability when AI contributes to adverse outcomes? How should AI tools be validated before deployment?

This uncertainty creates challenges for organizations developing and deploying healthcare AI. Requirements may change. Investments in systems that don't meet emerging standards may be wasted. The prudent approach involves building flexibility into AI programs and staying closely engaged with regulatory developments.

8.7 Economic and Workforce Implications

The economic effects of generative AI in healthcare will ripple through the industry in ways that are only beginning to become clear. Some impacts are already visible. Others will emerge over time as adoption spreads and the technology matures.

8.7.1 Healthcare Economics

Healthcare spending in most developed countries consumes a substantial and growing share of economic output. In the United States, healthcare accounts for nearly one-fifth of GDP. Any technology that can bend the cost curve has enormous economic significance.

Generative AI offers multiple pathways to cost reduction. Administrative automation can reduce overhead. Clinical decision support can prevent costly complications. Drug discovery acceleration can lower development costs that ultimately get passed to patients and payers.[1] Each pathway addresses a different component of healthcare spending.

The administrative opportunity alone is substantial. Revenue cycle management, coding, billing, and prior authorization consume significant resources at every healthcare organization.[2] AI systems that automate portions of this work can reduce staffing requirements or redirect staff to higher-value activities. Cleveland Clinic has deployed AI, including generative approaches, in revenue-cycle workflows to reduce delays and improve patient experience.[3]

Healthcare organizations need technological systems that can adapt to changing conditions. The industry continues to see growth in mergers and acquisitions, ownership of physician practices by large organizations, and adoption of value-based care arrangements. AI systems need to be flexible enough to support these evolving business models.

8.7.2 Workforce Transformation

Healthcare faces a workforce crisis. Physician shortages are projected to worsen over the coming decade. Nursing turnover has accelerated. Burnout rates remain elevated across clinical roles. Generative AI enters this context as both a potential solution and a source of disruption.

The optimistic view holds that AI will augment rather than replace healthcare workers. By automating administrative tasks and supporting clinical decision-making, AI can make existing workers more productive and reduce the factors driving burnout.[4] A physician who spends less time on documentation has more capacity for patient care. A nurse freed from manual charting can focus on bedside care.

This view has merit, but it's incomplete. AI will also change the skills that healthcare workers need. Clinicians will need to understand how to work effectively with AI tools, when to trust their outputs, and when to override them. New roles will emerge for people who can bridge clinical and technical domains.

The transition won't be smooth for everyone. Some roles may contract as AI automates their core functions. Entry-level positions that have traditionally served as training grounds may be particularly affected. Healthcare organizations and educational institutions will need to adapt their workforce development strategies accordingly.

8.7.3 Medical Education

The implications for medical education deserve particular attention. How should medical schools prepare students for a profession where AI plays an increasingly prominent role? What skills will matter most when AI can generate differential diagnoses, draft clinical notes, and propose treatment plans?

Some traditional skills may become less central. If AI can reliably identify drug interactions, perhaps pharmacology education can focus more on principles and less on memorization. If AI can draft clinical documentation, perhaps medical students can spend more time learning communication and examination skills.

Other skills will become more important. Critical evaluation of AI outputs will be essential. Understanding the limitations and failure modes of AI systems will be necessary for safe practice. The ability to recognize when AI recommendations don't fit a particular patient's circumstances will distinguish excellent clinicians from adequate ones.

AI itself may transform how medical education is delivered. Large language models can generate practice cases, simulate patient encounters, and provide personalized tutoring.[5] Synthetic data can provide training material without exposing actual patient information.[6] These capabilities could make medical education more accessible and more effective.

8.8 Looking Ahead: The Future of Healthcare AI

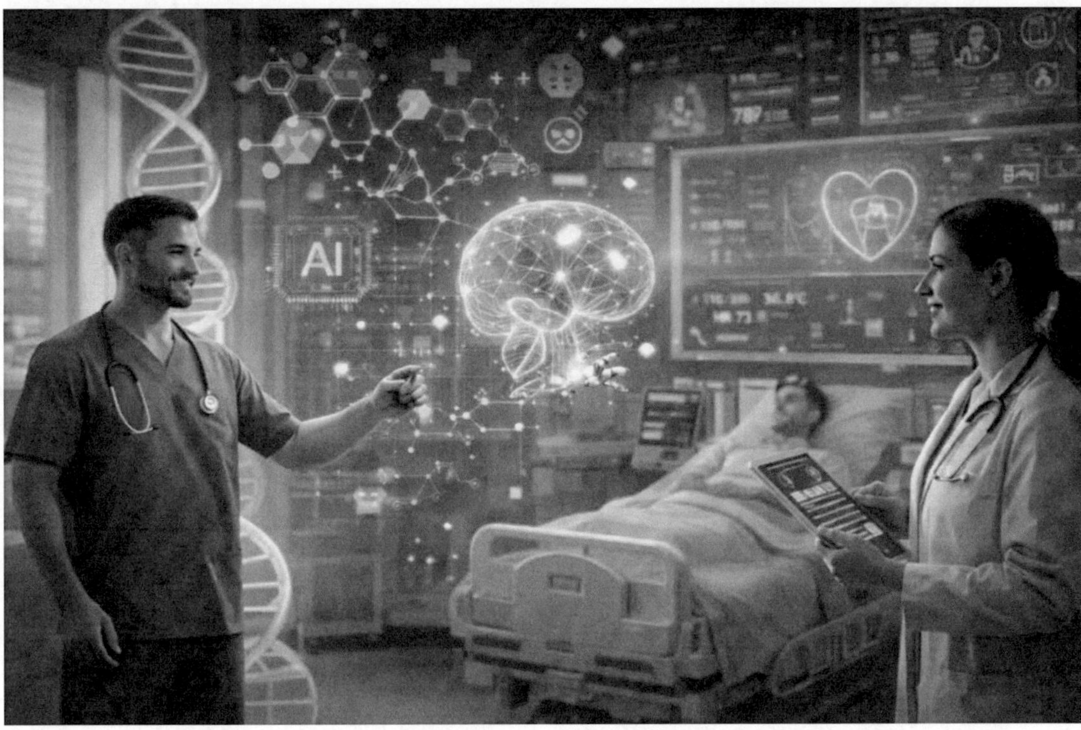

Figure 8-8. *The future of healthcare AI spanning agentic systems, personalized medicine, and integrated care platforms*

Predicting the future is a reliable way to be wrong. But certain trajectories seem likely to continue, and thinking through their implications can help healthcare organizations prepare for what's coming.

8.8.1 Integration and Convergence

The various applications of healthcare AI that exist today as separate tools will increasingly converge into integrated platforms. Rather than deploying one system for clinical documentation, another for diagnostic support, and a third for decision support, organizations will move toward unified platforms that share data and capabilities.

This convergence is already visible in how healthcare organizations describe themselves. These platforms and partnerships are crucial for using data and technology to drive the Quadruple Aim objectives: improving patient experience, improving population health, reducing care costs, and enhancing caregiver experiences.

Modern healthcare is evolving into an integrated ecosystem that connects traditional providers, health plans, pharmacies, and brick-and-mortar care organizations with cloud service providers, digital marketplaces, and connected medical devices. This ecosystem must be data-driven and, in turn, creates the data that can power innovative generative AI applications.

8.8.2 The Rise of Agentic AI

Healthcare is entering a new phase with the emergence of agentic AI, which goes beyond conventional AI technologies. Unlike traditional systems, agentic AI demonstrates autonomous decision-making capabilities, adaptive learning in complex healthcare environments, real-time monitoring of patient progress, dynamic coordination of care teams, and accelerated treatment plan development.

These intelligent systems are becoming embedded in healthcare operations, from enhancing diagnostic precision through advanced pattern recognition to optimizing clinical workflows and accelerating drug discovery processes. Agentic AI combines proactive problem-solving abilities with real-time adaptability so that healthcare professionals can focus on high-value, patient-centered activities, while the AI handles routine tasks and complex data analysis.

Consider the journey of a cancer patient today, marked by uncertainty and the weight of diagnosis. Clinicians must sift through mountains of data from various modalities and sources including medical images, lab results, and patient histories to develop treatment plans. Agentic AI systems can ease these burdens by providing real-time support to healthcare providers, handling complex tasks like deciphering intricate medical cases and coordinating care plans across multiple specialized departments.

8.8.3 Personalized Medicine at Scale

As we touched on in Chapter 7 in the "Organizational Transformation for Personalization Excellence" section, healthcare organizations develop programs that help clinicians integrate personalized care recommendations into their practice while maintaining clinical judgment and patient relationships. AI can further this and help create tailored treatment strategies for individual patients by processing vast amounts of medical literature along with patient data. Longitudinal risk models can predict disease risk across decades using multimodal clinical and registry data, supporting preventive care decisions.[7]

The rapid growth of medical information has made it challenging for patients to find reliable information about their conditions. Precision medicine adds to this challenge by taking into account individual differences in genes, environments, and lifestyles. When those variables are multiplied together, it becomes apparent that every individual is medically unique. AI systems can help unlock data from silos and make it available so patients can access personalized health information and get appropriate guidance.

8.8.4 Regulatory Evolution

The regulatory landscape continues to evolve. Agencies are developing frameworks for overseeing AI-based medical devices, and early adoption of AI can lead to substantial gains as regulatory bodies like the FDA issue clearer guidance on AI in clinical development.[8] The most successful organizations will be those that engage closely with regulatory developments while building flexibility into their AI programs.

8.9 Conclusion

The integration of generative AI into healthcare represents more than a technological upgrade; it marks a fundamental shift in how medicine is practiced, how drugs are discovered, and how patients experience care.

Throughout this chapter, we've traced the arc of AI across healthcare's full spectrum. In the exam room, ambient scribes are giving physicians back the time they lost to documentation, letting them focus on the person sitting across from them rather than the screen beside them.[9] In radiology departments, AI systems draft reports that radiologists can review and refine, increasing throughput without sacrificing quality.[10]

In research laboratories, generative models propose novel molecules and accelerate the search for new treatments.[11] In clinical trials, AI helps optimize protocols and match patients to studies.[12]

The opportunities are substantial. Healthcare organizations can use generative AI to enhance patient care, streamline operations, and accelerate medical research. AI-driven image analysis can provide rapid and precise insights, reducing the workload on medical professionals and minimizing the risk of human error. Predictive analytics can help organizations anticipate patient outcomes and personalize care plans accordingly.

But the risks deserve equal attention. AI systems can produce confident-sounding outputs that are wrong.[13] They can perpetuate biases present in their training data. They can create dependencies that prove difficult to manage. Healthcare organizations must approach these tools with appropriate caution, maintaining human oversight and building robust validation processes.

The workforce implications are significant. Clinicians struggle to balance patient care with the volume of routine tasks they perform every day. They grow frustrated when unable to access comprehensive patient-specific data at the point of care. Workloads are excessive, medical records incomplete, and working environments challenging. A modern approach to healthcare data and AI can help improve the work experience by automating administrative tasks and creating systems that facilitate the seamless exchange of records between providers.

The path forward requires balance. Healthcare organizations need technological systems that can adapt to changing conditions, including unexpected changes in healthcare needs. They need to invest in data infrastructure alongside AI capabilities. They need to train their workforce to work effectively with these new tools.

The question isn't whether AI will reshape healthcare. That's already happening. The question is whether we'll shape that transformation thoughtfully, capturing the benefits while managing the risks. The organizations that succeed will be those that treat AI as a tool to augment human judgment rather than replace it, that maintain appropriate skepticism about AI outputs, and that keep patient welfare at the center of every decision.

In the next chapter, we will explore how generative AI is transforming financial services through enhanced risk assessment, sophisticated fraud detection systems, and personalized banking experiences. This sector's data-rich environment and regulatory complexity provide compelling insights into enterprise AI implementation at scale.

CHAPTER 9

Financial Services: Risk Assessment, Fraud Detection, and Personalized Banking

The financial services industry stands at a critical juncture where artificial intelligence and generative AI are fundamentally transforming how institutions assess risk, detect fraud, and serve customers. As regulatory pressures intensify, customer expectations evolve, and competitive dynamics shift, financial institutions are discovering that AI capabilities are no longer optional enhancements but essential infrastructure for survival and growth. According to IDC research, AI investment in financial services is projected to grow significantly from 2025 to 2030, reflecting the industry's recognition of AI's transformative potential across key areas such as improving the speed and accuracy of fraud detection and prevention, automating compliance, bringing new levels of precision to all types of risk management, and delivering truly individualized experiences cost-effectively and at scale.

The convergence of traditional machine learning with generative AI creates unprecedented opportunities to address longstanding challenges in financial services. Institutions can now analyze vast amounts of structured and unstructured data in real time, identify subtle patterns indicative of fraud or risk, and deliver personalized experiences that were previously impossible at scale. Research demonstrates that over 70% of banks rank customer experience as a priority, with 81% making AI/ML investments to improve customer experience over the next 12 months, and banks focusing on personalization see a 20% improvement in customer satisfaction.

N. Sendas et al., *Building Generative AI Solutions for Industries with AWS*,
https://doi.org/10.1007/979-8-8688-2830-0_9

However, AI adoption in financial services requires careful navigation of complex challenges. Organizations must balance innovation and costs against stringent risk management and regulatory compliance while addressing critical requirements around data governance, ethical AI use, and the security of sensitive financial information. Success demands a strategic approach focused on building robust data foundations, upskilling the workforce, and establishing clear governance frameworks. Financial institutions that effectively address these challenges can harness AI's transformative potential today while maintaining the trust and security fundamental to their operations.

9.1 The Business Imperative for AI in Financial Services

The economic case for AI adoption in financial services has never been more compelling. Financial institutions implementing AI-powered fraud detection systems have reported meaningful reductions in fraud losses, with results varying significantly based on institutional maturity, fraud type, and implementation approach. Through GenAI and AI/ML, fraud reduction enables adaptive protection as fraud tactics evolve, with AI and machine learning systems continuously adapting to new threats. When fraud does occur, AI-driven systems can help businesses identify and resolve issues more quickly while staying compliant with evolving regulations and industry standards related to fraud prevention and data protection.

Beyond fraud prevention, AI transforms core banking operations across multiple dimensions. In credit decisioning, institutions leverage ML across internal and external unstructured data sets to better assess customers' credit risk and ongoing default and impairment risk. Pre-built and custom AI/ML capabilities provide customer recommendations on loan affordability and alternatives. For digital lending, AI-driven approaches enable alternative credit scoring models that expand financial inclusion. By leveraging AI-driven credit scoring, lenders can assess creditworthiness using non-traditional data sources such as utility payments, rental history, and social media activity, enabling them to serve previously underbanked populations.

The customer experience transformation enabled by AI delivers measurable business impact. Banks are listening and responding to customer demands, with 74% of consumers desiring more personalized services from their financial institutions. According to research by Kantar, a focus on customer experience could mean an increase in banks' share of deposits by up to 16.5%, while Foundry research shows that personalized messaging converts 20% more qualified leads than traditional broadly targeted communications. McKinsey research demonstrates that personalization drives a 10–15% revenue lift, with the better a company becomes in utilizing data to grow customer knowledge and intimacy, the greater the returns.

The operational efficiency gains from AI implementation prove equally significant. Financial institutions report substantial improvements in processing times and cost reductions. For example, PENNYMAC's AI solution processes 144,000 loans annually with 99% accuracy, saving nearly $1 million yearly while significantly reducing manual review needs and improving employee satisfaction by eliminating repetitive tasks. Travelers' generative AI solution reduces claim processing from months to days, enabling the company to handle higher volumes of claims and drastically cut claim handlers' call times, realizing massive returns on investment.

However, realizing these benefits requires more than technology deployment. Organizations must develop comprehensive strategies that address data quality, model governance, regulatory compliance, and organizational change management. The most successful implementations treat AI as a strategic capability requiring sustained investment and continuous optimization rather than a one-time technology project.

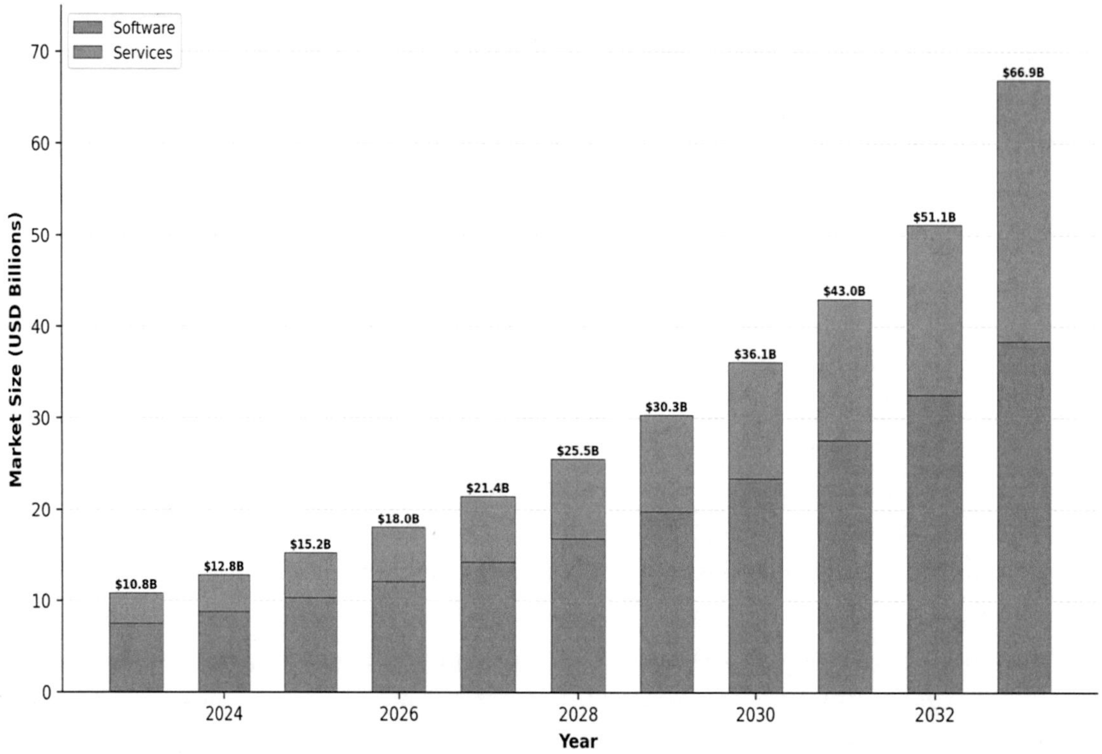

***Figure 9-1.** Global AI in fraud management market size projection (2023–2033), showing growth from $10.8B to $66.9B split between software and services segments*

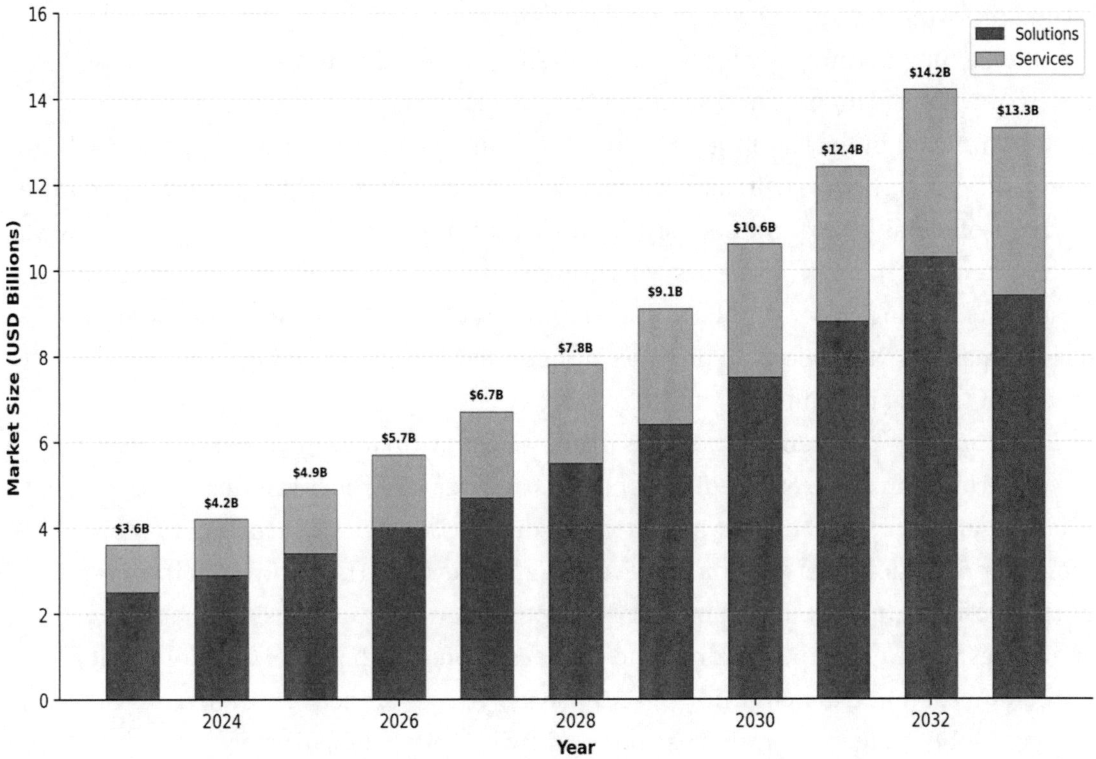

Figure 9-2. *Credit card fraud detection platform market size (2023–2033), showing growth from $3.6B to $13.3B across solutions and services*

9.2 AI-Powered Risk Assessment and Credit Decisioning

Risk assessment represents one of the most transformative applications of AI in financial services. Traditional credit scoring models, while effective, often fail to capture the full complexity of creditworthiness, particularly for individuals with limited credit histories or non-traditional financial profiles. AI and machine learning enable more sophisticated, nuanced approaches to credit risk assessment that expand access to financial services while maintaining appropriate risk management.

Alternative credit scoring models leverage machine learning to analyze diverse data sources beyond traditional credit bureau information. These models incorporate utility payment histories, rental payments, employment stability, educational background, and even behavioral patterns to assess creditworthiness. Research shows that alternative credit scoring can expand financial inclusion by enabling assessment of previously underbanked populations while maintaining or improving default prediction accuracy. Financial institutions implementing these approaches report significant improvements in approval rates for previously underserved segments while maintaining portfolio quality.

Real-time credit decisioning powered by AI transforms the lending experience from a multi-day process to near-instantaneous decisions. Machine learning models analyze hundreds of variables simultaneously, identifying patterns and relationships that human underwriters might miss. These systems continuously learn from new data, adapting to changing economic conditions and emerging risk factors. On-the-fly decisioning enables financial institutions to provide immediate responses to credit applications while maintaining rigorous risk standards.

Portfolio risk management benefits from AI's ability to identify emerging risks before they materialize into losses. Predictive models analyze macroeconomic indicators, industry trends, customer behavior patterns, and market signals to forecast potential defaults and portfolio deterioration. Leveraging LLMs for synthetic model training data generation and automated model documentation enhances risk management capabilities while reducing the time and cost associated with model development and maintenance. Financial institutions use these insights to proactively adjust lending criteria, modify collection strategies, and optimize capital allocation.

The integration of generative AI into credit decisioning processes enables new capabilities in document analysis and decision explanation. Large language models can extract relevant information from unstructured documents such as financial statements, tax returns, and business plans, synthesizing insights that inform credit decisions. Automated credit memos and investigation reports generated by AI reduce the time analysts spend on documentation while ensuring consistency and completeness. This automation allows credit professionals to focus on complex cases requiring human judgment, while AI handles routine analysis and documentation.

However, AI-powered credit decisioning raises important considerations around fairness, transparency, and regulatory compliance. Models must be carefully designed and monitored to avoid perpetuating or amplifying biases present in historical data. Explainability becomes critical, as regulators and customers increasingly demand understanding of how credit decisions are made. Financial institutions must implement robust model governance frameworks that ensure AI-driven credit decisions meet regulatory requirements while delivering business value.

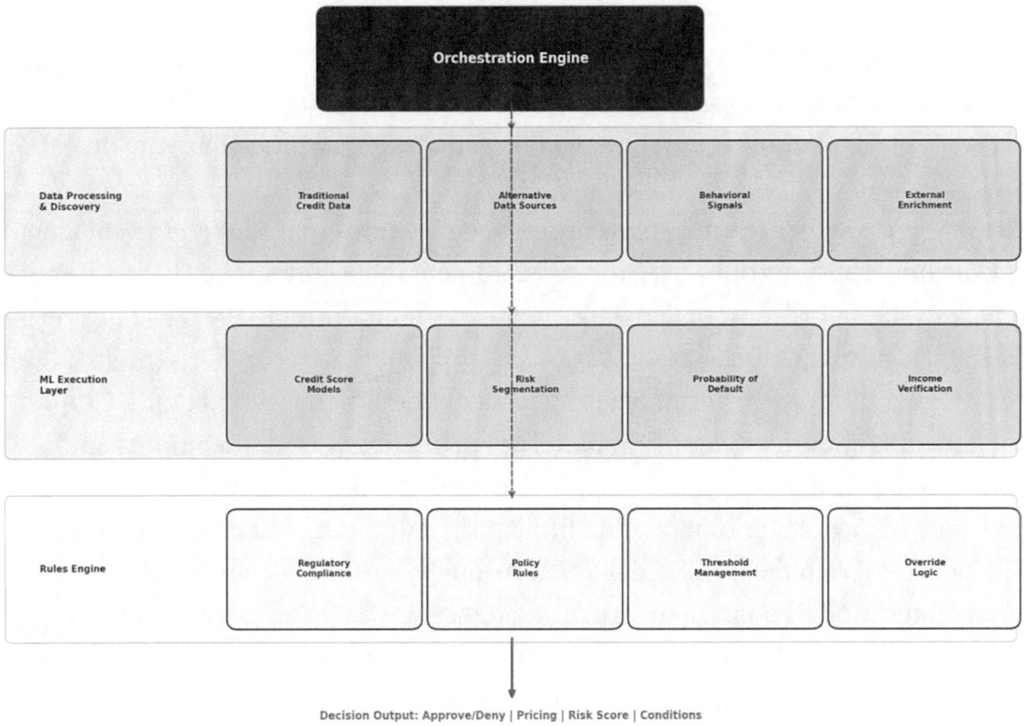

Figure 9-3. *AI-powered credit decisioning orchestration workflow showing data processing, ML execution, and rules engine layers coordinated by an orchestration engine*

9.3 Advanced Fraud Detection and Prevention

Fraud detection represents one of the most mature and impactful applications of AI in financial services. The sophistication of fraudulent activities continues to evolve, with criminals leveraging technology to execute increasingly complex schemes at scale. Traditional rule-based fraud detection systems struggle to keep pace with these evolving threats, generating high false positive rates that frustrate customers while missing novel fraud patterns. AI and machine learning provide the adaptive, intelligent capabilities needed to combat modern financial crime effectively.

Machine learning models for fraud detection analyze vast amounts of transaction data in real time, identifying subtle patterns and anomalies indicative of fraudulent activity. These models consider hundreds of features including transaction amounts, merchant categories, geographic locations, device characteristics, and behavioral patterns. Unlike rule-based systems that flag transactions based on predetermined thresholds, ML models learn complex relationships between features that distinguish legitimate from fraudulent transactions. Research demonstrates that AI-powered fraud detection can reduce fraud investigation time by 33% while improving detection accuracy.

Real-time fraud detection systems process transactions in milliseconds, making accept/decline decisions before customers complete their purchases. These systems must balance fraud prevention with customer experience, minimizing false positives that decline legitimate transactions. Advanced implementations use ensemble models that combine multiple algorithms, each specialized for different fraud types. Graph neural networks analyze relationship patterns between accounts, merchants, and transactions to identify fraud rings and coordinated attacks. Deep learning models detect subtle behavioral anomalies that indicate account takeover or identity theft.

Generative AI enhances fraud detection through multiple mechanisms. Large language models analyze unstructured data sources including customer communications, social media, and news reports to identify emerging fraud trends and schemes. Natural language processing extracts entities and relationships from fraud investigation reports, building knowledge graphs that reveal connections between seemingly unrelated cases. Synthetic data generation creates realistic fraud scenarios for model training, addressing the challenge of imbalanced datasets where fraudulent transactions represent a tiny fraction of total volume.

The integration of AI with traditional fraud prevention measures creates layered defense strategies. Behavioral biometrics analyzes how customers interact with devices, detecting anomalies in typing patterns, mouse movements, and navigation behaviors that indicate account takeover. Device fingerprinting identifies suspicious devices attempting to access accounts. Network analysis reveals coordinated fraud attempts across multiple accounts. When these signals combine with transaction-level ML models, financial institutions achieve detection rates exceeding 90% while reducing false positives by 60–80%.

However, fraudsters continuously adapt their tactics to evade detection systems. This adversarial dynamic requires continuous model retraining and monitoring. Financial institutions must implement robust MLOps practices that enable rapid model updates in response to emerging threats. Explainability tools help fraud +analysts understand why transactions were flagged, enabling them to validate model decisions and identify new fraud patterns. Collaboration across institutions through information-sharing networks amplifies the effectiveness of fraud detection by enabling collective learning from fraud attempts across the industry.

The regulatory environment for fraud detection continues to evolve, with increasing emphasis on customer protection and data privacy. Financial institutions must ensure their fraud detection systems comply with regulations while maintaining effectiveness. This includes implementing appropriate data governance, ensuring model fairness across customer segments, and providing transparency into fraud detection decisions when required. The balance between fraud prevention, customer experience, and regulatory compliance requires careful orchestration of technology, processes, and human oversight.

9.4 Personalized Banking and Customer Experience

Personalization has emerged as a critical differentiator in financial services, with customers increasingly expecting experiences tailored to their individual needs, preferences, and financial situations. Research shows that 74% of consumers want more personalized services from their financial institutions, and banks focusing on personalization see a 20% improvement in customer satisfaction. AI and generative AI enable financial institutions to deliver personalization at scale, transforming how they acquire, onboard, serve, and retain customers.

Customer acquisition benefits from AI-powered targeting and personalization. Financial institutions leverage external and internal data sources to gain a deeper understanding of prospects' investments, interests, connections, and financial needs prior to first contact. Generative AI transforms corporate sales activities including draft proposal creation to be more efficient and scalable, with implementations showing a 10× increase in prospecting activities and 30% boost in conversion rates. Target prospects based on needs and provide recommendations that resonate with individual circumstances rather than broad demographic segments.

Digital onboarding powered by AI streamlines the customer acquisition process while reducing friction and fraud risk. Identity verification solutions using computer vision and liveness detection ensure legitimate customers can quickly open accounts while preventing fraudulent applications. Intelligent document processing extracts information from identity documents, financial statements, and other required paperwork, automatically populating application forms and reducing manual data entry. Enhanced chatbots and conversational search powered by generative AI guide customers through the onboarding process, answering questions and providing assistance 24/7.

Personalized financial advice represents a transformative application of AI in banking. Traditional financial advisory services were limited to high-net-worth individuals due to the cost of human advisors. AI enables democratization of financial advice, providing personalized recommendations to customers across all wealth segments. Real-time advice engines leverage insights like retirement age, savings, spending, investment behaviors, and goal parameters to create customized financial plans that help clients meet their financial goals. Recommendation systems produce next best actions tailored to the goals of the client, enabling advisers to best serve customers.

Customer service transformation through AI improves both efficiency and experience quality. Omni-channel support powered by AI enables customers to seamlessly transition between self-service, chatbot, and human agent assistance based on their needs and preferences. Post-call analytics extract insights from customer service interactions, identifying common issues, sentiment trends, and opportunities for service improvement. Live-call analytics provide real-time guidance to agents, surfacing relevant information and suggesting responses that improve first-call resolution rates. Agent assist capabilities reduce average handle time while improving customer satisfaction.

Retention and growth strategies leverage AI to predict churn risk and identify cross-sell opportunities. Personalized recommendations suggest products and services aligned with customers' financial situations and goals. Churn prediction models identify customers at risk of leaving, enabling proactive retention efforts. Gamification elements powered by AI encourage desired behaviors such as increased savings or financial education engagement. NatWest's implementation of generative AI to create personalized, branded content resulted in a 4× improvement in message click-through rates and a 900% increase in savings account applications.

The technology infrastructure for personalized banking requires integration of customer data platforms, machine learning models, real-time decisioning engines, and omni-channel delivery systems. Customer 360 platforms unify data from disparate sources to create comprehensive customer profiles. Feature stores maintain consistent customer attributes across multiple models and applications. Real-time decisioning engines orchestrate personalization across touchpoints, determining what content, offers, or recommendations to present based on current context and customer state.

However, personalization in financial services must navigate strict regulatory requirements and customer privacy expectations. Financial institutions must implement robust consent management, provide transparency into how customer data is used, and enable customers to control their personalization preferences. Bias monitoring ensures personalization doesn't disadvantage certain customer segments. The balance between personalization effectiveness and privacy protection requires careful design of data architectures, governance frameworks, and customer communication strategies.

9.5 Regulatory Compliance and Responsible AI

The regulatory environment for AI in financial services continues to evolve rapidly, with regulators worldwide developing frameworks to ensure AI systems are safe, fair, and transparent. Financial institutions must navigate complex requirements from multiple sources including the EU AI Act, industry-specific regulations, and data protection laws like GDPR and CCPA. According to AWS research, financial institutions need comprehensive governance frameworks covering AI governance and management, risk management, and regulatory compliance to ensure responsible AI adoption.

AI governance frameworks establish the organizational structures, policies, and processes needed to ensure responsible AI development and deployment. These frameworks define roles and responsibilities for AI oversight, establish approval processes for new AI use cases, and specify monitoring requirements for deployed systems. Cross-functional governance committees review AI strategies for alignment with brand values, regulatory requirements, and ethical standards. All three lines of defense must be aligned on AI definitions, with reporting processes clearly defined for safety issues and incidents.

Risk management for AI systems requires systematic identification, assessment, and mitigation of unique risks such as hallucinations, prompt injections, and data poisoning. Organizations must implement automated monitoring, clear governance frameworks, and continuous process improvement to maintain regulatory compliance in the rapidly evolving GenAI landscape. Risk management activities are tiered, with high-risk use cases undergoing more extensive scrutiny. AI-specific risk assessment activities align with corporate governance structures, and individuals responsible for risk management activities receive appropriate training.

Model transparency and explainability requirements present particular challenges in regulated industries. Organizations must develop capabilities to explain and justify AI decision-making processes, while also managing the complexities of cross-border data transfers and varying jurisdictional requirements. This necessitates robust governance frameworks and continuous monitoring of regulatory developments. Financial institutions implement explainable AI techniques that allow customers to understand why specific products or services were recommended, building confidence in AI-driven advisory services.

Compliance monitoring serves as a crucial ongoing process involving continuous tracking of regulatory requirements and internal policies as they evolve. Organizations must implement automated monitoring systems to track compliance metrics, conduct regular audits and assessments, and maintain detailed documentation of model lineage and decisions. This documentation becomes particularly valuable during regulatory reviews and internal governance processes. Policies and procedures are updated for AI adoption, and appropriate disclosures are made for both external and internal facing AI use cases.

Bias detection and mitigation represent critical components of responsible AI in financial services. Models trained on historical data can perpetuate or amplify existing biases, leading to unfair treatment of certain customer groups. Financial institutions implement rigorous bias testing to ensure lending recommendations and credit decisions don't discriminate based on protected characteristics. Regular audits of AI systems for performance, fairness, and compliance help identify and address potential issues before they impact customers.

Data governance and privacy protection require careful attention in AI implementations. Financial institutions must ensure their AI systems comply with data protection regulations while maintaining effectiveness. This includes implementing appropriate data governance, ensuring model fairness across customer segments, and providing transparency into AI decisions when required. Privacy-preserving techniques including federated learning and differential privacy enable effective AI while protecting customer data.

The regulatory landscape varies significantly across jurisdictions, requiring financial institutions to adapt their AI governance frameworks to local requirements. In the Asia-Pacific region, approximately 95% of retailers recognize the importance of clear laws and regulations to provide guidance, consistency, and accountability in how AI is used and developed in their industry. This suggests that, without regulatory frameworks, financial institutions may face uncertainty or risks that hinder AI adoption and that well-defined rules are seen as essential to enabling responsible innovation and long-term growth.

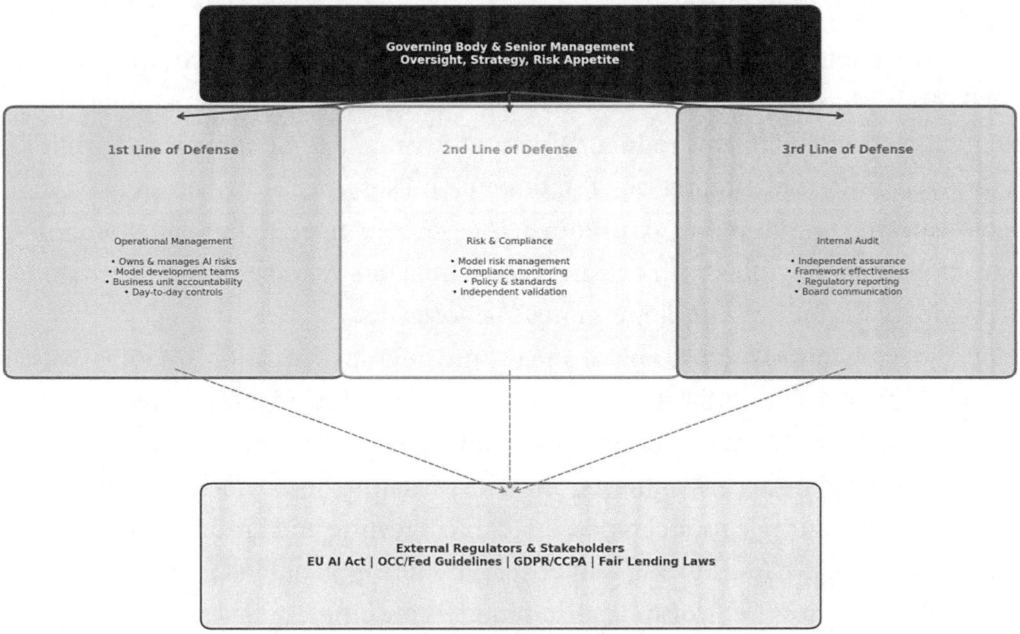

Figure 9-4. *AI governance framework based on the three lines of defense model: operational management, risk and compliance, and internal audit with regulatory oversight*

9.6 Technology Architecture and Implementation

Building effective AI capabilities in financial services requires assembling a technology architecture that balances capability, integration, security, and regulatory compliance. Organizations face build-vs.-buy decisions across multiple layers of the AI stack, from data infrastructure through model development to application delivery. These decisions significantly impact time-to-value, flexibility, and long-term scalability while ensuring adherence to stringent financial services requirements.

Data infrastructure forms the foundation of AI capabilities in financial services. Modern data platforms integrate structured data from core banking systems, unstructured data from documents and communications, and external data from market feeds and third-party providers. Data lakes built on cloud storage provide scalable, cost-effective repositories for diverse data types. Data warehouses optimized for analytics enable efficient querying and reporting. Feature stores maintain consistent feature definitions across training and serving environments, solving the training-serving skew problem that degrades model performance.

Machine learning platforms provide infrastructure for developing, training, and deploying AI models. Cloud-based ML platforms offer managed services for common financial services tasks including fraud detection, credit scoring, and customer segmentation. These platforms reduce infrastructure management overhead while providing scalability and integration with other cloud services. However, organizations with sophisticated requirements or unique use cases may need to build custom ML infrastructure that integrates with existing risk management and compliance systems while providing flexibility to implement novel algorithms.

Model serving infrastructure enables real-time inference at scale. Financial services applications often require sub-100 millisecond response times for fraud detection and credit decisioning. Achieving this performance requires careful optimization of model complexity, data access patterns, and infrastructure deployment. Model serving platforms support multiple model types, enable A/B testing and gradual rollouts, and provide comprehensive monitoring and observability. Financial institutions often maintain dozens or hundreds of specialized models for different tasks, customer segments, and product categories, requiring sophisticated orchestration.

Generative AI platforms provide capabilities for creating personalized content, conversational interactions, and document analysis. Organizations must decide whether to use general-purpose large language models through APIs, fine-tune models on proprietary data, or develop specialized models for specific tasks. Financial services firms often fine-tune models on historical customer communications and financial content to generate personalized investment commentary and advice that maintains appropriate tone and regulatory compliance. Amazon Bedrock provides a fully managed service that makes foundation models accessible via an API to build and scale generative AI applications while meeting stringent security standards required in regulated banking environments.

Integration architecture determines how AI capabilities connect with existing systems including core banking platforms, CRM systems, customer service applications, and regulatory reporting tools. API-first architectures enable flexible integration while maintaining separation of concerns between AI logic and application delivery. Financial institutions implement integration layers that enable AI systems to interact with multiple back-end systems while maintaining appropriate security, audit trails, and compliance controls.

Security and compliance infrastructure ensures AI systems meet financial services requirements. This includes encryption of data at rest and in transit, access controls based on least privilege principles, comprehensive audit logging, and monitoring for security threats. AI-specific security measures address risks including prompt injection, data poisoning, and model extraction. Integration with existing security information and event management (SIEM) systems provides unified visibility across AI and traditional infrastructure.

Observability and monitoring infrastructure provides visibility into AI system performance, model behavior, and business impact. Comprehensive monitoring tracks technical metrics like latency and error rates alongside business metrics including approval rates, fraud detection accuracy, and customer satisfaction. Anomaly detection identifies when AI systems behave unexpectedly, triggering alerts and potentially automatic rollbacks. Model performance monitoring tracks prediction accuracy, data drift, and concept drift, enabling proactive model retraining before performance degrades.

MLOps practices enable efficient development, deployment, and maintenance of AI systems at scale. Automated pipelines handle model training, validation, deployment, and monitoring. Version control tracks changes to models, data, and code. Automated testing validates model performance before deployment. Continuous integration and continuous deployment (CI/CD) practices enable rapid iteration while maintaining quality and compliance. Financial institutions implementing mature MLOps practices report 30–50% faster deployment to production, 80% increase in automation and reproducibility of ML workflows, and 30% lower cost in model maintenance.

Figure 9-5. *Generative AI applications in financial services: fraud detection, credit scoring, portfolio optimization, algorithmic trading, synthetic data generation, financial text generation, and risk management*

9.7 Organizational Transformation and Change Management

Successful AI adoption in financial services requires fundamental changes in organizational structure, processes, culture, and skills. Traditional functional silos between risk, compliance, technology, and business units create barriers to effective AI implementation. Leading financial institutions restructure around AI capabilities, creating cross-functional teams with shared accountability for AI outcomes across the organization.

AI Centers of Excellence (CoEs) provide centralized expertise and governance while enabling distributed AI development across business units. CoEs establish standards for AI development, maintain reusable components and accelerators, provide training and support, and ensure consistency in AI governance and risk management. The CoE model balances the need for specialized AI expertise with the importance of embedding AI capabilities within business units that understand domain-specific requirements and use cases.

Skill development represents a critical investment for AI success in financial services. Organizations need talent that combines domain expertise with data science, machine learning, and AI engineering capabilities. Training programs help existing employees develop skills in data analysis, model development, and AI-assisted decision-making. Financial institutions train risk analysts to leverage AI-powered tools effectively, understanding both the technical capabilities and limitations of AI-driven recommendations. Compliance teams develop expertise in AI governance and regulatory requirements specific to AI systems.

Data literacy programs extend beyond technical teams to business users, executives, and board members. Understanding how AI systems work, what they can and cannot do, and how to interpret their outputs becomes essential for effective decision-making. Financial institutions implement training programs that demystify AI, explain key concepts in accessible terms, and provide hands-on experience with AI tools. This broad-based data literacy enables more effective collaboration between technical and business teams.

Change management proves critical as AI transforms how financial institutions operate. Employees accustomed to traditional processes and decision-making approaches must adapt to AI-augmented workflows. Clear communication about AI strategy, comprehensive training, and visible leadership support help organizations navigate this transition. Financial institutions that successfully implement AI at scale invest heavily in change management, ensuring employees understand how AI enhances rather than replaces their expertise and judgment.

Cultural transformation toward experimentation and continuous learning underpins sustainable AI success. Organizations must embrace testing, accept that not all AI initiatives will succeed, and systematically learn from both successes and failures. This requires psychological safety where teams feel comfortable proposing and testing new approaches without fear of failure. Financial institutions foster experimentation cultures by celebrating learning from failed AI experiments as much as successful ones, recognizing that systematic experimentation drives long-term improvement.

Governance and decision rights must evolve to support AI-driven operations. Traditional approval processes designed for manual decision-making often create bottlenecks for AI systems that operate in real time. Financial institutions develop new governance models that provide appropriate oversight while enabling the speed and automation that AI enables. This includes establishing clear decision rights for AI systems, defining escalation paths for edge cases, and implementing monitoring that ensures AI systems operate within approved parameters.

Measurement and accountability systems align organizational incentives with AI objectives. Traditional metrics focused on individual function performance often create conflicts between optimizing AI systems and maintaining existing processes. Leading financial institutions implement AI-centric metrics that measure end-to-end outcomes, with shared accountability across teams. Risk management tracks not just traditional risk metrics but also AI-specific risks including model performance, bias, and compliance. Business units measure the impact of AI on customer outcomes, operational efficiency, and financial performance.

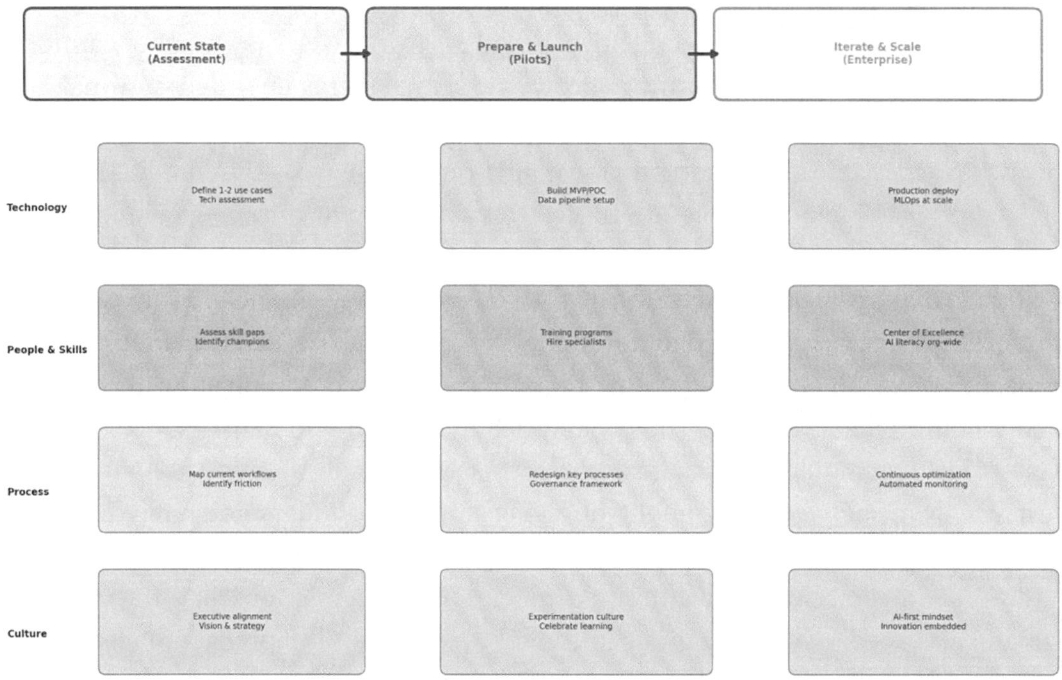

Figure 9-6. *Organizational AI transformation roadmap showing parallel tracks for technology, people, process, and culture across assessment, pilot, and scale phases*

9.8 Industry Case Studies and Implementation Patterns

Real-world implementations of AI in financial services demonstrate both the transformative potential and practical challenges of AI adoption. Leading institutions have achieved significant business outcomes through strategic AI investments, providing valuable lessons for organizations at various stages of their AI journeys.

S&P Global Ratings used generative AI to accelerate the delivery of financial analysis and creation of supporting documentation, increasing capacity and improving time to market. In financial services and credit analysis, time is a precious resource. These documents are complex, with a variety of sections that require deep subject matter expertise to create, which is a time-consuming process. AWS collaborated with the Ratings team to develop a comprehensive AI solution for document analysis and generation. This solution ingests a wide variety of internal documentation to retrieve, extract, and then generate documents section-by-section to augment analyst efforts. The solution empowers analysts to deliver faster results, driving value for S&P customers. It reduced manual effort, enhanced operational efficiency and time-to-market, and generated consistent positive user feedback with high engagement metrics.

Travelers Insurance partnered with the GenAI Innovation Center to create a general liability assistant that can break down insurance coverages, policy amendments, and claims details into concise and understandable summaries and clearly outline the specific insurance coverages and claim handling responsibilities that Travelers is required to fulfill during the claim approval process. The generative AI solution reduces claim processing from months to days, enabling Travelers to handle a higher volume of claims and drastically cut claim handlers' call times, realizing massive returns on their investment. The system processes complex legal documents like deeds of trust and promissory notes while maintaining 100% compliance with state-specific regulations.

Nasdaq partnered with the GenAIIC to create a market surveillance solution that can distill and analyze relevant information from multiple sources quickly and produce consolidated tables and summaries of key data points such as regulatory filings, company news, and other relevant information. The solution increased operational efficiency by reducing investigation time by 33%. The solution is more effectively able to detect potential market abuse, thereby maintaining trust and integrity in global capital markets. The traditional process of investigating alerts and suspicious activity is highly resource-intensive, involving manual collation and analysis of extensive data from multiple sources.

NatWest Group leveraged generative AI to enhance its existing ML personalization products, including tools like NatWest Digital Financial Health Check and the Know Your Credit Score service. By working closely with AWS to co-create responsible AI products on top of foundation models available through Amazon Bedrock, NatWest achieved a 4× improvement in message click-through rates and a 900% increase in savings account applications. Combining AWS's leading data, analytics, machine learning, and generative AI capabilities with the bank's 300 years of financial services experience resulted in tailored banking experiences that deliver personalized communications, financial education, products, and services to NatWest Group's customers.

Mitsubishi UFJ Bank developed a generative AI solution using Anthropic's Claude Sonnet 3.5 on Amazon Bedrock to improve the efficiency and effectiveness of sales proposal activities. The solution efficiently extracts insights from unstructured data like securities reports, understands the client's business strategy, analyzes the market environment, and supports the proposal of optimal financial products. Mitsubishi UFJ Bank's implementation of generative AI increased prospecting activities tenfold and boosted conversion rates by 30%. Sales representatives achieved higher efficiency and productivity with the generative AI solution.

Experian plc, a global leader in data broker and consumer credit reporting, processes 6 million dispute documents annually through manual review processes. AWS built a solution using state-of-the-art generative AI tools to extract customer information for identity matching and automate dispute reason code categorization. The system analyzes extracted content alongside credit report data, demonstrating reliable accuracy. As a result, the system went to production and achieved a 19% target reduction in handle time. Agents in a live environment are using automated dispute categorization and one-click AI suggestions. The system significantly improved one-shot and first-pass acceptance accuracy of the dispute handling volume.

These implementations share common patterns that contribute to success. Organizations start with clear business objectives and measurable success criteria. They invest in data quality and infrastructure before attempting sophisticated AI implementations. They implement robust governance and risk management frameworks from the beginning rather than treating them as afterthoughts. They focus on change management and user adoption, recognizing that technology alone doesn't drive transformation. They iterate rapidly, learning from both successes and failures to continuously improve their AI capabilities.

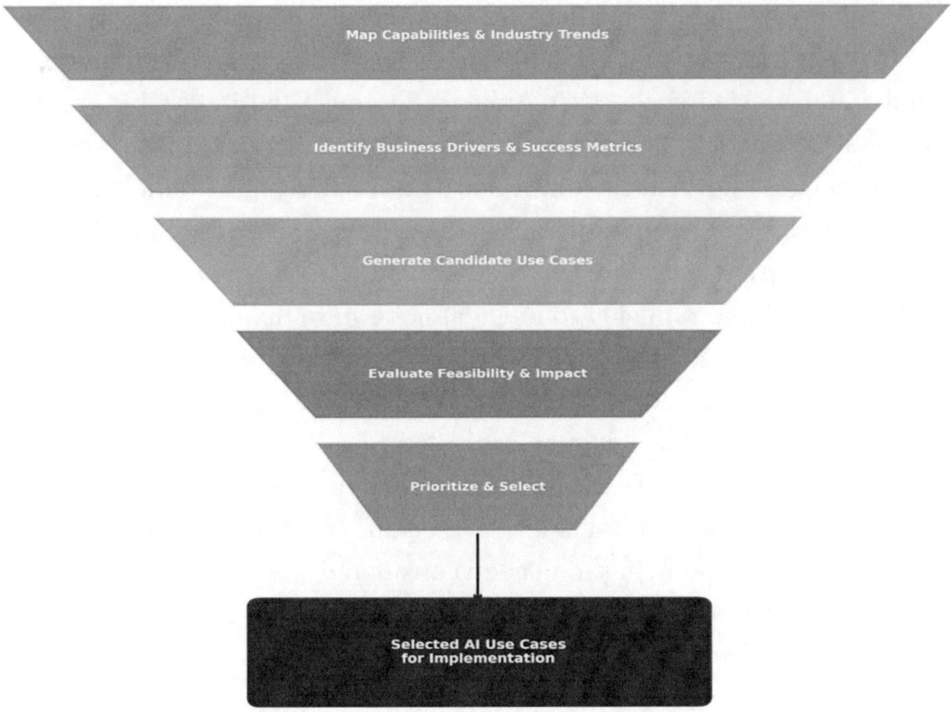

Figure 9-7. *AI use case selection and prioritization funnel: from capability mapping through business driver identification, candidate generation, feasibility evaluation, to final selection*

9.9 Future Directions and Strategic Implications

The trajectory of AI in financial services points toward increasingly sophisticated, autonomous systems that transform how institutions operate, manage risk, and serve customers. Several emerging trends will shape the future of AI in financial services over the coming years, creating both opportunities and challenges for institutions at all stages of AI maturity.

Agentic AI represents the next frontier in financial services automation. AI agents are emerging as a transformative force, with these systems thinking iteratively and executing complex workflows, helping to reinvent services like lending, underwriting, and claims processing. Organizations are using these capabilities to accelerate technology modernization, perform advanced research, identify novel investment opportunities, and develop deeply customized products and services. Recent studies indicate that foundation models and generative AI are approaching the "trough of disillusionment" in Gartner's Hype Cycle for AI, as organizations seek reliable solutions for enterprise use.

AWS is addressing reliability challenges by combining generative AI with automated reasoning. AWS has integrated automated reasoning into its generative AI offerings through automated reasoning checks in Amazon Bedrock Guardrails. This approach, also known as symbolic AI or formal verification, provides mathematical, logic-based verification that aligns outputs with known facts rather than hallucinations. This is particularly crucial for regulated industries where precision is important. Through Automated Reasoning checks in Amazon Bedrock Guardrails, organizations can transform their compliance policies and regulatory requirements into a mathematical format, enabling verification of AI outputs to be much simpler and guarded.

Personalization will reach new levels of sophistication as AI systems integrate more data sources and develop a deeper understanding of individual customer needs and preferences. The boundary between personalization and product customization will blur as AI enables mass customization of financial products based on individual circumstances. Personalization has long been considered a key part of enhancing the customer relationship, thus improving customer retention and satisfaction, which results in improved lifetime value. The next and much more productive level of personalization involves communication and cooperation between autonomous agents responsible for customer engagement and core banking solution agents to adapt product settings through differentiated parameters.

Privacy-preserving AI techniques will become increasingly important as regulations tighten and customer expectations for data protection grow. Organizations that master privacy-preserving AI will gain competitive advantages through enhanced customer trust. Federated learning, differential privacy, and synthetic data generation will evolve from research topics to standard practices in financial services AI implementations. These techniques enable effective AI while protecting customer data and maintaining regulatory compliance.

The integration of AI across financial services ecosystems will create new opportunities and challenges. AI-powered capabilities will extend beyond individual institutions to encompass payment networks, regulatory reporting systems, and industry utilities. These ecosystem-level AI capabilities will require new forms of collaboration, data sharing, and governance. Industry standards for AI interoperability and data exchange will emerge to enable these collaborative capabilities.

Regulatory frameworks for AI will continue to evolve, with increasing emphasis on transparency, fairness, and accountability. Financial institutions must develop capabilities to adapt quickly to changing regulatory requirements while maintaining AI effectiveness. This includes implementing flexible governance frameworks, maintaining comprehensive documentation of AI systems, and developing explainability capabilities that can satisfy diverse regulatory requirements across jurisdictions.

The competitive landscape will increasingly differentiate between institutions that master AI and those that lag. AI capabilities will become table stakes in financial services, with customers expecting intelligent, personalized experiences as standard. However, AI alone will not guarantee success; it must be part of comprehensive strategies that deliver genuine customer value while managing risk effectively. Organizations that fail to develop AI capabilities risk commoditization and customer attrition to more innovative competitors.

Strategic implications extend beyond customer-facing applications to internal operations and business models. AI will optimize employee experiences, streamline operations, and enable new business models. Financial institutions will develop AI-as-a-service offerings, providing AI capabilities to smaller institutions and fintech partners. Data cooperatives will enable collaborative AI development while maintaining data sovereignty and privacy.

The organizations that thrive in this AI-powered future will be those that view AI not as a technology project but as a fundamental capability requiring sustained investment, continuous innovation, and deep integration into strategy and operations. They will balance technological sophistication with ethical responsibility, business objectives with customer value creation, and automation with human judgment. Most importantly, they will recognize that AI is not an end in itself but a means to build stronger, more valuable customer relationships, more effective risk management, and more efficient operations that drive sustainable business success.

9.10 Conclusion: The Path Forward for AI in Financial Services

The transformation of financial services through AI represents one of the most significant shifts in the industry's history. AI capabilities in risk assessment, fraud detection, and personalized banking have evolved from experimental initiatives to an essential infrastructure that determines competitive success. Financial institutions that successfully navigate this transformation create substantial advantages in operational efficiency, risk management, customer experience, and innovation capacity.

The business case for AI investment in financial services is compelling and well-documented. Fraud reduction of 50–90%, credit decisioning improvements, customer satisfaction increases of 20%, and operational cost reductions of 30–60% demonstrate the tangible value AI delivers. However, these benefits require more than technology deployment. Success demands comprehensive strategies that address data quality, model governance, regulatory compliance, organizational change, and cultural transformation.

The technical foundations for AI excellence in financial services are now accessible to organizations of all sizes. Cloud-based platforms, managed AI services, and pre-built models democratize capabilities that were previously available only to the largest institutions with massive technology investments. However, technology alone does not guarantee success. Organizations must develop complementary capabilities in data management, organizational alignment, ethical governance, and continuous optimization to realize AI's full potential.

The regulatory environment for AI in financial services will continue to evolve, requiring institutions to develop adaptive governance frameworks that can respond to changing requirements while maintaining AI effectiveness. Organizations that build robust governance, implement comprehensive risk management, and prioritize transparency and explainability will be better positioned to navigate regulatory changes while maintaining customer trust and competitive advantage.

Organizational transformation proves as critical as technical implementation. Cross-functional collaboration, skill development, and cultural change toward experimentation and continuous learning enable AI at scale. Financial institutions must restructure around AI capabilities, creating centers of excellence that provide expertise and governance while enabling distributed AI development across business units. Change management investments help employees adapt to AI-augmented workflows, ensuring technology enhances rather than replaces human expertise.

The measurement frameworks organizations employ determine whether AI investments deliver expected returns. Comprehensive measurement spanning technical performance, business outcomes, and customer experience provides visibility into AI effectiveness. Leading indicators enable rapid course correction while lagging metrics confirm long-term value creation. Organizations that implement rigorous measurement and continuous optimization achieve superior outcomes from their AI investments.

Looking forward, AI in financial services will become increasingly sophisticated and autonomous. Agentic AI will transform complex workflows in lending, underwriting, and claims processing. Personalization will reach new levels of sophistication as AI systems integrate more data sources and develop a deeper understanding of individual needs. Privacy-preserving techniques will become standard practice as regulations tighten and customer expectations evolve. Ecosystem-level AI capabilities will require new forms of collaboration and governance across institutions.

The competitive landscape will increasingly differentiate between institutions that master AI and those that lag. AI capabilities will become table stakes, with customers expecting intelligent, personalized experiences as standard. Organizations that fail to develop AI capabilities risk commoditization and customer attrition. However, AI alone will not guarantee success; it must be part of comprehensive strategies that deliver genuine customer value while managing risk effectively.

Strategic implications extend beyond customer-facing applications to internal operations and business models. AI will optimize employee experiences, streamline operations, and enable new business models including AI-as-a-service offerings and data cooperatives. The organizations that thrive will view AI not as a technology project but as a fundamental capability requiring sustained investment, continuous innovation, and deep integration into strategy and operations.

The transformation of financial services through AI represents both a tremendous opportunity and a significant challenge. Institutions that successfully navigate this transformation will create substantial competitive advantages in operational efficiency, risk management, customer experience, and innovation capacity. The journey requires vision, investment, persistence, and careful attention to governance, ethics, and regulatory compliance. However, the rewards for organizations that achieve AI excellence are substantial and sustainable, defining which institutions lead and which struggle to remain competitive in an increasingly AI-powered financial services landscape.

CHAPTER 10

GenAI in Manufacturing: Design Optimization and Supply Chain Intelligence CAD Software

Generative AI in manufacturing automates the processes and enhances the operations, from instant product design and customer services to advanced predictive maintenance and supply chain optimization, which enables strategic decision-making at every step.

The manufacturer operates under never-ending pressure and quickly adapts to the dynamic market trends. It continuously strives to enhance the production processes, optimize supply chains, and deliver high-quality products to the customers. Manufacturing industries are now adopting generative AI for smart manufacturing operations and highly efficient outcomes.

10.1 Introduction to GenAI in Manufacturing

Manufacturing is a data-rich industry encompassing design, manufacturing, and quality assurance. With the revolution of generative AI, the manufacturing industry has been transformed into an intelligent, creative, accelerated, customized, and cost-optimized goods manufacturing sector.

According to the Gartner CIO and Technology Executive Survey, approximately 83% of manufacturing executives increased their spending in AI in 2025.

N. Sendas et al., *Building Generative AI Solutions for Industries with AWS*,
https://doi.org/10.1007/979-8-8688-2830-0_10

10.1.1 Evolution of AI in Manufacturing: From Automation to Generative Intelligence

Artificial intelligence has made significant strides in the manufacturing sector, from simple automation to complex generative intelligence. AI provides robotic and rule-based applications to improve accuracy and efficiency. Machine learning improved the predictive capabilities of manufacturing industries, and deep learning leads to real-time decision-making and real-time adaptive systems. Now, generative AI takes a huge leap with design creation, simulating production scenarios and generating solutions autonomously that result in continuous improvements to the design, production, and supply chain ecosystems.

10.1.2 Current Pain Points in Design and Supply Chain Operations

There are many pain points in design and supply chain operations that increase the time to market and increase cost.

Figure 10-1. *Pain Points in the Manufacturing Industry (Self)*

10.1.3 The Generative AI Opportunity: Cost Reduction, Speed, and Innovation

There are numerous opportunities for generative AI in the manufacturing industry, which help address pain points in design, development, and supply chain operations, as mentioned below:

- From design optimization to waste reduction and prototype and engineering costs, everything leads to cost reduction with GenAI.
- Generative AI accelerated time-to-market by shortening the design cycle and automating documentation, simulation, and prototyping.
- The manufacturing industry has been transformed into an adaptive, data-driven ecosystem driven by generative AI, intelligent automation, and continuous innovation.

10.1.4 Chapter Scope and Learning Objectives

The objective of this chapter is to understand how generative AI is evolving the manufacturing sector, resulting in improvements in product engineering, enhancing production, and optimizing worker training and productivity.

The learning objective is to analyze how generative AI can be implemented in different manufacturing processes, like

1. Production management
2. Design and engineering optimization
3. Supply chain optimization
4. Inventory optimization
5. Quality management
6. Conversional assistance
7. Predictive maintenance
8. Change management

10.1.5 Overview of AWS AI/ML Stack for Manufacturing

AWS is continuously innovating and evolving and now offers the AWS generative AI stack with three layers. AWS's generative AI stack is designed to efficiently build, customize, deploy, and scale generative AI applications.

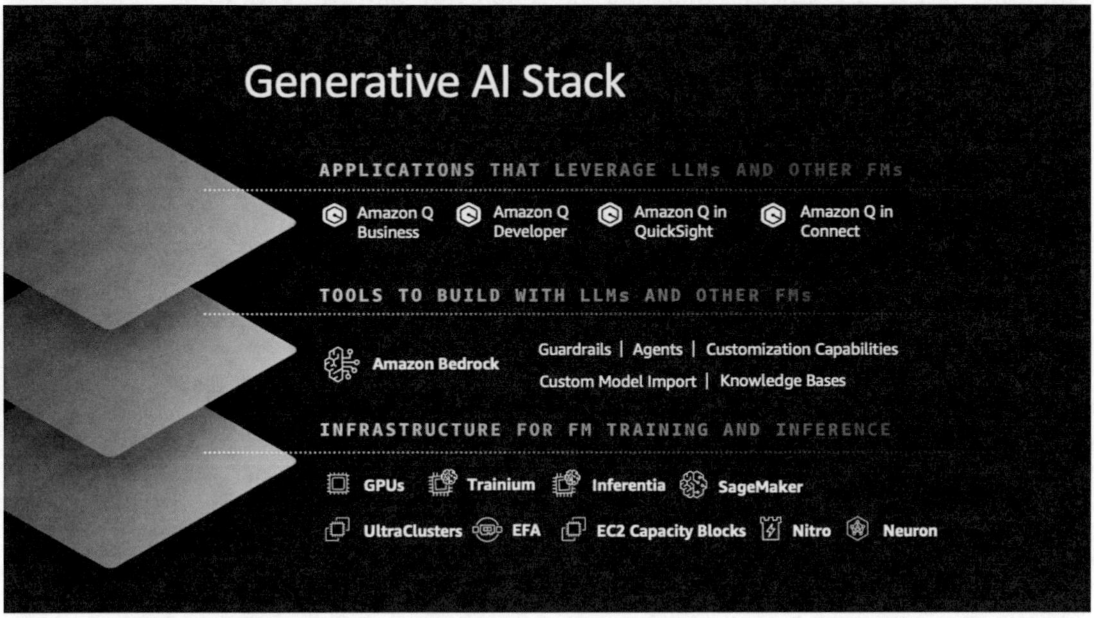

Figure 10-2. *AWS Generative AI Stack*

The bottom layer consists of SageMaker. GPU sets the base infrastructure to train LLMs and FMs to produce predictions and inferences. The middle layer consists of Bedrock, which provides models and tools to build and scale generative AI applications with security and access control services offered by AWS. The topmost layer is for applications that leverage LLMs, and its key area is generative AI-based coding.

Manufacturers trust AWS to accelerate generative AI technologies with enterprise-grade security and privacy and low-cost infrastructure to bring new products and services to market in less time and at a low cost.

10.2 Generative Design and Engineering Optimization

In manufacturing, generative AI revolutionizes product development by shifting the focus from a rule-based approach to a generative design and engineering optimization approach. Generative AI generates various features, geometries, and suggests materials to produce innovative and cost-effective solutions with real-time trade-offs.

10.2.1 Fundamentals of Generative Design vs. Traditional CAD Workflows

Generative AI shifts engineers from modeling to AI-driver exploration, innovation, and accelerative manufacturing. Let's compare traditional CAD and generative design in a tabular format.

Table 10-1. *Traditional CAD and generative design*

Aspect	Traditional CAD	Generative Design
Approach	The designer creates geometry features manually.	AI autonomously explores design features.
Input	Take fixed dimensions, sketches, and constraints.	Clear objectives are stated for GenAI, such as minimizing mass and maximizing stiffness.
Output	One or a few user-defined models are created.	Generated thousands of AI-generated variants.
Computation	Computations are deterministic in nature.	Probabilistic or simulation-driven computation.
Iteration Speed	Slow as interactions are done manually.	Automated and optimized iteration process.

10.2.2 Multi-objective Optimization (Weight, Cost, Strength, Manufacturability, Sustainability)

Generative AI algorithms can optimize for multiple engineering goals simultaneously, as follows:

- **Weight Reduction**: Focus on minimizing mass without compromising stiffness.
- **Cost Optimization**: Optimize cost with manufacturing raw material and process trade-offs.
- **Strength**: Focuses on the durability of the product, including its stress and fatigue performance.
- **Manufacturability**: GenAI considers all geometry limits for CNC, such as tool access, casting by material flow, cooling dynamics, additive manufacturing, etc.
- **Sustainability**: Consider various parameters like carbon footprint, recyclability, and energy efficiency to produce a sustainable and environmentally friendly product.

After predicting the results of thousands of variations using AI-driven models via tools such as AWS SageMaker, the optimization loop, with the help of GenAI analysis, chooses the best trade-offs.

10.2.3 Topology Optimization Using Foundation Models

Generative AI foundation models trained on millions of CAD geometries to learn structural patterns to optimize the topology.

- **Input**: For the foundation model, load different cases, various boundary conditions, design space, and constraints to train.
- **Output**: Output topology layout maps show optimal material distribution.
- **Implementation**: Before performing a full finite-element (FEA) study, fine-tune a foundation model such as Amazon Bedrock's

custom model capabilities on company-specific part geometry to anticipate optimal topology layouts.

- **Result:** With topology optimization, there is a significant speed-up in the manufacturing pipeline process and a reduced computational cost.

10.2.4 Parametric Design Exploration with Amazon SageMaker and Bedrock

Follow the steps below for parametric design exploration:

- Amazon SageMaker processing is used to generate parametric variations of CAD inputs (through external CAD APIs).
- Feed these parameters into a trained generative model hosted on Amazon Bedrock.
- SageMaker Pipelines is used to run batch simulations for performance metrics evaluation.
- The cost and weight optimization function is used to rank the results automatically.

By following these steps, an AI-powered loop is created that continuously improves designs to reach ideal goals.

10.2.5 Integration with Existing PLM/CAD Systems (Siemens NX, Catia, SolidWorks)

Generative AI can be integrated into current engineering ecosystems:

- **Siemens NX**: Via REST APIs or AWS IoT SiteWise connectors for design-simulation data
- **Dassault CATIA**: Plug-in invoking Bedrock or SageMaker endpoints for geometry generation
- **SolidWorks:** Python-based add-ins using AWS SDK (Boto3) to call optimization results directly into the CAD model tree

This hybrid workflow ensures AI-generated geometries are version-controlled within SolidWorks, maintaining digital-thread integrity.

10.2.6 Custom Model Training for Domain-Specific Design Constraints

Different manufacturing verticals have domain-specific constraints, and custom model training is required accordingly. Custom model training makes GenAI outputs practical, compliant, and production-ready for different sectors.

10.2.7 Case Study: Aerospace Component Weight Reduction Using GenAI

Objective: To reduce the weight of a titanium aerospace bracket by redesigning it using GenAI while maintaining safety factors and exceeding performance.

Baseline: Titanium aeroscape bracket designed traditionally.

Process:

- Engineers define load conditions, constraints, material properties, and weight requirements.
- Generative AI with AWS SageMaker and Bedrock generates more than 500 variants.
- Finite elements simulations filter feasible candidates based on weight, performance, durability, and structural integrity.
- Among these models, the top design is manufactured via metal additive manufacturing.

Outcome

- Weight reduced by approximately 38%.
- Material cost reduced by 22%.
- Development cycle reduced from six weeks to two weeks.
- Performance has been improved and meets all safety standards.

10.2.8 Code Example: Design Optimization API with AWS Lambda and Bedrock

Workflow to optimize the design of bracket variants, minimizing weight and cost using AWS Lambda and Bedrock:

AWS Lambda triggers on a CAD submission, which calls the Bedrock generative model and returns optimized parameter sets.

Sample Code

```
import boto3, json

bedrock = boto3.client('bedrock-runtime')
def lambda_handler(event, context):
    # Design parameters
    objectives = {
        "target_weight": 0.8,
        "max_stress": 250,
        "material": "Ti6Al4V",
        "process": "AdditiveManufacturing"
    }

    prompt = f"""
    Generate 3 optimized bracket design variants, minimizing weight
    and cost.
    under these constraints: {json.dumps(objectives)}.
    Output JSON with parameter sets and rationale.
    """

    response = bedrock.invoke_model(
        modelId='anthropic.claude-3-sonnet',
        contentType='application/json',
        body=json.dumps({"input": prompt})
    )

    result = json.loads(response['body'].read())
    return {"statusCode": 200, "body": json.dumps(result)}
```

10.3 Supply Chain Demand Forecasting and Planning

Beyond conventional time-series methods, generative AI incorporates a multimodal, contextual approach to deliver real-time demand forecasting insights. Manufacturers can transition from reactive planning to proactive, self-adaptive supply chain planning by utilizing Amazon's AI/ML stack, which includes Forecast, SageMaker, and Bedrock.

10.3.1 Traditional Forecasting Limitations vs. GenAI Approaches

For resilient and sustainable forecasting, GenAI integrates disruptions, market sentiment, and macroeconomic data to provide contextual awareness, while traditional models concentrate on time-series continuity. Let's see the difference in their approach.

Table 10-2. *GenAI vs. traditional forecasting approach*

Aspect	Traditional Forecasting Approach	Generative AI Forecasting Approach
Inputs	Historical data	Structured, unstructured data, and external signals
Method	ARIMA, exponential smoothing	Foundation models and multimodal and contextual learning
Adaptability	Static models, which are updated infrequently	Self-learning and real-time analysis
Scenario Planning and Analysis	Manual approach with a limited use case	Automated analysis of "what-if" scenarios
Outcome	Lagging indicator	Prescriptive and predictive insights

10.3.2 Time-Series Analysis with Foundation Models

AWS offers a high-performing foundation model, Amazon Titan, which can be fine-tuned according to business needs, like the following:

- To capture long-term dependencies like seasonality, trends, and cyclic patterns in time-series data.

- To handle and adapt to non-linear behaviors like spikes with promotion, launch of a new product, successful marketing strategy, etc.
- Express uncertainty in data by generating probabilistic forecasts.

10.3.3 Multimodal Forecasting: Combining Structured Data, Text, and External Signals

Generative AI focuses on a multimodal approach that combines different types of data, such as structured, unstructured, text, or any external signals for demand forecasting, and explains the reason behind the demand change. Data can be

- **Structured data** like inventory and logistics metrics, or ERP and POS data.
- **Text data** like supplier notes, news articles, and customer reviews.
- **External signals** like weather, commodity prices, and geopolitical events.

10.3.4 Demand Sensing and Real-Time Adjustments

Demand sensing is short-term demand forecasting that updates every few hours or days.

Generative AI enables manufacturers to adjust to real-time fluctuations in orders, logistics delays, or disruptions.

10.3.5 Scenario Planning and What-If Analysis

GenAI can simulate multiple possible futures and suggest a mitigation plan as well.

Users can create structured "what-if" datasets by querying natural language questions with Bedrock LLMs. Then, Amazon SageMaker or Amazon Forecast is used on these datasets to predict the impact on inventory, lead time, and cost.

10.3.6 Amazon Forecast Integration with Generative Models

Amazon Forecast uses machine learning algorithms like DeepAR+ and Prophet and offers automated forecasting with excellent accuracy. Generative AI integrates with Amazon Forecast and turns raw forecasts into decision-ready insights in the following ways:

- Bedrock LLMs preprocess input data and produce clean and enriched text-based data.
- LLMs interpret output and explain forecast anomalies in business language.
- Planners enter various variables as input to Amazon Forecast. Analyzing these variables, several alternate forecast scenarios are generated.

10.3.7 Building Custom Forecasting Models with SageMaker Jumpstart

The workflow to build a customized forecasting model with SageMaker Jumpstart is as follows:

- The first step is to load pre-trained forecasting models like DeepAR+ via SageMaker JumpStart.
- Fine-tune the model based on the defined SKU-level.
- AWS SageMaker Clarify is used to detect bias.
- After detecting bias, the inference endpoint is deployed.
- Integrate with Bedrock LLMs for natural language interaction and narrative explanations.

10.3.8 Code Example: Implementing a GenAI-Powered Demand Forecasting Pipeline

The workflow to implement a GenAI-powered demand forecast pipeline is as follows:

- After loading data, Amazon Forecast is used to provide numerical predictions.
- Amazon Bedrock LLM is implemented to interpret results, explain them, identify potential causes of demand change, suggest what-if scenarios, and generate actionable business insights.

Source Code

```
import boto3, json, pandas as pd
from datetime import datetime

# Initialize clients
forecast = boto3.client('forecast')
bedrock = boto3.client('bedrock-runtime')

def lambda_handler(event, context):
    # 1. Load structured demand data
    df = pd.read_csv('s3://my-bucket/sales_history.csv')

    # 2. Call Amazon Forecast for base prediction
    forecast_response = forecast.query_forecast(
        ForecastArn='arn:aws:forecast:region:123:forecast/my_model',
        Filters={"item_id": "SKU-123"}
    )
    predicted_values = forecast_response['Forecast']['Predictions']['p50']

    # 3. Use Bedrock LLM to explain and simulate scenarios
    prompt = f"""
    Based on the following predicted values {predicted_values},
    Identify potential causes of demand change and suggest 2 what-if scenarios.
    """

    llm_response = bedrock.invoke_model(
        modelId='anthropic.claude-3-sonnet',
        contentType='application/json',
```

```
        body=json.dumps({"input": prompt})
    )

    result = json.loads(llm_response['body'].read())
    return {
        "statusCode": 200,
        "body": json.dumps({
            "forecast": predicted_values,
            "insights": result
        })
    }
```

10.4 Inventory Optimization and Warehouse Intelligence

Inventory management is a crucial task for the manufacturing industry, which has evolved with GenAI by combining probabilistic forecasting, spatial optimization, and autonomous replenishment. An intelligent, adaptive warehouse ecosystem has been established with GenAI-driven, multi-echelon predictive systems.

10.4.1 Multi-echelon Inventory Optimization with GenAI

Generative AI enables inventory optimization at multiple echelons, like factories, retail outlets, and regional DCs. It helps in learning interdependencies among supply nodes and demand centers. It also helps in identifying trade-offs between services, cost, and time taken to execute.

GenAI models trained in SageMaker can identify diminishing demand trends across SKUs, including marketing, seasonality, and product lifecycle information, as slow or obsolete inventory locks working capital.

10.4.2 Safety Stock Calculations Using Probabilistic Models

Real-time safety stock recalibration as per market conditions helps in avoiding both shortages and excess. Generative AI relies on probabilistic models (like Normal, Gamma, or Poisson) of demand and lead time using SageMaker PyMC3 for safety stock calculations rather than on fixed averages. Creating informative summaries and recommending confidence levels for plans using Bedrock LLMs helps in determining dynamic safety stocks for varying service levels.

10.4.3 Warehouse Layout Optimization

The layout optimization of the warehouse directly impacts picking efficiency and storage utilization. Gen-AI assisted SageMaker in simulating picking routes via reinforcement learning, and Bedrock LLM easily interprets constraints and visualizes layout suggestions.

10.4.4 Automated Replenishment Strategies

Generative AI can autonomously design and implement replenishment strategies by analyzing real-time consumption patterns, supplier performance, and logistics capacity using Amazon Kinesis, Bedrock LLM, and AWS Lambda. With GenAI, it becomes capable of following these features:

- Dynamically predicting reorder timings
- Suggesting alternate suppliers or shipping modes
- Simulating intelligent, hands-free replenishment outcomes under disruptions aligned with real-time demand sensing.

10.4.5 Integration with WMS and ERP Systems

Generative AI insights are most valuable when integrated directly into operational systems:

- Warehouse Management Systems (WMS) automate slotting, picking, and replenishment tasks.
- Enterprise Resource Planning (ERP) updates material requirements, safety stock, and PO parameters.

10.5 Quality Control and Defect Detection

The traditional method involves lots of manual, rule-based quality checks, but generative AI augments quality management and defect detection systems to ensure the quality of products across all plants.

10.5.1 Computer Vision for Automated Visual Inspection

GenAI-driven deep learning models are implemented to detect surface defects, color deviation, assembly errors, or dimensional inconsistencies in real time. With GenAI, it is easy to detect subtle defects that are invisible to traditional methods. Manual inspection has been replaced with high-speed, consistent automation.

AWS SageMaker Vision models or Amazon Rekognition Custom Labels are trained on annotated defect images. Use AWS IoT Greengrass to deploy edge cameras for production line real-time inference.

10.5.2 Generative Models for Synthetic Defect Data Augmentation

One of the main issues with AI quality inspection is the lack of labeled defect data. Generative methods such as diffusion methods and GANs (Generative Adversarial Networks) are used to create artificial defective images in order to balance training datasets. Consequently, it reduces labeling costs and improves model generalization.

10.5.3 Anomaly Detection in Production Processes

GenAI models can spot unusual patterns by examining sensor streams, process logs, and equipment telemetry. For unsupervised anomaly detection, autoencoders and Variational Autoencoders (VAEs) are used. Foundation models such as Amazon Titan are used for identifying correlated process deviations.

10.5.4 Root Cause Analysis Using Multimodal AI

Generative AI performs multimodal root cause analysis on multiple data types like text, images, time series, and sensor data. Bedrock LLMs are implemented to analyze correlations between events and defect types. GenAI helps in generating a summary of probable root cause and corrective action in natural language.

10.5.5 Predictive Quality Assurance

GenAI learns from historical defect patterns, supplier quality, and machine data to forecast future quality risks. It helps in modeling "what-if" scenarios, such as modifications to the machine or material batch, and Bedrock LLM generates proactive recommendations to maintain quality assurance.

10.5.6 Integration with MES (Manufacturing Execution Systems)

To produce quality with generative AI, seamless integration of operations with the Manufacturing Execution System (MES) is essential. For ongoing development, MES offers process traceability back into the GenAI pipeline. GenAI insights automatically trigger quality alerts or rework orders within MES.

10.5.7 Amazon Rekognition Custom Labels and SageMaker Integration

SageMaker provides sophisticated, domain-specific CNN architectures like ResNet and EfficientNet for specialized defect detection categories, while Rekognition manages common visual tasks like classification/localization. We need to integrate both for a hybrid approach.

Integration Workflow

- Firstly, defect images are uploaded to S3.
- Create a Custom Labels model in Amazon Rekognition and train it.
- Use SageMaker Ground Truth for annotation and model comparison.
- Integrate Rekognition API into production monitoring dashboards or Lambda triggers.

10.5.8 Deployment Patterns for Edge Inference with AWS IoT Greengrass

AWS IoT edge inference is done by deploying SageMaker-trained models to industrial devices. Greengrass facilitates real-time defect detection and process monitoring. It ensures consistent, dependable AI performance across dispersed manufacturing sites by supporting low-latency, offline operation, automatic model upgrades, and secure synchronization with cloud services like S3 and CloudWatch.

10.6 Digital Twin and Simulation Environments

Digital twins enable scenario testing, diagnostics, and performance forecasts by producing synchronized virtual replicas of machinery, lines, or facilities. When paired with GenAI, twins transition from descriptive mirrors to generative copilots that suggest process variations, design modifications, and remedial strategies, resulting in shortening of the physical test cycle and speeding up validation.

10.6.1 Digital Twin Fundamentals in Manufacturing

In order to reproduce behavior under actual working settings, a manufacturing digital twin models asset geometry, telemetry, process logic, and past performance. Lineage (digital thread), fidelity (model correctness), and latency (real-time synchronization) are important characteristics of high-quality twins for continuous optimization, virtual commissioning, and predictive analytics.

10.6.2 AWS IoT TwinMaker for Asset Modeling

AWS IoT TwinMaker offers a managed platform for creating rich asset models by combining 3D sceneries, time-series telemetry, and contextual data from enterprise systems. It facilitates model-driven applications for monitoring, visualization, and scenario playback at scale and speeds up connector-based twin creation.

10.6.3 GenAI-Enhanced Simulation and Scenario Testing

Generative AI enhances simulation by producing realistic testing scenario variations, artificial sensor traces, and multi-step interventions for "what-if" analysis. GenAI reduces costly compute and concentrates validation on high-risk instances by proposing high-value perturbations, prioritizing runs, and summarizing results in human-readable recommendations rather than using fixed param sweeps.

10.6.4 Predictive Maintenance Integration

Digital twins power predictive maintenance integration that consumes both past failure data and real-time telemetry. To increase model robustness, GenAI generates causal hypotheses and synthetic failure-mode examples. It may recommend inspection schedules and spare parts policies based on predicted degradation paths, optimizing uptime and maintenance costs.

10.6.5 Real-Time Optimization Feedback Loops

GenAI-generated policies, along with real-time analytics, allow for continuous setpoint, scheduling, and routing optimization when twins operate in a closed loop with control systems. Fast feedback allows operations to respond to drift, demand shocks, or energy price signals while maintaining safety and restrictions.

10.6.6 Virtual Commissioning and Process Validation

Virtual commissioning verifies PLC logic, robotic routes, and material flows using a twin before physical deployment. Advanced twins enhanced with GenAI can identify integration problems early and reduce ramp-up times from weeks to days while intricating production reconfigurations.

10.7 Natural Language Interfaces and Knowledge Management

Generative AI turns static manuals into interactive knowledge systems using conversational agents, RAG-augmented search, and multilingual assistants. This reduces the cognitive strain, expedites troubleshooting, and maintains implicit knowledge across shifts and locations in manufacturing.

10.7.1 Conversational AI for Manufacturing Operations

Conversational AI agents can take work instructions, KPI searches, and incident logging without any manual effort. Role-based prompts provide operator-level assistance and engineering diagnostics, while MES and IoT integrations allow context-aware responses.

10.7.2 Technical Documentation Generation and Maintenance

GenAI automates the generation, standardization, and versioning of technical documents, such as repair manuals, inspection checklists, and control logic descriptions. While human-in-the-loop review maintains compliance and traceability, automated diffs speed up the policy-aware creation and updates.

10.7.3 RAG (Retrieval-Augmented Generation) for Engineering Knowledge Bases

RAG using LLM generation combines vector retrieval with engineering documents such as drawings, test logs, and change notes to provide accurate, source-based answers. RAG facilitates explainable suggestions to engineers for design modifications or remedial actions, lessens hallucinations, and offers citations to drawings and procedures.

10.7.4 Multi-language Support for Global Operations

Each jurisdiction has its own privacy and data governance laws, so each global plant requires localized helpers for regional data augmentation, translation, cultural alignment, and refined multilingual LLMs to preserve language parity.

10.7.5 Amazon Lex and Bedrock Integration Patterns

Amazon Lex manages conversational routing and slot filling, and Bedrock provides knowledge-driven generation and document grounding (RAG). The integration between Amazon Lex and Bedrock LLM enables auditable, low-latency business chatbots.

10.7.6 Code Example: Building a Manufacturing Knowledge Assistant

Here is the step-by-step guide to building a manufacturing knowledge assistant.

1. Amazon Lex is a conversational interface that captures the user's question.
2. Lambda is used for embedding for the query.
3. Retrieve similar documents from OpenSearch.
4. Generate context-based grounded answers using the Bedrock LLM model.
5. Return a traceable response with sources.

Sample Code

```
import json, boto3
from opensearchpy import OpenSearch

bedrock = boto3.client('bedrock-runtime')
os_client = OpenSearch("https://<your-opensearch-endpoint>")

EMBED_MODEL = "amazon.titan-embed-text-v1"
LLM_MODEL = "anthropic.claude-3-sonnet"

def lambda_handler(event, context):
    question = event.get("question", "")

    # Create embedding for query
    emb = bedrock.invoke_model(
        modelId=EMBED_MODEL,
        body=json.dumps({"inputText": question})
    )
```

```
qvec = json.loads(emb['body'].read())["embedding"]

# Retrieve top documents from OpenSearch
query = {
    "size": 3,
    "query": {
        "script_score": {
            "query": {"match_all": {}},
            "script": {
                "source": "cosineSimilarity(params.query_vector,
                'embedding') + 1.0",
                "params": {"query_vector": qvec}
            }
        }
    }
}
docs = os_client.search(body=query, index="manufacturing_docs")["hits"]
["hits"]
context_text = "\n\n".join([d["_source"]["text"] for d in docs])

# Generate grounded answer
prompt = f"Use the context below to answer:\n{context_text}\n\nQ:
{question}\nA:"
resp = bedrock.invoke_model(
    modelId=LLM_MODEL,
    body=json.dumps({"input": prompt, "max_tokens": 300})
)
answer = json.loads(resp['body'].read())

return {"answer": answer, "sources": [d["_source"]["id"] for d in docs]}
```

10.8 Implementation Architecture and Best Practices

To implement generative AI in the manufacturing industry, an infrastructure is necessary that unifies data, models, and operations across design, production, and supply chain. AWS offers many components to implement GenAI in manufacturing architecture, such as S3 for data lakes, SageMaker for the ML lifecycle, Bedrock for foundation models, and IoT/Greengrass for edge deployment that guarantees scalability, compliance, and business alignment.

10.8.1 Reference Architecture for GenAI in Manufacturing

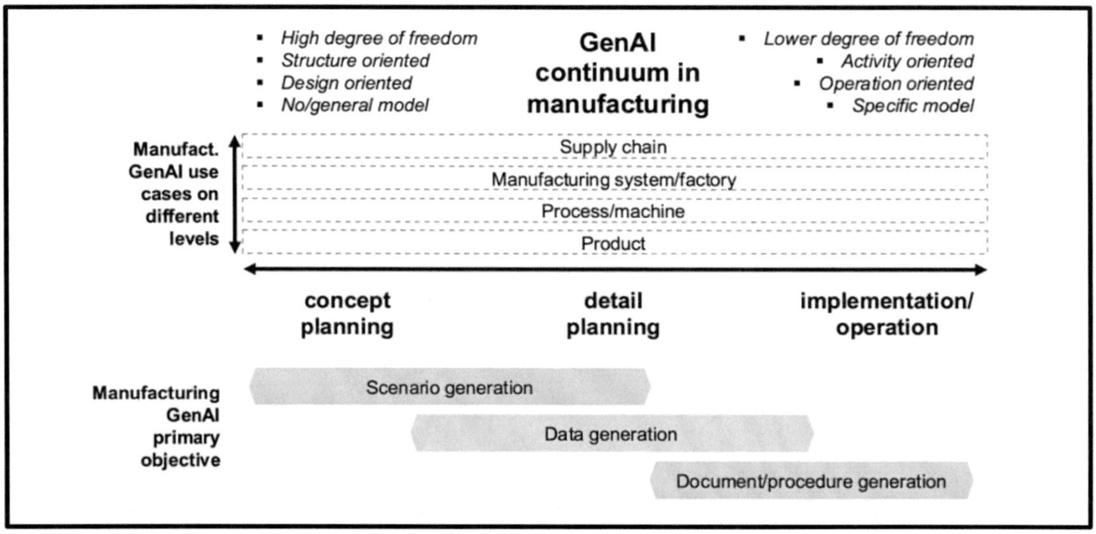

Figure 10-3. *Generative AI Reference Framework in Manufacturing*

AWS offers **Amazon Bedrock** to build and scale generative AI-based applications using FMs. It offers **SageMaker** for bespoke machine learning, **TwinMaker/IoT Core** for operational data, **Amazon Titan FMs** for responsible innovation, and **OpenSearch** for RAG pipelines to make up a typical reference stack. FM integration with MES/PLM/ERP ensures context-rich intelligence across the product lifecycle and enables design optimization, predictive operations, and AI-driven decision loops.

10.8.2 Data Pipeline Design: Ingestion, Processing, and Storage

Data pipelines start with data being ingested into Amazon Kinesis or IoT Core from various sensors, MES, ERP, and design repositories. Ingested data is being processed by AWS Glue and stored in S3 or Redshift. Data must be vectorized, versioned, and semantically enriched for GenAI to support RAG search and foundation model fine-tuning.

10.8.3 Model Deployment Strategies (Batch vs. Real-Time)

SageMaker Batch Transform and Step Functions automate runs with planning, quality analysis, and cost modeling. Real-time inference is implemented for line inspection, adaptive control, and operator assistants, using SageMaker Endpoints. For ongoing optimization, hybrid patterns provide a balance between latency, cost, and throughput.

10.8.4 Security Considerations: Data Encryption, Access Control, and Compliance

Manufacturing AI workload must adhere to GDPR, NIST, and ISO 27001 guidelines. Use PrivateLink for Bedrock/SageMaker, IAM for least-privilege access, KMS for encryption, and VPC isolation. Data governance frameworks are implemented as they take necessary measures like IP protection, data segregation, and secure GenAI prompting to avoid sensitive data disclosure.

10.8.5 Scalability Patterns for Enterprise Manufacturing

Auto-scaling clusters, serverless orchestration, and distributed data access via Glue and Lake Formation are ways to accomplish elasticity. Workload division by plant or business unit increases resilience. Real-time global operations across R&D, production, and logistics teams are supported by cross-region replication.

10.8.6 Cost Optimization Strategies (Spot Instances, Auto-Scaling, Model Caching)

To optimize GenAI operating expenses, EC2 Spot Instances and SageMaker Managed Spot Training for model development are implemented. Enable model caching and auto-scaling endpoints to handle frequently called generative workloads. For storage efficiency, S3 Intelligent-Tiering is used, and CloudWatch Metrics and AWS Cost Explorer are implemented to track consumption and ongoing improvement.

10.8.7 MLOps for Continuous Model Improvement

MLOps guarantees automatic retraining of GenAI models and managed data versioning, model lineage, and bias detection via SageMaker Pipelines. Adaptive fine-tuning for domain-specific manufacturing operations is made possible by ongoing learning loops via edge devices or operator feedback.

10.8.8 Monitoring and Observability with Amazon CloudWatch and SageMaker Model Monitor

Monitoring and observability are necessary to keep a check on data quality, inference delay, and model drift with Amazon CloudWatch. SageMaker Model Monitor detects bias drift, feature drift, and any violations in the data schema. These are integrated with QuickSight dashboards to optimize performance and compliance visibility.

10.9 Change Management and Organizational Readiness

A successful generative AI transformation in manufacturing requires a strategic blend of technology and human adaptation. Organizations must drive the change management and organizational readiness to guarantee the long-term integration of GenAI throughout the industrial, design, and supply chain ecosystems.

10.9.1 Workforce Training and Upskilling Requirements

Since generative AI is new to the manufacturing sector, all departments, like engineering, operations, and quality, must become trained and knowledgeable about it. The primary areas of upskilling are AI-driven decision support, prompt engineering, and data interpretation. With the help of AWS Skill Builder, engineers and operators can learn gradually and get prepared to apply GenAI solutions in real-time scenarios to increase creativity and productivity.

10.9.2 Stakeholder Alignment and Executive Buy-In

Executive sponsorship and stakeholder alignment are essential for the growth of GenAI in manufacturing. Stakeholders and leadership must ensure ROI, risk management, and rules compliance. Long-term commitment and enterprise-wide adoption are facilitated by structured communication that emphasizes cost reductions, quality improvements, and sustainability.

10.9.3 Pilot Program Design and Success Metrics

Supply chain forecasting, predictive maintenance, or design optimization are the primary pillars for the successful deployment of GenAI with reduced cost, reduced cycle time, and improved accuracy. AWS CloudWatch dashboards are used to measure operational and business impact for quick prototyping.

10.9.4 Integration with Existing IT Infrastructure

For a successful manufacturing pipeline, engineers need to ensure that the GenAI system integrates with MES, ERP, and PLM systems smoothly. AWS AppFlow and EventBridge ensure secure integration between legacy systems and GenAI pipelines. Integration is done gradually with minimum disturbance, with the help of hybrid design implementation.

10.9.5 Cultural Transformation Considerations

Faith in machine intelligence is crucial for AI-driven manufacturing, and leaders must promote effective AI practices and foster cross-functional collaboration while considering the need for cultural transformation. Leaders need to ensure that generative tools complement rather than replace human expertise and should acknowledge employee contributions while building ethical GenAI frameworks.

10.10 Future Trends and Emerging Technologies

The future of manufacturing industries will be a combination of generative AI, autonomous systems, and intelligent networks to create an innovative, creative, and self-adaptive environment. Integration of quantum computing, robotics, blockchain, and sustainability will redefine industries to an autonomous, independent, and self-reliant ecosystem.

10.10.1 Autonomous Manufacturing Facilities

For minimal human intervention and real-time decision-making, autonomous factories combine robotics, IoT, and GenAI. AWS services like RoboRunner and IoT Greengrass will be used to establish decentralized orchestration of smart devices with self-adaptive production properties.

Use Case: Autonomous Production Lines

In autonomous production lines, AI agents extract data from sensors and digital twins to autonomously tune and process equipment parameters and reconfigure workflows for maximum throughput, yield, and reduce energy consumption without any intervention.

10.10.2 Blockchain Integration for Supply Chain Transparency

Blockchain technology will be implemented to establish immutable, decentralized ledgers for material sourcing, compliance, and quality assurance to improve traceability and trust in industrial networks. When blockchain is combined with GenAI, it makes fraud detection and intelligent audits possible, resulting in safe, expandable deployments throughout networks.

Use Case: Automated Vendor Payments

Blockchain records and keeps track of every stage of the component lifecycle. It verifies all the contractual milestones, quality inspection results, and proof-of-delivery, and then the vendor payment is executed automatically with the implementation of generative AI.

10.10.3 Quantum Computing Applications in Optimization

Quantum computing applications can solve multi-variable optimization problems in energy management, material design, and supply chain scenarios more quickly than classical systems. AWS Braket implements generative optimization models to manage the environment for investigating quantum-enhanced industrial use cases.

Use Case: Quantum-Enhanced Production Scheduling

Quantum-enhanced GenAI algorithms compute the most efficient arrangement of machines, equipment, robots, and conveyors and evaluate millions of scheduling permutations. Based on energy consumption, production requirements, and maintenance windows, production scheduling can be optimized for faster output.

10.10.4 Advanced Robotics with GenAI

Generative AI enhances robotics through motion planning, adaptive learning, and human–robot cooperation. GenAI robots can analyze unstructured data, create new work methods on their own, and are adaptable to changing circumstances. The combination of Bedrock and AWS RoboMaker enables dynamic simulation, control tuning, and continuous, adaptable learning from operational feedback across distributed production sites.

Use Case: Intelligent Motion Planning

GenAI optimized robot paths, reducing energy consumption and cycle time while avoiding collisions or bottlenecks to implement intelligent motion planning.

10.10.5 Sustainable Manufacturing and Circular Economy

GenAI prompts sustainable manufacturing by modeling waste reduction, closed-loop material flows, and eco-efficient designs. GenAI-powered lifecycle assessment tools to optimize energy consumption and predict environmental impacts. AWS Clean Rooms and Supply Chain are paired to provide sustainability data and resource efficiency across the entire circular economy value chain to the manufacturers.

Use Case: Generative Eco-Design Optimization

GenAI can create design variants that minimize material usage, weight, carbon footprint, and energy consumption while maintaining strength and sustainable manufacturing. With GenAI eco-design optimization, raw material consumption is reduced, recyclability is optimized, and sustainability targets are achieved early in the design phase.

10.10.6 Industry 5.0 Vision

Industry 5.0 vision emphasizes human-centered, resilient, and sustainable production strongly, where humans and generative AI work together to increase efficiency, creativity, adaptability, and innovation. With the use of robotics, edge intelligence, and cognitive AI systems, the focus shifts from automation to augmentation, enabling flexible, compassionate manufacturing that aligns with social and environmental goals.

Use Case: Human–AI Co-creation Workflows

GenAI targets to achieve industry vision 5.0 of collaborating with design engineers with GenAI for co-development workflows to co-create products that balance manufacturability, sustainability, and innovation.

10.11 Shop Floor Conversational AI Assistants

Conversational AI assistants on the shop floor are the amalgamation of human expertise and digital intelligence. They deliver real-time insights, automated documents, and guided operators leveraging a complex workflow of generative AI, voice recognition, and NLP. These AI assistants improve productivity, safety, and knowledge retention in manufacturing settings when integrated with AWS Bedrock and Amazon Lex.

10.11.1 Voice-Enabled Operator Assistance

Voice-enabled operator assistance empowers operators with hands-free access to SOPs, machine data, and performance metrics. Operators can verbally query process parameters or maintenance records using Bedrock LLMs for contextual reasoning and Amazon Lex for voice recognition, increasing efficiency and reducing downtime without interfering with manual operations.

Use Case: Hands-Free Operations

In the manufacturing industry, there is a high-speed and hazardous environment where manual operations are not safe. Here, operators can use voice commands to run standard operating procedures, set machine setpoints, check quality, and maintain a history of working equipment. This eliminates manual checks and operations, increases safety, and reduces downtime as well.

10.11.2 Real-Time Troubleshooting Guidance

Conversational AI systems offer real-time troubleshooting guidance, informed by GenAI-driven reasoning and historical defect data. AI assistants that are integrated with IoT Core and predictive analytics can identify sensor irregularities instantly and recommend remedial measures for mitigation. This speeds up troubleshooting scenarios on the manufacturing floor and reduces the need for human intervention.

Use Case: AI-Driven Fault Diagnosis and Repair

Real-time troubleshooting and repair can be done using an AI-driven conversational assistant. Whenever any alarm raises, the AI-driven conversational assistant analyzes sensor data, checks logs, cross-checks historical failures, and finds out the root cause of failure. It then guides the operator to take corrective measures without any senior intervention, thus reducing mean time to repair (MTTR).

10.11.3 Training and Onboarding Support

AI assistants trained in natural language serve as interactive training partners for novice operators, explaining process steps, safety procedures, and equipment functioning to the trainers. They can judge the user's competency and employ reinforcement learning to modify training accordingly. AWS SageMaker Canvas helps in drafting personalized, multimodal onboard programs to reduce learning curves and increase retention.

Use Case: Interactive AI Trainer for New Operators

An interactive AI trainer interacts with new operators and trains them with personalized training modules, equipment walkthroughs, safety briefings, and interactive quizzes. It accelerates the onboarding of new operators, improves their efficiency, and ensures standardized knowledge transfer across global manufacturing sites.

10.11.4 Integration with Amazon Lex and Bedrock

Integration of Amazon Lex and Bedrock results in a link to MES, ERP, and IOT systems with scalable conversational interfaces. This is possible as Amazon Bedrock foundation models offer generative reasoning and contextual memory using external storage, while Amazon Lex handles natural language interactions. Manufacturers can ensure low latency, security, and multilingual operations by implementing AI assistants on AR headsets or edge devices.

Use Case: Integrated Multilingual Manufacturing Assistant

Manufacturers can deploy a multilingual manufacturing assistant integrated with MES, ERP, and IOT systems. This assistant can answer various queries of operators, like production status, quality deviation, and machine status, in preferred languages across the globe.

In the next chapter, we will discuss GenAI personalization in the automotive industry.

10.12 References

1. Getting Started with Generative AI in Manufacturing. https://www.linkedin.com/pulse/getting-started-generative-ai-manufacturing-flavio-diniz-xvikf/

2. AWS Generative AI Stack. https://docs.aws.amazon.com/whitepapers/latest/aws-overview/machine-learning.html

3. Future of Manufacturing with Generative AI. https://d1.awsstatic.com/psc-digital/2024/gc-a4ind/gen-ai-mi-ebook/future-of-manufacturing-with-generative-AI.pdf

4. Design Optimization API with Amazon Lambda and Bedrock. https://repost.aws/articles/ARixmsXALpSWuxIO2zHgv1YA/bedrock-unveiled-a-quick-lambda-example

5. Amazon Forecast Time-Series Forecasting. https://aws.amazon.com/blogs/machine-learning/automate-the-deployment-of-an-amazon-forecast-time-series-forecasting-model/

6. Amazon Bedrock. https://aws.amazon.com/bedrock/

7. Amazon SageMaker Jumpstart. https://aws.amazon.com/blogs/machine-learning/deep-demand-forecasting-with-amazon-sagemaker/

8. Amazon Rekognition Custom Labels. https://aws.amazon.com/rekognition/custom-labels-features/
9. Digital twin for smart manufacturing: A review. https://www.sciencedirect.com/science/article/pii/S2667344423000099
10. AWS GenerativeAI in Manufacturing. https://aws.amazon.com/manufacturing/
11. Generative AI Reference Framework in Manufacturing. https://www.sciencedirect.com/science/article/pii/S2212827124012356
12. How Generative AI will transform manufacturing. https://aws.amazon.com/blogs/industries/generative-ai-in-manufacturing/
13. How blockchain and IoT are making supply chain smarter. https://www.ibm.com/think/topics/blockchain-for-supply-chain
14. Improve customer experience with chatbots and virtual assistants. https://aws.amazon.com/ai/generative-ai/use-cases/chatbots-and-virtual-assistants/
15. Generative AI's Role in the Factory of the Future. https://www.bcg.com/publications/2023/gen-ai-role-in-factory-of-future
16. https://docs.aws.amazon.com/whitepapers/latest/aws-overview/machine-learning.html

CHAPTER 11

Automotive Industry: Personalization at Scale

GenAI is revolutionizing the automotive industry by redefining the customer experience through personalization at scale, predictive maintenance, and real-time assistance. With the rise in automated-driven capabilities, Software-Defined Vehicles (SDV), and Advanced Driver Assistance Systems (ADAS), the automotive industry finds itself at the cutting edge of this GenAI-powered transformation.

By investing billions to incorporate AI into their products, Original Equipment Manufacturers (OEMs) are expanding the possibilities for automobiles and drivers. GenAI is being used to optimize the vehicle for a personalized experience. GenAI-driven operating models can allow companies to develop automotive software more easily, safely, and innovatively. The global automotive AI market is expected to be substantial in the near future.

A survey conducted by McKinsey found that approximately 75% of surveyed automotive enterprises are experimenting with at least one GenAI application for automobiles.

11.1 Strategic Context: Why Personalization Matters in Automotive

Personalization enables brands in various domains to design experiences that are unique to each consumer. Customers are more likely to buy personalized goods. According to statistics, marketers achieve a positive ROI when they incorporate personalization into their campaigns, and often they gain repeat customers following a positive customized shopping experience. According to McKinsey, a company's income can increase by up to 40% with the implementation of personalization.

N. Sendas et al., *Building Generative AI Solutions for Industries with AWS*,
https://doi.org/10.1007/979-8-8688-2830-0_11

Similarly, in the automotive industry, consumers expect vehicles to be tailored according to their preferences in terms of design features and performance capabilities. Personalization done using a traditional approach faces several limitations, including time intensity, dependence on human resources, and scalability constraints, whereas the use of GenAI reduces human resource dependence while achieving high customer engagement and quick enterprise-scale personalization.

Personalization with GenAI shifts the focus from product-centric to experience-centric vehicles for the customers. An automobile is not just a piece of hardware but an emotional bond to showcase one's individual taste. GenAI transforms software development capabilities for the automotive industry to improve customers' driving experiences with increased personalization. Personalization has a direct impact on business KPIs like customer lifetime value, retention, upsell, safety, and brand loyalty.

11.1.1 Shift from Product-Centric to Experience-Centric Vehicles

The automotive industry is shifting from product-centric to experience-centric vehicles with context-aware digital interactions. Today's customers expect tailored car interfaces, adaptive climate control, personalized infotainment, Advanced Driver Assistance Systems (ADAS), personalized voice assistance tailored to their preferences, predictive maintenance services, and real-time assistance for faults.

Let's take the example of ADAS: ADAS are electronic systems designed to improve vehicle safety and comfort by assisting drivers with parking and driving and sometimes take control of the vehicle to avoid accidents if needed. It has complex features like adaptive cruise control and lane-keeping, aiming to reduce human error with the help of mainly three sensors: RADAR, LIDAR, and a camera.

When ADAS is integrated with GenAI, it can transform into an adaptive partner that can understand complex, unseen scenarios and simulate scenarios for training. It increases safety, reliability, and personalizes the user experience and shifts the perspective from product-centric to experience-centric vehicle.

Key ADAS Features Powered by GenAI

- Adaptive Cruise Control (ACC)

  It maintains safe following distances and adjusts speed based on real-time traffic flow.

- Automatic Emergency Braking (AEB)

  It detects potential collisions and autonomously applies brakes to avoid a collision.

- Lane Departure Warning/Correction

  It uses cameras to detect lane markings and keep the vehicle within them.

- Driver Monitoring Systems

  It uses interior cameras and AI to detect the driver's drowsiness or distraction through eye-tracking.

- Autonomous Parking

  It uses ultrasonic sensors and AI to park the vehicle without human intervention.

11.1.2 Personalization As a Competitive Moat: Differentiation Beyond Hardware

The automotive industry is vast and crowded, and today's customers require strategic differentiation in road vehicles with a personalized touch, such as body style or engine performance. AI and generative AI analyze customer data, curate tailored services with real-time recommendations, smart user interfaces, and individualized maintenance prompts that foster deeper brand affinity.

Data-driven personalization redefines value beyond hardware, forming an emotional bond, perceived value, happiness, and individual taste, by transforming touchpoints throughout the driving, purchasing, and after-sales journeys. As product characteristics alone become increasingly commoditized, brands that provide distinctive, relevant experiences can maintain customer loyalty, protect market dominance, and reduce the churn rate.

11.1.3 Convergence of Software-Defined Vehicles (SDV), Connectivity, and AI

Software-Defined Vehicles (SDV) combined with generative AI to pave the way for AI-defined vehicles that will drive themselves and evolve with every update. Vehicles will become smarter, safer, more intelligent, customized, and more personalized to meet the customer's demands.

The promise of smooth, continuously improving driving experiences is undermined when new SDV features are not promptly and contextually communicated to drivers through traditional channels like manuals, emails, and cellphone notifications, and GenAI comes to the rescue.

Reference Architecture: Implementing a GenAI-Based Vehicle User Guide

The reference architecture illustrates the implementation of a GenAI-based vehicle user guide that powers a voice assistant used by drivers. In the architecture below, a Small Language Model (SLM) is stored locally in the vehicle, allowing drivers to query about vehicle features and operations using their natural language, thereby implementing a GenAI-based voice assistant. This GenAI voice assistant functions as a more accessible vehicle owner's manual by using the SLM to respond to enquiries from car occupants. Additionally, it potentially increases customers' interest and trust in the car brand.

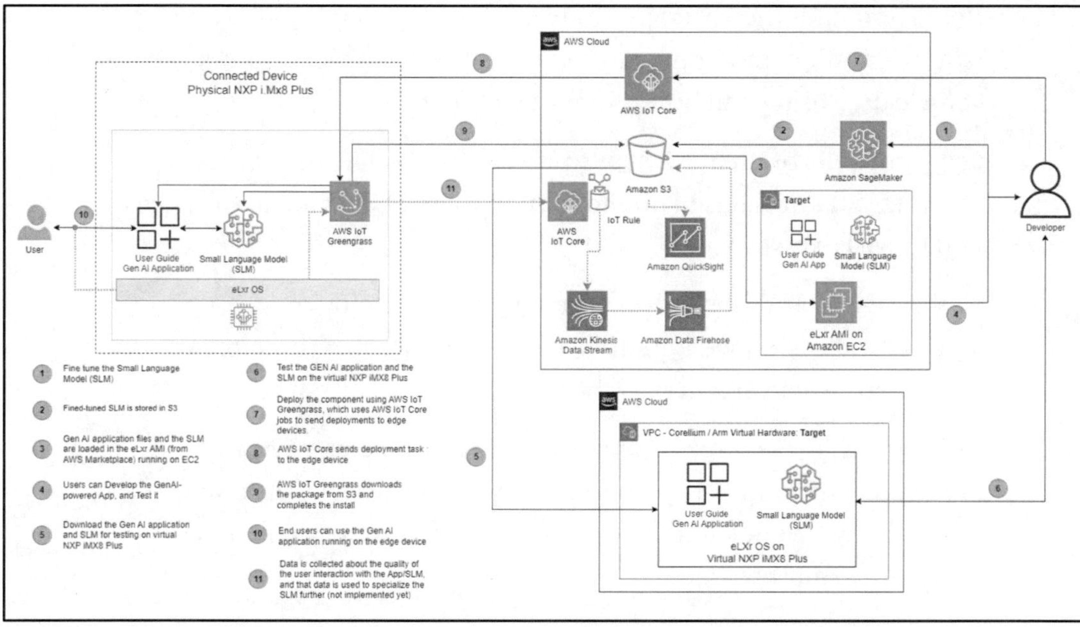

Figure 11-1. *Reference Architecture for GenAI-Based Vehicle User Guide*

For the implementation of the GenAI voice assistant use case, OEMs start by utilizing their current car user manual to create curated content, and they keep enhancing features and capabilities throughout the vehicle lifecycle using software updates. Amazon SageMaker Studio is used to fine-tune the pre-trained SLM model and store it in S3.

11.1.4 Business KPIs: Customer Lifetime Value (CLV), Retention, Upsell, Safety, and Brand Loyalty

GenAI has a direct impact on business KPIs like customer lifetime value (CLV), retention, upselling, safety, and brand loyalty by enabling hyper-personalization, accelerating development, and improving operational efficiency across the vehicle lifecycle.

- **Customer lifetime value (CLV)** can be enhanced using GenAI through repeat service engagements, personalized marketing, and various digital subscription offerings.

- **Retention** rates increased by 10–15% through proactive, personalized communication and improved service experience that reduces vehicle downtime and builds long-term trust.
- GenAI **upsells** by creating hyper-personalized offers and recommendations based on individual driving behavior, preferences, and browsing history.
- GenAI significantly can improve **safety** by enhancing the ADAS system, and customized predictive maintenance leads to more robust and reliable safety features in the vehicle.
- Collectively, these three capabilities cultivate long-term **brand loyalty**, transforming transactional purchasers into loyalty and maintaining revenue long beyond the initial transaction in this competitive market.

11.2 Personalization Dimensions Across the Automotive Value Chain

According to towardautomotive.com, the vehicle personalization market is projected to increase at a compound annual growth rate (CAGR) of 14.68%, from USD 13.9 billion in 2025 to USD 47.68 billion by 2034. Personalization in the automotive value chain is evolving from simple, aesthetic, predefined design to hyper-personalization that spans multiple dimensions, including design, manufacturing, and the long ownership cycle.

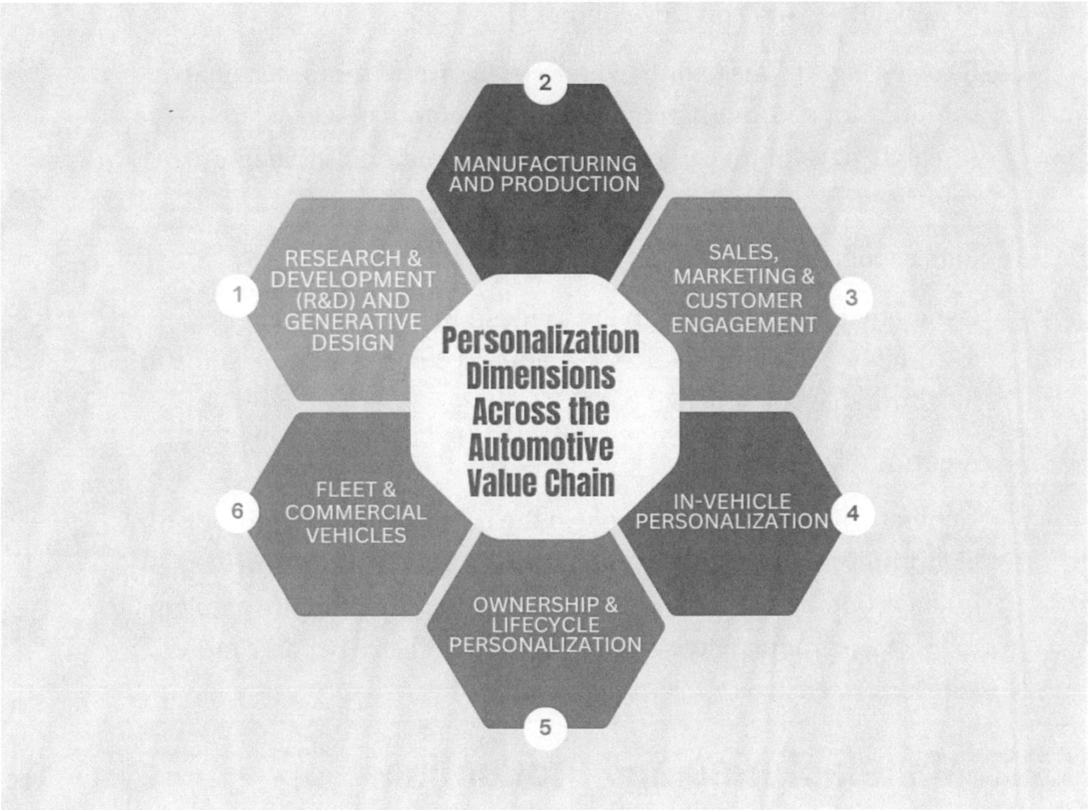

Figure 11-2. *Key Personalization Dimensions*

Here are the personalization dimensions across the automotive value chain.

11.2.1 Research and Development (R&D) and Generative Design

Generative AI analyzes massive datasets, identifies optimal material, generates designs, research, and innovates for an enhanced personalized product. Some use cases of generative design, research, and development are as follows:

- Vehicle Design Personalization

  Generative AI implements advanced models and evaluates many car designs, finding the best combinations of materials, forms, layouts, and personalized choices to improve design, safety, economy, and aerodynamics.

- Material Research and Development

  By using algorithms to find lighter, stronger, and more sustainable solutions for automotive components, generative AI accelerates the research, development, and testing of new materials that improve vehicle efficiency and sustainability.

- Battery Innovation

  Generative AI contributes to the innovation of vehicle battery technology by analyzing diverse chemical compositions, leading to more durable and efficient batteries.

- Algorithm Development

  Generative AI plays a major role in the development and testing of algorithms for autonomous vehicles. GenAI helps teams write high-quality code, create test cases, describe APIs, and identify problems to increase productivity and reliability, as vehicles become more software-intensive.

11.2.2 Manufacturing and Production

Generative AI significantly enhanced manufacturing and production in the automotive industry by streamlining production processes, autonomous manufacturing, reducing waste material production, and enhancing quality control. Some use cases of manufacturing and production with GenAI are as follows:

- Streamline Production Process

  GenAI analyzes vast data from production lines, identifies inefficiencies, predicts market demands, improves efficiency, and streamlines the entire production process. GenAI not only accelerates development cycles but also reduces costs with high precision and innovation in manufacturing operations.

- Autonomous Manufacturing

  GenAI reduces the human effort and automates the entire manufacturing line, thus reducing the chances of error and reducing the time taken at optimized cost with minimum human oversight.

- Quality Control and Inspection

  GenAI analyzes real-time data from manufacturing lines and automatically detects defects and keeps a check on quality in case of any deviation from set standards. This approach not only improves product quality, consistency, and reliability but also reduces the time and cost of manual inspection.

- Material Waste Reduction

  Streamline the manufacturing and production line, optimize the sequence of operations, and reduce waste material production. Reduction in waste production leads to better resource utilization and increased production efficiency.

11.2.3 Sales, Marketing, and Customer Engagement

Deploying GenAI benefits all areas of automotive marketing, sales, and customer engagement, transforming marketing and sales operations across the board. It analyzes the data available on the customers' journey and helps personalize the sales effort by offering individualized configurations, product recommendations, and personalized pricing to their customers. Some use cases of sales, marketing, and customer engagement with GenAI are as follows:

- Personalized Marketing Campaigns

  GenAI helps in personalized marketing campaigns by creating unique content based on the customers' requirements, preferences, tastes, and behavior. It adapts dynamically according to market trends with engaging strategies resulting in better outcomes.

- Virtual Showrooms and Product Demos

  GenAI produces dynamic product demos and immersive virtual showrooms that provide real-time customization and interactivity for a more captivating consumer experience, which is not possible with traditional AI.

- Predictive Sales Analytics

  Generative AI enhances sales analytics by generating future scenarios and insights rather than just focusing on past data like traditional AI, resulting in more accurate sales forecasting.

- Customer Feedback Analysis

  GenAI analyzes customer feedback, identifies their sentiments and behavior, studies future trends, and suggests improvements accordingly.

- Automated Content Generation for Marketing

  GenAI automates content generation for marketing, diversifies products, and innovates ideas to enhance efficiency in marketing strategies, resulting in increased sales.

11.2.4 In-Vehicle Personalization

GenAI enables the following in-vehicle personalization with dynamic vehicle settings adaptation, based on stored data, personal patterns, and contextual signals. It helps to improve comfort, safety, and customer engagement continuously. Some use cases of in-vehicle personalization with GenAI are as follows:

- Enhanced ADAS

  GenAI improves vehicle safety with an enhanced ADAS system that can predict potential threats and take control of driving and accelerating functions in case of emergency, thus reducing accidents and improving overall safety. GenAI analyses data from multiple sensors to understand a vehicle's surroundings and ensure a smooth transition between automated ADAS systems and human drivers.

- Personalized Voice Assistant

  Personalized voice assistants utilize generative AI in automotive applications to enable natural, context-aware interaction between the vehicle and drivers. It uses deep learning and natural language processing to accurately understand complicated voice commands and comprehend user preferences to dynamically adjust controls in real time.

- Intelligent Navigation

  GenAI empowers drivers to make smarter decisions on the road by transforming a navigation system that can analyze real-time data of accidents, road closures, prevailing road conditions, and traffic congestion. This intelligent understanding enables the navigation system to guide the driver to a more efficient and optimized route for a smoother and stress-free journey.

- Personalized In-Car Infotainment

  GenAI delivers a personalized experience for in-car infotainment tailored to individual preferences. It analyzed driver and passenger historical data, understood their mood and preferences, and recommended music, podcasts, and media accordingly. Infotainment systems adapt to real-time data such as mood and driving conditions and provide options accordingly to enhance the driving experience and make long trips enjoyable.

- Personalized Recommendations

  GenAI helps in providing personal recommendations based on historical data, driver behavior, preferences, and real-time scenarios analysis, offering automated climate control, automated display, automated camera, automotive HVAC (Heating, Ventilation, and Air Conditioning), and ambient lighting.

11.2.5 Ownership and Lifecycle Personalization

With the help of GenAI, personalization across ownership and the lifecycle is possible by interpreting usage patterns, vehicle health, maintenance schedules, and driver behavior insights that improve safety and reduce costs. It enhances brand value throughout the lifecycle and strengthens owner-brand relationships with seamless digital enhancements. Some use cases of ownership and lifecycle personalization with GenAI are as follows:

- Scenario Generation

  GenAI helps in generating diverse virtual scenarios by analyzing real-world data for testing autonomous driving systems. GenAI tries to mimic real-world driving situations, future market and trends, demand, and customer behavior scenarios to test the vehicle efficiently.

- Anomaly Detection

  GenAI detects an anomaly by analyzing sensor data and driving patterns during simulation testing. It can easily detect system failures, hidden risks, and abnormal situations beforehand to avoid any potential system failures. It improves the safety and reliability of autonomous vehicles and ensures optimal performance in various driving conditions.

- Battery Health Estimation

  GenAI estimates the health of vehicle batteries by analyzing historical data, current voltage, timing, and cycle information. It can predict the remaining useful life of batteries and ensure timely maintenance, thus reducing the risk of unexpected battery failures and ensuring optimal performance.

- Resource Allocation

  GenAI enables dynamic and optimal resource allocation by predicting future demand and enhancing the entire supply chain experience, a major advancement over conventional techniques that just use historical data.

- Supply Chain Optimization

  GenAI creates a highly accurate predictive model to forecast demand for the upcoming season, quarter, or year, managing the entire supply chain. It helps in optimizing supply chains by determining inventory levels, thus saving the industry from both overstock and stockout scenarios.

11.2.6 Fleet and Commercial Vehicles

In fleets and commercial vehicles, personalization optimizes operations using GenAI, which integrates and analyzes real-time data to improve uptime and reduce the total cost of ownership across complex fleet and commercial vehicle deployments. Some use cases of fleet and commercial vehicles personalization with GenAI are as follows:

- Driver-Centric Personalization

  GenAI implements personalization as per driver safety and comfort, like seating arrangement, ADAS settings, and display configurations. Personalized coaching is also provided to drivers to get the maximum benefits of personalized services.

- Brand and Aesthetic Personalization

  GenAI personalized graphics, dashboard, wraps, paint schemas, and vehicle aesthetics according to the company's identity, which justify the brand's personalization.

- Predictive Maintenance

  GenAI can predict and personalize vehicles and their equipment maintenance based on real-time data analysis, preventing unexpected breakdowns and extending vehicle lifespan.

- Intelligent Scheduling and Dynamic Route Optimization

  GenAI implements intelligent scheduling of fleet and commercial vehicle trips, maintenance scheduling, and route optimization to improve their efficiency.

11.3 Role of Generative AI vs. Traditional ML in Automotive Personalization

Both traditional ML and generative AI play an important role in automotive personalization, maintaining their individuality. Traditional ML specializes in predictive, rule-based optimization, while GenAI enables humanlike, interactive, contextual content creation.

11.3.1 Deterministic Rules and Predictive ML vs. Generative Systems

Deterministic rule-based systems follow predefined rules to predict outputs. Predictive ML models learn patterns from historical data to predict outputs. Both combine to make traditional AI, which emphasizes precision and explainability. Generative systems are designed to generate text, images, voice, and other types of data by learning from underlying multimodal unstructured data and understanding context to create content on demand.

11.3.2 Role of Traditional ML in Automotive Personalization

Traditional ML adds value in the automotive industry, as mentioned below:

- It helps in driver profiling by analyzing the driver's past behavior.
- It helps in vehicle damage assessment based on real-time sensor data.
- It helps in vehicle insurance fraud detection.
- It helps in detecting pedestrians, line markers, and traffic signals for road safety using object detection.
- It helps in predicting music or a destination based on past choices using the recommendation engine.
- It enables easily accessible chatbots for customer service.

11.3.3 Role of Generative ML in Automotive Personalization

Generative AI adds value in the automotive industry in various domains discussed in the section "Personalization Dimensions Across the Automotive Value Chain" above.

11.3.4 Hybrid Architectures: ML for Prediction + GenAI for Interaction and Orchestration

Predictive machine learning models (for forecasting, classification, and optimization) and generative systems (for interaction, synthesis, and explanation) are combined in hybrid AI architectures. While GenAI translates, contextualizes, and orchestrates responses, predictive models manage dependable, repeatable outputs. This enables structured logic with innovative interface layers, perfect for complex situations that require both accuracy and conversational flexibility.

11.4 Automotive Data Foundation for Personalization at Scale

Today's vehicles comprise Electronic Control Units (ECU) and sensors that store GBs of data every day. It is important to analyze this robust data and extract the relevant information for personalization. This data contains real-time vehicle telemetry, behavioral signals, infotainment data, CRM, and supply chain data that support both low-latency personalization and deep historical learning. This data foundation is utilized by predictive ML and generative AI systems to deliver consistent, context-aware experiences throughout the entire automotive value chain when combined with data governance and robust identity resolution.

11.4.1 Data Sources

An automotive data foundation consists of raw and heterogeneous multimodal sources and is then transformed into an input format for an ML model that provides real-time inference. Data sources are as follows:

- Vehicle Telemetry, CAN Bus Data, and Sensor Streams capture real-time engine data, including tire pressure monitoring, fuel, brake, transmission, camera inputs, radar, LIDAR data, and more.
- Driver Behavior, Infotainment Usage, and Mobile Apps capture driving analytics, including speeding, braking system usage, infotainment system use, and various mobile apps connected to the vehicle, along with their usage and logs.
- CRM, Dealer Systems, and Supply Chain Systems capture customer analytics, their history, sales patterns, and component traceability, enriching models for personalization across ownership timelines, service experiences, and product planning.

11.4.2 Data Challenges

Automotive systems generate high volumes of high velocity with varied data from telematics, sensors, CRM systems, and external sources. This type of data presents storage, processing, and model training challenges at scale, and unified schemas and standards must be established to prevent silos.

Cross-OEM and Multi-region Data Governance, which incorporates regulatory compliance with GDPR/CCPA, regional privacy laws, consent management, and standardized metadata, is essential for trust, interoperability, and secure personalization without infringing on ownership rights or disclosing sensitive information.

11.4.3 Real-Time vs. Batch Personalization Pipelines

Real-time and batch personalization pipelines serve different purposes in the automotive sector based on the data required for immediate action or long-term analysis. Real-time pipelines require continuous processing for immediate personalization, such as safety alerts, dynamic telemetry, and behavioral events. Real-time pipeline data can face consistency issues, be complex to handle, and be a costly affair.

Batch personalization pipelines handle large, accumulated historical data for model training, deep analytics, and periodic features. These are suitable for scheduled tasks such as monthly servicing reports, odometer readings, historical maintenance records, CRM systems, customer satisfaction surveys, and aggregated telematics data. These are moderately complex, low-cost solutions that often rely on stale data and do not take immediate action.

11.5 Reference Architecture for GenAI-Driven Personalization

GenAI-driven personalization architecture in the automotive industry involves contextual awareness, scalability, features, stores, and personalization knowledge graphs and raw event ingestion to enable real-time contexts, utilizing a hybrid edge-cloud approach.

In this section, we will see how Audi has improved their enterprise chat experience through a generative AI chatbot using Amazon Web Services (AWS), and the solution is based on a Retrieval-Augmented Generation (RAG).

11.5.1 Reference Architecture of Generative AI Chatbot

Over the past few years, as the internal knowledge of Audi was expanding, they have been facing challenges in accessing and navigating their internal documents in different locations filled with important as well as redundant information. So, a chatbot is designed with generative AI for conversational contexts where the GenAI model responds to users' queries in a natural and engaged manner.

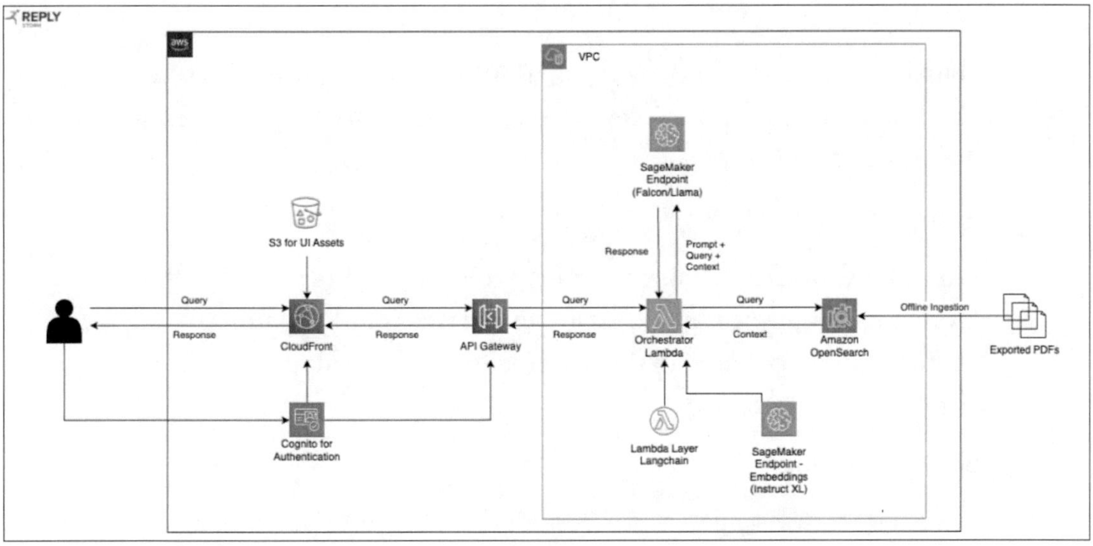

Figure 11-3. *High-Level Architecture of Generative AI Chatbot Implemented by Audi*

Audi has improved its internal search experience by deploying a generative AI chatbot, significantly reducing search times from hours to seconds while improving response accuracy. The solution ingests documentation into a vector database and combines semantic retrieval with large language models to provide contextual answers. Hosted securely within AWS services, it integrates multiple data sources and optimizes for performance, security, and scalability.

11.5.2 Key Components of Generative AI Architecture

Some of the key components of generative AI implementation are as follows:

- Event-Driven Ingestion (Vehicle ➤ Cloud ➤ Edge)

  Event-driven architecture is a decoupled system that runs in response to events. It has three key components: event producers, event routers, and event consumers. In GenAI, personalization relies on event-driven ingestion pipelines that stream vehicles' real-time telemetry, sensor data, and user interaction data. Vehicle data triggers events, which are sent to the cloud, and then, after processing and updation, commands are sent back to the vehicle.

Vehicle-to-Cloud (V2C)

Vehicles utilize IoT protocols, such as AWS IoT Core, to stream sensor data, telemetry flow data, user interaction data, and diagnostic event data to the cloud.

Event-Driven Pipeline

Amazon EventBridge is used to create rules that route specific vehicle event data to appropriate downstream services, and streaming platforms like Apache Kafka are used to process the data into a data lake (Amazon S3).

Edge Processing

Critical inferences, such as safety alerts and in-cabin personalization, are processed on edge gateways, while non-critical data is sent to the cloud for intensive processing to minimize latency.

- Feature Stores

  Feature stores personalize in the automotive industry by standardizing real-time and batch features, such as driver signals, choices, patterns, and contextual language, to be used across GenAI and ML systems.

- Personalization Knowledge Graphs

  Personalization knowledge graphs establish a relationship between vehicles, drivers, services, and surroundings to develop a better, richer, more contextual, and explainable environment across data sources.

- Retrieval-Augmented Generation (RAG) for Contextual Responses

  Retrieval-Augmented Generation is a GenAI implementation used for contextual responses by extracting data from vehicle telemetry, manuals, policies, and user preferences. RAG architecture utilizes LLM for context-aware recommendations for vehicles based on vehicle telemetry, driver behavior, and different situations. RAG implementation for contextual response increases accuracy and decreases hallucination.

- Edge vs. Cloud Inference Trade-Offs

  Edge inference is ideal for low-latency and privacy-sensitive use cases, such as safety triggers and real-time voice assistance for drivers. In contrast, cloud inference is ideal for powerful, highly complex models and cross-fleet optimization. GenAI personalization architecture for automotive balances latency, bandwidth, complexity, cost, and regulation by selectively deploying models across edge and cloud tiers.

- Multi-tenant Personalization Platforms for Global Scale

  To implement personalization for millions of vehicles, the platform must be designed for multi-tenancy across OEMs, brands, regions, and fleets while sharing core capabilities. Data privacy and security must be ensured between different tenants when sharing the same architecture. Multi-tenancy enables horizontal scaling using cloud services based on demand. Regional edge nodes and cloud instances have been deployed to minimize latency, and governance regulations should be followed.

11.6 In-Vehicle GenAI Experiences

In-vehicle GenAI experiences transform vehicles into personalized machines, marking the shift from a human interface to conversational, context-aware, safe, and multimodal intelligent cars. They understand driver intent, situational awareness, adapt, and interact dynamically due to the large language model implementation and real-time vehicle data accessibility.

11.6.1 Conversational Assistants Beyond Voice Commands

Personalization helps in establishing a conversational assistant that not only takes voice commands but also understands context, emotions, and driver needs.

- Voice assistants understand the driver in natural language dialogue, their context, intent, maintain conversational memory, adapt responses based on the driver's state, and follow up on questions.

- Multimodal interaction is possible by combining requests such as "navigate home" and "play my favorite playlist."
- An assistant is trained to understand user emotions and respond empathetically, thereby building trust.
- It understands the history and context of vehicles, enabling proactive assistance compared to rigid voice commands.

11.6.2 Context-Aware Recommendations (Navigation, Music, Comfort)

GenAI enables personalized recommendations that are context-aware and proactive.

- Personalized music, climate control, comfort settings based on habits, past data, and real-time situations.
- Adapt navigation rules based on needs, traffic, and driving conditions.
- It balances multiple objectives intelligently, such as time, safety, and energy efficiency, according to the situation.
- It continually learns from acceptance, overrides, and behavioral feedback, adapting accordingly.

11.6.3 Personalized Safety and Driving Insights

GenAI humanizes and personalizes safety analytics, driving insights that increase its effectiveness and adaptation in concerned situations.

- GenAI helps in ML models and ADAS outputs by translating them into human-understandable language.
- It raises personalized alerts based on the driver's profile, history, and behavior.
- Share feedback and summaries post-drive.
- Provide safety interventions tailored to the context to foster trust and compliance.

11.6.4 Multimodal AI: Voice + Vision + Sensor Fusion

Multimodal GenAI enables richer perception and natural interaction in voice and vision.

- Data is gathered and trained for voice, radar, vehicle sensors, cabin vision using a camera, and gaze tracking using multimodal AI.
- It can infer driver intention, attention span, fatigue, and emotional state and adapt its decision accordingly.
- It enables gesture-based interaction with the driver and makes decisions based on the situation.
- It enables seamless collaboration between humans and machines during driving and exhibits robust behavior in noisy, ambiguous, and high-speed environments.

11.6.5 Latency, Offline Inference, and Edge Constraints

Automotive personalized implemented architecture optimizes intelligence while handling various situations without compromising on safety.

- Architecture must meet automotive acceptable safety standards, reliability, and power constraints.
- Sub-second, predictable latency is required for safety-critical interactions.
- In case of poor or no connectivity, offline inference support must be available.
- Cloud-based implementation, edge constraints, and orchestration need to be balanced.

11.7 Personalization Across the Customer Journey

GenAI-driven personalization helps automotive brands to deliver more connected, safe, seamless, and one-to-one-tailored customer journeys. Personalization has become a critical strategy for manufacturers, and dealers have shifted from mass marketing to deeply personal, individually tailored experiences. Using Customer Data Platforms (CDPs), brands can interact with individual customers, understand their needs, tailor their products, and deliver high-quality personalized results, leading to higher revenue and stronger loyalty. The future of automotive users is driven by AI technology.

11.7.1 AI-Driven Vehicle Configuration and Virtual Assistants

Generative AI-driven vehicle configuration has changed from rule-based options selection to intelligent and conversational virtual assistants. Virtual AI assistants guide customers through manuals and configurations using natural language, intent inference, and contextual reasoning. It also recommends features and packages aligned with their profile, lifestyle, choices, budget, and usage patterns. Virtual assistance boosts confidence, lessens choice overload, and improves conversion rates by intelligent trade-offs, adaptable configurations, and simulates real-time scenarios across digital or showroom journeys.

11.7.2 Personalized Financing, Warranty, and Service Offers

GenAI-driven personalization tailors finances, warranty, and service offers packages based on customer driving patterns, emotional quotient, ownership intent, risk profiles, lifestyle, and to ensure safety. Machine learning predictive models can predict mileage, affordability, price, or service need. Still, GenAI helps in understanding intent, behavior, and emotion in natural language. This opens a window for dynamic pricing, targeted upselling, flexible subscription models, improves acceptance, and fosters trust through long-term customer relationships.

11.7.3 Post-Purchase Engagement and Loyalty Programs

Personalized automotive also offers post-purchase sustainable engagement and loyalty programs through AI-driven insights, recommendations, and contextual communications. GenAI analyzes vehicle data to provide personalized tips, maintenance reminders, loyalty rewards, and knowledge about vehicle features. OEMs deepen emotional connection, evolve royalty programs to increase retention, and maintain a continuous value-driven relationship throughout the ownership lifecycle.

11.7.4 Integration with Dealer Ecosystems and Partner Platforms

Seamless integration with dealer ecosystems and partner platforms is necessary for effective personalization. All data from CRM, DMS, finance, insurance, and service providers is unified to ensure consistent and persistent personalization across all touch points. While preserving tenant isolation and governance, generative AI enables shared intelligence, supporting dealer sales assistants, service advisors, and partner platforms. This alignment continuously improves the customer experience, operational efficiency, and a wide range of values across the ecosystem.

11.8 Personalization for Manufacturing, Supply Chain, and Operations

GenAI is personalizing manufacturing, supply chain, and operations, which applies to people, process, and decisions, not only the manufactured products. It utilizes insights and interventions tailored to specific skills and contexts to reduce manufacturing unit load and errors, resulting in improved efficiency, execution quality in high-variable environments, and economical production of custom goods at scale.

11.8.1 GenAI-Driven Role-Based Dashboards for Plant Managers

GenAI enables role-based dashboards for plant managers, transforming complex manufacturing data into actionable insights. Dashboard dynamically detects risks, bottlenecks, and optimization opportunities using natural language assistance, context-awareness, and scenario reasoning. It not only improves speed, efficiency, decision-making, quality, throughput, energy, and workforce dimensions but also reduces cognitive overload.

11.8.2 Personalized Alerts and Recommendations for Operators

GenAI personalized alerts and recommendations for operators based on their role, skill level, shift context, and machine state. GenAI not only raises alarms but also explains root causes and takes corrective actions to fix the issue in human-understandable language. It recommends proactive actions to the operators to avoid future failure scenarios. This reduces error rates, improves response times, and gives operators the confidence to act confidently in a highly variable manufacturing environment.

11.8.3 Mass Customization Feedback Loops into Manufacturing

GenAI-driven insights can be used to feed personalization data from customer configurations, usage patterns, and post-sale feedback back into manufacturing, which is known as mass customization feedback loops. Production and supply chain modifications are made based on system identification of new demand patterns, option combinations, and design problems. Scalable mass customization is made possible by closing the loop between operational execution and demand personalization.

11.9 Platform and Technology Considerations for Architects

The architects need to balance the platform, technology, scalability, intelligence, cost management strategy, and observability mechanisms before making any decisions to build a robust GenAI-driven personalization system. Model strategy, cost optimization, infrastructure location, data isolation, and operational observability are all crucial choices that have a direct bearing on experience quality and financial sustainability.

11.9.1 Model Selection: Foundation Models vs. Domain-Tuned Models

Architects need to balance generality and speciality while making model selections between foundation models and domain-tuned models. Foundation models provide broad reasoning, linguistic comprehension, and cross-domain adaptation, while domain-tuned models deliver determinism, higher precision, and safety in automotive-specific tasks.

Automotive architects can adopt a hybrid approach by combining both foundation and domain-tuned models, which delivers fine-tuning, adapters, and domain grounding without sacrificing scalability and evolves continuously with changing requirements.

11.9.2 Cost Optimization: Inference Cost, Caching, and Tiered Personalization

For personalization at scale, an architect needs to optimize cost per query, inference, storage, and orchestration layer cost and minimize unnecessary computation. Response caching, embedding reuse, quick compression, and layered personalization are some strategies that use predictive machine learning or rules for routine decisions and GenAI reasoning for high-value interactions. Architects need to balance between cost optimization, quality, and operational efficiency.

11.9.3 Scalability Patterns: Regionalization, Sharding, and Tenant Isolation

Personalization at global platforms must scale across regions, brands, and customer segments while meeting governance regulations, latency constraints, and data residency requirements. Architects implement regionalization, data and feature sharding, and strict tenant isolation to ensure high-quality performance and customer satisfaction. Without causing cross-tenant data leakage, these patterns facilitate multi-brand OEMs, dealer ecosystems, and partner integrations.

11.9.4 Observability and Feedback Loops for Personalization Quality

Observability and feedback loops are crucial for maintaining personalization quality and trust in the automotive industry. It is necessary to detect bias, drift, and degradation by tracking model outputs, customer interaction, and other outcomes. Closed-loop feedback pipelines continuously optimized the personalized experiences by feeding human and machine signals back into model retraining, prompt refinement, and policy updates.

11.10 Privacy, Safety, and Regulatory Considerations

The integration of GenAI in the automotive personalization space needs a robust framework to balance the customer's experience with privacy, safety, and regulatory compliance at its core. They follow regional regulatory adherence, such as GDPR, CCPA, and automotive standards, with data minimization and explicit consent management. Explainability, auditability, and policy-enforced safeguards foster trust while facilitating responsible customization and large-scale innovation.

11.10.1 Data Minimization and Consent Management

The automotive GenAI system must adopt data minimization principles to strictly collect, process, and store only the data necessary for a defined purpose. User consent for data collection is essential across all vehicle, mobile, and cloud touchpoints. To support privacy and reduce exposure, architects are now supporting minimal transmission of personal information to the cloud.

11.10.2 Regional Compliance (GDPR, CCPA, Automotive Data Regulations)

Automotive GenAI personalization platforms must operate across divergent privacy, regional, and global regulations regarding driver data. GDPR, CCPA/CPRA, are emerging regulations that mandate automotive data to take care of users' rights, data, and auditability. To guarantee that personalization scales internationally without regulatory risk, architectures must support regionalized deployments, policy-aware data routing, and compliance-by-design.

11.10.3 AI Explainability and Transparency in Recommendations

In GenAI-driven personalization, it is crucial to establish transparency and AI explainability to build trust with customers. GenAI systems must be able to provide understandable explanations for their decisions, recommendations regarding price, features, and safety. Rationale generation, confidence indicators, and traceability to input signals are some techniques that can improve user acceptability of AI-driven decisions and choices, as well as alignment with regulatory requirements.

11.10.4 Safety-Critical vs. Non-safety-critical Personalization Boundaries

Maintaining a clear difference between safety-critical and non-safety-critical personalization is mandatory. Safety-critical functions, such as alerts and ADAS, rely on deterministic validated models, while GenAI is typically restricted to explanation, interaction, or advisory roles. Architects ensure adherence to functional safety standards by preventing the generation of outputs that directly control vehicle behavior.

11.11 Security and Trust Architecture

The foundation architecture layer for deploying automotive GenAI is a security and trust architecture to provide safety, privacy, and trust for brands. A robust architecture needs secure vehicle-to-cloud communication with trust, mutual authentication, and secure OTA as its roots. GenAI operates strictly by following policy enforcement and guardrails, maintaining safe identity management, and reducing data leakage and hallucination risks.

11.11.1 Reference Architecture of Generative AI Network Defense

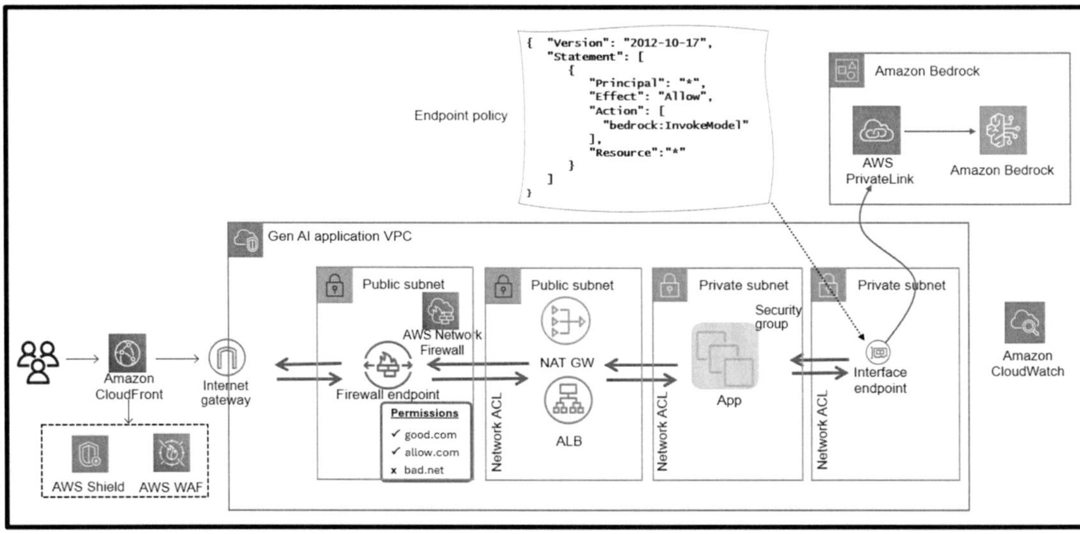

Figure 11-4. *Generative AI Network Defense Workflow Using AWS*

Let's understand how to build a network defense architecture for GenAI applications using AWS services. The above architecture secures a generative AI application using layered AWS protections. Client traffic flows through CloudFront, AWS WAF, and Shield for DDoS and application-layer defense, then through Network Firewall and an ALB to private subnets. The app securely accesses Amazon Bedrock via PrivateLink and IAM endpoint policies, while CloudWatch provides end-to-end monitoring and observability.

11.11.2 Secure Vehicle-to-Cloud Communication

Secure vehicle-to-cloud communication featuring mutual authentication, certificate-based identity, and end-to-end encryption is necessary for GenAI-driven personalization. In addition to low-latency, high-availability connectivity across international automobile fleets, secure boot, trusted execution environments (TEE), and over-the-air (OTA) updates provide security guarantees, ensuring data integrity and preventing data tampering to ensure secure communication.

11.11.3 Identity Management for Drivers and Vehicles

Strong identity management and resolution across drivers, cars, and digital channels is necessary for personalization. Personalization architecture utilizes a privacy-preserving identity federation to integrate driver profiles, vehicle identities, and customer accounts. Access management ensures that the right data and AI rights are activated for each driver, role, and context while sharing vehicles and fleets.

11.11.4 Prompt Injection, Data Leakage, and Hallucination Risks

GenAI systems are vulnerable to various types of attacks, including prompt injection, data leakage, and hallucination risks. Automotive platforms need to validate outputs against reliable systems, segregate sensitive data, limit prompts, and sanitize inputs. Some in-depth defense approaches, like retrieval constraints, output filtering, and confidence scoring, reduce the risk of unsafe or misleading responses.

11.11.5 Guardrails and Policy Enforcement for GenAI Systems

Guardrails and policy enforcement for the GenAI system enforce safety, security, and brand policy across various interactions. These include role-based access controls, content moderation, deterministic fallbacks, and explicit boundaries between advisory and control functions. To ensure compliance with safety standards, privacy commitments, and regulatory requirements at scale, policy engines dynamically control what GenAI can access, say, or recommend.

11.12 Organizational and Operating Model Implications

GenAI-driven personalization needs new operating models to balance the centralized AI platform in the organization with different domain teams. OEMs need to think about build-vs.-buy strategies, invest in data, ML, and AI architecture. They also work on cross-functional collaboration across IT, sales, marketing, and legal teams. Innovation that aligns with governance, common platforms, and transparent accountability throughout the automotive value chain is essential for success.

11.12.1 Centralized AI Platforms vs. Federated OEM Teams

Organizations must choose between centralized AI platforms and federated OEM teams to balance speed, efficiency, cost, knowledge, and compliance. Centralization enables scale, governance, cost efficiency, and model reuse, while federated teams preserve domain expertise and speed. A practical solution that balances innovation pace with safety, compliance, and architectural consistency is a hub-and-spoke model, which consists of central AI foundations with domain-owned personalization use cases.

11.12.2 Build vs. Buy Decisions for Personalization Engines

OEMs often need to decide whether to build or buy personalization engines based on data sensitivity, strategic differentiation, and time-to-market considerations. When a brand invests in core personalization according to brand value, driver behavior, and customer data, it chooses to build its own personalization engines. Some commodity components, such as LLMs, orchestration frameworks, and analytics tools, can be sourced externally to accelerate time to market while maintaining control over proprietary intelligence.

11.12.3 Skills Transformation: Data Engineers, ML Engineers, and AI Architects

Organizations must invest in upskilling, skill transformation, new technology, new roles, and cross-disciplinary expertise to sustain and accelerate personalization in the automotive industry. GenAI implementation requires an upgrade in skill set with cross-disciplinary expertise. AI architects create scalable, safe, and compliant systems; ML engineers balance predictive and generative pipelines in hybrid mode, and data engineers concentrate on streaming, feature stores, and governance.

11.12.4 Cross-Functional Collaboration (IT, Engineering, Marketing, Legal)

The cross-functional collaboration model combines IT, engineering, marketing, legal, and data teams, resulting in reduced silos, accelerating decision-making, and responsible innovation across the vehicle lifecycle. When cross-functional teams work iteratively on the GenAI-driven vehicle lifecycle, then only projects are converted into products.

11.13 Measuring Success of Personalization at Scale

Measuring the success of personalization at scale requires aligning technical performance with business needs. There are some technical metrics to measure success, such as latency, accuracy, drift, and cost per interaction. Additionally, various business indicators, including engagement, conversion, retention, and lifetime value, confirm the impact of personalization throughout the customer journey. Continuous experimentation, A/B testing, and closed-loop feedback from vehicles into model retraining enable sustained optimization, relevance, and trust at scale.

11.13.1 Technical Metrics: Latency, Accuracy, Drift, and Cost per Interaction

There are some technical metrics to monitor the performance, health, efficiency, and accuracy of the personalization system.

- Latency

  Latency is critical for real-time applications as it can directly impact the in-vehicle experience and safety boundaries. High latency can lead to poor user experience, as optimization is necessary for better responses.

- Accuracy

  Accuracy is relevant to measure how correctly the model predicts user recommendation quality.

- Drift Detection

  Drift detection monitors changing driver behavior and degradation in model performance over time.

- Cost per Interaction

  It measures all expenses, including computation, architectural, and financial expenses, to deliver personalized content at scale.

11.13.2 Business Metrics: Engagement, Conversion, and Retention

Three key business metrics reflect financial and user-centric value achieved through personalization. These metrics validate whether personalization strengthens customer relationships rather than adding isolated functionality.

- Engagement

  Engagement measures usage frequency and the depth of personalized features.

- Conversion

  Conversion tracks the rate at which personalized interactions lead to the uptake of configurations, subscriptions, feature adoption, or other offers.

- Retention

  Retention and lifetime value indicate long-term success, loyalty, and satisfaction across ownership cycles, thus reducing churn rate.

11.13.3 Continuous Experimentation and A/B Testing

Quality of personalization in automobiles improves through continuous experimentation. Experimental frameworks must be integrated with business, technical, safety metrics, and user interactions for informed decision-making.

A/B testing compares architectural designs, models, prompts, and recommendation strategies across regions, companies, and groups. With GenAI, faster hypothesis testing is possible, but caution must be exercised to prevent the dangerous or biased variations.

11.13.4 Feedback Loops from Vehicle to Model Retraining

GenAI benefits from human-in-the-loop feedback to refine prompts, recommendations, strategies, and explanations, ensuring continuous alignment with real-world vehicles, users, and drivers' behavior and needs, as well as their expectations.

Closed-loop feedback is also crucial for personalization at scale, as signals, usage patterns, outcomes, and overrides all contribute to feature strokes and retraining pipelines for continuous learning and improvement.

11.14 Future Outlook: From Personalization to Autonomy of Experience

Automotive personalization is evolving, and its next stage is the automotive experience, in which GenAI actively plans mobility outcomes rather than only responding to preferences.

GenAI agents coordinate vehicles, homes, and city infrastructure, while personalization expands across multimodal mobility signals to anticipate needs across emotion-aware and intent-driven vehicles. GenAI is continuously optimized for comfort, safety, cost, and sustainability with a focus on goal-driven and adaptive mobility experiences.

11.14.1 Emotion-Aware and Intent-Driven Vehicles

Future automobiles will use multimodal AI, which combines voice, vision, biometrics, and contextual signals, to infer driver intent and emotion. GenAI takes input as a prompt to contextually understand, analyze, and simulate and adapt to recommendations, interaction style, and interventions dynamically. This enhances comfort, safety, and trust by shifting personalization away from reactive preference matching and toward anticipatory, emotionally intelligent experiences.

11.14.2 Personalization Across Multimodal Mobility Ecosystems

Personalization will extend across multimodal mobility ecosystems like public transit, spanning care and ride services rather than individual vehicles. GenAI offers end-to-end experiences that optimize routes and prices while preserving persistent user context across modes. This enables seamless, personalized journeys rather than fragmented interactions across disconnected mobility services.

11.14.3 GenAI Agents Coordinating Vehicle, Home, and City Infrastructure

GenAI agents will orchestrate coordination across vehicles, smart homes, and city infrastructure. By considering all dynamic parameters such as traffic, schedules, energy availability, and user preferences, agents coordinate routing, charging, climate control, and mobility timing. This leads to system-level optimization, converting vehicles into intelligent nodes within large urban and energy ecosystems.

11.14.4 Transition from "Personalized Features" to "Personalized Mobility Experiences"

The future shifts focus from isolated personalized features to outcome-driven personalized mobility experience. GenAI helps in optimizing time, comfort, sustainability, and cost through the lifecycle. Instead of providing static personalization, vehicles become adaptive service platforms that continuously learn, predict, and coordinate dynamically.

11.15 Key Takeaways for Technology Leaders

Personalization at scale requires shared data, identity, and AI foundations with disciplined architecture, governance, and cost controls. It is not a standalone feature but a platform capability that delivers quality output with high-quality governed data. In order to promote distinction, continuously evolving customer lifetime value, and future mobility experiences, winning OEMs will consider personalization as a key digital product.

11.15.1 Personalization Is a Platform Capability, Not a Feature

At scale, personalization cannot be delivered as an isolated feature in an individual vehicle but as a platform capability. It required a common platform that consists of data ingestion, identity, models, orchestration, and governance. Personalization as a platform capability enables consistency, reusability, and rapid innovation across customers, vehicles, dealers, and operational domains.

11.15.2 GenAI Amplifies Value When Combined with Strong Data Foundations

GenAI delivers amplified value when combined with strong, high-quality, governed data foundations. To build trust and prove relevance, real-time telemetry, feature stores, customer content, and feedback loops are crucial. Strong data foundations enhance insights, explanation, and user experience throughout the automotive value chain, and in the lack of these, GenAI runs the risk of hallucination and inconsistency.

11.15.3 Scale Requires Disciplined Architecture, Governance, and Cost Controls

Scaling personalization across millions of users requires disciplined architecture, governance, and cost controls. To implement disciplined architecture, it follows tiered model strategies, edge-cloud optimization, tenant isolation, and cost-aware inference routing. As the use of GenAI increases, strong governance that addresses safety, privacy, security, and observability is crucial to preserve dependability, legal compliance, and economic viability.

11.15.4 Winning OEMs Will Treat Personalization As a Core Digital Product

Leading OEMs treat personalization as a core digital product with KPIs, road maps, and continuous improvement cycles. This shifts the mindset by emphasizing from one-time features to long-term value creation across operations, ecosystems, and client lifetimes. Personalization turns into a tactical differentiator that shapes brand identification, loyalty, safety, and future mobility experiences in complex real-world environments.

11.16 References

1. Generative AI for Automotive. https://aws.amazon.com/automotive/automotive-generative-ai/
2. How GenAI Is Personalizing Customer Experience at Scale. https://www.movate.com/how-genai-is-personalizing-customer-experience-at-scale/
3. Revolutionizing the Automotive Customer Experience with Generative AI. https://medium.com/@romeopartners/revolutionizing-the-automotive-customer-experience-with-generative-ai-3d10ed9af20a
4. Gen AI in automotive software development. https://www.mckinsey.com/features/mckinsey-center-for-future-mobility/our-insights/from-engines-to-algorithms-gen-ai-in-automotive-software-development
5. AI in the automotive industry. https://www.itransition.com/ai/automotive
6. Software-defined Vehicles, GenAI, IoT – The Path to AI-Defined Vehicles. https://aws.amazon.com/blogs/industries/software-defined-vehicles-genai-iot-the-path-to-ai-defined-vehicles/
7. Generative AI in the automotive industry: Use cases, architecture, implementation, and future trends. https://www.leewayhertz.com/generative-ai-in-automotive-industry/

8. Vehicle Personalization Market Growth with Logistics and Distribution Solutions. https://www.towardsautomotive.com/insights/vehicle-personalization-market-sizing

9. Winning tomorrow's car buyers using artificial intelligence in marketing and sales .https://www.mckinsey.com/industries/automotive-and-assembly/our-insights/winning-tomorrows-car-buyers-using-artificial-intelligence-in-marketing-and-sales

10. Software-defined Vehicles, GenAI, IoT – The Path to AI-Defined Vehicles. https://aws.amazon.com/blogs/industries/software-defined-vehicles-genai-iot-the-path-to-ai-defined-vehicles/

11. How Audi improved their chat experience with Generative AI on Amazon SageMaker. https://aws.amazon.com/blogs/industries/how-audi-improved-their-chat-experience-with-generative-ai-on-amazon-sagemaker/

12. AI-driven customer experience: Enhancing personalisation in the automotive industry. https://yourstory.com/2025/01/ai-driven-customer-experience-enhancing-personalisation-automotive

13. Role of Generative AI in Automotive Industry. https://www.antiersolutions.com/blogs/role-of-generative-ai-in-automotive-industry-top-use-cases-examples/

14. NVIDIA Autonomous Vehicles. https://www.nvidia.com/en-us/solutions/autonomous-vehicles/

15. What is an Event-Driven Architecture? https://aws.amazon.com/event-driven-architecture/

16. Build secure network architectures for generative AI applications using AWS services. https://aws.amazon.com/blogs/security/build-secure-network-architectures-for-generative-ai-applications-using-aws-services/

17. https://aws.amazon.com/blogs/industries/how-audi-improved-their-chat-experience-with-generative-ai-on-amazon-sagemaker/

CHAPTER 12

Media and Entertainment: Content Creation and Audience Engagement

The media and entertainment industry stands at a transformative crossroads. As streaming platforms proliferate and content consumption patterns fragment across devices and platforms, companies face unprecedented challenges in capturing and retaining audience attention. Generative AI has emerged as a powerful catalyst for addressing these challenges, fundamentally reshaping how content is created, personalized, and delivered to audiences worldwide.

This chapter explores how leading media and entertainment companies are leveraging generative AI to revolutionize content creation workflows, enhance audience engagement through hyper-personalization, and unlock new monetization opportunities. We examine real-world implementations from industry leaders including Netflix, Disney, Spotify, Warner Bros. Discovery, and Amazon Prime Video, alongside emerging applications in gaming, sports broadcasting, and news media.

12.1 The Media Industry's AI Inflection Point

The media and entertainment landscape has undergone seismic shifts over the past decade. Traditional broadcast models have given way to on-demand streaming, social media platforms have democratized content creation, and audiences increasingly expect personalized experiences tailored to their preferences. According to a 2025 HubSpot

N. Sendas et al., *Building Generative AI Solutions for Industries with AWS*,
https://doi.org/10.1007/979-8-8688-2830-0_12

survey, 96% of marketers reported that personalized experiences have increased sales, with brands like Netflix, Spotify, and Amazon leading the charge by using data about past behavior to predict future preferences. However, it is worth noting that this figure reflects self-reported perceptions from marketers rather than independently measured sales outcomes, and survey respondents may skew toward those already invested in personalization strategies, potentially introducing selection and confirmation bias.

The volume of content being produced has exploded. Media companies now manage petabytes of video, audio, and image assets while simultaneously facing pressure to produce more content faster and at lower cost. The PGA TOUR, for instance, manages over 25 petabytes of content, including footage dating back to 1920. This scale presents both opportunities and challenges that generative AI is uniquely positioned to address.

12.1.1 Current Industry Challenges

Media organizations face several interconnected challenges that generative AI can help solve:

> **Content Discovery and Searchability**: With vast archives of media assets, finding relevant content for production teams becomes increasingly difficult. Traditional keyword-based search provides limited value when dealing with unstructured video and audio data.
>
> **Production Costs and Timelines**: Creating high-quality content remains expensive and time-intensive. Studios face pressure to localize assets quickly for global distribution, develop creative concepts rapidly, and maintain consistent quality across increasing volumes of content.
>
> **Audience Fragmentation**: Viewers consume content across multiple platforms—streaming services, social media, and mobile devices—each with different format requirements and audience expectations. Content must be adapted and personalized for these diverse contexts.
>
> **Monetization Pressure**: As subscription fatigue sets in and advertising markets evolve, media companies seek new revenue streams through contextual advertising, personalized recommendations, and enhanced viewer engagement.

12.2 Content Creation Revolution

Generative AI is transforming every stage of the content creation pipeline, from initial concept development through post-production and distribution. Leading companies are implementing AI-powered workflows that augment human creativity while dramatically reducing production timelines and costs.

12.2.1 Automated Metadata Generation and Asset Management

One of the most immediate applications of generative AI in media is automated metadata generation. The PGA TOUR provides a compelling example of this transformation. By integrating Amazon Transcribe to convert speech to text, they increased metadata entries from 9 million to 16 million in just five months. This significant increase in volume reflects the system's ability to process and tag content at a scale that would be impractical through manual effort alone. However, higher metadata volume does not inherently equate to higher metadata quality—increased entries could include inaccurate transcriptions, mislabeled content, or irrelevant tags if not properly validated. To address this, the PGA TOUR further enhanced accuracy by incorporating Amazon Bedrock with Claude 3 Sonnet to improve recognition of golf-specific terms and player names, targeting the domain-specific precision challenges that general-purpose transcription models often struggle with. The distinction between metadata quantity and quality is important: the value of automated metadata generation ultimately depends not just on how many entries are produced, but on their precision, consistency, and usefulness for downstream applications like search, content discovery, and personalization.

This automation delivers significant benefits beyond simple time savings. Rich, accurate metadata enables

Faster Content Discovery: Production teams can quickly locate specific moments within vast archives using natural language queries.

Enhanced Searchability: Semantic search capabilities allow users to find content based on concepts and context rather than exact keyword matches.

Improved Rights Management: Automated tracking of content usage, licensing, and distribution rights.

Contextual Advertising Opportunities: Detailed metadata enables precise ad placement based on content context.

Bloomberg Media has implemented similar capabilities, using AI to analyze and manage their large media libraries with a focus on speed, accuracy, and trust in media processing. Their system emphasizes metadata creation, content ingestion, hybrid search, and AI-driven workflows to ensure journalists can quickly access relevant footage for breaking news coverage.

12.2.2 Video Summarization and Content Transformation

Generative AI excels at transforming long-form content into engaging short-form formats optimized for different platforms and audiences. This capability addresses the growing demand for social media content, promotional materials, and highlight reels.

AWS provides guidance for video summarization that enables media companies to produce short-form summary videos from longer files by extracting and summarizing speech, identifying the most relevant video segments, and compiling final video output. This process, which previously required hours of manual editing, can now be largely automated while maintaining editorial quality through human oversight.

Prime Video demonstrates this capability through their X-Ray Recaps feature, which uses generative AI to create personalized episode summaries. This helps viewers catch up on content more efficiently and reduces barriers to re-engagement with series they may have paused watching.

The transformation extends beyond simple summarization. AI can now

Generate Multiple Versions: Create platform-specific versions optimized for TikTok, Instagram Reels, YouTube Shorts, and other formats from a single source video.

Add Localization: Automatically generate subtitles, dubbing, and culturally adapted content for global audiences.

Create Promotional Materials: Generate trailers, teasers, and social media content that highlight the most engaging moments.

Produce Highlight Reels: Automatically identify and compile key moments from sports events or long-form content.

12.2.3 Content Localization and Accessibility

Media companies face increasing pressure to localize content quickly for global audiences. Traditional localization—involving translation, voice dubbing, and lip-syncing—is expensive and time-consuming. Generative AI is transforming this process.

AWS guidance on video localization demonstrates how companies can leverage AI services like Amazon Transcribe and Amazon Translate in conjunction with open source generative AI models to create realistic voice dubbing with optional lip-syncing. This approach can also potentially reduce localization costs by up to 35% or more while dramatically accelerating time-to-market for international releases.

Prime Video's Dialogue Boost feature exemplifies AI-enhanced accessibility. Using AI to enhance speech clarity, the feature makes content more accessible across multiple languages, improving the viewing experience for audiences with hearing difficulties or those watching in noisy environments.

12.2.4 Creative Content Generation

While content creation remains an area where human creativity is paramount, generative AI is proving valuable for specific creative tasks:

Concept Art and Storyboarding: LG AI Research used Amazon SageMaker to develop EXAONE, a 300-billion-parameter multimodal foundation model that powers Tilda, an AI-powered visual artist. When designing clothing, the time required decreased from nine months to just one month with AI assistance.

Character Development: Gaming studios and animation companies use AI to generate character variations, costume designs, and environmental concepts that human artists can refine. This accelerates the creative exploration phase and allows artists to evaluate more options quickly.

Background and Asset Generation: AI can generate backgrounds, textures, and secondary visual elements, allowing human artists to focus on primary creative elements. Adobe's Firefly, integrated into Creative Cloud applications, enables users to generate backgrounds, illustrations, and typographic effects directly within their existing workflows.

Music and Audio Generation: While still emerging, AI-powered music generation tools can create background scores, ambient sounds, and musical variations that composers can use as starting points.

The key insight from successful implementations is that AI augments rather than replaces human creativity. As one media executive noted, "AI-generated content won't be immediately ready to include in a game without human refinement and curation. However, AI can quickly produce placeholders, prototypes, and starter assets so that humans can focus on selection and refinement".

12.3 Audience Engagement Through Hyper-personalization

The most transformative application of generative AI in media may be hyper-personalization—delivering content experiences tailored to individual preferences, viewing history, and real-time context. Leading streaming platforms have pioneered this approach, setting new standards for audience engagement.

12.3.1 Recommendation Systems and Content Discovery

Netflix, Spotify, and Amazon have set the benchmark for AI-powered recommendations. These systems analyze user behavior—viewing history, listening patterns, purchase behavior, browsing activity, and engagement signals—to predict preferences and surface relevant content. The measurable impact of these systems is well-documented: Netflix has reported that its recommendation engine influences approximately 80% of content watched on the platform, reducing churn by helping users find content they enjoy more quickly. Spotify's Discover Weekly, powered by collaborative filtering and natural language processing, reportedly drives billions of streams annually and has become a key driver of user engagement and retention. Amazon has attributed a significant portion of its revenue to its recommendation engine, with cross-sell and upsell suggestions driving measurable increases in average order value. These systems are typically evaluated on metrics such as click-through rate (CTR), watch/listen time, conversion rate, and user retention—not subjective notions of accuracy—because the business value of recommendations lies in measurable behavioral outcomes.

According to HubSpot research, brands like these "use data about your past behavior to predict your future preferences—whether that's a TV show, a playlist, or a product recommendation".

These systems analyze user behavior to predict preferences with remarkable accuracy.

Warner Bros. Discovery provides a concrete example of recommendation system implementation. The company uses Amazon Personalize to enhance user experience by customizing show and movie recommendations based on user preferences. Through Amazon Personalize, Warner Bros. Discovery can "quickly analyze user preferences from their other web properties and build the most relevant real-time recommendations".

The technical architecture underlying these systems combines multiple AI approaches:

> **Collaborative Filtering**: Analyzing patterns across users with similar viewing histories to identify content that specific users are likely to enjoy
>
> **Content-Based Filtering**: Matching content attributes (genre, actors, themes) to user preferences derived from viewing history
>
> **Hybrid Approaches**: Combining collaborative and content-based methods with contextual signals like time of day, device type, and viewing location
>
> **Real-Time Adaptation**: Continuously updating recommendations based on immediate user behavior and engagement signals

Hisense TV System demonstrates the business impact of sophisticated recommendation systems. By developing an AI-powered intelligent recommendation system on AWS using Amazon SageMaker, they built user profile libraries catering to diverse tastes while supporting business expansion in advertising and customer engagement.

12.3.2 Personalized Content Experiences

Beyond recommendations, generative AI enables truly personalized content experiences that adapt to individual viewers:

Dynamic Content Assembly: Prime Video uses AI to create personalized episode recaps through their X-Ray Recaps feature, helping viewers catch up on series they're watching. This addresses a common pain point—viewers who pause a series and struggle to remember plot details when returning.

Adaptive Streaming Experiences: AI can adjust content presentation based on viewer preferences, device capabilities, and network conditions. This includes optimizing video quality, adjusting subtitle presentation, and even modifying content pacing.

Personalized Marketing: Media companies use generative AI to create customized promotional materials for different audience segments. As noted in AWS guidance, this includes "creating customized ads, product recommendations, and website content based on user data and preferences, leading to higher engagement and conversion rates".

Interactive Experiences: Gaming companies are pioneering AI-powered interactive narratives where character responses and story progression adapt to player choices in real time. This technology is beginning to influence interactive streaming content as well.

12.3.3 Contextual Advertising and Monetization

Generative AI is transforming advertising in media by enabling contextual targeting that respects privacy while delivering relevant ads. Rather than relying solely on user tracking, AI analyzes content context to place appropriate advertisements.

AWS provides guidance on contextual intelligence for advertising, demonstrating how to implement contextual advertising approaches with enhanced machine learning capabilities. This involves

Content Analysis: Using AI to understand the themes, sentiment, and context of content at a granular level

Brand Safety: Automatically identifying moments in content that are appropriate or inappropriate for specific advertisers

Dynamic Ad Insertion: Placing ads at contextually relevant moments rather than fixed time intervals

Performance Optimization: Continuously learning which ad placements drive the best engagement and conversion

The PGA TOUR exemplifies this approach in sports broadcasting. They use AI to generate automated commentary through their TOURCAST application, providing personalized insights for different viewers while creating opportunities for contextually relevant advertising.

12.4 Technical Architecture and Implementation

Implementing generative AI for media and entertainment requires sophisticated technical architecture that balances performance, cost, and scalability. Leading companies have developed reference architectures that others can learn from.

12.4.1 Media Asset Management and Processing

The foundation of AI-powered media workflows is robust asset management. The PGA TOUR's migration to AWS provides a blueprint for modernizing media asset management systems:

Cloud-Native Storage: Migrating from on-premises systems to cloud storage (Amazon S3) enables global access, automatic scaling, and integration with AI services.

Automated Processing Pipelines: Using AWS services like Amazon Transcribe, Amazon Rekognition, and Amazon Bedrock to automatically extract metadata, identify objects, and generate descriptions.

Hybrid Search Capabilities: Combining traditional keyword search with semantic search powered by vector embeddings to enable natural language queries.

Version Control and Workflow Management: Maintaining multiple versions of assets (raw footage, edited versions, localized variants) with clear lineage and approval workflows.

Media2Cloud, an AWS solution, provides a comprehensive framework for placing video, image, audio, and document assets and associated metadata in the cloud. The latest version (v.4.0) includes capabilities where metadata can be enriched using generative AI to produce image captions, transcript summaries, and content classifications powered by Amazon Bedrock.

12.4.2 Real-Time Processing and Low-Latency Requirements

Live sports and news broadcasting present unique challenges requiring real-time AI processing with minimal latency. The PGA TOUR's implementation of AI commentary demonstrates how to operationalize generative AI for live events:

Observability and Monitoring: Using Amazon CloudWatch to collect metrics at both component and user levels, ensuring system reliability during live events

LLM As a Judge: Employing AI models to evaluate AI-generated content quality, enabling assessment of over 10,000 shots per day—unfeasible through human evaluation alone

Deployment Pipelines: Treating prompts as "soft code" and using CI/CD pipelines for rapid iteration and deployment

Model Selection: Using different models for different tasks—faster models for real-time generation, more sophisticated models for quality evaluation

12.4.3 Scalability and Cost Optimization

Media workloads exhibit significant variability—peak demand during live events or content releases, followed by quieter periods. Cloud-native architectures enable cost-effective scaling:

Serverless Processing: Using AWS Lambda and other serverless services to process media assets on demand, paying only for actual usage

Batch Processing: Scheduling non-urgent tasks (like archive metadata generation) during off-peak hours to reduce costs

Model Optimization: Selecting appropriate model sizes and capabilities for each task—using smaller, faster models where sufficient and reserving larger models for complex tasks

Caching and Reuse: Caching frequently accessed content and AI-generated results to reduce redundant processing

12.5 Industry-Specific Applications

Different segments of the media and entertainment industry face unique challenges and opportunities for generative AI applications.

12.5.1 Streaming Platforms

Netflix, Disney+, HBO Max, and other streaming services compete intensely for subscriber attention and retention. Generative AI helps them differentiate through

Content Curation: Creating personalized home pages where every user sees different featured content based on their preferences

Thumbnail Optimization: Generating and testing multiple thumbnail variations to maximize click-through rates for different audience segments

Viewing Experience Enhancement: Features like Prime Video's X-Ray Recaps and Dialogue Boost that use AI to improve accessibility and engagement

Content Planning: Analyzing viewing patterns to inform content acquisition and production decisions

12.5.2 Gaming Industry

Gaming represents one of the most advanced applications of generative AI in entertainment, with use cases spanning development, live operations, and player engagement:

Accelerated Development: AI generates game assets, environments, and character variations, allowing developers to "spend more time on refinement and finding the fun".

Dynamic Player Experiences: AI creates personalized content, adaptive difficulty, and responsive non-player characters that react intelligently to player actions.

User-Generated Content: Tools that enable players to create custom content using AI assistance, increasing engagement and extending game longevity.

Content Moderation: AI-powered systems like those from Spectrum Labs help gaming platforms manage toxic behavior and illegal content without expanding Trust and Safety teams.

12.5.3 Sports Broadcasting

Sports present unique challenges—multiple simultaneous events, vast amounts of footage, and the need for real-time processing. AI is transforming sports media:

Automated Commentary: The PGA TOUR's AI commentary system provides personalized insights for viewers, addressing the challenge of covering multiple players across vast courses.

Highlight Generation: Automatically identifying and compiling key moments from games, reducing the time from event to published highlight from hours to minutes.

Enhanced Analytics: FOX Sports uses Amazon SageMaker to streamline production of relevant in-game storylines for commentators during live broadcasts, creating more natural-sounding narratives compared to rule-based templates.

Multi-angle Coverage: AI helps determine optimal camera angles and shot selection for different distribution channels and audience preferences.

12.5.4 News and Journalism

News organizations face pressure to produce content quickly while maintaining accuracy and editorial standards. Bloomberg Media's implementation demonstrates AI's role in modern journalism:

Rapid Asset Retrieval: AI-powered search enables journalists to quickly find relevant footage from vast archives for breaking news coverage.

Automated Transcription: Converting speech to text in real time for live events and interviews, enabling faster story development.

Content Verification: Using AI to help identify potential misinformation or verify source authenticity.

Multi-platform Distribution: Automatically adapting content for different platforms (web, mobile, social media) while maintaining editorial consistency.

12.6 Ethical Considerations and Responsible AI

The media and entertainment industry faces unique ethical challenges in deploying generative AI, particularly around authenticity, copyright, and creative labor.

12.6.1 Authenticity and Deepfakes

The same technology that enables beneficial applications can also create convincing deepfakes and misinformation. Responsible media companies must

Implement Detection Systems: Using AI to identify synthetic content and potential deepfakes with a high degree of accuracy

Establish Clear Labeling: Transparently disclosing when content is AI-generated or AI-enhanced

Maintain Editorial Oversight: Ensuring human review of AI-generated content before publication, particularly for news and factual content

Develop Industry Standards: Participating in industry-wide efforts to establish norms and best practices for AI use in media

12.6.2 Copyright and Intellectual Property

Generative AI models trained on copyrighted content raise complex legal questions. Leading companies are addressing these concerns:

Licensed Training Data: Adobe's Firefly is trained exclusively on licensed, high-quality content including Adobe Stock, openly licensed media, and public domain content. This approach addresses copyright concerns, particularly for enterprise users.

Clear Rights Management: Implementing systems to track content provenance and ensure proper licensing for AI-generated derivatives.

Creator Compensation: Developing models for compensating creators whose work contributes to AI training datasets.

Indemnification: AWS offers copyright indemnity for outputs from Amazon Titan models and other services, protecting customers from IP infringement claims.

12.6.3 Impact on Creative Labor

The 2023 Hollywood strikes highlighted concerns about AI's impact on creative jobs. Successful implementations balance efficiency gains with respect for creative labor:

Augmentation over Replacement: Positioning AI as a tool that enhances human creativity rather than replacing creative professionals

Reskilling and Training: Investing in programs to help creative professionals develop AI-related skills

Clear Boundaries: Establishing contractual protections around AI use, as achieved in recent union agreements

Human-in-the-Loop: Maintaining human oversight and final creative control over AI-generated content

12.7 Organizational Transformation

Successfully implementing generative AI requires more than technology—it demands organizational change, new skills, and evolved workflows.

12.7.1 Building AI-Ready Teams

Media organizations need teams that combine domain expertise with AI capabilities:

Cross-Functional Collaboration: Bringing together creative professionals, technologists, and data scientists to design AI-powered workflows

New Roles: Creating positions like AI content strategists, prompt engineers, and AI ethics officers

Continuous Learning: Establishing training programs to help existing staff develop AI literacy and skills

External Partnerships: Collaborating with technology providers, academic institutions, and industry consortia to access cutting-edge capabilities

12.7.2 Change Management

Introducing AI into creative workflows can face resistance. Successful organizations

Start with Pain Points: Identifying specific problems that AI can solve rather than implementing "AI for AI's sake"

Demonstrate Value Quickly: Running pilot projects that deliver measurable benefits in weeks or months

Involve Stakeholders Early: Engaging creative professionals in designing AI tools and workflows to ensure they meet real needs

Communicate Transparently: Being clear about AI's role, limitations, and impact on jobs and workflows

12.7.3 Measuring Success

Media companies should establish clear metrics for AI initiatives:

Efficiency Metrics: Time saved in content production, metadata generation, or asset discovery

Quality Metrics: Accuracy of AI-generated metadata, viewer satisfaction with recommendations, and engagement with personalized content

Business Metrics: Cost reduction, revenue from new monetization opportunities, and subscriber retention improvements

Creative Metrics: Number of creative concepts explored, speed of iteration, and diversity of content produced

12.8 Future Outlook

The application of generative AI in media and entertainment is still in its early stages. Several trends will shape the industry's future.

12.8.1 Increasingly Personalized Experiences

Personalization will extend beyond recommendations to encompass entire viewing experiences. Imagine content that adapts in real time—adjusting pacing based on viewer attention, offering alternative storylines based on preferences, or even generating personalized endings.

12.8.2 AI-Powered Interactive Content

The boundary between gaming and traditional media has been narrowing for years, and AI-powered tools are likely to accelerate this convergence. Interactive narrative formats, AI-assisted content creation, and game-engine-driven production pipelines are already bridging the two industries, suggesting that more deeply interactive experiences in film and television are a plausible near-term evolution rather than a distant possibility.

12.8.3 Democratization of Content Creation

As AI tools become more accessible, the barrier to high-quality content creation will be lowered dramatically. Individual creators and small studios will access capabilities previously available only to major studios, leading to an explosion of diverse content.

12.8.4 Enhanced Live Experiences

Real-time AI processing will transform live events—sports, concerts, and news—with personalized commentary, dynamic camera angles, and interactive features tailored to individual viewers.

12.8.5 Synthetic Media and Virtual Performers

AI-generated characters, virtual influencers, and synthetic media will become increasingly sophisticated and prevalent, raising new questions about authenticity and audience relationships.

12.9 Strategic Recommendations

For media and entertainment companies looking to leverage generative AI effectively:

12.9.1 Start with Clear Business Objectives

Don't implement AI for its own sake. Identify specific business problems—reducing production costs, improving content discovery, and increasing engagement—and design AI solutions to address them.

12.9.2 Invest in Data Infrastructure

AI's effectiveness depends on data quality and accessibility. Prioritize building a robust data infrastructure, including cloud-native storage, automated metadata generation, and unified search capabilities.

12.9.3 Adopt a Hybrid Approach

Combine AI capabilities with human expertise. The most successful implementations use AI to handle repetitive tasks and generate options while keeping humans in creative and editorial control.

12.9.4 Build Responsibly

Address ethical considerations proactively. Implement clear policies around AI use, ensure transparency with audiences, respect creator rights, and maintain editorial standards.

12.9.5 Foster Experimentation

Create space for experimentation and learning. As one marketing expert advises, "Eighty percent of your work should be low- to mid-risk, but carve out 20% for the stuff your competitors are too scared to try".

12.9.6 Develop Partnerships

No single company can master all aspects of AI. Build partnerships with technology providers, creative agencies, and industry peers to access capabilities and share learnings.

12.10 Conclusion

Generative AI represents a fundamental shift in how media and entertainment content is created, distributed, and experienced. Companies like Netflix, Disney, Spotify, Warner Bros. Discovery, and the PGA TOUR are demonstrating that AI can simultaneously reduce costs, accelerate production, and enhance audience engagement when implemented thoughtfully.

The technology's impact extends across the entire media value chain—from initial concept development through production, post-production, distribution, and audience engagement. It enables personalization at a scale previously impossible, unlocks value in vast content archives, and creates new monetization opportunities through contextual advertising and enhanced viewer experiences.

However, success requires more than adopting new technology. It demands organizational transformation, new skills, evolved workflows, and careful attention to ethical considerations around authenticity, copyright, and creative labor. The companies that will thrive are those that view AI as a tool to augment human creativity rather than replace it, that invest in both technology and people, and that maintain focus on delivering genuine value to audiences.

As we look ahead, the pace of innovation will only accelerate. The media and entertainment companies that begin building AI capabilities now—developing the infrastructure, skills, and organizational culture needed to leverage these technologies effectively—will be best positioned to thrive in an increasingly competitive and fragmented landscape. The future of media is not just about creating content; it's about creating personalized, engaging experiences that resonate with individual viewers at scale. Generative AI is the key to unlocking that future.

CHAPTER 13

Conclusion

13.1 The Generative Intelligence Imperative: A Call to Lead, Not Follow

This book began with a declaration: generative AI represents not an incremental improvement to the tools we already use, but a fundamental paradigm shift in how intelligence is applied to business problems. Twelve chapters later, that claim has been tested across the full breadth of modern industry—from the exam rooms of healthcare providers to the assembly lines of automotive manufacturers, from the trading floors of global banks to the recording studios of entertainment companies.

What emerged from that survey is not a uniform picture of AI-driven transformation, but something more nuanced and more instructive: a set of common patterns, recurring tensions, and universal truths that transcend any single industry or use case. This conclusion draws those threads together. It offers not a summary of what has already been written, but a synthesis of what it all means—and what leaders must now do about it.

We are—to use the language of Chapter 1, at wave 3: the Emergence phase—where AI is no longer a tool for optimizing existing workflows but the engine of entirely new business models, value propositions, and competitive dynamics. The organizations that understand this—and act on it with discipline and urgency—will define the markets of the next decade. Those that treat it as a technology experiment will find themselves unable to catch up.

N. Sendas et al., *Building Generative AI Solutions for Industries with AWS*,
https://doi.org/10.1007/979-8-8688-2830-0_13

13.2 The Unifying Thread: AI As Force Multiplier, Not Replacement

Across every industry examined in this book, one insight recurs with striking consistency: generative AI creates its greatest value not by replacing human judgment, but by amplifying it.

In healthcare, ambient AI scribes give physicians back the hours they spent on documentation—not to eliminate clinicians, but to restore the human quality of the clinical encounter. In software engineering, vibe coding powered by tools like GitHub Copilot does not replace developers; it transforms them from line-by-line coders into curators and architects of AI-generated output. In financial services, AI-powered fraud detection does not remove analysts; it frees them to focus on complex cases and emerging threat patterns that require human reasoning. In manufacturing, generative design tools do not displace engineers; they give engineers the ability to explore thousands of design variants in the time it once took to evaluate one.

This pattern is not accidental. It reflects a deep truth about the current state of generative AI technology: these systems are extraordinarily capable at generating, synthesizing, and pattern-matching across large datasets, but they require human judgment for validation, context-setting, and accountability. The human-in-the-loop is not a temporary workaround until AI becomes smarter. It is a feature—the essential bridge between machine capability and real-world trustworthiness.

Leaders who understand this will invest in AI differently than those who do not. They will not simply seek to automate headcount away. They will redesign workflows so that human expertise is deployed where it creates the most value: in decisions that require ethical judgment, contextual nuance, accountability, and creative vision. They will measure AI success not by how many roles it eliminates, but by how much it expands what each person in the organization can achieve.

This is the force multiplier principle, and it is the foundation upon which every successful generative AI implementation in this book was built.

13.3 The Five Universal Patterns of Successful GenAI Adoption

Beyond the force multiplier principle, the case studies, industry analyses, and implementation frameworks presented across these twelve chapters reveal five patterns that distinguish organizations achieving durable value from those still searching for it.

13.3.1 Pattern 1: Data Before Models

Without exception, the organizations achieving the most compelling results from generative AI had invested—often for years before AI became mainstream—in the foundations that make AI work: clean, governed, accessible data; unified customer or operational data platforms; and robust pipelines that connect data sources to decision systems. The Starbucks "Never-Out" failure, described in Chapter 4, is an instructive counterexample. The AI system was sophisticated; the data infrastructure was not. The result was widespread product shortages and a costly rollback.

Generative AI amplifies what is already true about your data. If your data is fragmented, siloed, and inconsistently governed, AI will produce fragmented, inconsistent, and unreliable outputs at scale. If your data is high-quality, unified, and semantically rich, AI will generate insights and experiences that no amount of human effort could replicate. The investment in data infrastructure is not a prerequisite to AI—it is an AI strategy, expressed at its most fundamental level.

13.3.2 Pattern 2: Governance As Enabler, Not Obstacle

In financial services, healthcare, and automotive sectors—industries where regulatory scrutiny is intense—the organizations that moved fastest on AI adoption were not those that treated governance as a friction to be minimized. They were the organizations that built governance into their AI programs from day one, giving them the confidence to scale.

Morgan Stanley's deployment of GPT-4 for 16,000 financial advisors involved months of compliance design before a single user logged in. NatWest's generative AI personalization program was built on a foundation of responsible AI principles before it achieved a 900% increase in savings account applications. The PGA TOUR's AI commentary system was developed with human editorial oversight baked into the architecture before it went live at scale.

Governance—comprising model risk management, bias monitoring, explainability, data privacy, and acceptable use policies—is not the part of the AI program that slows you down. It is the infrastructure that allows you to run faster and further without catastrophic failure. The Center of Excellence model described in Chapter 4 exists precisely to make governance a shared capability rather than a bureaucratic bottleneck.

13.3.3 Pattern 3: Start Narrow, Scale Deliberately

The 90-Day AI Adoption Playbook in Chapter 4, the phased personalization roadmap in Chapter 7, and the pilot program structures in Chapters 9, 10, and 11—all reflect the same underlying logic: start with a clearly scoped, high-value use case, validate it rigorously, and then use that evidence to justify and guide broader deployment.

This is not timidity. It is a recognition that generative AI implementation is a capability-building exercise, not a technology purchase. Each pilot teaches the organization something essential about data readiness, workflow integration, change management requirements, and governance gaps. Organizations that skip this learning phase by attempting organization-wide deployment too quickly consistently underperform those that proceed in structured stages.

The organizations achieving the most dramatic results—NatWest, Travelers, Nasdaq, the PGA TOUR, and National Australia Bank—all followed this pattern. They identified a problem worth solving, built for that problem specifically, measured the outcomes rigorously, and used that foundation to expand.

13.3.4 Pattern 4: Change Management Is the Hardest Part

Technology rarely fails AI programs. Organizations do. Research cited in Chapter 4 suggests that 70–85% of AI projects fail to deliver expected value, and the primary cause is not model accuracy or infrastructure limitations—it is the human side of the transformation: inadequate training, insufficient executive sponsorship, poor communication, and the absence of the cultural infrastructure that allows experimentation to thrive.

Microsoft's 2024 Work Trend Index, referenced in Chapter 4, captures the gap precisely: 75% of knowledge workers are already using generative AI, but only 39% have received formal training. That 36-percentage-point gap is a governance failure, a risk exposure, and a missed productivity opportunity rolled into one.

The organizations building durable AI capability are investing in AI literacy as a foundational competency—not just for data scientists and engineers, but for every role that will interact with AI-generated outputs, make decisions informed by AI, or be held accountable for AI-assisted actions. They are also creating the psychological safety that makes experimentation possible: the willingness to fail in controlled settings, learn from those failures, and iterate faster than competitors.

13.3.5 Pattern 5: Human Judgment Remains the Ultimate Filter

From radiology AI that drafts reports for radiologist review, to manufacturing quality systems that flag anomalies for human inspection, to financial AI that recommends trades for advisor evaluation—every mature implementation in this book preserves a meaningful role for human judgment at the point where the stakes are highest.

This is not merely a compliance requirement or a hedge against AI error. It reflects the current reality of generative AI systems: they are powerful pattern-recognizers and content generators, but they do not possess the contextual wisdom, ethical accountability, or lived experience that human experts bring to high-stakes decisions. The goal of AI augmentation is to make humans better at being human—more available, more informed, and more capable—not to route around human judgment entirely.

As agentic AI matures and AI systems begin to make decisions and execute actions with greater autonomy, this principle will require more sophisticated expression—not its abandonment. Defining the boundaries between autonomous AI action and required human oversight will be one of the defining governance challenges of the next five years.

13.4 The Competitive Divide Is Already Opening

Chapter 1 introduced the framework of early adopters vs. late adopters, and the case studies across this book give that framework concrete meaning. The divide is not theoretical—it is already opening, and it is widening faster than most organizations appreciate.

Early adopters are building proprietary data assets and model fine-tuning capabilities that will be increasingly difficult for latecomers to replicate. They are accumulating the organizational learning—the prompt engineering expertise, the governance frameworks, and the change management muscle—that takes time to develop regardless of budget. They are establishing the customer trust and brand equity that accrues to organizations perceived as innovators in AI-driven experience. And they are creating the feedback loops—the continuous learning systems that improve model performance with each interaction—that compound their advantage over time.

The patterns are visible across every sector examined in this book. In financial services, institutions that have mastered AI-driven personalization are seeing 20% improvements in customer satisfaction and 900% increases in product adoption for targeted campaigns. In healthcare, organizations with mature ambient AI scribe deployments are recovering thousands of clinician hours annually and reporting measurably lower physician burnout. In manufacturing, companies using generative design are reducing development cycles from weeks to days and cutting material costs by more than 20%. In automotive, OEMs treating personalization as a platform capability are building the loyalty and lifetime value metrics that will sustain them through market cycles.

None of these advantages is available to organizations still treating generative AI as a proof-of-concept exercise.

The question is not whether to invest in generative AI. That question has been answered. The question is where to invest, how to sequence that investment, and how to build the organizational capabilities that allow technology investment to translate into a durable competitive advantage.

13.5 The Emerging Frontier: From Generative to Agentic Intelligence

If the central theme of this book is the transformative impact of generative AI on knowledge work, creative industries, and sector-specific applications, then the closing theme must be the next transformation already underway: the rise of agentic AI.

Generative AI responds. Agentic AI acts.

The distinction matters enormously. Generative AI systems, as described throughout this book, produce outputs in response to prompts—text, code, images, analysis—that humans then evaluate and act upon. Agentic AI systems are designed to pursue goals autonomously across multi-step workflows, making decisions, calling tools, managing information, and adapting their approach based on intermediate results—with minimal human intervention at each step.

Chapter 8 describes this transition in healthcare: the rise of agentic systems that go beyond conventional AI to demonstrate autonomous decision-making, adaptive learning, dynamic coordination of care teams, and real-time patient monitoring. Chapter 9 describes agentic AI transforming financial workflows in lending, underwriting, and claims processing—with AI agents executing complex multi-step tasks that previously required human orchestration. Chapter 4 distinguishes between AI copilots, which keep humans in the loop, and AI agents, which execute independently, and notes that agents require careful governance precisely because their autonomy introduces new categories of risk.

The emergence of agentic AI does not invalidate the lessons of this book. It intensifies them. Data quality becomes more critical when AI agents are making autonomous decisions based on that data. Governance frameworks become more consequential when AI actions have real-world effects that cannot be easily reversed. Change management becomes more complex when the workforce must adapt not just to AI-generated recommendations, but to AI-executed workflows.

For leaders planning their AI strategy beyond the immediate horizon, agentic AI demands attention now—not because mass deployment is imminent, but because the organizational foundations required to deploy it safely and effectively are the same foundations that make today's generative AI work. Building those foundations is the priority of the present moment.

13.6 The Ethical Imperative Is Non-negotiable

Across every chapter of this book, the ethical dimensions of generative AI emerge not as peripheral concerns but as central to whether AI programs succeed or fail over the long term.

Bias in training data produces AI systems that perpetuate and sometimes amplify existing inequities—in credit decisions that disadvantage underserved populations, in healthcare recommendations that perform differently across demographic groups, and in creative tools that reflect cultural homogenization at the expense of diversity. Organizations that fail to monitor and mitigate bias do not merely expose themselves to regulatory risk; they undermine the trust that is the foundation of every customer relationship.

Privacy violations enabled by AI—through data misuse, model memorization of sensitive information, or inadequate consent management—can destroy in hours the customer trust that took years to build. The regulatory frameworks governing data privacy, from GDPR and CCPA to sector-specific regulations in healthcare and financial services, are not obstacles to AI innovation. They are the guardrails that make AI-driven personalization sustainable.

Transparency—the obligation to be clear with customers, employees, and the public about when and how AI is being used—is becoming both a regulatory requirement and a competitive differentiator. Organizations that are honest about AI's role in their products and services, that provide meaningful human oversight of AI-generated outputs, and that build explainability into their systems will earn a level of trust that opaque AI programs cannot achieve.

And accountability—the clarity about who is responsible when AI systems produce harmful outcomes—is not just a legal question. It is an organizational design question that every leader deploying AI must answer before deployment, not after an incident.

The organizations that will lead in generative AI are not those that treat ethics as a compliance checkbox. They are the organizations that recognize ethical AI as a business imperative—because customers, regulators, employees, and the broader public are all watching and all reaching conclusions about which organizations deserve their trust.

13.7 A Framework for the Next Five Years

Synthesizing the lessons of this book into actionable guidance, leaders navigating the generative AI landscape over the next five years should organize their thinking around four strategic imperatives.

13.7.1 Imperative 1: Build the Foundation Before Scaling the Application

The data infrastructure, governance frameworks, talent capabilities, and organizational culture required for sustained AI success are long-lead-time investments. They cannot be rushed, and they cannot be shortcut. Organizations that are not yet investing in these foundations are not just behind on AI adoption—they are making a durable AI advantage structurally impossible.

Concretely, this means unifying customer and operational data into governed, accessible platforms; establishing AI governance bodies with real authority and cross-functional composition; building AI literacy across the workforce, not just within technical teams; and creating the Center of Excellence structures that allow AI learnings to compound across use cases rather than remaining siloed in individual pilots.

13.7.2 Imperative 2: Sequence Use Cases by Impact, Feasibility, and Risk

Not all AI use cases are created equal. The most successful implementations in this book shared a common discipline: choosing initial use cases that offered high impact, strong data availability, and manageable risk—then using those wins to build the organizational credibility and capability required for more ambitious applications.

The framework for use case selection should consider: the magnitude of business impact if the use case succeeds; the quality and availability of data required; the regulatory and reputational risk if the AI system fails or behaves unexpectedly; the change management requirements for adoption; and the speed at which value can be demonstrated. Use cases that score well across all five dimensions should be prioritized. Use cases that score poorly on data availability or risk management should be deferred until the foundation is in place to execute them safely.

13.7.3 Imperative 3: Treat AI Talent As a Strategic Capability

The shortage of AI-capable talent is real, but its scope is often misunderstood. The most critical shortage is not of data scientists and ML engineers—though those roles matter. It is of the hybrid professionals who can bridge technical AI capability with deep domain expertise: the healthcare informaticists who can evaluate AI-generated clinical notes, the financial analysts who can assess AI-driven credit recommendations, and the creative directors who can guide AI-assisted content production toward distinctive outcomes.

Building this talent requires investment in both hiring and development. It requires creating career paths that reward AI fluency across functions, not just within technology departments. And it requires the organizational culture changes—the psychological safety, the tolerance for experimentation, and the celebration of learning—that make AI-capable people want to build their careers within your organization rather than elsewhere.

13.7.4 Imperative 4: Maintain Strategic Patience While Executing with Urgency

The tension at the heart of every AI program is the conflict between the urgency that the competitive situation demands and the patience that building durable capability requires. Organizations that sacrifice the latter in service of the former—that rush deployments before foundations are ready, that declare victory on pilots before outcomes are validated, and that scale applications before governance is in place—consistently underperform those that hold both imperatives in tension.

Strategic patience means accepting that the payoff from foundational investments will lag the investment by months or years—and making those investments anyway, because the organizations that do not will find themselves unable to compete when the landscape matures. Operational urgency means moving quickly within each phase, not getting stuck in planning cycles when piloting is possible, and not allowing governance processes to become an excuse for inaction.

The organizations that get this balance right—that move with the speed the moment demands while building with the discipline the future requires—are the ones that will look back on this period as the moment they established an enduring competitive advantage.

13.8 The Larger Stakes

This book has focused primarily on the business implications of generative AI: the competitive dynamics, the implementation frameworks, the ROI evidence, and the organizational transformations. But as we conclude, it is worth stepping back to acknowledge the larger stakes that make this moment significant beyond the boundaries of any individual organization.

Generative AI is not merely a business technology. It is a general-purpose technology—like electricity, like the internet—with the potential to reshape how human societies create and distribute knowledge, provide and access healthcare, allocate capital, and express culture. The decisions being made right now by technology developers, business leaders, policymakers, and regulators will shape the trajectory of that transformation for decades.

The healthcare applications described in Chapter 8 have the potential to make specialist-level diagnostic capability available in underserved rural communities that have never had access to it. The personalization capabilities described in Chapter 9 have the potential to extend financial advisory services to individuals who have never been able to afford a human advisor. The creative tools described in Chapter 5 have the potential to give voice to creators in cultural traditions that have been historically underrepresented in mainstream media.

But these same technologies, deployed without adequate governance, transparency, and ethical commitment, can also deepen inequalities, amplify biases, erode privacy, and concentrate power in ways that serve narrow interests rather than broad human welfare.

The difference between these outcomes will not be determined by the technology itself. It will be determined by the choices made by the leaders reading this book and by the standards, governance frameworks, and accountability structures they build into their AI programs.

The AI inflection point is not just a business opportunity. It is a moment of genuine consequence. The organizations and leaders who approach it with both ambition and responsibility—who pursue competitive advantage while upholding ethical obligations and who move fast while building with integrity—will be the ones who look back on this period with pride, not regret.

13.9 A Final Word

Twelve chapters. Twelve industries and functions. Thousands of case studies, implementation frameworks, research citations, and strategic insights. And yet the essential message can be stated simply:

Generative AI is the most powerful technology available to business leaders today. It is not magic, and it is not without risk. It requires investment, discipline, governance, and the courage to build for a future that is arriving faster than most organizations are prepared for.

The organizations that will win are not the ones with the most sophisticated models or the largest AI budgets. They are the organizations that combine technical ambition with organizational readiness—that build the data foundations, governance structures, talent capabilities, and cultural conditions that allow technology investment to translate into durable human and business value.

The inflection point is now. Wave 3 is underway. The question before every leader is not whether generative AI will transform their industry—it is whether their organization will lead that transformation or be transformed by it.

Lead.

End of Book

Index

A

N. Sendas et al., *Building Generative AI Solutions for Industries with AWS*,
https://doi.org/10.1007/979-8-8688-2830-0

B

C

D

E

F

G

H

I, J

K

L

M

N

O

P

Q

R

S

T

U

FSC
www.fsc.org
MIX
Papier | Fördert gute Waldnutzung
FSC® C083411

Kolibri 360 GmbH
Ferdinand-Jühlke-Straße 7
99095 Erfurt, Deutschland
produktsicherheit@kolibri360.de